THE FUNDING GAP

WHAT SUCCESSFUL BORROWERS DO
WHEN TRADITIONAL FINANCE FALLS SHORT

ANDREW CROSSLEY

#1 BEST SELLING AUTHOR

ISBN: Paperback: 978-1-923501-90-4
Hardcover: 978-1-923501-91-1
Ebook: 978-1-923501-92-8

Cover image: Busybird Publishing
Cover design: Andrew Crossley, Chris Maamoun
Layout and typesetting: Busybird Publishing

busybird publishing

Busybird Publishing
2/118 Para Road
Montmorency VIC
Australia 3094

Disclaimer

The content of this book – including its strategies, ideas, concepts, explanations, definitions and opinions – does not constitute legal, financial, property, credit, compliance or any other type of advice. All information is general in nature. Everyone's personal situation is different, and expert advice must be sought in each case from a suitability-qualified individual. You will realise that this book has not taken into account your personal situation, goals, attempts at fact-finding, your risk profile or a multitude of other factors. This book is for educational purposes and provides no warranties as to the up-to-date nature of the information contained. Risks are inherent in all investments, so you must seek appropriate advice before making any decision; we disclaim all liability for any decision you make.

I have taken every reasonable effort to ensure the accuracy of the contents in this book; however, we do not warrant or make any undertakings as to the completeness or accuracy of any information provided. Neither I, nor anyone involved in this book, in any manner whatsoever, accepts any responsibility for any action that you take as a result of the motivation or education that you will hopefully receive from the contents of this book.

Obtain expert advice before you implement anything.

Acknowledgments

I would like to thank my family, friends and colleagues for their support and encouragement. Also, Daniel Uzelac from 'Lendier', (one of the industry's best mortgage brokers) who contributed the bulk of chapter 14.

Table of Contents

Preface

Consider Your Current Reality

Do you lack the borrowing capacity to achieve your goals or meet your needs? Are you considered too old or too risky for a loan? Do you need to settle your loan quickly? Do you require finance that a traditional lender does not offer? Want to invest in a property or develop a property? Are you an owner-builder, or do you have an incomplete build? Want to buy a business or enter a business and don't have an ABN, or have an ABN established for too short a time? Have a tax debt that needs to be paid? Want to buy before you sell? Have credit impairment or insufficient financial information for a standard loan? Need to settle a loan quickly? Then this book is for you.

As a borrower, have you ever faced the following challenges?

- Been overwhelmed by the number of choices in the mortgage broker market
- Don't know which lender to choose
- Struggled to get a loan
- Lacked the borrowing capacity to do what you need to or want to
- Are you struggling to find funding for a deal?
- Has your finance been declined?
- Do you require fast access to capital?

- Have you lost funding halfway through your construction project?
- Need to buy before you sell?
- Owner builder?
- Need a development loan but do not have borrowing capacity or pre-sales?
- Have you been sprung with changes to terms during the application process?

Achieving what you need requires knowledge. No matter what your age or current circumstances, consider talking to a good mortgage advisor /mortgage broker, to better understand your ability to borrow from a lender that can help you, and it will not be the banks if you lack borrowing capacity or have a different type of property.

Whether you're an investor, builder or developer, or whether you're upsizing, downsizing, extending, refinancing, consolidating, or considering purchasing your second or tenth property, or need finance for a business, the most important consideration and requirement, besides the property itself, is finance.

- **Will you get a loan?**
- **How can you maximise your borrowing capacity?**
- **How can you apply for a loan with less or NO borrowing capacity required?**
- **How to buy before you sell without requiring any additional borrowing capacity or no borrowing capacity?**
- **How can you be more prepared?**

Often 'would be' borrowers listen to their parents and friends' or even inexperienced mortgage brokers or bank employees' opinions about where to apply for a loan, or whether the type of loan needed is even possible.

The best advice I can offer is to do your own research. It's important to seek appropriate and qualified advice. If the person offering their opinion is consistently successful at securing finance or is a mortgage broker who does not rely on a single niche (for example, they do not deal only with first home buyers or simple loans), then please value their opinion. If not, then ignore them.

Bank employees are often trained within the policies and procedures of their own institution and may have limited exposure to solutions available elsewhere. Anecdotally, they so often have no idea, and if they do, they would likely be unwilling to share, what is possible outside of the very narrow world of where they work.

Be aware that the property and lending landscape is always changing. Lending has become unpredictable, and the goalposts are constantly moving, so seek up-to-date advice.

Many borrowers struggle to plan successfully or structure their finances adequately. Many struggle to successfully apply for a loan. This book will provide answers on useful types of loans that many simply do not know are available.

This book is intended as an insider's guide to help you understand more about how a finance provider can make or break a loan. It will also explain how to find an appropriate mortgage broker to access all available options, helping you make better decisions and streamline the process. But most importantly better help you get the loan you need.

Standard loans

The cost of the mortgage should never be based solely on current interest rates, but rather on the future cost of debt in repayment-figure terms. There are many cases where a lower rate can lead to higher repayments, whereas a slightly higher rate may result in lower repayments due to lower fees.

The problem is that most people focus on the 'now' rather than the 'what if'. Modelling holding costs — considering interest rates, lending criteria, income earned, and unexpected changes in personal circumstances — and being better prepared are so important.

Not factoring in the potential future cost of debt in conjunction with actual living expenses, which may differ from the standard expenses the lender will factor in, is crazy.

Whether you're an investor, buyer of a house to live in, or a refinancer, most people by default are 'borrowers'. Very few have an inheritance or a gift or have saved enough to purchase a property with no debt.

Non-standard loans (which is what this book is focused on)

The cost of the mortgage should never be based just on current interest rates, but rather the solution you are seeking. If you lack the borrowing capacity to get the loan you want when you need, or the property is of a type that the banks don't want, then it's the solution that matters, not the rate. Interest rates for the solutions this book focuses on often start at roughly 1.5% higher than a normal bank rate but again, it's the solution not the rate when a bank says no.

The problem is that most people focus on a standard 30-year loan term, but solutions that nonstandard lenders may offer are based on a shorter loan term to assist with the immediate requirements, loan terms may often range from 1-36 months. Once your need has been addressed, it is often simpler to refinance to a standard rate with a lender that was not able to provide the original solution. Additionally, the exit strategy may often include the sale of a property, and if this extinguishes the debt, then the rate ought not to be the focus, especially if it meant you did not require borrowing capacity for the loan.

The focus may be profit. For example, the goal may be to buy, renovate, then flip or sell the property for a profit. The lender may well use the property's on-completion value, not its current value. So, if a loan can be provided by basing the loan-to-value ratio on the end value rather than the current value, the loan may be higher, allowing you to complete the project. In this example, the profit is the goal, not the interest rate.

The secret to getting the loan you need, when most lenders won't offer the solutions this book discusses, is accepting the short term additional cost associated with the loan which can then enable you to refinance, sell or pay off the debt some other way, such as through cash flow, a term deposit reaching its end, maybe superannuation, gift from parents which may not have been available when you need it, sale of other assets or inheritance.

Using a short-term lender to solve a problem often involves two key considerations. The property type and the exit strategy. If the exit strategy is to sell the property, and provided this is acceptable (the acceptability of it will be discussed later) then if it is acceptable, no borrowing capacity is required.

Can you answer the following two questions without doubt as to the accuracy of your response?

- **Unsure which lender to use, whether to use a broker or a bank, or how to structure your finance?**
- **Should you consider a solution rather than focusing on the best interest rate?**

If you have just one of these questions unanswered then you will benefit from reading this book. It does not matter where in Australia you live, or what you have done up to this point, what matters is what you do next, to help improve the likelihood of getting the loan you want for your desired outcome, whether it be; buying before selling, buying your first or next investment property, finishing an incomplete build, becoming an owner builder, development to maximize profit from the project, buying a farm, or acreage, or simply consolidating debt or seeking a loan increase for another need.

About This Book

After reading this book, you will have a much better understanding of the importance of choosing the most appropriate lender and borrowing strategy. More importantly, you will walk away with greater awareness of what is possible. Everyone needs a team or people around them, as none of us knows everything.

Most people have a pain or problem they need to address and overcome. The problem could be not knowing where or how to borrow money without sufficient borrowing capacity, while also reducing risk and lessening the impact on your lifestyle when buying, selling, developing, or simply obtaining a loan that most lenders say you cannot get. This book will provide you with answers to overcoming these problems.

This book provides essential tips for:

- bridging finance (buy before you sell);
- upsizing or downsizing homebuyers;
- first time and 'would be' property investors;
- business owners, or someone wanting to buy or invest in a business;
- owner builders;
- completing a partially completed commercial or residential build;
- development finance without the need for pre-sales or income evidence

- credit impaired;
- retirees with equity in a property;
- those that simply lack the borrowing capacity required for their needs.

Having the right mortgage broker is the most important thing you can do.

People often listen to those who have an uneducated opinion, formed from little experience or hearsay, and backed by limited knowledge or facts. Every successful borrower assesses their situation and what they want to achieve. They establish a plan and follow it, taking action to implement it. They undertake the required research and put in place finance strategies.

About The Author

Growing up in Melbourne, Andrew Crossley left Australia at a young age and soon began working in London for an advertising and marketing firm, which led to his landing a role at a prestigious investment firm serving shareholders in the share market. In 1996, at the age of twenty-four, Andrew was headhunted and moved to Rotterdam to work for a private equity firm. For eight years, he worked in the Netherlands, Cayman Islands and Italy, with high-net-worth clients, handling investments in venture capital projects, international property funds, IPOs and off-market derivatives.

Andrew drew strength from completing four master's degrees — an MBA, a Master of Commerce, a Master of Commercial Law, and a Master of Laws — and holds a Bachelor of Laws. He became a qualified financial planner, mortgage broker, and estate agent (in Victoria, NSW and QLD), and later a qualified property advisor.

Andrew has worked in the finance industry for over 30 years, 20 of those years in Australia, including for the largest non-bank, the largest mortgage manager and Australia's leading short-term property lender during that time, and has worked overseas in private wealth management on several continents

Throughout his career in finance, property, lending, and business development, Andrew has been featured extensively across Australian print media, newspapers, online publications, television, radio, podcasts, and industry journals. His commentary, educational material, and market analysis have appeared across a broad range of consumer, property, finance, business, and investment publications, reflecting a long-standing involvement in the Australian lending and property industry.

Andrew's print magazine features and contributions have included *API Magazine*, *Australian Property Investor*, *Australian Property Journal*, *Better Homes and Gardens*, *Brisbane and Beyond Magazine*, *Business First*, *CEO World*, *Country Style*, *Fitness First*, *Franchise Business*, *Get It*, *Gold Coast*, *Home Beautiful*, the inflight magazine of Regional Express Airlines, *Inside Small Business*, *LABEL Magazine*, *Ladies Golf Magazine*, *Ladies in Racing*, *Ladies in Sport*, *Maroondah Leader*, *MedicSA*, *MindFood*, *Minestyle – West Australian Publishers*, *Modern Business Magazine*, *Money Magazine*, *Mortgage Professional / Your Mortgage*, *Mortgage Professional Australia Magazine*, *MPA Magazine*, *NETT Magazine*, *New Idea*, *Optimum Health*, *OutThere / Rocks Magazine*, *OutThere Magazine*, *Owner Builder Magazine*, *PrimoLife*, *Property Observer*, *Quest Kudos*, *Q-Magazine*, *REIQ Book Review*, *SALife*, *Smart Property Investment*, *Starting Out Magazine*, *The New Daily*, *The CEO Magazine*, *Think & Grow Rich*, *Women's Weekly*, *Working Women*, *Yahoo Finance*, and *Your Investment Property Magazine.*

His work and commentary have also appeared in a number of newspapers and syndicated publications, including *APN articles distributed across New South Wales and Queensland*, *Australian Financial Review – Time Out*, *Financial Review*, *Herald Sun – Property*, *Huffington Post Australia*, *Leader Newspapers*, *Maroondah Leader*, *The Age – Domain*, and *The Queensland Times.* These contributions often focused on lending practices, property investment, financial strategy, borrower behaviour, and broader housing market commentary.

Andrew has also contributed to, or been featured across, a substantial number of online and digital publications, including

AFR Smart Investor, AAMI Blog, Business Woman Media, CEO World, Domain, Dynamic Business, Femail.com.au, How to Property, House and Garden, Homes to Love, Kochie's Business Builders, My Business, News.com.au, PIAA, Property Observer, PS News, Public Service News, Real Estate View, Realcommercial.com.au, Sheinspires, Smart Property Investment, The Cusp, and WYZA.

Across these platforms, Andrew has provided practical insights into financial structuring, property investing, mortgage strategy, credit policy, and the realities faced by borrowers navigating the Australian lending system.

In television and broadcast media, Andrew has appeared on *Sky News Business – Property, Channel 72, and Channel 31's Dollars With Sense,* discussing property trends, financial solutions, lending markets, and investment-related topics. His ability to communicate technical lending concepts in straightforward, practical terms has led to ongoing engagement across both consumer- and industry-facing media.

Andrew's radio and podcast appearances have also been extensive and nationally recognised. These appearances have included *4BC – Real Estate Talk, 4CA – Mornings, 4RO – Afternoons, 5MU – Breakfast, ABC Illawarra, ABC South East NSW – Mornings, ABC Tropical North Queensland – Mornings, Easymix Ten-71, FiveAA – Evenings, 198FM – Breakfast, Grant Broadcasters, David Koch's Business Builders, Luke & Susie syndicated nationally across more than 40 radio stations, Property Investory Podcast, Public Service News, Qantas Inflight Radio's Talking Business program with Alan Kohler, Real Estate Talk with Kevin Turner, RED FM, Smart Property Investment Podcast, Spirit FM – Weekends, Spirit Radio – Mornings, Talking Lifestyle Property across Sydney, Melbourne, and Brisbane, WAY FM – Mornings, interviews with* journalist Nathan Mawby, and *Ultra106five – Afternoons.* His appearance on Qantas Inflight Radio's *Talking Business* program was replayed nationally after being voted one of the program's top interviews.

Throughout this period, Andrew also received substantial industry recognition for his work in the finance and mortgage sectors. His achievements included winning the MFAA Best BDM in Victoria in 2017 and 2020, winning the AMA Best BDM nationally in 2018, and winning the MFAA Best BDM nationally in 2017. He was also recognised as a finalist in the MFAA Best BDM awards in 2014, 2015, 2016, 2017, 2020, and 2021; a finalist in the Better Business Awards from 2017 through to 2021; and a finalist in the Australian Mortgage Awards in 2008, 2015, and 2016. These recognitions reflected Andrew's long-standing commitment to broker education, lender relationships, borrower outcomes, and practical lending solutions across the Australian property and finance sectors.

Andrew has published an online training course on property and finance, and a 'how to write a children's book' course. He is an Austrian-qualified ski instructor and a PADI-qualified advanced scuba diving instructor. He holds a black belt in Japanese freestyle Karate, has travelled to 86 countries and lived in 6, and has earned his wings on fixed-wing gliders. He also enjoys the gym.

Andrew Crossley lives in Melbourne and is the #1 best-selling and award-winning author of seven property and finance books. He was also a #1 best-selling author of 6 children's books in the Billy and Harry Adventure book series.

Andrew's Property and Finance books include:

- Property Investing Made Simple: 1st Edition 2014
- Property Investing Made Simple: 2nd Edition 2019

- Property Finance Made Simple
- The Australian Property Investment Handbook
- The 100k Property Plan
- Commercial Property and Residential Development Made Simple
- Make Your Property Dreams Come True: 2022-2023

Andrew's children's books include:

- Billy and Harry Go on a Winter's Holiday
- Billy and Harry Go to the Beach
- Billy and Harry Go to the Camping
- Billy and Harry Go to the Playground
- Billy and Harry Go to the Zoo
- Billy and Harry Love to Play

1.

Influences on Securing Finance

This chapter explains why it has become more difficult to successfully obtain a mortgage through a traditional lender.

Responsible Lending to Protect Lenders and Consumers

When applying for a loan, people often think that if the loan fits within policy, it will be approved. Too often, people go to an auction, for example, and in an auction process, the buyer cannot insert a 'subject to finance' clause in the purchase contract, or even worse, they sign a contract after buying a property through a private sale situation, without exercising their entitlement to have the clause inserted in the contract. Perhaps they have been told by their bank that it would easily be approved easily, but the reality can be quite different

In addition to credit assessment, lenders and brokers must comply with the requirements of 'responsible lending'. When applying for a loan, by law, every lender and broker must ensure that the two conditions of responsible lending laws are met.

These laws are designed to protect borrowers and are:

1. The consumer's objectives and requirements are met.
2. The consumer can repay the loan without substantial hardship.

Whether the scalability of lending causes confusion and hinders the smooth, uniform implementation of these two points remains to be seen.

(That is, the level of inquiry necessary can depend on a few things; for example, the type of loan, such as whether it is a reverse mortgage, and on the borrower's capacity to understand the contract, perhaps English is not their first language.) One size does not fit all, and it could lead to differing interpretations and opinions. More on reverse mortgages later.

I have seen instances where, during the assessment of a deal, there's some confusion between a broker's interpretation of the deal's strengths and worthiness and a lender's interpretation of the applicant's worthiness. The most confusion arises around the two main points of 'a client's objectives' and 'avoiding substantial hardship'.

The requirements that both brokers and lenders must follow are quite clear: they must make a reasonable enquiry to verify the information they gather from the borrower and make a preliminary assessment of whether the contract will be unsuitable or 'not unsuitable'. The loan does not have to be 'suitable' for the borrower — this point is important… borrowers may need this point reiterated.

Once reasonable steps have been undertaken, a final assessment is conducted to ascertain if the loan will be 'not unsuitable'. These obligations will apply if a new contract is being entered, which also includes loan increases and new loans; however, a variation of an existing contract will not normally trigger the process of responsible lending requirements being applied (although a lender may undertake some due diligence as part of its own credit criteria). A variation of a loan might include changing it from a fixed to a variable interest rate, from interest-only to principal and interest, or from fortnightly to monthly repayments; it would not include an increase in the loan amount.

The National Consumer Credit Protection Act (NCCP Act), which, among other things, introduced the responsible lending obligations,commenced on 1 July 2010, and any regulated credit contracts entered into on or after that date come under the act. This legislation was designed to professionalise the finance industry by requiring licensing for lenders and brokers.

Non-regulated Loan

Loans that do not fall under the NCCP Act (also known as non-regulated loans) are commercial loans and loans that are 'wholly or predominantly' for business purposes. If, however, the loan is in a company or trust name, even if for standard residential purposes, it may be treated as an unregulated loan.

Private lenders generally require a borrower to be a company or trust. This is fraught with danger for the borrower and the broker. If a property ownership on title is an individual and a company or trust is set up to be the borrower, the risk in the eyes of the regulators is that the borrower, broker or lender is intentionally attempting to circumvent responsible lending and compliance if the loan is not 'wholly or predominantly' for business purposes.

As in any industry, there are those who seek to avoid compliance or responsibility requirements, leaving the borrower less protected. Be very careful when advised setting up the borrowing entity in the name of a company or trust, when an individual is on title, and the purpose of the loan is not more than 50% for business purposes.

There are, in my opinion, better private lenders who do the right thing by recognising the purpose of the debt for what it is. Only certain professionals, for example, accountants who may provide advice on borrowing structures, can advise on ownership structures. Mortgage brokers and lenders cannot do so unless licensed to do so.

Non-regulated loans serve a very important purpose, however, as they enable a borrower to apply for a loan with fewer documentary requirements.

A regulated loan is generally provided to a borrower in an individual name (based on being a natural person or strata corporation) and/or where the loan is not wholly or predominantly for business purposes.

So, what does *"regulated"* versus *"unregulated"* mean for the buyer? Well, lenders may not have to be responsible in protecting your interests if the loan is not in your own name, depending on whether they're a bank or a mutual company who has signed up to the Code of Banking Practice (or the COBA code) in these cases, they will have limited responsible lending obligations to small business customers and other borrowers whom indeed may benefit and legitimately be entitled to a non-code loan.

If the lender does have limited responsibility pertaining to a specific loan, they may not have to make reasonable enquiry into the borrowers financial situation, or objectives and requirements (which would include the amount required, the term of the loan, features of the loan and purpose of the loan) or to determine the borrowers financial situation to the degree they otherwise would. The lender may not have to be as diligent, under the 'act' in understanding whether repaying the loan will cause substantial hardship. All they might need to do is assess the loan against risk of loss to them (the lender)!

Requirements for *NCCP Act* include a lender having to provide a comparison rate; this rate includes the interest rate plus many of the fees and charges the lender is charging. This provides greater transparency to the borrower as to the true cost of the loan.

Example

A 950K loan may have an interest rate of 6.5%; however, if there is an annual or monthly fee, or other recognised fees, excluding government fees, the repayment for the year could equate to more than 6.5% and is therefore higher in dollar terms as a cost to the borrower. This is where repayment figures rather than interest rates are so much more important in a traditional loan. Interest rate pales in significance to a comparison rate. A higher interest rate from one lender could prove cheaper than a lower interest rate elsewhere.

Comparison rates help the borrower compare loans based on cost. Be careful though, as it only allows the cost of a loan to be compared, and it does not allow the suitability or features of a loan to be compared, so it is limited in its benefit.

Unscrupulous lenders or brokers may coerce a borrower in signing a declaration for business purposes to avoid complying with the '*NCCP Act*' and this could leave the borrower more exposed. Borrowers must also take responsibility for understanding the implications of their decisions.

I believe our schools should do more to educate students about reality, financial literacy, and the importance of research and responsibility. I once ran seminars for mortgage brokers, including a presentation on the importance of paying bills on time that could be delivered to Year 11 and 12 students. Often, teenagers don't care about, nor do they understand, this responsibility. Many people applying for a loan don't understand the consequences of blemishes on their credit file either. Not paying a mobile phone bill can lead to a default appearing on the person's credit file. When this person matures and applies for a loan, the interest rate could end up being 2%+ higher than what everyone else is offered.

Research by MLC, part of National Australia Bank's wealth management division, also found one third of parents are concerned their children's quality of living will be of a lower standard to what the parents have been used to, and almost 66% of Australians believe the next generation will never be able to afford their own home.

Comprehensive/Positive Credit Reporting

In the past, the information lenders could share was limited to credit enquiries and credit blemishes, like defaults for example. This was known as 'negative' credit reporting.

Positive credit reporting is something that lenders have implemented. Previously, lenders have been assessing how good someone is as at 'now', they can now better determine how good someone will be 'tomorrow' with a complete picture of every credit card, personal loan and repayment history.

The information that appears on a personal credit report usually includes personal information (such as birthdate, name, and address), any directorships, credit enquiries, overdue debts (or those that have led to a default being listed), and more serious blemishes such as court judgements and bankruptcies.

(Source: Equifax)

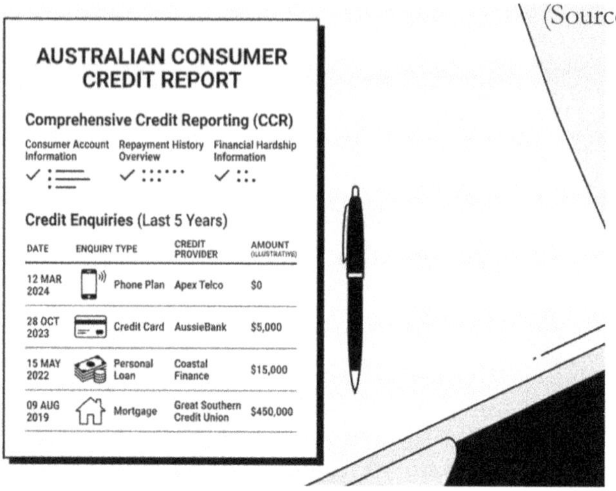

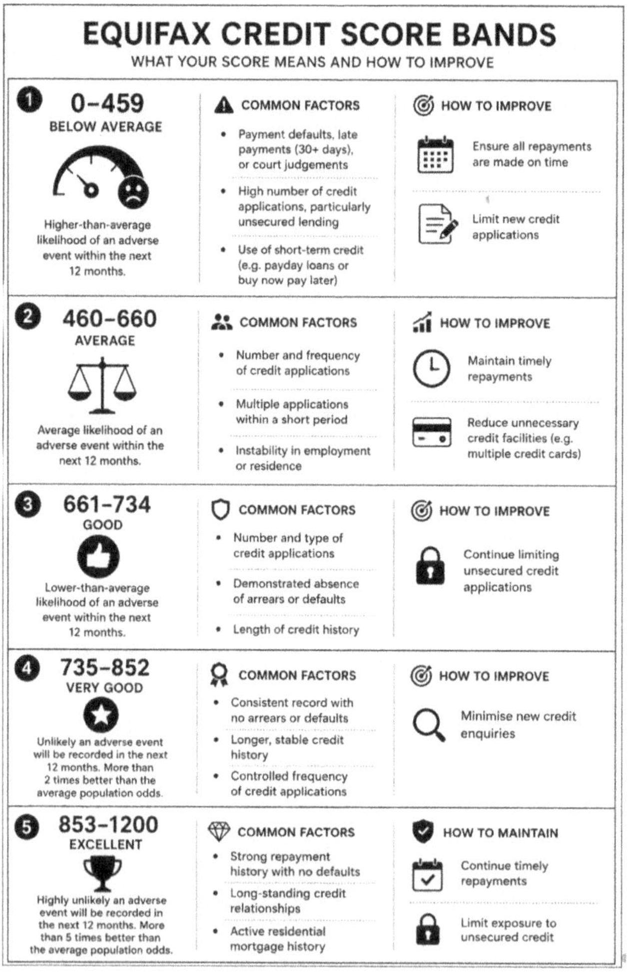

With credit reporting, it is easier to profile a client and the risk they pose to a lender. Those with a better profile will be rewarded, and those with a lesser profile could be put on a higher rate, have their LVR reduced, or be declined a loan.

Most traditional lenders have a credit scoring system in place, each with its own algorithm. It remains unclear what weight each lender places on each piece of information. The weight may be dialled up or down depending on the lender's appetite for that type of borrower at the time. Private lenders do not rely on credit score thresholds. In contrast, many traditional lenders use automated systems where a low score may result in an immediate decline. I have seen negative scores, i.e. with a minus sign in front of it; this is very bad, yet the loan may still occasionally be considered by a private lender.

The type of loan they have, the opening and closing dates of the debt facility — including the facility's credit limit and balance — and the repayment history on the loan generally appear on a borrower's credit report.

Many lenders, when receiving a loan application, ask to see the repayment history of debts held elsewhere. A 6-month repayment history is usually requested. Lenders can penalise people who frequently switch between lenders. The average time a borrower remains with a lender is roughly 3.5 years. The less loyal someone is, the more of an unwanted commodity they may become to a traditional lender. To a private lender, not usually at all.

One may be forgiven for thinking that the shareholders of the lender are the only ones that matter to the traditional lender, whether the lender is publicly listed or not. From what I have observed, the borrower is merely a contributor to the bottom line, and the more a borrower switches between lenders, the worse off they may be in the long run. Many traditional lenders may find short-term borrowers unpalatable, as these borrowers earn less for the lender if they refinance elsewhere.

As for the palatability of a private lending client migrating back to a bank as an exit strategy, once their needs have been satisfied may be simpler than you may think. Traditional lenders require evidence of repayments, and private lenders typically capitalise interest, so there are no repayments. However, the private lender may be able to provide a statement with monthly repayments, dividing the capitalised interest repayments into monthly payments for the loan.

There are some benefits to the borrower, though, including greater transparency that highlights how good someone's credit history is, as well as the transition from a not-so-good period in their life to a better, more reliable one. Showing a good credit history may provide greater entitlements on rate or loan-to-value ratio, for example.

Credit Enquiries

A borrower's credit file records every formal application for finance. An excessive number of enquiries within a short period is often viewed unfavourably by traditional lenders. From a banking perspective, frequent applications suggest either financial stress or an inability to secure approval, both of which elevate perceived risk.

It is not uncommon to see borrowers submit multiple applications in quick succession—sometimes five or more within a fortnight, or dozens over a year. While some borrowers believe this reflects diligence in seeking the best terms, lenders typically interpret it as instability. The greater the volume of enquiries, the more cautious a mainstream lender becomes.

Private lenders, however, often adopt a different approach. While they do consider enquiry history, it is rarely determinative. Instead, they place greater weight on the asset, the proposed exit strategy, and the overall transaction structure. As a result, a borrower with numerous enquiries may still obtain funding in the private market where a bank would decline.

Credit Scoring

Credit scores are used by many institutional lenders as a primary screening tool. They provide a numerical summary of a borrower's credit behaviour and are often embedded within automated decision-making systems.

Most private lenders do not use credit scores as a strict threshold at all. Their assessment is typically more qualitative, focusing on equity, security, and the plausibility of repayment or exit. This distinction is critical: a low credit score may preclude access to mainstream finance yet remain workable within a private lending framework.

Defaults, Judgments and Writs

A default arises when a borrower fails to meet a payment obligation within the required timeframe. Once recorded, it signifies a breach of financial responsibility and remains on the credit file for a substantial period, commonly up to five years.

More serious still is a judgment, which usually follows prolonged non-payment and involves court proceedings where liability is formally established. A writ represents a further escalation, reflecting a court order directing or restraining specific conduct.

Traditional lenders treat these events with considerable caution. Even relatively small defaults can restrict borrowing capacity, particularly if recent or unpaid. The nature, size, and recency of the default all influence the outcome, with more recent and larger defaults attracting stricter scrutiny.

Private lending again differs in its treatment. While defaults and judgments are not ignored, they are assessed in context. Many private lenders will consider applications with multiple or significant defaults, provided there is sufficient equity in the security property and a credible repayment plan. In the context of defaults, private lenders are more likely to assess the circumstances surrounding the issue rather than treat it as determinative. Pricing will adjust accordingly, but access to funding remains available.

Causes and Practical Realities of Defaults

In practice, defaults often arise from ordinary life events rather than deliberate non-payment. A change of address, administrative oversight, or reliance on a third party to manage payments can all result in a recorded default.

Disputes are also common. Borrowers frequently challenge the validity of a default, yet lenders generally adopt an objective stance: while the default remains on the credit file, liability is assumed. Attempts to explain or attribute fault rarely alter this position in a mainstream lending environment.

From a practical standpoint, it is often more effective to resolve the debt first and dispute it afterwards. This approach may improve borrowing prospects, particularly where timing is critical.

Private lenders tend to take a more pragmatic view. While they acknowledge the presence of a default, they are more willing to consider the surrounding circumstances, especially where the issue is isolated or adequately explained. The emphasis shifts from past conduct to present viability.

Interest Rates and Risk Allocation

Where adverse credit events exist, the cost of borrowing typically increases. Mainstream lenders may decline outright, whereas specialist or private lenders will often proceed but at a higher rate. The pricing reflects the perceived risk, including the number of defaults, their size, and their recency.

Importantly, private lending is structured with this risk in mind. The higher rate is not arbitrary; it compensates for the flexibility offered—such as accepting impaired credit, reduced documentation, or complex circumstances.

Arrears and Late Payments

Late payments and arrears are among the most common issues affecting a credit profile. Even minor lapses—such as missing a repayment date due to timing mismatches with income—can be recorded and influence lending decisions.

Lenders typically distinguish between:

Late payments, where the missed amount is rectified before the next due date; and

Arrears: debt that remains outstanding beyond the next repayment cycle.

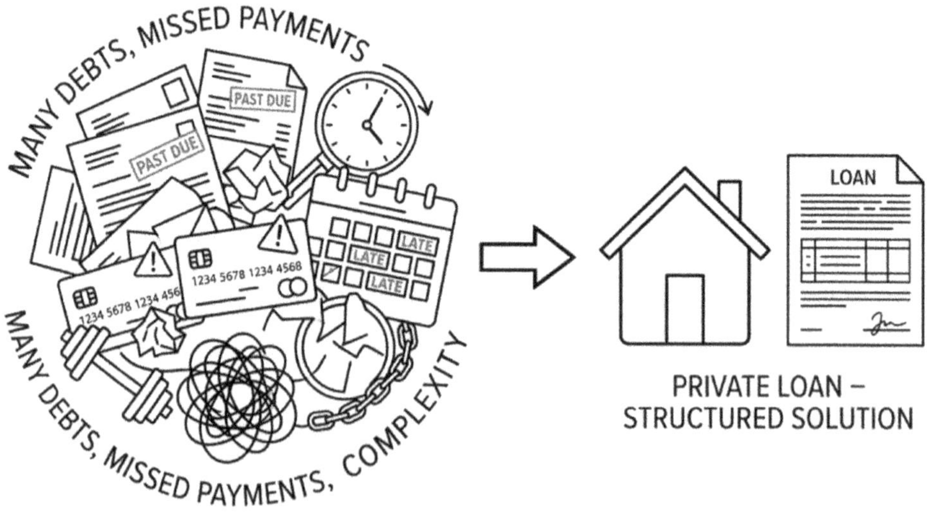

Repeated late payments or ongoing arrears signal an inability to manage financial obligations, regardless of the underlying reason. Explanations—whether for illness, overcommitment, or temporary cash-flow issues—are rarely persuasive to institutional lenders.

Private lenders, by contrast, often place greater emphasis on whether the issue is ongoing and can be resolved within the loan term. For instance, if arrears are historic or can be cleared as part of the transaction, the loan may still proceed.

Private Lending: A Different Lens

The central distinction between traditional and private lending lies in the method of assessment.

Banks assess the borrower first, then the asset. Private lenders assess the asset and exit strategy first, then the borrower.

This shift allows for a broader range of scenarios to be funded. Credit impairments—whether enquiries, defaults, or arrears—become factors to be priced rather than barriers to entry.

Private lending is therefore not a substitute for mainstream finance, but rather an alternative pathway where conventional criteria cannot be met. It provides flexibility in situations involving urgency, complexity, or impaired credit, albeit at a higher cost. A higher cost is better than no loan at all, especially given that in many instances interest is capitalised, so there are no repayments.

Case Study: Debt Consolidation and Serviceability

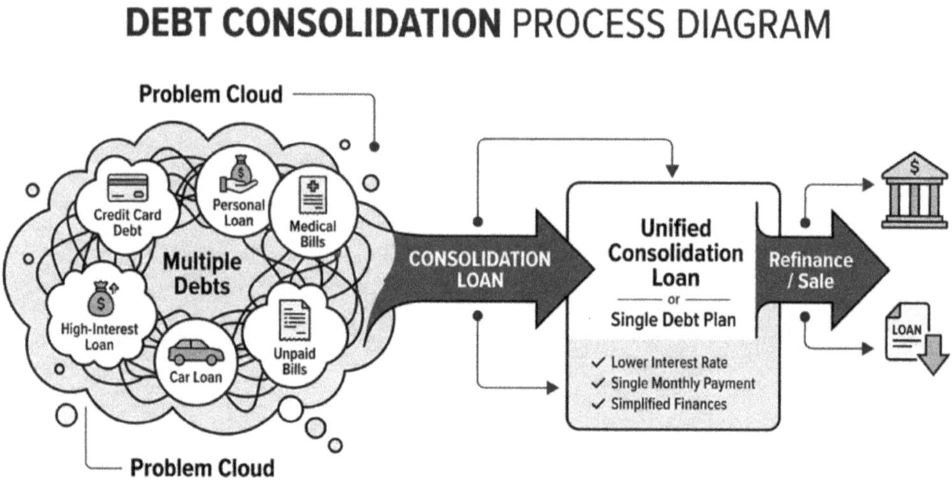

A married couple applied to refinance and consolidated multiple liabilities, including six credit cards, a personal loan, and their existing home loan. The total unsecured debt exceeded $80,000, with credit card interest rates averaging approximately 18% per annum. Their mortgage stood at $350,000 at 5%, and a personal loan of $30,000 was held at 8.5%.

Their combined monthly repayment obligations totalled $2,870.83.

The proposed solution involved refinancing all liabilities into a single facility at an interest rate of 6%. Notwithstanding the higher rate relative to their existing mortgage, the consolidation produced a materially lower monthly repayment of approximately $2,300. This resulted in a saving of $570.83 per month, or close to $7,000 annually.

This outcome illustrates a fundamental lending principle: **repayment capacity outweighs nominal interest rate**

considerations. While the blended rate increased in part, the overall financial position improved due to the reduction in total servicing burden.

A critical factor in the approval of this loan was the borrowers' demonstrated ability to meet the proposed repayment. Although they were struggling with the aggregate of multiple repayments, their financial conduct indicated that they could sustain a single, lower consolidated repayment.

Had the borrowers failed to demonstrate this capacity—either through actual repayments or by evidencing surplus funds equivalent to the proposed saving—the application would likely have been declined. Lenders assess not only historical conduct but also the plausibility of future performance under the new facility.

This principle applies across both traditional and private lending. However, private lenders may adopt a more pragmatic approach. Where a bank relies heavily on strict serviceability metrics, a private lender may instead consider whether the loan resolves an unsustainable position and whether an exit strategy exists.

The consolidation achieved two outcomes:

- A reduction in monthly financial obligations; and
- A simplification of the borrowers' financial position, reducing eight separate debts to a single facility.

While the latter provides psychological relief and administrative simplicity, lenders focus exclusively on **tangible financial benefit**. The decisive factor was the reduction in repayments, not the emotional convenience of managing fewer accounts.

Importantly, had the consolidation resulted in a higher monthly repayment—even if it simplified the borrowers' affairs—the loan would not have been approved. Lending decisions are grounded in measurable financial improvement, not subjective preference.

Interest Rate versus Repayment

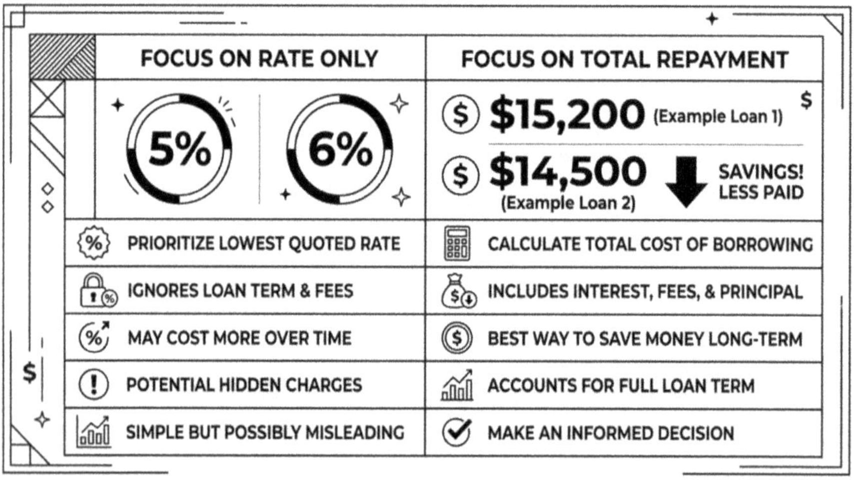

This case reinforces a point often misunderstood by borrowers: **the interest rate, in isolation, is not determinative in loan suitability.**

Despite the increase in the mortgage component from 5% to 6%, the overall position improved due to the elimination of significantly higher-rate unsecured debts. A narrow focus on the headline rate would have obscured the broader financial benefit.

This distinction is particularly relevant in private lending. Private facilities often carry higher interest rates; however, they are structured to achieve a defined outcome—such as debt consolidation, bridging finance, or asset repositioning. The appropriateness of the loan must therefore be assessed by reference to its purpose and outcome, rather than the rate alone.

Private Lending Perspective

In a traditional banking context, this application may have faced resistance due to:

- the number of debts being consolidated;
- prior missed payments on unsecured facilities; and;
- the overall complexity of the borrower's financial position.

In this scenario, a private lender is more likely to proceed, focusing on the property's security, the equity position, and the exit strategy.

Accordingly, even when a bank declines or imposes restrictive conditions, private lending can provide a workable solution, albeit at a higher cost reflecting the increased risk.

Bankruptcy, Part IX and Part X Arrangements

Borrowers with a history of bankruptcy or formal debt arrangements present heightened risk to lenders. Bankruptcy is generally regarded as a last resort, indicating a breakdown in the borrower's ability to manage financial obligations.

A **Part IX debt agreement** allows a borrower to reach a structured settlement with creditors, typically for unsecured debts. A **Part X arrangement** is more complex and is used in circumstances involving greater financial distress.

From a lending perspective:

- Undischarged bankrupts are generally ineligible for finance.
- Discharged bankrupts may be considered, subject to the time elapsed since discharge, and
- Part IX and Part X arrangements are treated similarly to bankruptcy in risk assessment.

Mainstream lenders often require a period of two to three years post-discharge before considering an application. Private lenders, however, may assess such borrowers earlier, particularly where the loan resolves outstanding liabilities and is supported by sufficient equity.

Tax Debts

Tax Debt and Lending Risk

Outstanding tax liabilities—particularly those owed to the Australian Taxation Office (ATO)— are a recurring feature in credit assessment, most commonly among self-employed borrowers and small to medium enterprises. These liabilities typically develop over time due to cash flow prioritisation, undercapitalisation, and deficiencies in financial management. The COVID-19 period did not create this issue but materially increased liabilities for many businesses.

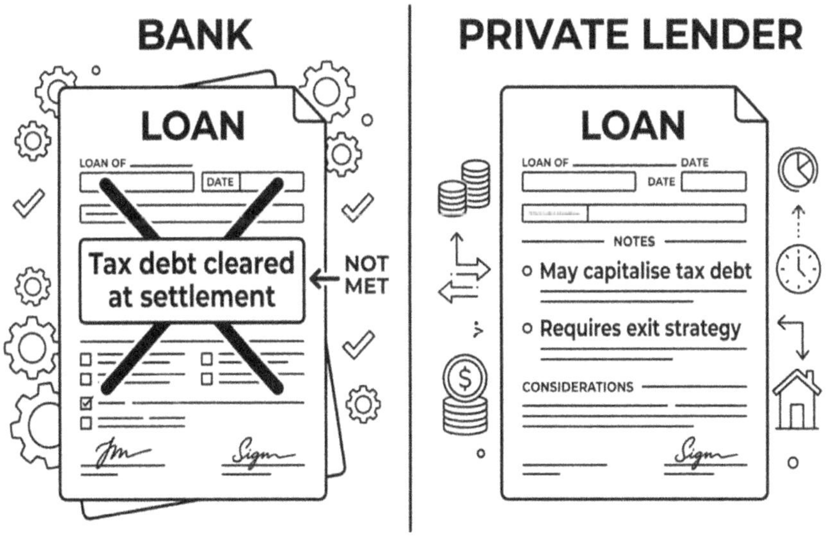

Why Businesses Accrue Tax Debt

Tax debt arises where a business generates revenue but fails to preserve or remit the portion attributable to statutory obligations. Contributing factors include:

- prioritisation of operational expenses over tax liabilities;
- failure to segregate GST and PAYG amounts;
- inadequate financial controls and forecasting;
- structural cash flow constraints;
- business growth without corresponding governance.

COVID-19 functioned as an aggravating factor. Reduced income combined with ATO enforcement leniency allowed existing patterns of deferral to expand into larger accumulated debts.

Characterisation of Tax Debt

Not all tax debt reflects incompetence. In some cases, it is a response to financial pressure. However, persistent or increasing tax debt without a structured repayment strategy indicates poor financial discipline. Where a business has earned income but failed to retain the tax component, this raises legitimate concerns about its ability to manage ongoing obligations.

Institutional Lenders vs Private Lenders

The divergence between lender types is most pronounced at this point.

Institutional Lenders (Banks) adopt a policy-driven approach. Tax debt is treated as a material impairment to both serviceability and borrower conduct. As a result:

- the liability will almost always need to be cleared at or prior to settlement;
- exceptions are rare and tightly controlled;
- any approved exception requires a formal ATO payment plan and clear servicing capacity;
- failure to comply typically results in an automatic decline.

The underlying rationale is that unpaid tax demonstrates an inability—or unwillingness—to meet statutory obligations, which directly informs credit risk.

Private and non-bank lenders, by contrast, assess the issue through a commercial and asset-based lens. Their approach is more flexible, but not more lenient in substance:

- Tax debt may be permitted to remain where there is a formal ATO arrangement.
- In most cases, the debt may be capitalised or addressed as part of the broader transaction.
- Emphasis is placed on the exit strategy (for example, sale, refinance, or business recovery), it is also on clearing the debt.
- Pricing reflects the elevated risk through higher interest rates and fees.
- Loan-to-value ratios may be reduced to preserve equity buffers.

The key distinction is that private lenders are less concerned with past conduct and more focused on whether the position can be stabilised and exited within the loan term. They are not ignoring the risk; they are structuring around it.

Priority and Enforcement Considerations

A further issue is the interaction between ATO enforcement powers and secured lending. A registered first mortgage generally takes priority over other real property interests. However, the Commissioner of Taxation has extensive statutory recovery mechanisms under the *Taxation Administration Act 1953 (Cth)*, including garnishee notices, director penalty notices, and judgment enforcement.

While these powers do not automatically displace a first mortgage, they can materially affect recovery outcomes. The ATO can intercept cash flow, enforce against assets, and act with speed and breadth that may disrupt a lender's position. In practical terms, this creates a level of leverage that lenders must factor into their risk assessment.

This is precisely why institutional lenders avoid the exposure altogether, whereas private lenders proceed only where the risk is mitigated through pricing, structure, and a clear exit.

Summary

Tax debt is a cumulative issue grounded in financial discipline and cash flow management. COVID-19 increased the scale of the problem but was not its origin. The key distinction in lending is not whether the debt exists, but how it is treated.

Institutional lenders generally require the elimination of the risk. Private lenders accept it conditionally, price it, and rely on a defined exit strategy.

In both cases, the underlying principle remains the same: unresolved tax debt introduces legal and commercial uncertainty and must be addressed in a structured and credible manner before funding can be sustained.

2.

Property Types, and Your Current Situation

Property Type and borrowing Capacity

To start with, let's consider the 3 main reasons a borrower would want a mortgage.

Buy and hold

This is perhaps the easiest of the three strategies. Buy and hold is what the majority of borrowers decide on.

Once a property is acquired, people often sit on it, typically because it's for owner-occupier use or long-term investment. Then the property's growing equity can be used to reward other things, such as debt consolidation, investing in other things, whether it be holidays, school fees, asset finance or just general living. These types of properties could be used for anything in the future.

Buy, Renovate and Flip

This requires a more hands-on approach or paying a premium to have someone renovate for you. The purchaser can generate more capital growth and cash flow independently of the market, so they're not solely reliant on the market for

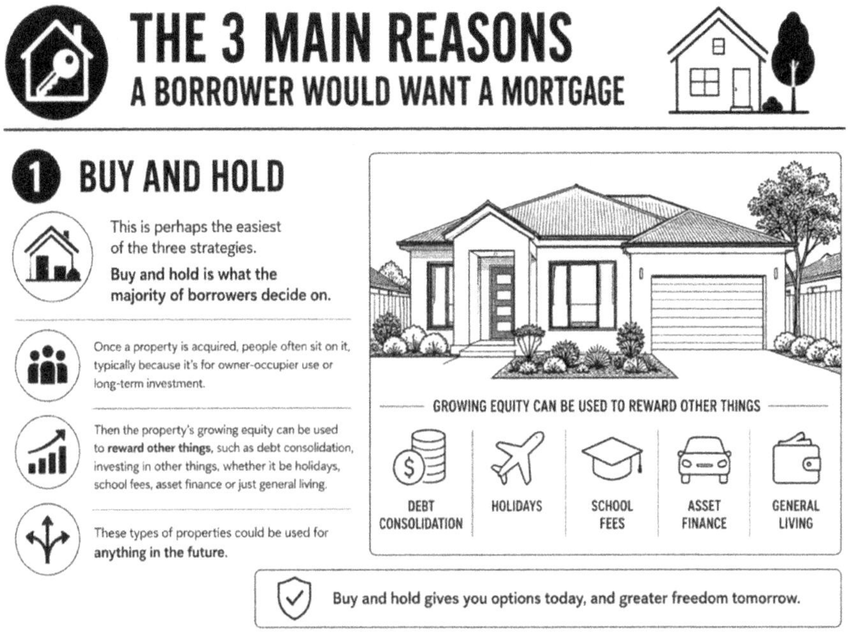

the property's performance. If too much emotion is involved and they over-capitalise, serious problems will arise. Leaving it vacant for an extended period while work is being carried out means incurring costs. Affordability could then be an issue, as it is more difficult to cover the costs of keeping a property vacant for an extended period.

The benefits are fantastic, and it is possible to borrow from a private lender providing up to roughly 70% of the as-is valuation. What banks typically won't do is use the end value (the value it will be worth after the renovations are completed) as the basis for the LVR. Some private lenders can use the end value, thereby providing a larger loan to help cover renovation costs. This would normally require the lender to control the disbursement of the funds as the works are completed. This helps ensure the work is completed, so the projected end value is more likely to be achieved.

If the end goal is to sell the property, private lenders will not require the borrower to demonstrate borrowing capacity to purchase it. This works from a compliance perspective, whether the purchase is by a company, trust, or individual, because interest is usually capitalised (the loan provided includes the interest), so no repayments are made during the loan term.

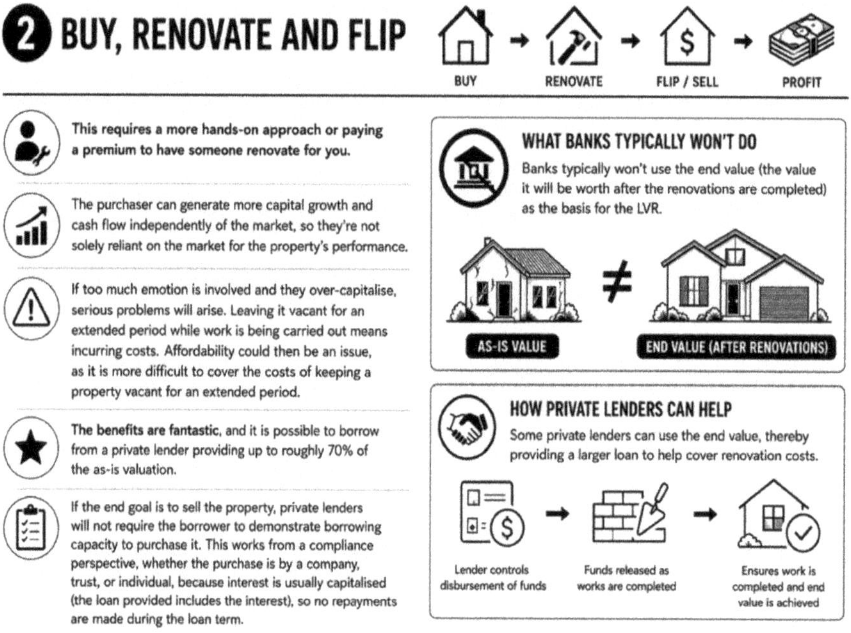

Construct/ Develop

This includes constructing another dwelling or several dwellings on the block, and/or subdividing. This is the riskiest due to time and cost, but it has the potential for significantly greater financial benefits in terms of cash flow and capital growth. A feasibility study would be required to determine whether the project will make money or lose money.

Property and borrower banks typically have a problem with

They are listed below and will be defined and expanded on later, with an explanation of why most of these property types are easy to get a loan for. As you read the list, please pause, grab a pen and write down which of these things interests you the most so you remember to review it later.

Property Type

There are several types of property that banks do not like, and an experienced bank employee or mortgage broker may tell you they are difficult or not possible, but that is not the case.

- Owner Builder
- Incomplete Dwellings
- Kit and Transportable Homes
- Acreage (with or without a house), Farms, Hobby Farms, Green wedge, Agricultural, Rural Zoned Properties
- Display Homes
- Multiple Dwellings on One Title
- Serviced Apartments and Student Accommodation
- Rooming houses
- NDIS property
- Residual stock
- Split contracts
- Self-Managed Super Fund lending
- Bridging
- Bridging construction

Borrower Type

- Self-employed without tax returns or BAS
- Not in your job long enough
- Credit impairment or lower credit score
- Pay out tax debt
- Cash out for working capital
- Buying a business, no ABN or short-term ABN
- Lack of income or no income (inability to service a loan)
- Living expenses too high compared to your income, on paper at least
- Over 60 years old and/or retired
- Being on a visa or being a non-resident

Your Current Situation

With anything important in life, it is far better to understand what you need to do before you try to do it. Without hope and goals, we merely exist; there is nothing to strive for or look forward to. Having a goal gives direction and purpose in life, whether it is a small or big goal, short-term or long-term.

A useful and considered outcome comes from determining your income requirement in retirement. The choices you make today about your borrowing ability and property will affect you tomorrow. The culmination of your actions in your working life will either positively or negatively affect your life in retirement.

So many borrowers have used a less experienced broker or a useless bank employee. If you go to one bank and they say no, and then you accept that, that's your mistake, and you will have to live with it, but it's never too late to change. Every lender has a different policy. Accessing lenders that will give you a loan that banks will not can significantly impact your future and the present.

Retirement age can be open-ended; for some people, it may be earlier than for others. The younger someone starts making wise borrowing and investment decisions, the more time those assets have to grow in value, and the greater the income potential from those assets or what those assets can be turned into (sold and the equity repurposed) in retirement. Retirement is not the end goal; many people in their 70's wish to downsize, and they will usually need a bridging loan (buy before selling, then sell their current home to pay off the debt).

Many people assume that if they work hard and save money, they will one day become wealthy. This is wishful thinking for most, as 80% will end up on the pension. With this mindset, they are more likely to end up with modest savings that are ultimately less useful. They are unlikely to be wealthy unless they own a business and sell it for a couple of million dollars. So opening your borrowing options is often crucial.

An income figure to aim for in retirement could be $40,000 or $200,000 pa; what matters is that the figure is right for you. Once you have a goal, you will need to work backwards. Knowing what you want and need in your retirement makes it easier to establish a plan of action. When you are still young and working, it is easier to leverage your assets, in particular property, whilst not overstretching yourself. You still need to have a life.

Once you have a goal, you need to consider your current situation. There is no point in having a goal that is completely unachievable. What is achievable can often be more than you might think, though, especially if you have equity but lack the borrowing capacity to access it. Some borrowers are naïve; they think that if they have equity in a property, they can access it irrespective of their income when using a bank. Accessing equity, in turn, becomes debt or a loan, and as the debt increases, more borrowing capacity is required from a bank.

However, these borrowers would be correct in assuming they can access equity without income or borrowing capacity if they use a private lender, provided it is not their only property, and they are not going from owning a property to owning no property, unless it is already unconditionally sold, then a private lender can consider this. Because with a suitable exit strategy, there is often no need for borrowing capacity. It is important to understand how to apply for a loan without sufficient borrowing capacity.

Non-Residents and Visa Holders

For many borrowers, obtaining finance in Australia is not simply a matter of income or assets. Residency status, visa category, country of origin, currency conversion policies and lending appetite all play a significant role in whether a loan is approved. This is an area where traditional bank lending and private lending often differ substantially.

Traditional banks in Australia operate within highly structured credit policies. Those policies are designed to reduce risk and create consistency across large volumes of applications. While this can work well for standard PAYG borrowers with permanent residency and stable Australian income, it can become restrictive for non-residents, temporary visa holders, foreign income earners and applicants with more complex circumstances.

One of the major issues faced by non-residents is country restriction policy. Many banks have internal lists of countries they are either unwilling to lend against or only willing to consider under limited circumstances. These restrictions are not always publicly advertised. A borrower may have substantial income, strong assets and an excellent repayment history, yet still find themselves declined simply because they reside in, earn income in, or hold citizenship from a country viewed by the lender as higher risk.

The reasons banks impose these restrictions vary. Some concerns relate to foreign regulatory systems, political instability, currency volatility, fraud prevention, sanctions exposure, enforcement difficulties or document verification issues. Other restrictions arise from internal risk appetite rather than any issue with the borrower personally. In practice, this means two borrowers with identical financial positions may receive entirely different outcomes purely because they originate from different countries.

Traditional lenders also commonly apply shading to foreign income. This means the borrower's overseas earnings are not accepted at full value when converted into Australian dollars. Instead, many banks only use approximately 90% of the Australian dollar (AUD) equivalent income for servicing calculations. Some lenders reduce this even further depending on the currency involved.

For example, if a borrower earns the equivalent of AUD $200,000 per annum overseas, a bank using a 90% acceptance policy may only recognise AUD $180,000 for borrowing capacity purposes. If further buffers or exchange rate adjustments apply, the usable income may be reduced again. This can significantly impact borrowing capacity, particularly where interest rates are assessed at sensitised rates above the actual loan rate.

Banks justify this approach on the basis that exchange rates fluctuate. A borrower who pays in a foreign currency may see their effective Australian dollar income decline if the currency weakens against the AUD. While this is a legitimate credit concern, the practical effect is that many otherwise strong borrowers cannot access sufficient funding through mainstream lenders.

Visa status creates another major challenge. Many traditional lenders have strict policies regarding which visa subclasses they will accept. Australian citizens and permanent residents generally have access to the broadest range of lending options. However, temporary visa holders often face reduced loan-to-value ratios, additional pricing margins, stricter employment requirements or outright ineligibility.

Certain visa subclasses may be acceptable to one bank but completely unacceptable to another. Some lenders only accept specific skilled migration visas. Others may refuse bridging visas, student visas, working holiday visas, or newly issued temporary visas altogether. In many cases, borrowers are required to demonstrate that their remaining visa terms are lengthy before settlement, even where they have stable employment and substantial equity.

This creates frustration for many borrowers living and working in Australia who are financially capable of servicing a loan but do not neatly fit within standard banking policy. It can also create uncertainty for brokers attempting to place transactions where residency status becomes the primary obstacle rather than the underlying strength of the deal.

Private lending approaches these scenarios differently.

Private lenders are generally more focused on the overall transaction, the available security property, the exit strategy and the equity position rather than relying exclusively on rigid residency or visa policies. Because private lenders are commonly asset-based, they often assess the strength of the security property and the borrower's proposed repayment strategy before applying standardised servicing metrics.

As a result, private lenders may consider borrowers from countries that traditional banks would automatically decline. Rather than imposing broad country exclusions, a private lender may review the applicant's individual circumstances, the location and value of the security property, the loan-to-value ratio, and the proposed exit strategy.

Similarly, private lenders are commonly far more flexible regarding visa categories. Borrowers holding temporary visas, investor visas, bridging visas, partner visas, working visas or less common subclasses may still be considered. The focus becomes whether the transaction itself makes commercial sense and whether sufficient security exists to protect the lender's position.

This flexibility can be particularly valuable for borrowers who have recently arrived in Australia, are self-employed internationally, earn offshore income, or are involved in cross-border business activities. Many such borrowers have strong asset positions but do not satisfy the rigid income-verification models used by mainstream banks.

Another important distinction is that private lending usually does not require the same level of traditional borrowing capacity as standard bank lending, particularly when there is a clear and realistic exit strategy. For example, if the intention is to sell a property within a short period, refinance after construction completion, receive an inheritance, complete a business transaction or repay the loan through another identifiable event, the private lender may place substantial weight on that strategy.

This differs significantly from bank lending, where long-term servicing capacity is often the dominant consideration regardless of short-term asset position or planned repayment events.

Foreign Investment Review Board (FIRB) approval remains an important consideration for many non-resident borrowers purchasing Australian property. FIRB approval is generally required for certain acquisitions by foreign persons and is separate from the lender's own credit assessment process. Whether finance is obtained from a traditional bank or a private lender, borrowers must still comply with Australian foreign investment rules, where applicable. Private lenders will still require evidence that FIRB requirements have been satisfied before settlement.

Timing is another area where private lending can provide advantages for non-resident and visa-holder borrowers. Traditional bank applications involving foreign income or overseas documentation often experience extended assessment periods. Documents may require translation; foreign tax returns may need specialist review; and additional compliance checks may significantly delay approval timeframes. Private lenders may typically not require tax returns anyway.

Private lenders are often able to assess these matters more quickly due to their commercial approach and streamlined decision-making processes. This can be critical where borrowers are seeking to secure a property purchase, complete a settlement urgently or refinance an existing debt under time pressure.

Of course, flexibility comes with trade-offs. Private lending generally involves higher interest rates and fees compared with standard bank lending. This reflects the increased risk profile, shorter loan terms and specialised nature of the transactions being considered. Private lending is therefore commonly used as a short-term solution rather than a long-term owner-occupier mortgage product.

Even so, for many non-residents and visa holders, access to finance is more important than simply obtaining the lowest possible rate. A borrower cannot benefit from a cheaper bank rate if the bank will not approve the transaction in the first place.

In many respects, private lending fills the gap left by traditional banking policy. It provides a pathway for borrowers who have genuine equity, strong assets and credible exit strategies but fall outside the increasingly narrow lending criteria imposed by mainstream institutions.

For brokers and borrowers alike, understanding these differences is essential. Residency status, country of origin and visa type can dramatically alter lending outcomes under traditional banking policy. Private lending offers an alternative pathway where the focus shifts away from rigid policy restrictions and toward the overall strength of the transaction itself.

3.

What Lenders Look At – A Practical Guide for Any Loan Application

Foundations of Lending

When most people first consider borrowing, their thinking tends to settle quickly on a single, seemingly straightforward question: how much can be borrowed? It is an understandable focus. Numbers provide clarity. They give shape to an otherwise abstract process and allow for comparisons to be made. Yet this focus, while useful at the outset, can also obscure the broader nature of lending.

Lending is not simply a numerical exercise. It is not a process that begins and ends with a calculation. Rather, it is an assessment that determines whether a particular financial arrangement can be coherent, sustainable, and adaptable to change. The amount borrowed is the visible outcome of that assessment, not its substance.

To understand lending more fully, it is necessary to move beyond the idea of borrowing as a single decision and instead view it as a relationship between multiple elements. These elements include income, expenses, assets, liabilities, structure, and time. Each plays a role, but none is decisive on its own. It is their interaction that determines whether a lending scenario is considered workable.

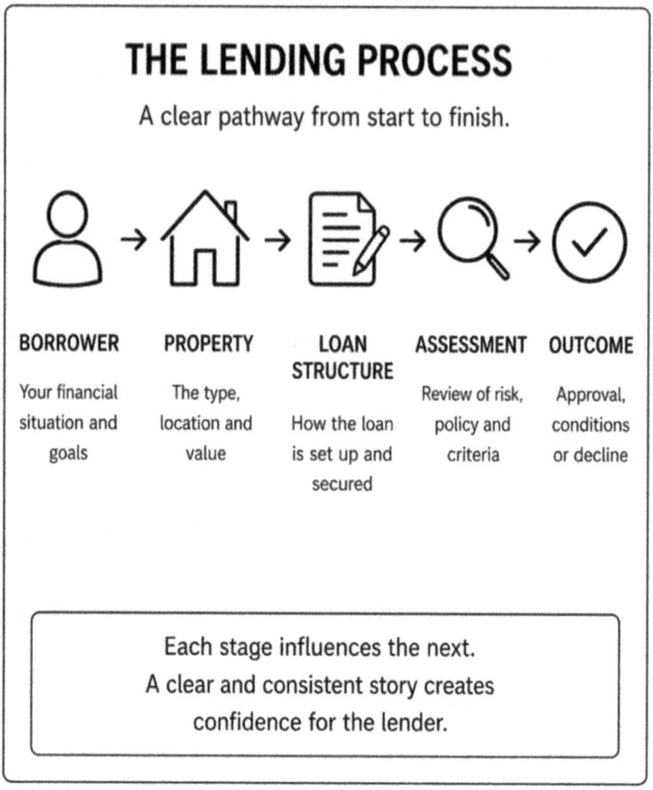

At the centre of this interaction sits the concept of confidence. A lender must be satisfied that the funds provided can be repaid not only under favourable conditions but also under circumstances that may change over time. This introduces a more nuanced question. The issue is not whether repayment is possible in a static sense, but whether it remains likely as conditions evolve.

Income is often treated as the starting point of this analysis. It represents the inflow of funds and provides the means through which obligations are met. However, income is not assessed solely by its size. Its reliability, consistency, and continuity are equally important. A high income that fluctuates significantly may offer less confidence than a lower, stable, and predictable income.

This reflects a broader principle within lending: stability often carries more weight than magnitude. A consistent pattern of behaviour, whether in income or expenditure, allows for a more reliable assessment. It reduces uncertainty and makes it easier to anticipate how a loan will perform over time. Of course, in many situations, income is not required with private lenders.

Expenses introduce another dimension. They represent the ongoing cost of maintaining a particular standard of living and fulfilling existing responsibilities. In practical terms, expenses determine what remains after essential obligations are met. This remaining portion, often referred to as surplus, is what supports additional commitments.

It is important to approach expenses with realism. They are not simply figures to be minimised to improve a borrowing position. They reflect actual living patterns and responsibilities. An artificially reduced estimate may improve a theoretical outcome, but it does not contribute to a sustainable arrangement. Lenders are therefore more concerned with consistency than optimisation. They seek to understand what is typical, rather than what is ideal.

Assets and liabilities extend the analysis further by providing a broader view of financial position. Assets represent accumulated value, while liabilities reflect existing obligations. Together, they show how a borrower's position has developed over time and how it is currently structured.

However, the presence of assets does not automatically translate into borrowing strength. Similarly, liabilities do not necessarily indicate weakness. What matters is how these elements interact. A borrower may hold significant assets, but if those assets are not readily accessible or realisable, their practical contribution may be limited. Conversely, liabilities that are well-managed and proportionate to income may not detract from a strong overall position.

This interplay between elements naturally leads to the concept of structure, which is often the least understood yet the most influential aspect of lending. Structure determines how a loan operates over time. It defines the pattern of obligations, the timing of payments, and the manner in which the loan progresses from commencement to conclusion.

A loan structured around regular repayments behaves predictably. The balance reduces gradually, if on principal and interest repayments, and the pathway to repayment is clear. In contrast, a loan structured around a defined future event introduces a different dynamic. The focus shifts from ongoing affordability to the feasibility of that event occurring as planned. This is the overarching benefit of short-term private lending.

Neither structure is inherently superior. Each serves a different purpose and suits different circumstances. The key consideration is alignment. The structure must reflect the borrower's position, the nature of the asset, and the intended outcome.

Alignment is a recurring theme in effective lending. A strong scenario is one in which all elements work together coherently. Income supports expenses; the structure supports the intended outcome, including the opportunity to avoid worrying about existing expenses or income; and the overall arrangement remains manageable under a range of conditions.

When alignment is present, the scenario becomes easier to understand and assess. The pathway from borrowing to repayment is clear, and confidence increases accordingly. When alignment is absent, the scenario may still be workable, but it requires more explanation and carries greater uncertainty.

Time is another critical factor that shapes lending outcomes. Every loan exists within a timeframe, whether short or long. Time introduces variability. Income may change, expenses may evolve, and external conditions may shift. A lending arrangement must therefore be capable of functioning not only at the outset, but throughout its duration.

Shorter timeframes tend to reduce uncertainty, simply because there is less opportunity for change. Longer timeframes introduce more variables, which may increase complexity. This does not make longer arrangements unsuitable, but it does require a more considered approach to structuring and planning.

It is also useful to distinguish between certainty and predictability. Certainty implies that outcomes are known in advance, which is rarely the case in financial matters. Predictability, on the other hand, suggests that outcomes are likely to follow a certain pattern based on available information. Lending relies on predictability rather than certainty.

This distinction reinforces the idea that lending is not about eliminating risk entirely. It is about understanding risk and structuring around it. A well-considered loan does not avoid uncertainty but manages it in a way that remains acceptable.

Behaviour introduces a more subtle but equally important element. While not always explicitly stated, the way a borrower manages their financial affairs can influence how a scenario is perceived. Consistency, clarity, and a demonstrated understanding of obligations contribute to overall confidence.

This does not make lending subjective in an arbitrary sense. Rather, it reflects the reality that financial decisions are made within a human context. Numbers provide structure, but interpretation gives them meaning.

As a result, lending outcomes are rarely determined by a single factor. They emerge from the combined effect of multiple elements, each influencing the others. This interconnectedness is what gives lending both its complexity and its flexibility.

Understanding this interconnectedness is perhaps the most valuable insight a borrower can gain. It shifts the focus from isolated measures to the overall picture. It encourages a more thoughtful approach, where decisions are made with reference to how all elements fit together.

Ultimately, the central question in lending is not simply whether a loan can be approved. It is whether the arrangement makes sense within the broader context of a person's financial position and objectives. When this question is addressed with clarity and realism, the process becomes more transparent, and the resulting decisions are more likely to be sustainable.

Borrowing Capacity and Structure

Borrowing capacity is one of the most widely discussed aspects of lending, yet it is often treated with more finality than it deserves. It is frequently presented as a clear, calculated number that defines what a borrower can and cannot do. While this presentation is useful in providing a reference point, it can create the impression that borrowing capacity represents an absolute boundary. In practice, it is more accurately understood as a **result within a specific framework**, rather than a universal limit.

The framework that produces borrowing capacity is built on a set of assumptions. These assumptions are designed to create consistency in how lending decisions are made. They typically include expectations regarding income stability, expenditure patterns, and how a loan will be repaid over time. Within this framework, borrowing capacity serves as a guide to what can be supported through regular repayments under standard conditions.

However, the presence of a framework also introduces constraints. Because borrowing capacity is calculated based on specific assumptions, it reflects what is possible within those assumptions. It does not necessarily capture the full range of possibilities that may exist when those assumptions change.

This is where confusion often arises. A borrower may receive a borrowing capacity figure and interpret it as a fixed limit. Yet when the structure of the loan is altered, or the purpose of the borrowing is reconsidered, the outcome may also change. The number itself has not become incorrect; rather, it has been applied within a different context, and that is why, in many contexts, not having a sufficient borrowing capacity is irrelevant.

Understanding this requires a shift in perspective. Borrowing capacity should not be viewed as a ceiling but as a **reference point within a particular model**. It provides direction, but it does not define every possible outcome.

This distinction becomes clearer when considering the role of structure. Structure determines how a loan behaves over time. It defines the pattern of obligations, the timing of payments, and the manner in which the loan progresses towards repayment.

In a traditional lending model, the structure is based on ongoing repayments. The borrower makes regular payments that gradually reduce the loan balance. In this context, borrowing capacity is directly linked to the ability to sustain those payments. The relationship between income, expenses, and commitments is central.

In other lending scenarios, the structure may differ. The loan may be designed around a defined outcome at a future point, rather than a series of regular repayments. In such cases, the emphasis shifts away from ongoing affordability and towards the feasibility of that outcome.

This does not mean that income becomes irrelevant. It remains an important factor because it can provide a choice of exit strategies. However, it is considered alongside other factors, such as the asset's strength and the clarity of the exit strategy. The framework has changed, and with it, the way borrowing capacity is applied.

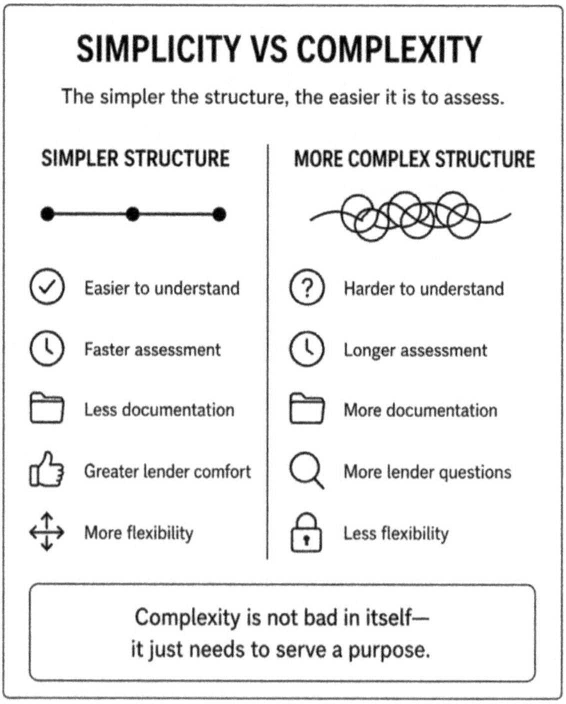

This highlights the relationship between borrowing capacity and structure. Borrowing capacity answers the question of what can be supported under a particular model. Structure answers the question of how that support is translated into a practical arrangement.

A borrower who focuses exclusively on borrowing capacity may overlook the opportunities that arise through structuring. Conversely, a borrower who focuses solely on structure, without regard for capacity, may create an arrangement that is difficult to sustain. The most effective approach involves understanding how the two interact.

Another important aspect of borrowing capacity is the role of assumptions within the model itself. These assumptions are designed to reflect reasonable expectations about financial behaviour. However, they are necessarily generalised. They cannot account for every individual circumstance.

For example, a model may apply standardised estimates of living expenses or assume certain levels of income variability. These assumptions provide a margin of safety, but they may not align perfectly with a specific borrower's situation. As a result, the borrowing capacity figure may feel conservative.

This conservatism is intentional. It reflects the need for lenders to manage risk across a wide range of scenarios. At the same time, it reinforces the idea that borrowing capacity is a guide rather than a precise measure of what is achievable in every case.

The interaction between borrowing capacity and structure also evolves over time. A borrower's financial position is not static. Income may change, expenses may shift, and priorities may develop. These changes can influence both capacity and the suitability of different structures.

For example, a borrower who initially relies on a traditional repayment model may later find that a different structure better suits their circumstances. Alternatively, a borrower who begins with a more flexible arrangement may transition to a more conventional structure as stability increases.

This dynamic aspect of lending is often overlooked. Borrowing capacity is not a fixed attribute, but a reflection of a particular point in time. Recognising this allows for a more adaptable approach. When the structure changes, the outcome may also change.

There is also a psychological dimension to borrowing capacity. Because it is presented as a clear number, it can create a sense of certainty. Borrowers may feel they have received a definitive answer, which can influence their decision-making.

This perception can lead to a focus on maximising borrowing capacity, rather than considering whether the resulting arrangement is appropriate. It may also discourage exploration of alternative structures that could better align with long-term objectives.

A more balanced approach involves recognising borrowing capacity as one piece of information among many. It provides useful insight, but it does not replace the need for judgment. Decisions should be guided by a combination of factors, including structure, timing, and overall suitability.

This brings into focus the distinction between ability and strategy. Borrowing capacity reflects the ability within a particular framework. Strategy involves choosing the most appropriate course of action within one's ability.

A borrower may have the capacity to pursue a certain option, but that does not necessarily mean it is the most suitable choice.

Suitability depends on how well the arrangement aligns with the borrower's circumstances and objectives.

This distinction encourages a more considered approach. Rather than focusing solely on what is possible, it emphasises what is appropriate. This shift in perspective leads to more sustainable outcomes.

Ultimately, borrowing capacity is best understood as a tool that informs decision-making. It provides a sense of what may be achievable under certain conditions, but it should be considered alongside other elements. When used in this way, it supports a more flexible and thoughtful approach to lending.

Equity, Leverage, and Positioning

Equity is one of the most frequently referenced concepts in lending, yet it is often approached in a simplified way that does not fully reflect its operation in practice. It is commonly defined as the difference between the value of an asset and the amount owed against it. While this definition is technically correct, it does not capture the practical realities of how equity is interpreted, applied, and relied upon within lending decisions.

From a lender's perspective, equity is not merely a calculation. It is a form of support, but one that must be assessed within context. The existence of equity does not automatically mean it can be accessed, nor does it guarantee that it will be treated uniformly across different scenarios. Its usefulness depends on how it interacts with other factors, including the nature of the asset, the structure of the loan, and the borrower's broader financial position.

One key distinction to understand is that equity is not static. While it may be measured at a particular point in time, its practical significance can change. Market conditions may influence the value of an asset, lending policies may affect how that value is interpreted, and the borrower's own position may alter how equity can be used. This means that equity should not be viewed as a fixed resource, but rather as a component that evolves within a changing environment.

Another important consideration is that not all equity carries the same practical weight. This is not a conceptual difference, but a functional one. Equity in an asset that is widely traded, easily valued, and broadly understood tends to inspire greater confidence than equity in an asset that is less frequently traded or more difficult to assess. The difference lies in how readily that equity can be relied upon if circumstances change.

For example, an asset with strong market activity provides a clearer reference point for value. It allows lenders to form a more confident view of what the asset represents in practical terms. In contrast, an asset with limited transaction history or more specialised characteristics may introduce greater uncertainty. This does not mean it lacks value, but it does influence how that value is considered within a lending framework.

This leads to a broader understanding of equity as something that must be interpreted, rather than simply measured. The figure itself is only part of the picture. Its relevance depends on how it fits within the overall structure of the scenario.

Closely related to equity is the concept of leverage. Leverage involves using existing assets to support additional borrowing. It allows a borrower to extend their position beyond what could be achieved through income alone. In doing so, it introduces both opportunity and complexity.

At a basic level, leverage enables expansion. It allows resources already accumulated to be used in new ways. However, it also establishes relationships among the different parts of a financial position. When one component is affected, others may be influenced as well.

This interconnectedness is central to how lenders assess leverage. The question is not simply how much leverage is being applied, but how that leverage is structured and whether the resulting position remains sustainable. A structure that relies heavily on interdependent elements may require closer scrutiny than one where each component stands more independently.

Leverage is not inherently positive or negative. Its effect depends on how it is used. When applied thoughtfully, it can provide flexibility and support progression. When applied without sufficient consideration, it can introduce pressure.

The distinction lies in control. Controlled leverage involves a deliberate approach in which each element of the structure is understood and managed. It considers how the arrangement will function not only under favourable conditions, but also under less predictable ones. Uncontrolled leverage, by contrast, tends to focus on expansion without fully accounting for how the structure will respond to change.

From a lending perspective, sustainability is the key measure. A leveraged position is considered stronger when it can remain stable under a range of conditions. This does not mean eliminating all risk but ensuring that risk is balanced and manageable.

Another aspect to consider is how leverage interacts with time. As with other elements of lending, time introduces variability. Over shorter periods, the effects of leverage may be more predictable. Over longer periods, the potential for change increases. Market conditions, asset values, and personal circumstances may all evolve, influencing how the leveraged position performs.

This reinforces the importance of structuring leverage with an awareness of the timeframe. A structure that is appropriate over a shorter horizon may require adjustment if extended over a longer period. Conversely, a structure designed for longer-term stability may appear more conservative initially but provide greater resilience over time.

The relationship between equity and leverage also highlights the importance of positioning. Positioning refers to how a borrower's overall financial arrangement is configured. It is not limited to individual assets or liabilities but also encompasses how these elements are combined.

A well-positioned scenario is one in which the various components support one another coherently. Equity is accessible where needed, leverage is applied in a controlled way, and the overall structure aligns with the borrower's objectives. Poor positioning, on the other hand, may involve elements that are individually acceptable but do not work effectively together. This is why some property types, and some remote locations, may present concerns for a lender, and so the loan-to-value ratio could be much lower to help mitigate the risk of stagnant or falling prices or prolonged sale period, which may then lead to the borrower having to reduce the sale price to sell it.

Positioning is particularly important when considering change. A well-structured financial position can adapt more easily to new conditions. It allows for adjustments without requiring fundamental changes to the entire arrangement. This flexibility contributes to stability, even when circumstances are uncertain.

Another dimension of positioning is the relationship between ability and intention. A borrower may have the capacity to apply leverage or access equity in a particular way, but the question remains whether doing so aligns with their broader objectives. This distinction between what can be done and what should be done is central to effective decision-making.

In practice, this means considering not only the immediate outcome, but also the longer-term implications. A decision that appears advantageous in the short term may introduce constraints later if it does not align with the overall direction. Conversely, a more measured approach may provide greater flexibility and sustainability.

Lenders, while primarily focused on risk, also indirectly assess positioning. They look for coherence in how a scenario is presented. A position that is clearly structured and logically aligned is easier to understand and assess. One that appears fragmented or inconsistent may raise questions, even if the individual components are acceptable.

This reinforces the importance of clarity. Equity and leverage are not abstract concepts; they are practical tools that must be applied in a way that is understandable. The clearer the positioning, the easier it is for a lender to form a view.

It is also worth recognising that equity and leverage do not operate in isolation from other elements of lending. They interact with income, expenses, and structure. A leveraged position that relies heavily on a particular outcome may require stronger support from other areas. Conversely, a position with strong income stability may accommodate a different approach.

This interconnectedness is what makes lending both complex and adaptable. It allows a range of approaches, but it also requires careful consideration of how they fit together.

Ultimately, the role of equity and leverage within lending is to provide flexibility within a structured framework. They expand what may be possible, but they do not remove the need for discipline. Their effectiveness depends on how they are applied, supported, and aligned with the overall position.

When understood in this way, equity and leverage become less about maximisation and more about balance. They are not ends in themselves but means through which a coherent and sustainable financial arrangement can be achieved.

Structure, Contracts, Time

The structure of a loan is one of the most influential yet often underappreciated aspects of lending. While much attention is given to figures such as borrowing capacity or asset value, structure determines how those figures are translated into a functioning arrangement. It defines how a loan behaves over time, how obligations are met, and how the arrangement progresses from commencement to conclusion.

At a practical level, structure answers a series of fundamental questions. When are payments required? How are they calculated? What events influence the progression of the loan? How does the arrangement respond if circumstances change? These questions are not always considered at the outset, yet they have a direct impact on the borrowing experience.

It is useful to think of structure not as a technical detail, but as the framework within which the loan operates. Two loans of the same size can feel entirely different depending on how they are structured. One may require consistent, predictable payments that gradually reduce the balance. Another may involve a different pattern of obligations, where repayment is linked to a defined future event. The difference lies not in the amount borrowed but in how the arrangement is designed to function.

Contract types play a central role in shaping this structure. They influence the timing, certainty, and sequence of events surrounding the loan. While contracts may appear to be legal documents that sit alongside the loan itself, in practice, they are closely connected to how the loan is assessed and managed. Each property type may have a different lending contract to accommodate its nature.

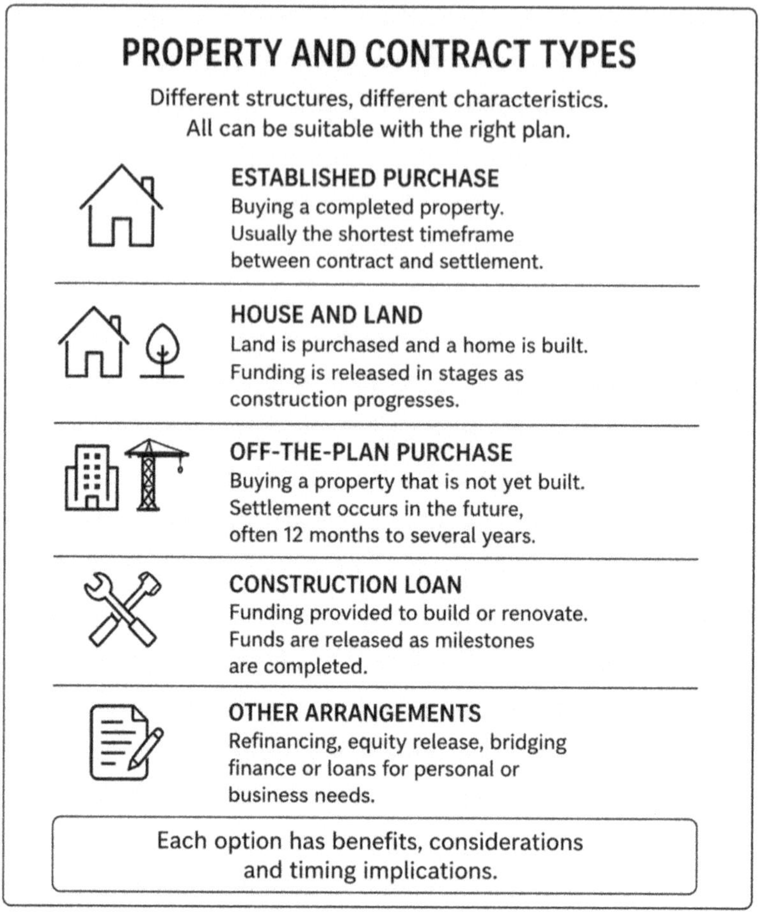

One of the most significant variables introduced by contract type is time. Some arrangements involve immediate completion, where the asset is acquired, and the loan is fully established at the same point. Others involve a delay between agreement and completion. During this period, the loan may not yet be fully in place, but the commitment has been made.

This distinction introduces a layer of complexity. When there is a delay between agreement and completion, circumstances may change. Income may fluctuate, expenses may evolve, and broader market conditions may shift. These changes do not necessarily create problems, but they do introduce uncertainty.

From a lending perspective, uncertainty is not something that must be eliminated entirely. Rather, it must be understood and managed. A structure that accounts for the passage of time is more resilient than one that assumes conditions will remain static. This is why lenders consider not only the current position, but also how that position may evolve.

Construction-based arrangements provide a clear example of how structure and time interact.

In these cases, funding is typically provided in stages, aligned with progress. The loan does not exist as a single, fixed amount from the outset. Instead, it develops over time as different phases of the project are completed.

This staged approach reflects practical reality. It ensures that funding corresponds with value as it is created. At each stage, progress is reassessed, and funds are released accordingly. This creates a dynamic structure in which the loan evolves rather than remains static.

However, this evolution also requires awareness. During the construction period, the borrower may be managing multiple elements simultaneously. Costs may increase gradually, and the asset itself may not yet be in a position to provide any form of return or utility. This does not make the arrangement unsuitable, but it highlights the importance of understanding how the structure behaves during this phase.

Timing is not limited to construction scenarios. It is a factor in all lending arrangements. Even in more straightforward cases, the duration of the loan influences how it is assessed. Shorter timeframes tend to reduce the potential for change, while longer timeframes introduce more variables.

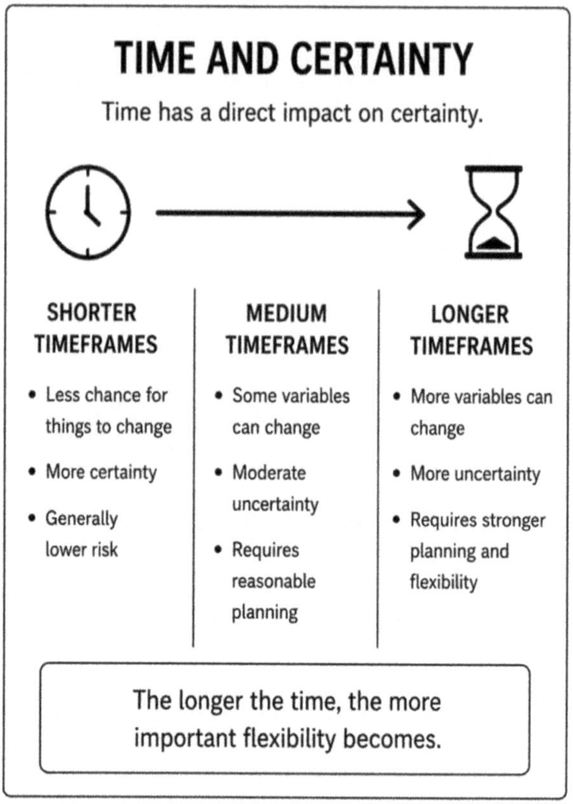

This introduces an important consideration: the relationship between time and certainty. Certainty is rarely absolute in financial matters, but shorter periods tend to offer greater predictability. There is less opportunity for external factors to influence the outcome. Over longer periods, the likelihood of change increases.

This does not mean that longer-term arrangements are inherently less suitable. In many cases, they are necessary and appropriate. However, they require a structure that can accommodate variation. A rigid arrangement may function well under stable conditions but become difficult if circumstances shift. A more flexible structure, while potentially less efficient in certain respects, may offer greater resilience.

Another aspect of structure closely linked to time is sequencing. This refers to the order in which events occur and how they influence one another. In some arrangements, events follow a straightforward progression. In others, multiple elements may occur simultaneously or in overlapping stages.

For example, a borrower may be managing an existing obligation while entering into a new arrangement. One property may be in the middle of being constructed, while another contract to purchase an existing property is being considered. There would be no rental income yet for the property under construction, and some lenders may not use projected rental income. The timing of these elements can influence how the overall position is assessed. If obligations overlap in a way that creates pressure, the structure may require adjustment. If they are sequenced in a more manageable way, the scenario may be easier to support.

Sequencing is therefore not just a matter of timing, but of coordination. It involves ensuring that different elements of a financial position align in a way that remains workable.

Contractual arrangements also influence the level of certainty within a structure. Some contracts provide clear, defined outcomes with limited variation. Others allow for a degree of flexibility, which may introduce additional considerations.

Flexibility within a contract can be beneficial, as it allows for adjustment if circumstances change. However, it also requires a greater level of understanding. The implications of different outcomes must be considered, and the structure must accommodate them.

This reinforces the idea that structure is not simply about meeting initial conditions. It is about creating an arrangement that can function over time, even as those conditions evolve. For example, if someone has an investment property with sufficient equity that, if sold, would clear the debt, a private lender can consider lending against it or their home without demonstrating borrowing capacity. This would be an arrangement discussed with the relevant lender; it will not be a bank.

From a lender's perspective, the clarity of structure is critical. A clearly defined arrangement is easier to assess because it provides a coherent picture of how the loan will operate. The lender can see how obligations will be met, how the loan will progress, and how it will ultimately be concluded.

Where structure is unclear or overly complex, the level of scrutiny increases. This is not because complexity is inherently problematic, but because it requires greater explanation. The lender must understand not only the individual components but how they interact.

This is why simplicity is often valued within lending. A straightforward structure reduces the potential for misunderstanding and makes the assessment process more efficient. However, simplicity should not be pursued at the expense of suitability. In some cases, a more complex structure may be necessary to achieve the desired outcome. Very often, what is complex in the eyes of a bank will be simple in the eyes of a private lender.

The key is to ensure that complexity serves a purpose. It should be introduced where it adds value, not simply as a matter of preference. A well-considered structure balances clarity with functionality, providing both understanding and flexibility.

Another important aspect of structure is how it responds to change. No financial arrangement exists in a static environment. Income, expenses, and external conditions may all evolve over time. A structure that is too rigid may struggle to accommodate these changes, while one that allows for adjustment can remain effective.

This adaptability does not mean that the structure should be uncertain or undefined. Rather, it should include mechanisms that allow for variation within a controlled framework. This may involve flexibility in repayment patterns, options for adjustment, or provisions that account for different scenarios.

In practical terms, this means considering not only how a loan will function under expected conditions, but also how it will respond if those conditions change. This forward-looking approach contributes to long-term sustainability. For example, if a person conveys to a private lender that they will sell an investment property, and it will clear the debt on the property being provided to the lender, they still have the flexibility to refinance it or pay it off another way, whilst at the same time avoiding the need for demonstrated borrowing capacity. Maybe later they will have enough income, or their financials will be in order, or their business cash flow can pay it off.

It is also useful to consider how structure influences behaviour. The way a loan is designed can shape how a borrower interacts with it. Regular, predictable obligations may encourage consistency, while more flexible arrangements may require a higher level of discipline.

This behavioural dimension is often overlooked, yet it plays a role in how a loan performs over time. A structure that aligns with a borrower's habits and preferences is more likely to be maintained effectively.

Ultimately, structure, contracts, and time are interconnected elements that define how a lending arrangement operates. They determine not only the initial assessment, but the ongoing experience of the loan.

Understanding these elements allows for more informed decision-making. It shifts the focus from individual components to how they fit together. This broader perspective supports the creation of arrangements that are not only workable at the outset but sustainable over time.

Advanced Structures and Refinancing

As a borrower's financial position develops, the question of structure often becomes more prominent. Early lending decisions are frequently made in relatively simple forms, typically involving direct ownership and straightforward repayment arrangements. Over time, however, circumstances may evolve. Assets accumulate, objectives broaden, and the need for more tailored structures begins to emerge.

At this stage, borrowers may consider holding assets or entering into lending arrangements through different legal or financial structures. These can include companies, trusts, or superannuation-based entities. While these structures are often associated with sophistication, their relevance lies not in their complexity, but in their suitability for a given situation.

From a lending perspective, the introduction of these structures changes the nature of the assessment. The focus is no longer limited to an individual's financial position. Instead, it extends to the interaction among the entity, the individuals associated with it, and the arrangement's purpose.

Companies, for example, operate as separate legal entities. This separation can provide certain advantages in terms of organisation and accountability. However, it also introduces additional considerations. Lenders must assess not only the company's financial position but also the individuals who stand behind it. In many cases, this involves guarantees, which effectively reconnect the company's obligations to personal responsibility.

This dual-layered assessment requires clarity. The lender must understand how the company functions, how decisions are made within it, and how its financial position is supported. Where this understanding is clear, such as the company existing purely as an asset-holding company, not a trading company, the structure can be assessed effectively, and the length of time they have had an ABN will not matter to private lenders. Where it is not, the process may become more involved.

Trusts introduce a different set of considerations. Unlike companies, which operate as entities in their own right, trusts function as arrangements in which assets are held and managed by one party for the benefit of others. This creates a structure defined by roles and relationships rather than by ownership in the traditional sense.

From a lending perspective, this requires a broader view. The lender must consider the trustee, the beneficiaries, and the terms of the trust itself. The trust deed becomes a central document, as it defines how the structure operates and what actions can be taken within it.

This additional layer of interpretation does not make trusts unsuitable. Rather, it highlights the importance of understanding how the structure functions. A well-documented and clearly defined trust can be assessed with confidence. One that lacks clarity may require further examination. Some banks, however, when the trustee is an individual, will treat this as a coded loan with greater compliance, whereas a private lender may still treat it as a non-coded loan. This can be very beneficial to the trustee.

Superannuation-based structures, particularly self-managed arrangements, introduce yet another dimension. These structures operate within a defined regulatory framework, which influences how borrowing can occur. Loans in this context are typically limited, with specific conditions governing their structure and the assets that can be involved.

For lenders, this means that the assessment must account not only for financial considerations but also for compliance with the relevant framework, the *Superannuation Industry (Supervision) Act (SIS)*. The structure is therefore shaped by both financial and regulatory factors, which must align for the arrangement to proceed.

Across all of these structures, a common principle applies: that complexity should serve a purpose. The introduction of an entity or arrangement should reflect a clear objective, rather than a preference for sophistication. Where a structure aligns with the borrower's position and goals, it can enhance clarity and organisation. Where it does not, it may introduce unnecessary complications.

This principle of alignment is particularly important when considering how structures interact with lending over time. A structure that is appropriate at one stage may require adjustment as circumstances evolve. This is where the concept of refinancing becomes relevant.

Refinancing is often described in simple terms as replacing one loan with another. While this description is accurate, it does not fully capture the role refinancing plays within a broader financial strategy. In practice, refinancing is a means of reassessing an existing arrangement and determining whether it remains suitable under current conditions.

Over time, a borrower's position may change. Income levels may increase or decrease, expenses may shift, and objectives may evolve. In addition, external factors such as lending policies, market conditions, and regulatory requirements may also change. These developments can alter the way a loan is viewed and how it functions.

Refinancing provides an opportunity to respond to these changes. It allows the borrower to revisit the loan structure, adjust its terms, and realign it with their current position. This may involve modifying repayment terms, extending the loan term, or restructuring the arrangement to improve flexibility.

However, it is important to recognise that refinancing is not a continuation of an existing approval. It is a new assessment, conducted under current conditions. This means that the outcome of a refinancing application is influenced by the borrower's current position rather than by the circumstances that existed when the original loan was established.

This distinction is significant. A loan that was appropriate and approved at one point in time may not be replicated under different conditions. Changes in income, expenses, or policy can all influence the outcome. For this reason, refinancing should be approached with a clear understanding of both its potential benefits and its limitations.

Another aspect of refinancing is its role in maintaining alignment. As discussed earlier, a strong lending scenario is one in which all elements work together coherently. Over time, this alignment may shift. A structure that once suited the borrower's needs may no longer be the most effective arrangement.

Refinancing allows for this alignment to be restored. By adjusting the loan structure, it is possible to bring it back into line with the borrower's current position and objectives. This process does not necessarily involve major changes. In some cases, small adjustments can have a meaningful impact.

It is also worth considering how refinancing interacts with broader financial planning. A loan does not exist in isolation. It forms part of a larger financial position that may include other assets, liabilities, and commitments. Changes to one element can affect others, and refinancing may be used to manage these relationships.

For example, a borrower may seek to consolidate multiple arrangements into a single structure, simplifying their overall position. Alternatively, they may adjust the structure of a loan to create greater flexibility for future decisions. In each case, refinancing is used not simply to alter a loan but to improve the coherence of the overall arrangement.

The timing of refinancing is another important consideration. Because lending conditions can change, the timing of a reassessment may influence the available options. A borrower who reviews their position at one point in time may encounter different conditions than at another.

This does not mean that timing should be approached speculatively. Rather, it highlights the importance of awareness. Understanding the current environment enables more informed decisions and helps explain why outcomes may vary.

Another dimension of refinancing is its behavioural aspect. The decision to revisit an existing arrangement requires a willingness to embrace change. It involves reassessing assumptions, considering alternatives, and adjusting where appropriate.

This process can be beneficial, as it encourages a more active approach to financial management. Rather than treating a loan as a fixed arrangement, it can evolve over time. This adaptability contributes to long-term sustainability.

At the same time, it is important to approach refinancing with clarity. Not every situation requires change. In some cases, the existing structure may continue to serve its purpose effectively. The decision to refinance should therefore be based on a clear understanding of what is being achieved.

Across both advanced structures and refinancing, a consistent theme emerges. Lending is not static. It is shaped by decisions made over time, which influence how the overall position evolves. Structures may become more complex or be simplified. Arrangements may be adjusted to reflect changing circumstances.

The effectiveness of these decisions depends on alignment. Each change should contribute to a more coherent and sustainable position. Where this is achieved, the overall structure becomes easier to manage and more resilient to change.

Ultimately, advanced structures and refinancing are tools. They provide ways to organise, adjust, and refine a financial position. Their value lies not in their complexity, but in their ability to support a clear and consistent approach to lending.

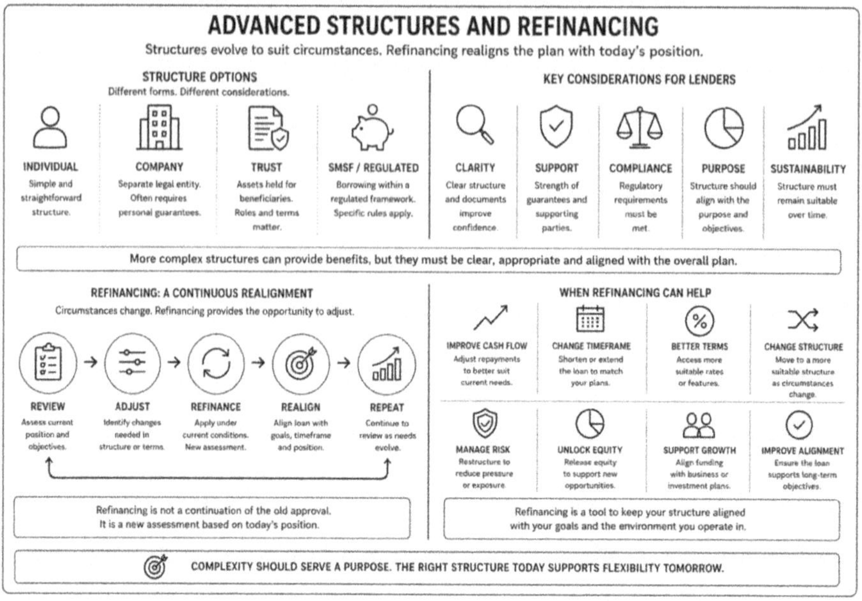

Risk, Decision-Making, and Real-World Application

Risk is an inherent part of lending, yet it is often misunderstood as something that can be reduced to a single measure. In practice, risk is not a standalone concept. It emerges from the interaction of multiple elements, each contributing to the overall position. Understanding how these elements combine is essential to understanding how lending decisions are made.

Lenders do not assess risk in isolation. They consider how different factors sit alongside one another and how they behave collectively. A single factor, when viewed on its own, may be entirely acceptable. However, when combined with other factors, the overall position may change. This process of combining elements is often referred to as layering.

Layering reflects the idea that risk is cumulative. It is not simply the presence of a factor that matters, but how that factor interacts with others. For example, a longer timeframe may be manageable in one context. A more complex structure may also be manageable in another. However, when both are present together, the level of uncertainty increases, and the scenario requires closer consideration.

This does not mean that complexity or variation should be avoided. Rather, it highlights the importance of balance. A well-structured scenario distributes different elements so that they do not unnecessarily compound. It ensures that no single aspect places undue pressure on the overall arrangement.

The concept of balance extends beyond individual factors to the entire lending scenario. Income, expenses, assets, structure, and time all contribute to the overall position. When these elements are aligned, the scenario becomes easier to understand and assess. When they are not, the level of uncertainty increases.

This naturally leads to an understanding of how lending decisions are made. From the outside, lending decisions can sometimes appear inconsistent. Similar scenarios may produce different outcomes, or a seemingly straightforward arrangement may require additional scrutiny. To understand this, we need to look at the process from the lender's perspective.

Lending decisions typically involve multiple layers of assessment. At an initial level, baseline criteria are reviewed. This includes income, expenses, existing commitments, and the nature of the asset. This stage establishes whether the scenario meets fundamental requirements.

Beyond this initial review, a more detailed assessment takes place. This is where the broader context is considered. The structure of the loan, the purpose of the borrowing, and the overall coherence of the arrangement are examined. It is at this stage that the scenario is evaluated not just in terms of numbers, but in terms of how those numbers fit together.

Decision-makers are not simply applying formulas. They are interpreting information. They are asking whether the scenario makes sense, is internally consistent, and is likely to remain workable over time. This interpretive aspect is what allows lending to accommodate a wide range of circumstances.

Institutional factors also play a role. Lenders operate within defined frameworks that are shaped by internal policies, regulatory requirements, and broader market conditions. These frameworks influence how decisions are made and what level of flexibility is available.

As a result, lending outcomes are influenced by both the specifics of the scenario and the environment in which it is assessed. This explains why outcomes may vary, even where the underlying details appear similar.

Another important aspect of lending is the concept of the exit strategy. Every loan has an endpoint, whether it is explicitly defined or implied through ongoing repayments. The exit strategy describes how the loan will be concluded.

In more straightforward arrangements, the exit is built into the structure. Regular repayments gradually reduce the balance until it is fully repaid. This type of exit is predictable and closely linked to income.

In other scenarios, the exit may depend on a specific event. This could involve completing a project, selling an asset, or transitioning to another form of lending. In these cases, the clarity of the exit becomes particularly important.

A well-defined exit strategy answers several key questions. What event will lead to repayment? When is that event expected to occur? What factors could influence its success? The strength of the exit lies in its realism. It should be grounded in current conditions and supported by evidence, rather than based on assumptions that may not hold.

It is also important to recognise that exit strategies are not static. As circumstances change, the most appropriate way to conclude a loan may also evolve. This reinforces the need for ongoing awareness and the ability to adjust where necessary.

The relationship between risk and exit strategy is significant. A clear and achievable exit reduces uncertainty, while an unclear or overly optimistic exit increases it. This does not mean that all scenarios must follow the same pattern. Rather, it highlights the importance of ensuring that the exit aligns with the overall structure.

Real-world scenarios provide a useful way to understand how these concepts come together. While each situation is unique, certain patterns can be observed.

In a straightforward scenario, a borrower with stable income and manageable expenses seeks a loan for a widely understood asset. The structure is simple, the timeframe is clear, and the exit is based on ongoing repayments. In this case, the elements align in a way that is easy to assess. The pathway from borrowing to repayment is predictable, and confidence is high.

In a more complex scenario, a borrower may be pursuing an arrangement that involves multiple elements. The structure may be layered, the timeframe extended, and the exit linked to a future event. Each of these elements may be acceptable on its own, but together they require careful consideration.

The outcome in such cases depends on how well the elements are balanced. If the structure is clear, the exit is realistic, and the overall arrangement remains coherent, the scenario may still be supported. If these elements are not aligned, the level of uncertainty increases.

Another scenario may involve a change over time. A borrower who was previously approved under certain conditions may seek to adjust their arrangement. Since the original approval, their financial position may have evolved, and lending conditions may have shifted. In this case, the assessment is based on current circumstances, not past approvals.

These examples illustrate that lending is not determined by a single factor. It is shaped by the interaction of multiple elements, each contributing to the overall position.

Decision-making within lending, therefore, involves both structure and judgement. It requires a consistent framework, but also the ability to interpret how that framework applies to a particular scenario. This combination allows for flexibility while maintaining discipline.

From a borrower's perspective, understanding this process can lead to more effective decision-making. It encourages a focus on alignment rather than maximisation. Instead of asking what is possible in isolation, the question becomes whether the overall arrangement makes sense.

This shift in perspective has practical implications. It supports more realistic expectations, reduces the likelihood of misalignment, and contributes to more sustainable outcomes. It also reinforces the importance of clarity. A well-presented scenario, where the elements are clearly defined and logically connected, is easier to assess and more likely to proceed.

Behaviour also plays a role in how scenarios are perceived. Consistency in financial management, clarity in communication, and a demonstrated understanding of obligations contribute to overall confidence. While these factors may not be quantified in the same way as income or assets, they influence how a scenario is interpreted.

Another dimension to consider is adaptability. Financial positions are not static, and lending arrangements must be capable of responding to change. A structure that allows for adjustment is more likely to remain effective over time than one that is rigid.

This does not mean that all arrangements should be flexible in the same way. Rather, it highlights the importance of considering how a structure will respond if conditions evolve. This forward-looking approach contributes to resilience.

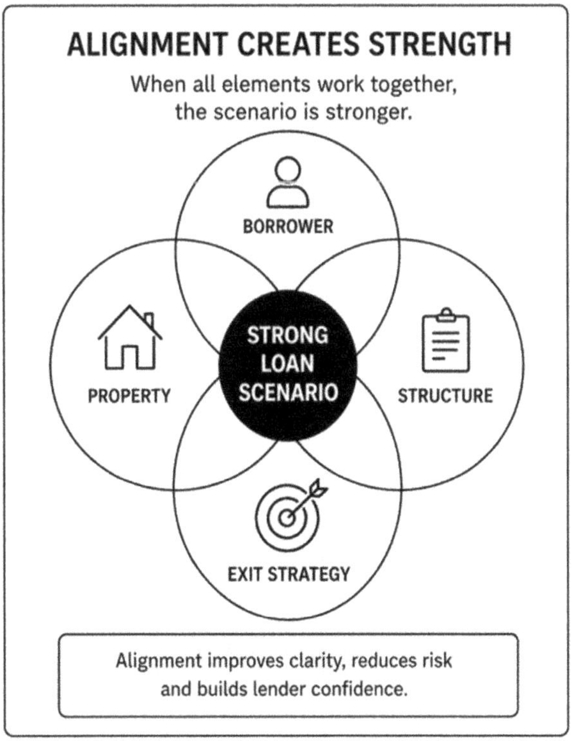

Ultimately, risk, decision-making, and exit strategy are interconnected elements that define how lending operates in practice. They influence not only whether a loan is approved, but how it performs over time.

When these elements are understood and aligned, the lending process becomes more transparent. Decisions are easier to interpret, expectations are more realistic, and outcomes are more likely to be sustainable.

At its core, lending is not about eliminating uncertainty. It is about managing it in a way that remains acceptable. This involves balancing different factors, structuring arrangements thoughtfully, and maintaining clarity throughout the process.

When this balance is achieved, lending becomes less about constraint and more about alignment. It supports decisions that are not only possible but appropriate for the circumstances in which they are made.

4.

Mortgage Lending Requirements Helping You Be Better Prepared

Now we get into some very practical and useful information to guide you in applying for finance, and how you can improve the experience you have as you go through the loan application process.

The most important thing a borrower needs to consider is what the loan will cost them each month (the repayment amount) and whether the loan is suitable for their needs. It should never be only about the interest rate. It is also important to recognise that not all loans are designed to operate in the same way.

Traditional lending relies heavily on income and the ability to meet ongoing repayment commitments. By contrast, most private lending arrangements are structured around the strength of the underlying asset and the borrower's ability to exit the loan within a defined timeframe. In these cases, the question is not at all whether the borrower can afford the loan each month, but whether the overall structure makes sense from beginning to end. There are no repayments; what would have been repayments are capitalised as interest-only.

'Would-be' borrowers must also consider, if currently renting, whether they should continue to rent or whether they should 'buy to live in' or 'buy as an investment' and continue to rent.

LOAN PURPOSE
(OUTSTANDING LOANS)
(ADIs ONLY)

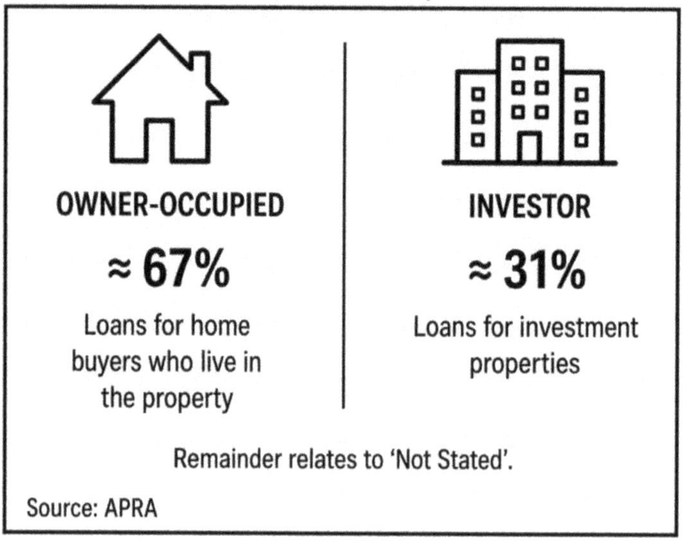

In some lending structures, particularly within private or short-term lending, this focus shifts slightly. Rather than assessing affordability through ongoing monthly repayments, the emphasis may instead be placed on how the loan will be repaid at the end of the term. This can include situations where no regular repayments are required during the loan period, provided there is a clearly defined and realistic exit strategy, such as the sale of a property or refinancing at a later stage.

Refinancing, for whatever reason, such as upsizing properties, extending, or debt consolidating, including freeing up equity for another property, should require the need to compare the repayment figure of the current loan to what another lender can offer. Often, what matters more is whether the loan provides everything the buyer needs, which may be a higher priority than just a better rate.

Borrowing capacity has risen to the top of the list as one of a borrower's most important needs. That said, borrowing capacity is not always the limiting factor in every lending scenario. In private lending, there are circumstances in which a borrower's income position may be less relevant, particularly when there is sufficient equity in a property and a clear pathway to repayment through sale. This does not remove risk, but it changes how that risk is assessed.

The question of which situation is superior (buying or renting a place to live) is one that's not as common as some might think, but I think it should be.

Emotion is a powerful force and, more often than not, eclipses pragmatism. In other words, people often want to live in their own house rather than buy a house to make money. The Australian Dream has been to own a house, pay it off over 30 years and live debt-free in retirement. This in itself has become difficult for many. The reality is that very few people actually end up living in their dream home. Likewise, it is too singularly minded just to focus on where to live. Many people have purchased a property, perhaps paid it off, perhaps not, but have a financially limited existence in retirement. The bigger picture needs to play a part, now, not later.

Selecting a property, if buying to live in it, is rarely a commercial decision-making process.

People like to own a house so they can do what they want to it. It provides a greater sense of freedom, particularly for those who work for someone rather than being self-employed. Many feel it's nice to be in control of their home life if someone else largely dictates their work life.

Whilst property may not be a short-term investment, finance may be, and often is, changed or varied. It's a bit like being part of the Millennials and Generation Y, and how they think about a job: generally, there's no loyalty, and transient behaviour is common and widespread.

It's always worth applying for a loan to buy a property, at a bare minimum for investment, if not to live, rather than just continuing on renting, and doing nothing to leverage off any capital growth.

Whether you escape the life of renting — or are unable to escape it — is not the main issue. It's what you do with your borrowing capacity that really matters. Weigh up trying to save for years, to stubbornly accumulate a deposit for a property to live in, in a better suburb perhaps, or close to parents, compared to buying something still in a good suburb, but a bit more affordable, much sooner. Then you can leverage the growth in that property to climb the property ladder.

You need money to make money. Leverage (debt) provides the money and, therefore, the opportunity to make money with it. This does not mean someone should purchase a $1.2 million house that only brings in $650 a week rent, when there may be an opportunity to buy a 700K property that could bring in $600 a week.

Leverage, however, can be applied in different ways depending on the lending structure used. In a traditional loan, leverage is supported by income and managed through ongoing repayments. In a private lending scenario, leverage may instead be supported by equity, with the expectation that the position will be resolved through a future event, most commonly the sale of the asset. This distinction is subtle, but important.

Renting to invest, or as some are labelling it, 'rentvesting' means a person continues to rent, while maximising and improving their borrowing capacity by buying an investment property. Borrowing capacity will often be higher when buying an investment property than when buying a home, depending on how much rent the borrower chooses to continue paying. Whilst renting allows someone to live in a better suburb than they might normally be able to, it does not mean they should spend all their money towards rent, just to live in a better suburb, especially if they're thinking smarter by lowering their rent expense and the effect of it on their borrowing capacity.

Owning a property can work out hundreds of thousands of dollars better long term if the borrower just buys somewhere less expensive (thought well-researched) than the narrow focus of simply comparing the cost of rent versus the cost of a mortgage. Buy somewhere just to get your foot in the door and on the capital growth ladder.

For investors, it's not as easy as it was to keep borrowing money and having many options for where to borrow is less likely than having fewer choices that work for structure, strategy, borrowing capacity, and lower risk.

Whatever the decision — whether to continue to rent/live at home, and buy an investment property, or whether to cease renting and actually buy a property to move into — it's important to understand how finance works, and to find the loan that best meets your needs.

Always bear in mind the costs associated with buying a property; these costs apply whether it's your principal place of residence or an investment (except for land tax and variances to stamp duty in some cases). Lenders will need to see, in an account, that the borrower has the money to pay the difference between the loan amount on offer and the purchase price when buying a property. Remember, you will need more than just the difference in order to settle on the property and own it.

These costs also become relevant when considering exit strategies. In a sale-based repayment scenario, it is not enough to consider the gross sale price of a property. The net proceeds, after accounting for selling costs, must still be sufficient to clear the loan. This is a key consideration in private lending, where the exit is central to the structure.

Costs of buying a property include:

- Stamp duty;
- Search fees, legal costs (including conveyancer fee);
- Lender costs (these could be application fees, legal costs, or sometimes valuation);
- Possibly lenders' mortgage insurance;
- Pest and property inspections.

Pest costs may not be necessary for brand-new properties. Property inspections are necessary for *every* property. You cannot just blindly trust the builder's quality or their finished product. Be careful who you rely on. If they're a real estate agent, they're a salesperson and do not represent the buyer. Some will definitely try to convince you not to get a property inspection.

Costs of owning a property include:

- water and council rates (other rates for an owner-occupier);
- insurance (building insurance if there's no body corporate, and landlord insurance if it's an investment property);

- repairs and maintenance costs;
- body corporate fees, for strata (typically more than two on a block);
- furbishing (depending on how much furniture the buyer already has).

Costs of selling a property include:

- advertising and marketing fees;
- capital gains for investment property;
- agent's fees (can often be negotiated, but let's say between 1.6–2.5%).

Requirements for Submitting a Loan Application to a Lender

These requirements apply primarily to traditional lending institutions. Private lenders may require a different set of information, often placing greater emphasis on the asset itself, the loan-to-value position, and the proposed exit strategy, rather than detailed income verification.

Requirements can vary by lender. The list below will suit most lenders.

- Two to three forms of ID totalling 100 points — one of them being a photo ID, such as driver's license (40 points), or passport (70 points) and one additional form of ID such as birth certificate (70 points), concession, healthcare card, student card (40 points), rates notice, letter from employer with name and address of applicant (35 points), utility statement, Medicare card/credit card (25 points). The points attributed may vary from lender to lender;

- Two forms of income evidence for an employee — starting with one to two pay slips or 3 months' salary credits plus one other form of verification, such as a letter from an employer/contract, and/or group certificate, tax return and assessment notice. Some employers do not have the professionalism or capability to produce anything beyond handwritten pay slips and group certificates, so we will need other evidence;
- Self-employed full documentation loan, 1–2 full financial years tax returns and assessment notices personally and 1–2 full financial years tax returns for the company/trust;
- If low/alternate documentation loans. BAS, and/or bank statements, and/or accountant or self-declaration;
- 6 months repayment history statements of any mortgage debt, if it is a refinance situation;
- 1–3 months of credit card statements, 3 months of statements for personal loan, and/or car loan;
- Council rates notice for refinances, sometimes required to evidence ownership of other properties;
- If you are making a purchase, you will need the purchase contract, the land transfer, a copy of the deposit receipt, and evidence of funds to complete the purchase. If it's for a 'house and land' or structural renovations/extensions, you'll also need to supply the *fixed-price* construction contract, plans, and specs;
- Rental statement/lease agreement for any investment properties or rent appraisal if buying one without a tenant in;
- Full 'stamped' trust deed if a trust is involved;
- *Please* include all credit card limits and amounts owing, including HECS debts, store cards and cards associated with buying furniture on interest-only terms.

Process of a Loan

The Process Involved in Applying for a Loan (Anyone):

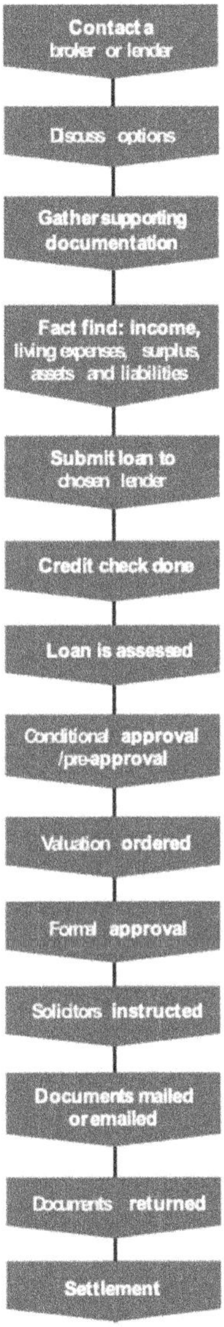

While this process reflects a standard lending pathway, private lending may follow a more streamlined sequence. Because the assessment is often centred on the asset and exit strategy, fewer steps may be required for income verification, while valuation and structural clarity become more critical.

Mortgage Brokers/Credit Advisors

Broker share of loans

- **76.7% of all new residential home loans** were written through brokers in the **December 2025 quarter**
- **77.3% (Sept 2025)** and **77.6% (June 2025)** — effectively the peak range
- Around **75%–77% throughout 2025,** depending on the quarter
- Australia is now one of the **most broker-reliant mortgage markets globally**, with some estimates placing it close to **80% of new lending. (Source: Reuters)**

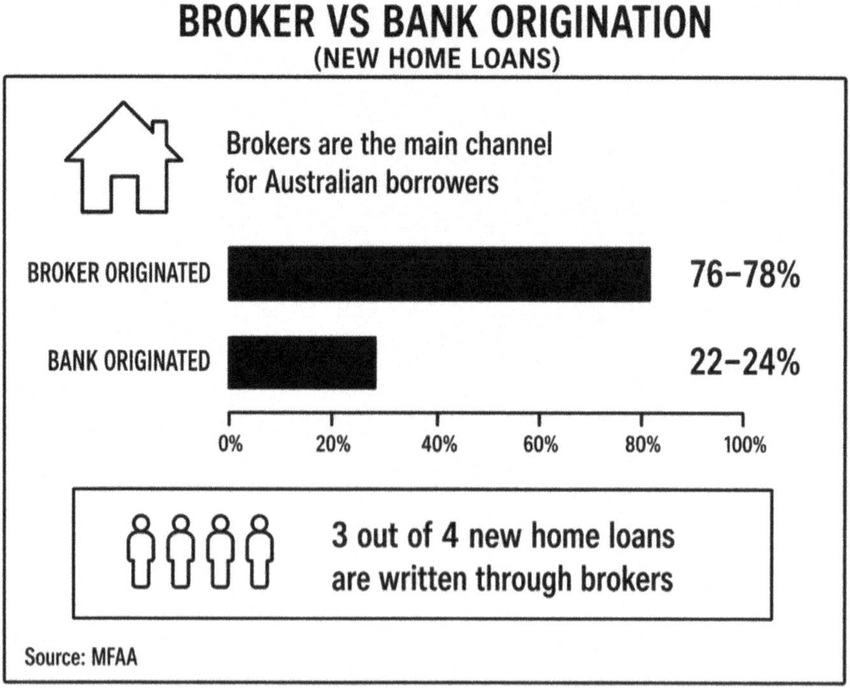

The industry they operate in is known as 'third party', because brokers

have access to a panel of lenders via the aggregator or franchise model they belong to, and brokers offer you the lenders' products. An aggregator/ franchise group acts as a wholesaler between mortgage brokers and lenders. Some brokers are directly accredited with some lenders, giving them direct access to those lenders rather than via the aggregator/group they're a member of (though they will usually belong to an aggregator). Therefore, the products are not being offered directly to you (the consumer) from the lender. They are offered through a third party (i.e. the broker).

Brokers may hold their own credit license, or more commonly, operate as a credit representative under another broker's license, the franchise's license, or the aggregator's license. A broker must be a member of either the Mortgage & Finance Association of Australia (MFAA) or the Finance Brokers Association of Australia (FBAA). Otherwise, it's recommended not to use them.

A mortgage broker is vital, and I recommend using one for many reasons. One that stands out for anyone, whether you're an up-sizer, downsizer, extender, refinancer, first homebuyer, first-time investor or growing property investor, is that the broker can compare the borrowing capacity calculators of various lenders and their differing policies on acceptable income.

Servicing a Debt

There are 3 main measures lenders use to determine a borrower's borrowing capacity.

Debt-to-income (DTI): How much debt you have

- Total debt ÷ income
- Measures leverage/exposure

Debt-to-income (DTI) is a central metric most lenders use to assess a borrower's ability to service debt relative to their income. It is expressed as a multiple rather than a percentage, comparing total debt obligations against gross annual income. For example, a borrower earning $100,000 with total debts of $400,000 has a DTI of 4.0x. This measure provides a straightforward indication of leverage and is widely used in credit risk assessment, particularly for residential lending.

DEBT-TO-INCOME (DTI) RATIOS
(NEW LOANS)
(ADIs ONLY)

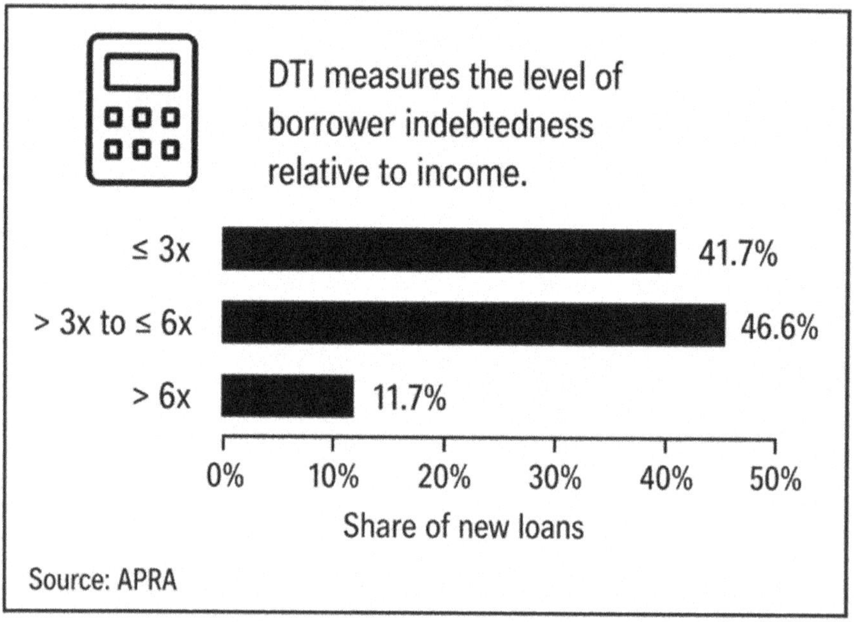

In practical terms, lower DTI ratios indicate a more conservative borrowing position. Borrowers with DTI levels at or below 3.0x are generally considered lower risk, as their debt burden is modest relative to income. As DTI increases beyond this level, lenders begin to exercise greater caution. The range between 3.0x and 6.0x is often viewed as moderate risk, where serviceability remains acceptable but is more sensitive to changes in interest rates, income stability, or living expenses. Once DTI exceeds 6.0x, the borrower is typically considered highly leveraged, and approval becomes more restrictive, often requiring stronger compensating factors, such as higher income stability, additional security, or a clear exit strategy.

DTI is not assessed in isolation. It operates alongside other metrics, including loan-to-value ratio (LVR), credit history, and expenditure analysis. However, its importance has increased in recent years due to regulatory focus on household indebtedness. Prudential guidance has encouraged lenders to monitor and limit the proportion of high-DTI lending, particularly in periods of rising property prices and interest rate volatility. This reflects a broader concern that highly leveraged borrowers are more vulnerable to economic shocks, including interest rate increases or income declines.

From a structural perspective, DTI also influences loan design. Borrowers with higher DTIs may face tighter loan terms, reduced borrowing capacity, or the need to adopt shorter loan durations or interest-only periods with defined exit strategies. In contrast, lower DTI borrowers typically benefit from greater flexibility, improved pricing, and a wider range of product options.

In the context of private lending, DTI can carry a different weight. While still relevant, private lenders may place greater emphasis on asset position, equity, and exit strategy rather than strict income-based servicing. This allows for scenarios where traditional lenders may decline an application despite strong underlying security.

Overall, DTI serves as a key indicator of financial resilience. It provides lenders with a clear, quantifiable measure of leverage while helping borrowers understand the relationship between income, debt, and long-term sustainability.

Net Surplus Ratio (NSR)

This is a percentage that every lender uses to underpin their decision to lend money, and it's non-negotiable if it doesn't meet it.

The basic version of the formula is gross income minus tax, liabilities, debt, and other commitments such as HECS or rent expense. Living expenses (basic and additional), then a buffer may be factored in, and this then equals the monthly surplus.

This is displayed in two ways on a calculator:

1. A ratio (which must be over 1:1; in some cases, it must be even higher than 1:1, up to, in fact, 1:1.25, like, for example, if the LVR is high or if all income is being used for servicing is Centrelink)
2. Cash surplus

Less common nowadays is the debt service ratio (below).

Debt Service Ratio (DSR)

How much of your income goes to repayments

- Loan repayments ÷ income
- Measures repayment burden

DSR provides the lender with an assessment of the borrower's debt relative to income. Basically, a ratio of gross income to debt payments. Whilst some lenders will accept 50%, most base their decision on 40%. If a person earns 80K per annum and their cost of debt is 30K per annum, they have a 37.4% exposure. Divide these figures by 12 or 52 to derive a monthly or weekly figure to help with household budgeting and cash flow.

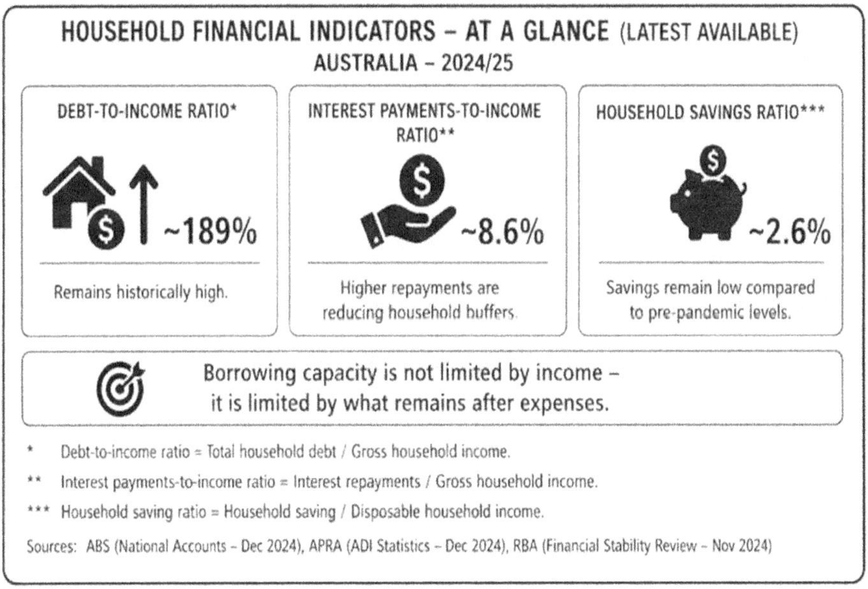

I explained earlier how someone's borrowing capacity may be increased. Always ask the question of how much you should borrow, rather than how much you can borrow, particularly if there is little surplus in the household. Please add 2% to the cost of the debt as a buffer.

It is wise to have a buffer/safety net and to be able to sleep at night. Don't end up in a situation where more than 40% of the household's salary is being spent on debt. Balance this with your lifestyle.

It's interesting: I find that many people I meet, whether they earn 80K or 400K per year, don't have much of a difference in their household budget surplus each month. One just has a bigger mortgage and spends more, leaving about the same as the person with the smaller mortgage who spends less.

Acceptable Income

The following types of income were mentioned earlier, but let's look at what lenders generally do, remembering that some lenders will take more or less than the general rule.

Income	How it's treated
Overtime	If it's a condition of employment a lender can accept 80–100%
Shift work	Same as overtime
Casual income	Minimum 12 months normally, can be 6 months with some lenders
Second job	Normally 2 years in the position
Rental	75–80%
Deductible Interest	The amount of interest on any investment property apportioned to those on title and based on the percentage ownership of title, not those on the loan.

Salary packaging/ sacrifice	Depends on if it is a condition of employment, and conditions surrounding it.
Maternity leave	Normally not if it is the government payment as this ends after 18 weeks, but half can be considered depending on the lender. Employer's sometimes pay for the leave, and if the female guarantees to return to work by the time the payments from the employer cease and the employer also confirm this, then it may be considered. There are lenders who will consider using the return-to-work income for a permanent part time or full-time employee, returning to the same employer, just by providing a date of returning, if there is a short fall providing there is sufficient savings or redraw to get them through that period of up to 12 months.
Pensions like carers' pension	Up to 100%, normally less than 50% of it though
Disability pension	
Centrelink support like Family Tax Benefit A and B	
Parenting payments	Normally not considered
Child maintenance payments	Normally require a child support agency agreement and 6 months evidence of receiving it.
Fringe benefits like a car allowance	Normally 5K, unless it is paid with wages, then the full amount may be used
Self- employed add backs, including depreciation	Normally on equipment, vehicles etc.

A study allowance is normally not acceptable.

Tenure

Note that none of this usually matters when using a private lender, subject to the property use and exit strategy.

Full-Time, Part-Time and Contract Work

Generally, 6 months of full-time or permanent part-time work in the same role with the same employer is acceptable.

As little as 1 day in a new job can be acceptable. There is even a lender who will accept an employment contract and the income in the contract, even before the person commences the new job. One day on probation is also acceptable, but once the LVR is over 80%, the probation period should be completed.

Contract Employment

Experience in industry required, with evidence of consistent work, some time remaining on the contract, and potential for renewal. The main point here is consistency and the ability to tell a story, which is why a good broker, not a bank, should be engaged. A broker will spend the time helping paint an accurate, but favourable picture.

Living Expenses

Lenders traditionally often use the higher of the two figures below in their servicing calculators for living expenses.

- What the client believes their living expenses are
- What the calculator uses as a default figure either HEM (household expenditure measure) or HPI (Henderson poverty index); these are based on the number of adults, couples and dependents in the households of the applicants/guarantors connected with the application.

SINGLE ADULT LIVING EXPENSES
(BANK BENCHMARKS)

HOUSEHOLD SEGMENTS	HEM RANGE PER MONTH	HPI RANGE PER MONTH
No dependants	$1,800 – $2,200	$1,400 – $1,700
1 dependant	$2,400 – $3,000	$1,900 – $2,400
2 dependants	$2,900 – $3,800	$2,300 – $3,000
3 dependants	$3,400 – $4,600	$2,700 – $3,600

Banks do not use what you say you spend.
They use a benchmark – and apply whichever is higher.
HEM is not a minimum – it is a conservative estimate of real spending.

Note: HEM = Household Expenditure Measure. HPI = Household Policy Index.
Source: Based on major lender benchmarks and MFAA Industry Studies.

LIVING EXPENSES INCREASE WITH INCOME
(HEM BENCHMARKS)

HOUSEHOLD INCOME (GROSS ANNUAL)	ESTIMATED MONTHLY LIVING EXPENSES (HEM RANGE)
Less than $60,000	$1,800 – $2,400
$60,000 – $100,000	$2,200 – $3,000
$100,000 – $150,000	$2,600 – $3,600
$150,000 and above	$3,000 – $4,200+

The more you earn, the more lenders assume you spend – even on basic living costs.
This is how banks calculate your repayment capacity.

Note: HEM (Household Expenditure Measure) benchmarks vary slightly between lenders.
Source: Major Lender Benchmarks & MFAA Industry Studies.

Another method is to tier a household's living expenses based on its income, in the belief that the more money people make, the more they spend and the better their lifestyle.

Many lenders are adding additional expenses as well. Some examples of additional living expenses that are not included in basic living expenses (since they are voluntary/incurred directly or indirectly from a decision or action the borrower had the choice of making are:

- non-government education;
- mobile phone, internet, Foxtel, Netflix;
- school sports;
- any type of insurance not covered by a super fund;
- private health cover;
- body corporate levies;
- childcare;
- additional car and its costs, such as maintenance, petrol, and registration;
- gym membership;
- child maintenance;
- subscriptions to magazines/newspapers, etc;
- building and contents insurance.

Some lenders are actually asking for the prior month's bank statement (at the time of application) of an applicant and scrutinising that to determine living expenses, while others attribute higher living expenses to people residing in better suburbs. For example, people living in Double Bay, New South Wales or Toorak, Victoria, will spend more than people living in Werribee, Victoria or Ipswich, Queensland.

The household expenditure measure (HEM) reflects the level of household expenditure across various family sizes; however, it does not necessarily represent true household living expenses. Some people smoke two packs of cigarettes a day, or have several subscriptions to streaming services, or their kids play every sport known to man. These are examples of how living expenses can quickly blow out of control.

Some lenders factor in an allowance for rental expense when buying an investment property, even if the borrower is living rent-free. This helps the borrower leave their current residence and be independent, and it ensures there is at least some allowance, so the borrower is not trapped. If the lender does not allow this and the borrowing capacity is very tight (just passing the calculator), it is obvious that they cannot avoid renting. Other lenders don't impose a rental cost if the borrower is living rent-free. This is in addition to living expenses. The upside is that they can borrow more from these lenders, which helps them better afford the debt on an investment property. Factoring in a rent cost negatively impacts servicing, but it makes servicing more realistic.

Title Ownership

If two people are on the title, it's the % ownership on the title that determines any entitlements, not who is on the loan. A borrower, whilst they must be included in decisions regarding the financing of the property, has no rights of ownership — they may have no benefit associated with the loan if they are not on title. There are exceptions for de facto and married couples, given they benefit from residing in the property. Additionally, there may be a joint venture agreement if it is an investment property.

Entitlements may include:

- ownership;
- equity;
- rental income (if any);
- profit;
- tax benefits

Example

Two friends, siblings or relatives buy a property together. If only one of them is on the title and both are on the loan, then both are responsible for the entire debt, but only the person on the title is entitled to the property and all that comes with it. The other applicant has no right to the profit, equity, property, or any rental income. Lenders generally dislike this because there are too many situations where two people take out a loan together, often just to leverage the second person's income. It's out of mere convenience to get the loan to pass serviceability by using both incomes.

The risk is also that the second applicant is ignorant and being taken advantage of, and lenders normally don't want to be complicit in such situations.

Most of the time, both applicants will be expected to go on the title. Perhaps the second person can have a minimum 20% ownership, so at least there's some benefit to them in taking joint responsibility for the entire debt. The minimum percentage may vary between lenders; I recommend that both applicants seek suitably qualified advice.

What lenders like even less are a parent and the child going on the loan. If the parent is over 55, there's no marriage license or binding relationship between these two, just as there's not between anyone other than married or de facto couples. Buying with someone over 55 has additional requirements, which will be covered in the exit strategy section of this book shortly.

Normally, the only time when both applicants don't have to both go on the title is when they are married or de facto, because in family court, each will get half of the property anyway if they split up, if not more.

Non-Genuine Savings

Once the loan-to-value ratio exceeds 80-85%, the borrower is normally required to demonstrate genuine savings to secure a better interest rate. So, what is genuine saving?

In short, it is the money (5% of the purchase price) someone has saved over a 3-month period from their income.

The four key elements in the above sentence each need to be explored in detail, as below ('save', '3-month period', 'from their income', '5%').

1. 'Saved': this is an important word. Strictly speaking, it excludes gifts because they are not savings. It excludes the sale of a non-investment asset (investment assets include property and shares). A term deposit would be acceptable if longer than 3 months. If money has been sitting in an account for 3 months, but has not accumulated over that time, or no further money has gone in the account, or if any lump sums arrived in the account during the 3 months, it would probably be a gift, sale of a non-investment item or tax rebate. If no lump sums have gone in, but no additional money has accrued over the 3 months, other than what was in there at the start, then it could look suspiciously like a gift had been provided, perhaps a few days prior to the 3 months period of

statements provided, and would look like the borrower simply has not been, and is incapable of, saving anything themselves.

2. Lenders may ask for 6 months' statements, so then it doesn't matter how the money arrived in the account. If a deposit has been paid toward a property, then a receipt will suffice as genuine savings if dated over 3–6 months earlier. If within 6 months, a statement showing who paid the receipt may be required to establish that the borrower paid it and that it was not a gift.

3. '3-month period': This demonstrates the ability to put aside money regularly and be disciplined. Any less time, and there is less discipline demonstrated to continually put aside money. A small tip to save what would be considered *genuine savings* could be to borrow some money from parents, in order to live off it, instead of using this borrowed money as a deposit; this enables more of the income being earned to remain in the account, as it would no longer be used for living expenses.

4. In some cases, someone may buy a block of land at 90% LVR, wait 3 months and refer to the other 10% equity in the land to have it recognised as genuine savings toward the construction contract. Whilst it may not be used or leveraged, a lender will normally consider this acceptable, even if a gift is ultimately used as 'funds to complete' for the construction contract.

5. 'From their income': this is important, as it excludes tax refunds and other things already mentioned. Bonuses are usually excluded—It must be from wages earned.

6. '5%' refers to the commonly acceptable amount for an owner-occupied property purchase. Some lenders apply it to investment properties as well, with a couple of lenders requiring 10% genuine savings. For low-documentation loans for self-employed people, 20% genuine savings may

be required, or, at a higher rate, no genuine savings are acceptable.

7. Other definitions applied to determine acceptable genuine savings vary between lenders. The one that is acceptable across the board is equity in another property or proceeds from the sale of an investment, such as shares or property, as mentioned.

8. Additionally, a few lenders have a non-genuine savings policy, under which historical rental payments made by the applicant (s) can be an acceptable form of genuine savings when the applicants are currently renting. What the banks glean from rental history is that the borrower can make regular, on-time payments, which demonstrates a commitment to meet their contracted obligations.

9. They are showing responsibility. The key point is that the applicant (s) are on a lease for 12 months or more, managed through a property management agency, and have an exemplary rental repayment history (it must be exemplary to be accepted).

10. Please keep in mind that evidence of adequate funds to complete the eventual settlement must still be provided with the application submitted to the lender.

Exit strategies are important, and lenders often require one when a borrower is between, or beyond, the ages of 55–60 years, and they need to show an ability to repay the loan as at the time the loan is taken out, or if their exit strategy is worded in the loan submission notes satisfactorily, when they cease work and retire. Their industry has a bearing, too. For example, if the borrower is employed in a labour-intensive role, they are more unlikely to work as long as someone in an office or administrative role. There is less wear and tear on the body; therefore, a person in an office or administrative role may be able to work for a few more years.

The next diagram highlights the number of people who are debt-free, think they will be, or won't be. Lenders need to be careful not to exacerbate the problem.

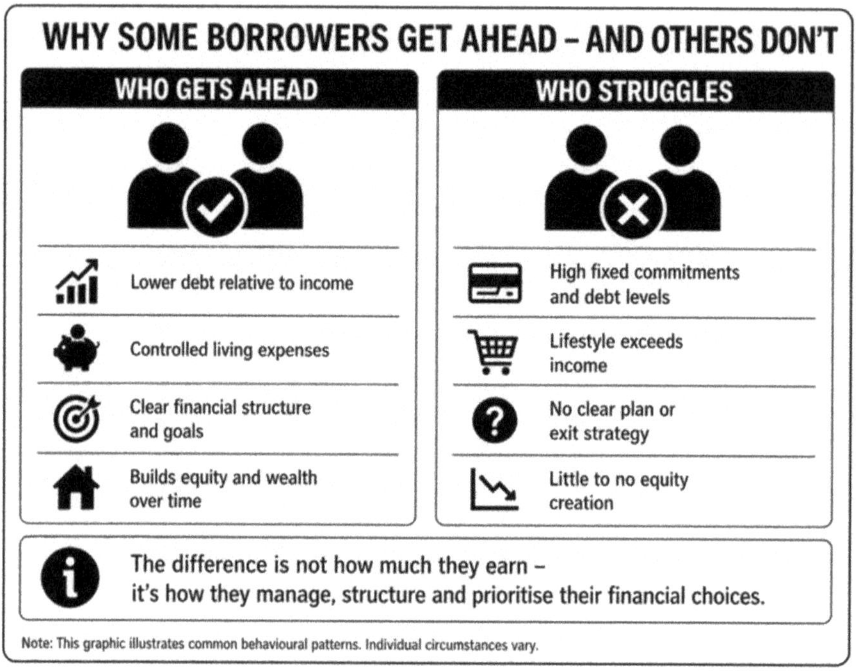

Lenders may offer the option of a shorter repayment history, particularly if the borrower is over 60 years old.

Nonetheless, these people normally must have equity in investment properties, or value in shares and superannuation, equivalent to the loan amount being sought, to pay off the loan at the time of assessment. Projected capital growth of other assets or statements that additional repayments will be made to pay down the debt are not normally acceptable, as they are considered speculation.

The simple strategy of downsizing properties is a common, generic response that applicants use to demonstrate an exit strategy. Downsizing can work with some lenders if there is enough equity in the property at the time of the loan to afford a respectable property.

Example

A house worth $1 million with a debt of 400K means there is 600K available to use for downsizing, less 2% agents' fees and, if any, capital gains tax. However, if the house is worth 300K with a 240K debt, downsizing as an exit strategy would make the borrower appear detached from reality in the lenders' eyes, as 60K, less selling commissions, leaves less than even the cost of a caravan. A caravan park or retirement home to downsize to is normally not acceptable. Lenders could then be accused of putting someone in a far worse situation than they were previously. The accusation could come from the industry regulator or from the borrowers themselves, who lack the integrity and intelligence to have taken responsibility for their own actions.

They may also state that they are planning to sell their business. Lenders don't want to be complicit, or implicated, in someone being forced to sell their house or business. People change their minds as they get older and could easily twist the situation around. They could then suddenly end up as a 'hard done by' story on a so-called 'current affairs' program, where someone is being sold up by a bank.

Not that I wish to judge the unfortunate situations people find themselves in, in life, but there are cases where a person has said they would downsize, then they get sick and cannot work anymore. The bank is then called to task for wanting their repayments made. It's best for lenders to avoid these situations under their interpretation of responsible lending. This is, at least, the opinion of many credit assessors.

If a 30-year-old and their parent go on the loan, and the parent is over 55-years-old, the parent will, most of the time, need to demonstrate an exit strategy equivalent to being able to pay out the entire debt, independent of the co-borrower if the co-borrower is anyone but their partner (de facto or married). If two people are over 55 and not in a relationship, each must be able to pay off the entire loan independently of the other. Read the earlier section on servicing a debt involving co-borrowers.

5.

Improve Borrowing Capacity, Increase Loan Size, Improve Repayment Commitments

Points to Improve Servicing (And the Ability to Obtain a Loan)

Investing in property requires planning and involves several strategies. Success in growing a property portfolio is not only about the property values increasing, but it's about balancing your accessible equity/cash available with your ability to service debt.

1. Consider reducing the number of credit cards: Some people feel special when they have a wallet full of credit cards, but this is the worst thing to do. Please reduce the number of credit cards to a minimum of one or two, if possible. Reduce the card limits to the minimum required. Borrowing capacity will increase immediately. Most lenders factor in 3% per month on a credit card limit, not on what is owed, but rather on the full limit. Reducing a credit card limit from 20K to 10K can typically free up $3,600 per year for servicing.

   To assist in reducing the debt on any credit card so that the limit to be reduced, consider using any redraw, not needed for emergencies, to pay these off as preparation for applying for another mortgage. Be careful not to eat into any genuine savings or deposits set aside for a property.

Apply this philosophy when trying to reduce or consolidate any unsecured debt, such as personal loans, HECS or car loans.

For every $1000 that you remove from your credit card limit, you can increase your borrowing capacity by up to $5500, depending on the lender — with every lender, it will make a difference.

For example, let's assume the borrower earns 80K per year, has a credit card with a 10K limit, no other debts, and is a single adult… the figures below show how much more can be borrowed with a 5K card limit versus a 10K limit.

10K card limit = borrowing capacity of $520,074

9K = $524,429

8K = $528,783

7K = $533,137

6K = $537,492

5K = $541,846

For every $1K increase in the credit card limit, the borrowing capacity in this instance increases by approximately $ 4,350. So, when your bank sends you an invitation to increase your credit card limit, think carefully before just blindly accepting their offer.

2. *Use a broker:* Don't shop around for the best rate, as it could result in several credit enquiries on your credit report. Every time you apply for a credit card, personal loan, or interest-free finance for furniture at a retail store, a credit hit occurs on your personal credit record. The more credit hits you have, the more of a risk you become to a lender. This means you could end up with a higher rate, sometimes 2%+.

Also, use a broker to find the best servicing calculator. This was discussed in more detail earlier, see Chapter 3. Different types of income are treated differently and can make or break a deal. Some lenders service existing debt at existing rates, and that means the servicing calculator can work in an investor's favour if they have other property debts.

Some calculators don't account for deductible interest, which negatively impacts servicing. Please speak with a good broker who compares products from banks and non-banks, as already suggested. A borrowing capacity can differ by many hundreds of thousands of dollars. Personally, I recently compared two lenders, a bank and a non-bank. The non-bank would allow me to borrow $600,000 more than the bank.

Some lenders offer a 40-year term; this increases the amount that can be borrowed with that funder, whether they load the rate you're on, or factor in a principal and interest repayment for conservatism's sake.

3. Cross-collateralising: When more than one property is used to secure a loan, this can work for or against you, mainly against you. Some would argue that doing this improves borrowing capacity, but the advantages are fewer than the disadvantages. Even if you can obtain a lower rate across the loans due to the size of the combined loans, it may still be higher than elsewhere.

Reasons not to cross-securitise include additional costs in refinancing one of the loans, more hassle in refinancing one of them, when not refinancing all of them, as they are all tied together, the valuation on one will affect all, and restrict one of the properties being sold or refinanced, or an increase in the loan being possible.

4. Prepared and organised: Keep your paperwork up to date, especially if self-employed. It can make a huge difference in the rate and borrowing power when tax returns and assessment notices are supplied to the lender. Two forms of ID, two forms of income verification, savings statements, a contract if a purchase or 6 months repayment history if a refinance (3 months for credit cards/personal loans if consolidating debt). Please fill in all sections of the application. Many lenders credit score and they could decline you for suspected non-disclosure.

5. Disclosure: Self-employed borrowers do sometimes prefer to avoid tax rather than to increase their taxable income on paper. If they increased their income on paper, it could help increase their borrowing capacity. They could also be eligible for a better rate, making it easier to borrow more for the next investment.

6. Age of property: Consider whether you are buying a new versus an established property, and the state of Australia in which you buy. The stamp duty differences between states are huge, as is the stamp duty paid for established rather than new property (again, avoid 'off-the-plan').

7. Repayment type and frequency: When there's a loan, and you would like it reduced, consider weekly or fortnightly repayments. Interest is compounded daily — you pay interest on interest, so every day that goes by is another day of interest added (after being calculated on the debt, plus all the days' interest charged prior to that, between the last repayment and the next).

8. Offset and access: Instead of putting money in the loan, an offset account could store the money, whilst saving interest on the loan. Let's compare a couple of choices.

   Put 50K into an interest-bearing account and perhaps make 3% per annum, equalling $1500, on which tax could be paid, depending on other income you earn. Put the same money into an offset account linked to the mortgage.

This 50K offset on a 750K loan at 6.5% would mean interest is charged only on 700K, saving 6.5% on the 50K for as long as it remains in the offset.

It is better to save 6.5% and not pay tax on these savings, rather than earn 3% and potentially pay tax on the earnings, walking away with maybe 2% instead of 3%.

Over the life of the loan, it could save $20,249 with only $5K sitting in the offset account. Naturally, the outcome is subject to the assumptions inputted in each calculator (but you get the point).

Reminder: Please ensure all income comes into the offset account and all expenses go out of it. Some authors advise setting up several accounts as buckets of money to help manage money better. Conceptually this is fine, but it can also be poor advice unless the accounts all serve as offset accounts.

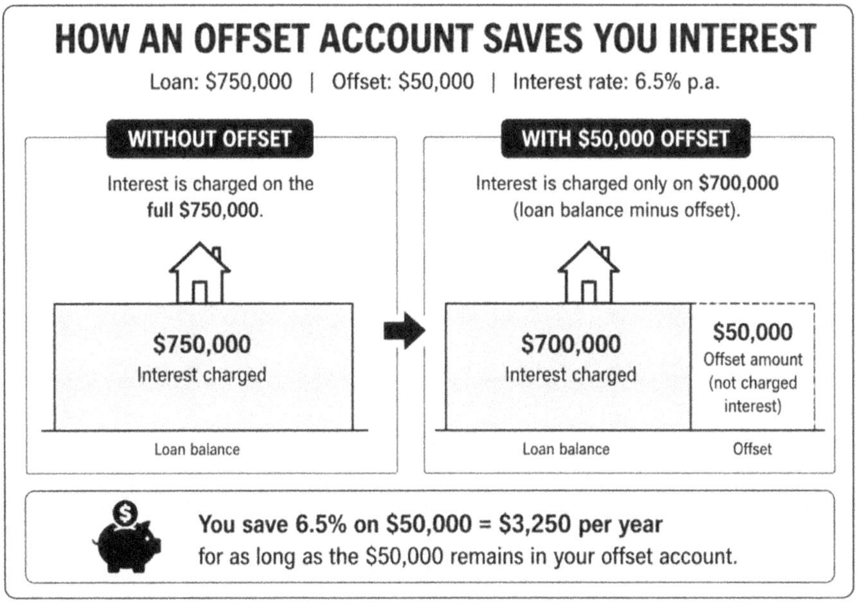

WHAT YOUR OFFSET SAVES YOU

Description	Amount	Details
Loan amount	$750,000	Total home loan balance
Offset balance	$50,000	Held in offset account
Effective balance charged	$700,000	$750,000 – $50,000
Interest rate	6.5% p.a.	Annual interest rate
Interest savings	**$3,250 per year**	**6.5% of $50,000**

By keeping $50,000 in your offset account, you reduce the interest charged on your loan. You save approximately $3,250 in interest each year, for as long as the $50,000 remains in the offset.

Note: Figures are an example only and assume interest is calculated daily.

9. *Refinancing:* Investigate options of refinancing. I have seen many instances where even 1% on the interest rate per annum has been saved. On a 350K loan that is a saving of $2500 per year, just by looking around, or changing between fixed and variable or vice versa. If the cost of the mortgage is reduced, it can improve your borrowing capacity.

10. Avoid family pledge and avoid being a guarantor or co-borrower: Avoid taking on a loan or guaranteeing one with anyone other than your spouse (most lenders will attribute 100% of the debt to you and only 50% of the rental income). If you're over 55, lenders typically require an exit strategy that excludes downsizing or selling a business.

11. Apply for a loan when you've been in your job for over 6 months: If you apply right after changing jobs, it can be difficult. If you apply when just becoming self-employed, it could prove impossible. Obtain a copy of your credit file as well, to ensure you are aware of what is on it. I have seen so many instances where someone has a default listed that they're not aware of. This will affect the interest rate you will receive and, therefore, the ability to service a loan.

12. Redraw: Set up a redraw facility, so you have the equity available and ready for the next opportunity. Lenders are not really your friend — they're a business out to make money, and the less you must deal with them for each purchase, the easier you can invest, and the quicker you can act on an opportunity. You would then be more in control of what you want to do.

13. Ownership structure: Establishing the correct foundation through structuring is vital, and it's very important to receive sound advice from an expert in this field—not a mate, a family member, or someone selling property.

Capital gains must be apportioned according to the ownership of the title, not according to who is on the loan; a borrower on the mortgage has no entitlement of ownership, or profit or rent associated with the property if they are not on title (of course, marriage and or de facto separation can lead to different outcomes).

There is no single ideal structure for holding investment property, but it is important to consider personal and work goals, as well as how long the property is likely to be held. If a couple is purchasing the property, is one of them likely to cease work in the short term or return to work? What are the projected incomes?

Does the client wish to build a property portfolio? Are the properties likely to become positively geared within the next few years, or is the investor able to positively gear some property?

What about asset protection? Maybe one of the parties owns a business, and it is important not to have valuable assets in their name.

Ownership as an individual or partnership: If a couple purchases a property under joint ownership, the default is 50:50 ownership.

However, if two or more people are purchasing a property and wish to vary the ownership ratio to suit their situation, the property needs to be purchased as 'tenants in common'. This not only allows flexibility in ownership percentages but also allows each party to 'will' their share of the property to a beneficiary of their choice upon death, which is not the case with joint ownership.

If the property is expected to be negatively geared for several years and the negative-gearing benefits are likely to be substantial, it might make sense for the higher-income earner to own more of the asset and offset the tax deduction against their higher income.

A disadvantage of this strategy is that if the asset becomes positively geared or is sold and a capital gain is made, that net profit or capital gain will be taxed at the tax margin of the person who owns a greater share of the property.

Trust: A significant disadvantage of holding a negatively geared property in a trust is that losses are 'trapped'. They cannot be used to offset the investor's taxable income with the intention to deliver an attractive refund to assist with the costs of holding the property.

The losses are carried forward in the trust and can be used to offset future profits generated. However, these losses don't offset future capital gains, much to the disappointment of many investors. Capital gains can only be offset by capital losses. Lenders don't generally factor in negative gearing into a borrowing capacity calculator if a property is purchased in a trust, but your income is earned outside the trust.

When considering a company structure, the most significant disadvantage of holding property in a company is that it is not entitled to the 50% discount on capital gains that an individual taxpayer is. Being unable to access the CGT discount is a disincentive to holding assets in companies.

A discretionary trust, however, provides superior asset protection because even if an individual taxpayer is bankrupted, the assets in the trust are protected, as the individual owns no interest in a discretionary trust.

A discretionary trust can be used to distribute capital gains to beneficiaries in an effective manner, and the individual beneficiary is also able to obtain a 50% discount on capital gains tax in their own individual returns.

Lenders' Mortgage Insurance (LMI)

Most lenders offering normal-priced rates will mortgage-insure their loans above 80% loan-to-valuation ratio (LVR) if it is a full-documentation loan, and over 60% LVR if it is a limited-documentation, alternative-documentation, or low-documentation loan (i.e., self-employed people who have not completed their tax returns). Some lenders can add the LMI to a 95% LVR, up to 99% LVR.

LMI may be able to be added on top of the loan. If the borrower wishes to avoid LMI, they will have to use more of their cash or equity, obtain a gift, or consider taking on more debt with a credit card or personal loan (this extra debt is problematic and will negatively affect servicing). Borrowing more for investment properties can provide more tax-deductible interest. It also uses less of the borrower's own money due to higher gearing/leverage, and it could help purchase more properties (depending on the overall cost of debt).

A borrower should consider a balanced approach when deciding whether to take on more debt, as doing so will have a greater negative impact on servicing due to the higher cost of debt. This also means starting with less equity in the property purchased (thereby exposing them to greater risk if the market has a downturn). Compare this to using more cash or equity reserves, which can also leave less money or equity available for future property purchases. LMI will be cheaper if the LVR (or debt) is lower. If you are using two properties, one as a refinance and one as a purchase, in addition to the other benefits of not cross-securing your assets with a single lender, this may also give you the benefit of paying less LMI to achieve the same outcome.

LMI: Should You Have It or Should You Avoid It?

Lenders' mortgage insurance (LMI) protects lenders and is paid by the client in the event of a loan default. It is a once-off premium that can be added to the loan. It's not a mortgage protection fee for the client; it's solely to protect the lender.

If using LMI, how do you do it safely? Whether to use or avoid LMI can be determined by the amount of equity a person has available.

The truth is that LMI isn't just black and white. It can be both a useful tool or a millstone, depending on how it is employed and the underlying asset. And while rules of thumb are helpful, there are always exceptions.

Used correctly, LMI can be a borrower's best friend, since it allows investors to enter the property market or apply for a loan increase without the cash they would otherwise need.

Lenders' mortgage insurers will credit-score any prospective borrower. This is done via a software program that analyses the loan application and assigns weighted scores to various aspects of the applicant's creditworthiness.

It could mean the application is declined before a credit assessor has had a chance to review it. It's a tough game, so if an application fails at the credit scoring point, often no amount of negotiation or rational discussion will swing things your way. There is, however, a way around it.

Some lenders charge a risk fee instead of LMI. This fee will typically work out similarly to LMI in dollar terms, but the borrower avoids the credit-scoring process.

It's important to remember that the more you borrow, the higher the repayments, of course, which in turn will eat into cash flow. LMI forms part of the property's cost base, meaning the property will need to increase in value more to compensate for the LMI cost if it is added to the loan.

LMI can be costly and increases with the loan amount and LVR. For example, the LMI charge on a $350,000 loan at an LVR of 85% could be around $ 4,600. The same charge on a $500,000 loan at 95% LVR could be $21,000.

However, there are restrictions you should be aware of. LMI providers may not offer their services on loans more than $1.2 million above 80% LVR.

At an LVR of 95%, the loan may be limited to around $650,000.

Exceptions may be considered, but on a 'per application' basis, of course. Plus, an applicant's exposure can be up to $2.5 million across several applications and properties. If this limit is reached with one insurer, another lender could be used. Some lenders only use one LMI provider, so a different lender may be required.

The aggregate amount of the debt can be even higher, spreading an investor's exposure across insurers. LMI may normally only be added to loans above 95% LVR if the home to be purchased will be owner-occupied. That way, a purchaser does not have to come up with the LMI funds out of their own cash or equity.

For an investment property, the maximum LMI level is 95% LVR. This means the loan will effectively be around 92% LVR. Refinancing a loan is normally capped at 90% LVR, plus LMI.

LMI is usually not portable. If a borrower refinances with another lender to secure a lower rate, they will pay LMI again if the new loan exceeds the 80% LVR threshold (based on a full-documentation loan). The premium paid the first time is, for the most part, gone. In some cases, a partial refund may be possible, so I recommend considering whether it is better to change lenders. It may simply be better to increase the loan if that's what you really needed to do in the first place. By applying for a loan increase with the lender you're already with, you would pay LMI only on the increase, if it's in LMI territory, not on the entire debt.

Buying a home is often a balancing act between borrowing more to preserve cash and borrowing less to preserve debt-servicing capacity. LMI can help borrowers walk this line with more confidence.

The cost of stamp duty may affect the need to use LMI, since a person's cash or equity may be enough to complete the purchase, but not cover stamp duty. This could lead to borrowing more against the property if there's room in the property's value.

Postcodes can be a determining factor in whether a lender wants to lend in a particular area. Some lenders have an internal sign-off with LMI policy (they can make their own decisions without consulting the credit assessment team at the LMI provider's office), so this can be overcome. Some lenders can avoid LMI. Please remember to base this decision on the merits of each transaction, assessing the risks and benefits, and ensure you remain in a strong financial position without overcommitting.

The broker can help the borrower by packaging the deal and selling it to the lender, convincing them to lend money to that borrower. Some borrowers need all the help they can get. It's not just a matter of giving the lender a bunch of statements and expecting a loan to be provided. Good brokers do a lot of work behind the scenes on their loan submission notes, highlighting the loan's strengths and painting a picture for the lender. They chase the deal, pushing it through the process, and have the right contacts. A bad broker is not helpful; they don't do any of the above.

This becomes even more important in non-traditional lending scenarios. A well-presented application is not simply a collection of documents, but a clear explanation of how the loan will work, particularly when repayment depends on a future event rather than ongoing income.

'Servicing' is what every traditional lender focuses on when deciding whether to approve a loan or continue saying 'yes' to the applicant. Borrowing capacity varies between lenders, as do policies and procedures. It is also what every responsible private lender focuses on when the exit strategy is refinance. Some naïve people, including some brokers, think that if interest is capitalised on a short-term facility, the private lender need not worry about it, but that is incorrect. The private lender needs to ensure the borrower is not stuck in that short-term facility.

Brokers can compare many choices — a service that a bank cannot offer you. Banks may try to mislead you into believing that they can offer the best loan for your needs, but I believe you should never go to any one lender. Please compare using a broker to do the legwork.

Not all brokers offer the value you would expect. Some use the big four Australian banks (NAB, Westpac, ANZ and CBA) more often than other lenders, and in fact some brokers only use the big four banks. This is possibly lazy and is evidence (in my mind) of poor business practice and poor sales skills.

Some brokers use motherhood statements (a vague, 'feel-good' platitude, which, whilst accurate in this case, is misleading). For example, they will tell you they have access to 25–35 different lenders on their approved panel of lenders, but if the broker has really only used four of those lenders on their panel, they lack experience of what the full panel can offer and are therefore best avoided.

Good brokers offer choices to their clients that may not always be available to the borrower simply by walking into a bank branch. They are solution providers.

A true broker compares loans and then offers their client the best and most objective choices, including products from both banks and non-banks. A bad broker is purely rate-driven; a good broker focuses on repayment figures, policy, servicing, turnaround times (the time from submitting your loan to settlement), and choosing a lender that provides timely communication.

Aggregators and franchise models make money from their brokers through either a fee or a percentage (clip) of the commission's brokers receive from lenders. They have also expanded into becoming white-label lenders.

A white-label offering is a normal home loan like any other; it is funding provided by a bank or lender that is rebranded as a self-branded home loan in the name the aggregator or mortgage manager gives it, a bit like a 'clean skin' bottle of wine. These 'white label' products are being provided to aggregators by funders such as Advantedge (owned by NAB), Macquarie, Pepper Money, and others to broaden their reach in the home loan market. It's like an 'in-house' product that brokers can offer and effectively call their own. This is great if it's operated as it is supposed to be — a competitor to the banks, often offering clients a valuable and differentiated solution.

Not too long ago, one of the major banks was accused of widespread corruption within its ranks; again, more reason to engage a broker from a good, respected aggregator.

Bad brokers may say 'no' to a prospective client simply because they do not want to offer the type of loan the borrower needs. Again, this is why consulting a good, versatile, and knowledgeable broker is important.

Applicants sometimes inadvertently create problems for themselves by shopping around for the best rate and making enquiries with different lenders, which can degrade the quality of their own credit history. Each time a person shops around, a hard credit inquiry may be generated, which can make it less palatable for a lender to work with that borrower.

Some of the reasons that I think using a good broker can be highly beneficial (besides saving time in finding a lender suitable for your needs) are that they chase documents for you, and you may get a better deal due to their relationships with some of the lenders (better than if you went direct sometimes). A good broker is there to help you understand the loan documents, and they shop around for you, without incurring credit hits on your credit file, before submitting your loan to the chosen lender.

There are many lenders who do not deal directly with the public; they do not have branches, yet they can often provide solutions that are equal to or much better than those offered by walking into a bank branch.

Bank branches can place a great deal of pressure on their 'in-house' loan writers, expecting them to cross-sell insurance, financial planning services, and other forms of debt, such as credit cards and personal loans. They have volume targets and therefore are less like relationship managers and more like 'order takers'.

It's important to source a broker suited to your individual needs. Many bank staff may lack the personal experience needed to truly understand clients' needs. They may have forgotten what it was like to apply for their first home loan, or they may be very young and have no investment properties, or they may not lend to more complex trust structures.

Finding a broker who specialises in a particular product or borrower types, such as first homebuyers or property investors, increases the likelihood of being offered a product that more suitably fits the borrower's needs, a tailored solution, not a product off the rack.

Brokers can save you time, manage the loan's progression from submission to settlement and be more easily contacted for updates than trying to get hold of someone at a branch.

Bank staff do understand their own products better than a broker does, and they may be able to provide exceptions to policy that a broker cannot, but these things are not necessarily useful if the product they have better knowledge of is not the most appropriate solution or the best repayment figure, borrowing capacity calculator, or rate for the client.

A borrower would simply not know this until several options had been explored, but who has the time for that? Hence, using a broker beats going to one or two lenders, or even several lenders, hands down.

Case Study

Jodi and Shane, who had just bought a property at auction, had obtained pre-approval with the help of a broker, so the only outstanding conditions of the pre-approval were to supply a contract of sale and to obtain a satisfactory valuation of the property.

The valuation was ordered to confirm the purchase price and the security's suitability for the lender. Guess what? The valuation came in less than the sale price. In this instance, the valuer was not convinced that Jodi and Shane had paid fair market value. This presented a dilemma to the borrowers, as they didn't have any more cash than what they had already put aside to put into the property, so the broker appealed the valuation, something a bank branch may not bother to think about doing, and disputing a valuation can sometimes work, but not often. Unfortunately, the loan was declined due to the low valuation and LVR (loan-to-value ratio) limitations.

So, with a $29,000 shortfall, that was the end of the deal with that particular lender. Welcome to the world of valuations, where nothing is clear-cut.

This is a situation where having a broker can help. In this instance, the broker was able to order an upfront valuation from another lender, who accepted the contract price. The borrowers proceeded with the deal, and it was completed within two weeks.

If the borrowers had gone directly to the bank and the valuation didn't stack up, they would have had to plead with family or friends for more money, which they really did not want to do. Keep in mind that if they did not settle, they would have been in breach of the contract for not settling, as the contract was 'unconditional' (not subject to finance), and it was purchased at auction. They would have lost the deposit and may have been charged re-advertising costs if the property had been placed back on the market.

Situations like this also highlight where alternative lending approaches may be considered. A private lender may take a different view of the same asset, particularly if the overall equity position remains strong and there is a clear strategy to resolve the loan within a defined period.

How some borrowers may be eligible to avoid LMI when borrowing as much as 95% of the value of the property:

The Government 5% Deposit Scheme and Help to Buy Explained

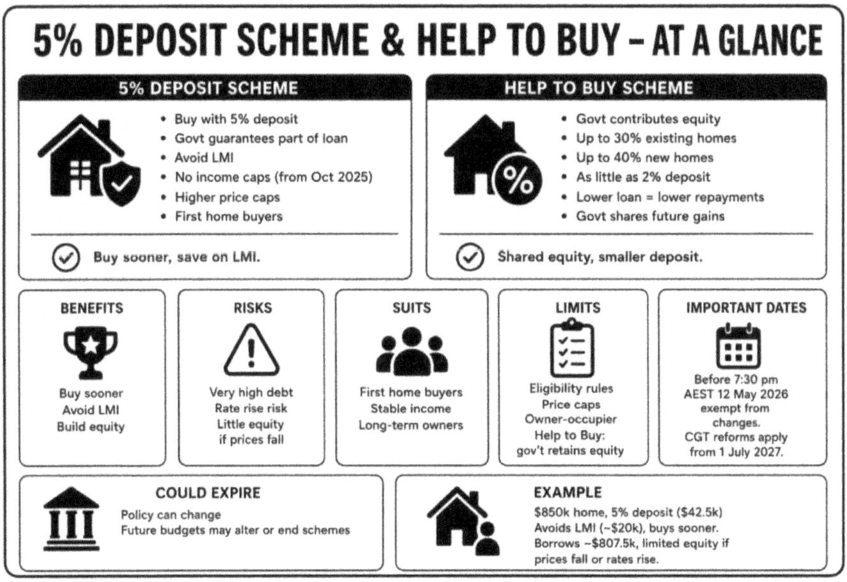

For many Australians, saving a traditional 20% deposit to purchase a property has become increasingly difficult. Rising property prices, higher rents, and overall living costs have created a situation where many borrowers can comfortably afford loan repayments but struggle to save a large enough deposit to enter the market. In response to this issue, the Australian Government introduced a range of housing support initiatives, including the expanded 5% Deposit Scheme and the newer Help to Buy shared equity program.

These schemes are designed to assist eligible borrowers in purchasing a home sooner while reducing some of the traditional barriers associated with homeownership. Although these initiatives can create significant opportunities for buyers, they also involve important risks and limitations that borrowers should properly understand before proceeding.

What is the 5% Deposit Scheme?

Traditionally, Australian lenders have preferred borrowers to contribute a 20% deposit when purchasing a property. If a borrower had less than this amount, lenders would generally require the borrower to pay Lenders Mortgage Insurance (LMI), which can add many thousands of dollars to the cost of buying a property.

Under the government-backed 5% Deposit Scheme, eligible borrowers may purchase a property with as little as a 5% deposit while avoiding LMI altogether. This is possible because the government effectively guarantees part of the loan to the lender. In practical terms, the lender treats the loan as if it had a larger deposit because the government is providing additional security.

The scheme was significantly expanded in 2025, with the government removing many of the previous restrictions, increasing property price caps, and broadening eligibility criteria. This expansion caused a substantial increase in demand for high-loan-to-value-ratio lending across Australia, particularly among first-home buyers seeking to enter the market before prices increased even further.

What Is the Help to Buy Scheme?

Separate from the 5% Deposit Scheme is the Help to Buy shared equity program. This arrangement works differently because the government does not simply provide a guarantee — it actually contributes part of the purchase price and takes an ownership interest in the property.

Under this arrangement, the government may contribute up to 30% of the purchase price for an existing property and up to 40% for a newly constructed property. This allows some borrowers to purchase property with deposits as low as 2%.

Because the borrower is borrowing less money from the bank, loan repayments may be significantly lower than those for a traditional purchase. However, the government will retain an ownership interest in the property and therefore share in part of any future capital growth when the property is sold or refinanced.

Why These Schemes Have Become So Popular

The primary attraction of these schemes is simple: they allow borrowers to enter the property market much earlier than they otherwise could.

In many parts of Australia, property prices have increased faster than wages for a prolonged period. Many borrowers have found themselves trapped in a cycle in which property prices rise faster than they can save for a deposit. Even disciplined savers can struggle to accumulate a 20% deposit while simultaneously paying rent and everyday living expenses.

By reducing the deposit requirement to 5%, or even 2% under Help to Buy, these schemes substantially reduce the upfront cash needed to purchase a property. This can bring forward home ownership by many years.

Another major benefit is avoiding Lenders Mortgage Insurance. On higher-value properties, LMI premiums can easily exceed $20,000. Avoiding this expense can make a very substantial difference to the affordability of entering the market.

The Help to Buy scheme may also improve borrowing capacity by allowing the borrower to take out a smaller loan from the bank. This can reduce repayment pressure and improve overall cash flow.

Who These Schemes May Suit

These schemes may suit borrowers with stable employment, reliable income, and long-term intentions to remain in the property.

They may work particularly well for younger professionals early in their careers who expect their income to increase over time. They may also suit borrowers who have demonstrated strong rental repayment history but have struggled to save a large deposit due to increasing living costs.

Borrowers who are financially disciplined and intend to hold the property for the long term may benefit significantly from entering the property market earlier. Over time, capital growth and debt reduction may substantially improve their financial position.

These schemes may also assist borrowers who are paying high rental amounts and find that mortgage repayments would be similar to, or even lower than, their existing rent.

The Risks of Borrowing with a Small Deposit

Although these schemes provide opportunities, they also create additional financial risk.

The most significant issue is that borrowers are still taking on very high levels of debt relative to the property value. Purchasing with a 5% deposit effectively means the borrower is borrowing 95% of the property value. This leaves very little equity buffer if property prices decline.

Even a relatively small decline in property values could place the borrower in negative equity, meaning the loan balance exceeds the property's value. This can create major issues if the borrower needs to sell the property unexpectedly.

Higher debt levels also generally mean larger repayments and significantly more interest paid over the life of the loan. Although the schemes reduce the upfront deposit requirement, they do not reduce the property's actual cost.

Interest rate increases also pose a greater risk to borrowers with very high loan balances. A relatively modest increase in rates can materially increase repayments when the debt level is large.

There is also concern amongst regulators that these schemes may encourage excessive leverage within the housing market. APRA has already flagged increasing levels of high-LVR lending associated with the scheme expansion, particularly amongst first home buyers.

Potential Impact on Property Prices

Critics of these schemes argue that they may unintentionally contribute to rising property prices.

When buyers suddenly gain access to increased borrowing power, competition for property may intensify. If housing supply does not increase at the same rate, property prices may rise further, ultimately reducing overall affordability.

In effect, some critics argue that the schemes may assist current buyers in the short term while simultaneously increasing prices for future buyers.

This does not necessarily mean the schemes are ineffective, but it does highlight that government housing policy can sometimes produce unintended market consequences.

Limitations and Eligibility Requirements

These schemes are not available to every borrower and do contain various restrictions.

Eligibility requirements may include Australian citizenship or permanent residency, owner-occupancy requirements, income thresholds, and maximum property price caps, depending on the scheme and location.

The Help to Buy shared equity program also involves ongoing obligations because the government retains an ownership interest in the property. This means borrowers do not receive the full benefit of future capital growth attributable to the government's ownership percentage.

There may also be limitations regarding refinancing, selling the property, or buying out the government's share in the future.

Borrowers should carefully review all scheme conditions and seek appropriate financial and legal advice before proceeding.

Could These Schemes Expire or Change?

Government housing schemes are ultimately policy decisions and can change over time.

Although the current government has strongly supported these initiatives, future governments may alter eligibility requirements, reduce funding, tighten restrictions, or replace the schemes entirely, depending on economic conditions, housing affordability pressures, or regulatory concerns.

The original versions of the schemes contained stricter caps and fewer places before their later expansion. This demonstrates that government housing policy can evolve significantly over time.

Borrowers should therefore avoid assuming these schemes will remain unchanged indefinitely.

Example Scenario

Consider Sarah, a 29-year-old nurse earning $105,000 per annum. She has managed to save $45,000 while renting in Melbourne.

Under traditional lending requirements, Sarah may struggle to purchase an $850,000 property because a 20% deposit would require approximately $170,000 plus purchasing costs. Saving this amount could take many more years, especially as property prices continue to rise.

Under the 5% Deposit Scheme, however, Sarah may require only approximately $42,500 in addition to purchasing costs. The government guarantee allows her to avoid Lenders Mortgage Insurance, potentially saving more than $20,000.

As a result, Sarah is able to enter the property market far earlier than she otherwise could have.

However, Sarah also takes on a loan exceeding $800,000. If interest rates rise substantially, or if property values decline, she may experience financial pressure and have limited equity available if she needs to sell unexpectedly.

The scheme has created an opportunity, but it has also increased her financial exposure.

Final Thoughts

The Australian Government's 5% Deposit Scheme and Help to Buy shared equity program have created genuine opportunities for many Australians to enter the property market sooner than would otherwise be possible.

For the right borrower, these schemes may provide a pathway into homeownership that would have taken many additional years through traditional savings methods. Reduced deposit requirements and avoidance of LMI can create significant financial advantages.

However, borrowers should not confuse a smaller deposit with a smaller financial commitment. In many cases, these schemes simply shift more debt into the future through larger loans and increased leverage.

As with all property and lending decisions, these schemes work best when approached carefully, with realistic expectations, strong financial discipline, and a clear understanding of the opportunities and risks involved.

Unacceptable Properties for Many Lenders (not all)

Something within 50m of high-tension power lines is considered an unacceptable property, as future capital growth and purchaser demand are adversely affected.

Having no services connected (no gas or sewerage is normally okay, but water and electricity need to be connected) is unacceptable, though having a generator for electricity and only tank water is less acceptable to a lender, as it can make the property less appealing and less marketable.

It is preferable that properties (normally apartments, where this applies) have more than 50 sqm of internal living space (some lenders will accept 35 sqm). A few will accept less, but it is uncommon. Others will consider less than 35 sqm of living space if the total size on the title is over 50 sqm. Items that may be included in the title are a courtyard, a balcony, a car park, or a storage room.

Types of properties that present problems include converted churches, warehouses, factories, and properties in resorts. Student accommodation (see *Property Investing Made Simple,* for an explanation of why this is often considered a problematic investment), serviced apartments, kit and portable homes, and studios are also problematic. Large Acreage may be unacceptable to a traditional lender. Titles with more than three-on-one (not for private lenders), leasehold (such as in a ski resort), over-55s accommodation, display homes (not for private lenders), and often defence housing are also unpopular with most traditional lenders. Rural zoning, land with covenants, and land with high-risk ratings due to flood or fire are also problematic. Mud brick homes and homes made from shipping containers are also unpopular with most lenders.

Private lenders can consider many of these properties, therefore providing solutions that many banks cannot.

UNACCEPTABLE PROPERTIES
FOR MANY LENDERS (NOT ALL)

- Within 50m of high-tension power lines.
- No services connected (water and electricity must be connected).
- Less than 50 sqm of internal living space (some accept 35 sqm).
- Converted churches, warehouses, resorts, studios, large acreage, leasehold, rural zoning, high-risk land, and more.

Valuations

Valuations can make or break a deal, but the property remains with the lender until the borrower pays off the debt. Naturally, the lender wants to ensure the property is marketable and acceptable should it ever be repossessed and sold. A lender will normally want a valuation undertaken on a property. The method by which this is completed can vary between lenders and is often based on compliance, the property's contract price, the loan amount, and the property's location.

Some lenders require a valuer to go to the property. Others just want the valuer to do a 'drive by', whilst some others will use a 'research' software program provider; this platform is designed to provide an approximate value without someone visiting the property.

The process of ordering a valuation is as follows: the lender orders the valuation. The valuer then contacts the appropriate person for access (the owner, if it is a refinance, and the sales agent, for example, if it is a purchase). Lenders have a list of valuers they accept for valuing a property they're considering lending against.

A valuation is ordered as part of the assessment process, but typically occurs after the 'conditional' approval of a loan.

Any valuation for lending purposes involves researching comparable sales, not what the property will sell for. The benefit of using a broker is that they can order an upfront valuation on a property through the lender, prior to submitting the loan application, and if the valuation stacks up, a loan can be submitted.

It can be difficult for a lender or individual to have a valuation reassigned to another lender, but it is certainly possible. There may, however, be a charge for another valuation to be conducted, even if it's with the same valuation firm — and even the same valuer.

One reason valuations are not reassigned across the industry so readily is that each lender has specific criteria it wants the valuer to address in the report. So, one lender's criteria may differ from another's, and what one lender wants may be less meaningful to another lender.

Valuations can range from being free to costing thousands of dollars for commercial, development, or high-priced properties.

If a valuation comes in low, there are six choices the buyer has:

1. Do not proceed with finance.
2. Proceed by putting in additional cash/equity from another property, or a gift, etc.

3. Borrow a higher loan-to-value ratio (LVR) against the property, if there's room for this (the initial LVR being sought could already be 95%, so this option could prove difficult, particularly for a first homebuyer).

4. Choose another property to purchase.

5. Choose another lender so that, hopefully, another valuer is used and the property comes in at a higher value (often lenders won't accept another lender's valuation). This is a double-edged sword. If you had a good valuation but, for some other reason, the lender could not be used, it would be handy to reuse the valuation. Alas, it's not so easy with most lenders. Even obtaining a copy of the valuation is difficult. Likewise, if there's another lender that can assist, they will get their own valuation done, giving the borrower a chance for a better outcome.

6. Go back to the lender to request the valuer to reconsider their decision. To support the request to re-examine the valuation, please provide additional comparable sales to help the valuer justify an increase in the price they believe the property is worth. As mentioned, valuers seldom change their opinion. Even if you cannot obtain a list of the comparable sales the valuer has used, you can still look for other comparable sales that you believe support the value of your property.

'Existing' (already built, excluding off-the-plan) property valuations are more likely to come in on the money than 'new' property valuations. If there's emotion creeping into the mix during a bid at auction, it may not necessarily be related to what the property is worth. The intelligent bidders will bid only up to the property's fair market value, or, more importantly, their budget. A less experienced bidder could become too excited and offer too much for a property; hopefully, they're not foolish enough to bid above their budget, but it does happen and not as infrequently as you might think.

I went to one auction where the property was on the market for 440K+. The margin above the advertised price in this suburb at which properties would sell is usually 8%. I knew the agent had advertised the property for too much below what it would go for. It was reasonable to expect the property to sell for around 520K (this was not a salubrious suburb or a suburb, and it was not in a good high school zone, yet the first offer was 470K, then 520K, and it worked its way up to 579K.

The higher bidder was proud of himself in front of his girlfriend and the crowd. I later heard that, due to his ill-advised approach, he lost his 10% deposit because he could not complete the purchase; the bank valuation came in far too low, and he did not have the funds to proceed.

Things that may not be taken into account in a valuation for a new property are more numerous. This may be due to developer overcharging, involvement of property marketing companies, environmental factors, a lack of third-party comparable sales, valuers' conservatism, and many other factors.

Some common reasons why a valuation on a new property may not stack up may include, but are not limited to, the following points:

- Level of finish or quality, site costs (e.g., soil tests, fences, blinds); better quality or more inclusions mean the construction contract price is higher, but a valuation will not necessarily reflect this.

- Comparable sales in the location within the last 3 months are not available. Undervaluations occur in newer estates because the surrounding properties are much older, and there are fewer usable comparable sales.
- Valuers not understanding the product (e.g., comparing a dual-occupancy to a five-bedroom house).

These things in their own right may not necessarily impact future value. Often a valuation firm will recognise the contract price as being acceptable by stipulating a replacement dollar figure for the dwelling as the same or higher than the contract price of the construction; hence, they're indirectly supporting the sale price, but they may not be able to state this figure to be the same as contract price as this has to be supported by comparable third party sales, not other developer/ builder sales.

Another factor that negatively affects a new property is oversupply in an area.

Valuations on new properties can range from coming in above contract price (very rare) to coming in 10%+ below contract price, more than $50K+ on some 'off-the-plan' developments. I once saw an instance where someone built a mansion, and thought it was worth 3 million, but it was in a suburb with a median price of 350K. There were no comparable sales, so the valuation was $1.9 million.

If you commit to an 'off-the-plan' contract and wait 12 months to 4 years until it is built, then at that time, whichever lender you may have obtained a pre-approval from at the start of the process has absolutely no obligation to re-approve you for finance.

VALUATIONS

Valuations can make or break a deal, but the property remains with the lender until the borrower pays off the debt. Lenders want to ensure the property is marketable and acceptable should it ever be repossessed and sold. A lender will normally want a valuation undertaken on a property.

Some lenders require a valuer to go to the property. Others just want the valuer to do a 'drive by', whilst some others will use a 'research' software program provider; this platform is designed to provide an approximate value without someone visiting the property.

The process of ordering a valuation is as follows: the lender orders the valuation. The valuer then contacts the appropriate person for access (the owner, if it is a refinance, and the sales agent, for example, if it is a purchase). Lenders have a list of valuers they accept for valuing a property they're considering lending against.

A valuation is ordered as part of the assessment process, but typically occurs after the 'conditional' approval of a loan.

Any valuation for lending purposes involves researching comparable sales, not what the property will sell for. The benefit of using a broker is that they can order an upfront valuation on a property through the lender, prior to submitting the loan application, and if the valuation stacks up, a loan can be submitted.

It can be difficult to have a valuation reassigned to another lender, but it is possible. There may be a charge for another valuation to be conducted, even if it's with the same valuation firm — and even the same valuer.

Each lender has specific criteria it wants the valuer to address in the report. So, one lender's criteria may differ from another's, and what one lender wants may be less meaningful to another lender.

Valuations can range from being free to costing thousands of dollars for commercial, development, or high-priced properties.

IF A VALUATION COMES IN LOW, THERE ARE SIX CHOICES THE BUYER HAS:

1. Do not proceed with finance.
2. Proceed by putting in additional cash/equity from another property, or a gift, etc.
3. Borrow a higher loan-to-value ratio (LVR) against the property, if there's room for this.
4. Choose another property to purchase.
5. Choose another lender in hopes a different valuer is used and the value is higher.
6. Go back to the lender to request the valuer to reconsider their decision, providing additional comparable sales to support the request.

SOME COMMON REASONS WHY A VALUATION ON A NEW PROPERTY MAY NOT STACK UP:

- Level of finish or quality, site costs (e.g., soil tests, fences, blinds); better quality or more inclusions mean the construction contract price is higher, but a valuation will not necessarily reflect this.
- Comparable sales in the location within the last 3 months are not available. Undervaluations occur in newer estates because the surrounding properties are much older, and therefore not considered a true comparison.
- Developer overcharging, involvement of property marketing companies, environmental factors, lack of third-party comparable sales, valuers' conservatism, and many other factors.

Different Types of Loans

Before choosing a loan, it's important to determine your requirements and understand your financial objectives or seek advice on which loan is not unsuitable for you. Please keep flexibility in mind, as your needs may change over time.

In this section, I've applied a general overlay to what is most common. There are always exceptions; each lender has its own idiosyncrasies. Private lenders offer a wide range of loan types that banks won't. Many borrowers have failed in their endeavours because they did not know a solution was possible, but borrowers have now recognised the rapidly evolving private lending space.

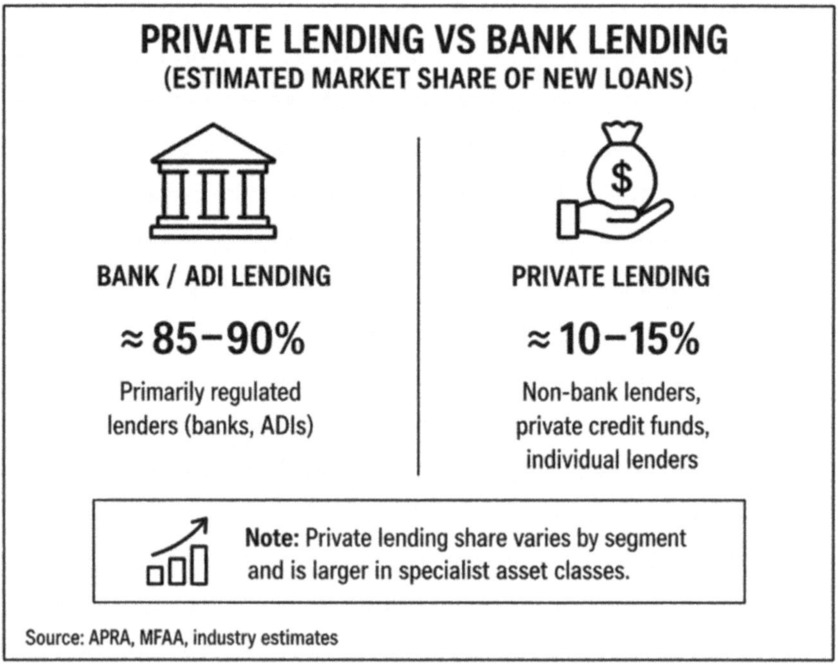

Standard Variable

This is by far the most popular product borrowers choose; it has more features than many other products. It can come with an annual fee or no annual fee. The annual-fee product is known as a professional package. Both can offer offset, redraw, split-loan capabilities, security portability, or credit cards. Some have frequent flyer points programs and may allow unlimited splits on the loan. This provides more benefits, options, flexibility and adaptability.

Most major lenders advertise their standard variable rates. Don't be misled by this. The actual rate is almost always much lower, between 0.7% and 1.45% lower. *Never* accept the standard variable rate if you can help it.

Basic Variable

No annual fee, no bells and whistles. This is commonly referred to as a no-frills home loan and is often chosen by a first homebuyer who wants to keep the loan costs down. Typically, this would not be suitable for an investor, since it may not allow loan splits that separate tax-deductible debt from non-tax-deductible debt.

Variable rates provide much more flexibility, including being able to refinance or sell your property without very large 'break' costs. Fixed rates carry with them exit fees. With some private lenders, it may only be a few hundred dollars.

Fixed Rate

Ultimately, it's a question of risk appetite. If a person has a low-risk appetite, fixed rates may be important. It is not necessarily about making or saving money as much as it is about minimising future risk. Variable rates used to be tied to the market, but they're now at regular and ongoing 'risk' at being changed as and when, and to what, the given lender feels in the mood for at the time.

To hedge your bets, perhaps consider half fixed and half variable; it's a personal decision. The majority of lenders won't provide an offset account against a fixed-rate loan, so if you wish to reduce debt by saving money in an offset account, you will not be able to find this easily unless using a broker. The surplus income you have, or will save, may or may not have a bearing on your decision to fix your rate.

There are two main reasons to consider splitting a loan into fixed and variable components.

- You're a good saver and want an accessible offset facility with redraw.
- Only partial protection is required against rate increases.

In my opinion, fixed rates can be a prudent risk management strategy, depending on your individual circumstances. They are great for budgeting, and you may have a happier life knowing what your repayments will be in 2 years' time or 4 years' time. If you have a fixed-rate loan and you sell your house, repay the loan, or refinance during the fixed-rate period, it will cost you. The cost will depend on the lender, the loan amount, and the term remaining in the fixed-rate period.

The borrower agrees to fix their interest rate for a period of time, normally 1–5 years; naturally, the borrower can continue to fix as often as they like at the end or thereafter, of a fixed rate period, what normally happens is the rate reverts to the lender's standard variable rate, and the borrower can end up being ripped off. Remember: always negotiate down the standard variable rate with the lender, especially at the end of a fixed-rate period. The borrower can never rely on the lender doing the right thing by automatically offering the largest discount possible. Why would they? Remember, they normally care about their shareholders more than their customers.

Fixing the rate is a risk reduction strategy. It provides peace of mind that, for the selected period, the interest rate won't change, and the repayment will remain the same. Please keep in mind that the lender has priced the fixed rate to the projected market, so they have more resources than you or I do, and you generally cannot outsmart them. Nonetheless, no one can predict with certainty how low rates will go in a declining-rate market, or how high they will go in a rising-rate market.

Once you've signed a contract, you cannot break your agreement and decide that you don't like it anymore (especially just because interest rates are going down further). Fixed rates are good if variable rates are rising, but not if they are falling. You're gambling when choosing between fixed rates and variable rates, and it's a gamble you need to live with if it's a fixed rate you want. If it's

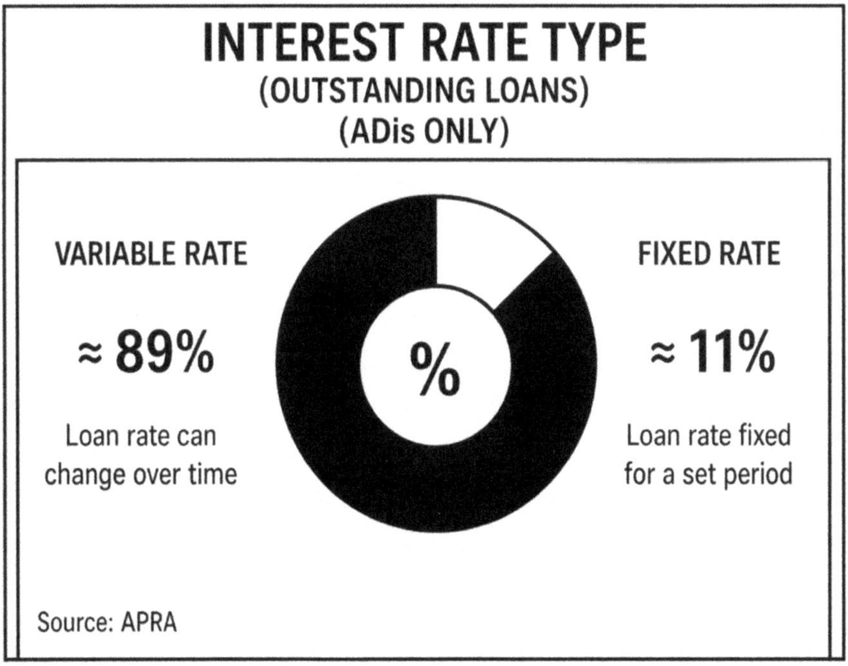

a variable rate you want, then you can always fix it later. The exception to this is using a private lender; it's a short-term loan anyway, it provides a solution you cannot obtain elsewhere, and there are often no repayments during the short loan term.

Be careful here; there is never an absolutely perfect time to fix your rate without the benefit of hindsight. Plan, do your homework and prepare to decide whether fixing your rates is the right thing to do.

Split Loans

When a split loan is taken, the total loan amount is split into two or more smaller loans. Each split can have either a fixed rate or variable rate. Most lenders allow you to name each split. One or two lenders allow different applicants to be on each split without incurring liability to the other borrower's loan split.

If you're buying with a friend, and wish to keep payments and responsibilities separate, then a loan split can help. Bear in mind that, in almost every instance, you'll be jointly and severally liable for the entire debt — even though you may only be 50% on the title. Even if you are less than 50% on title you are still liable for the entire debt in most instances.

100% Offset

An offset account is a separate, standalone account linked to the loan, with the primary purpose of helping reduce interest repayments on the loan and allowing easy access to any accrued savings you have built up. It offsets the loan limit by the amount sitting in there at a given time. Interest is calculated on the loan principal, less any monies you have saved in the offset account, known as the loan balance. This is a powerful tool that often is underutilised by borrowers; it can save many hundreds or thousands of dollars per year, depending on the amount in there and the size of the loan it's offsetting.

Example

A $900,000 loan at 6.75% interest, on an interest-only basis, would normally have a monthly repayment of $5,062.50. If $100,000 sat in the offset account for the entire month, the interest repayment would be ($800,000 x 6.75%)/12 = $4,500.00. If you have P&I repayments, your monthly repayment would be $5,837. With $100,000 in the offset account, the repayment remains the same, but a larger portion of the loan is paid off because interest is charged on $800,000 rather than $900,000. This would enable the borrower to pay off the loan more quickly. If the savings parked in the offset account increase, the loan will be paid off even more quickly—potentially many years sooner.

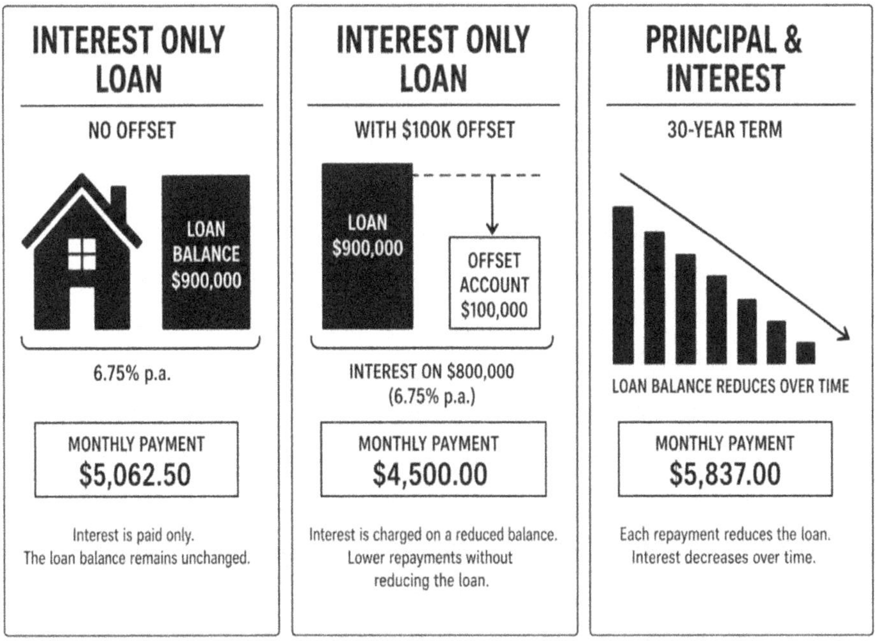

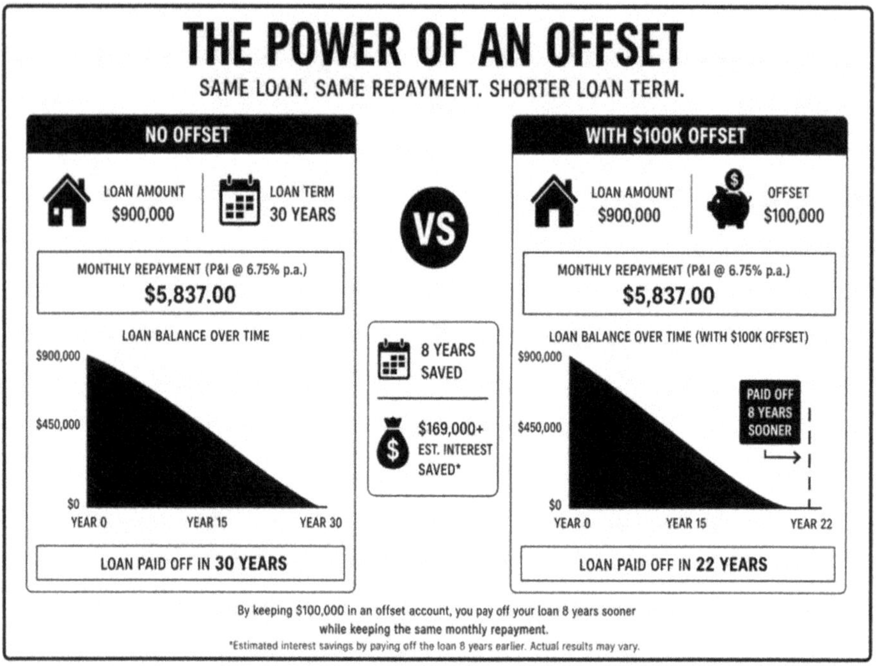

LOAN FEATURES – OFFSET ACCOUNTS (ADIs ONLY)

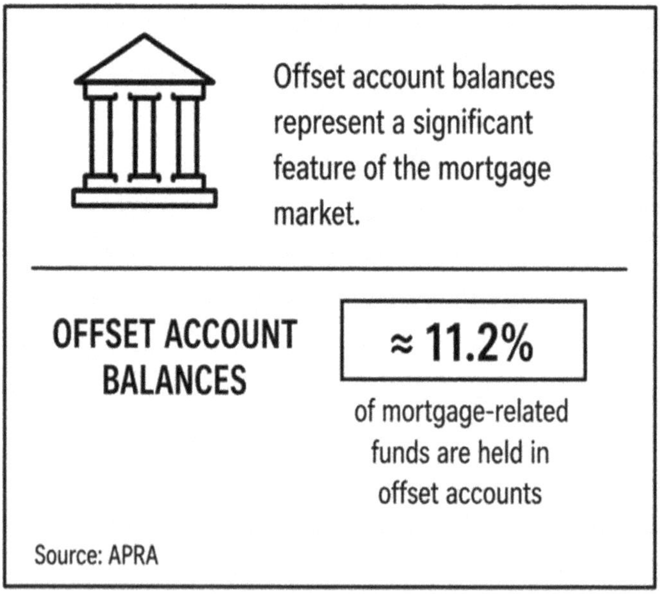

Leaving the money in an offset account allows redraw when required. If you pay any savings into the loan rather than an offset account, the borrower typically cannot access them unless the loan facility allows redraw.

Redraw accounts are different because they often refer to the loan itself, the ability to put extra money directly into the loan, and the ability to redraw those funds. Sometimes, a minimum amount must be withdrawn when accessing your money/accessible figure. There may be a charge to withdraw it, and it may not offset the loan amount beyond the initial month it's paid into the loan. If you have an investment property and a redraw facility within the loan, be careful: you cannot take money out after putting money in and then claim more interest expense. The ATO will not be happy with you because if you take money out and it's not for investment purposes, you cannot claim the resulting higher interest expense.

Partial Offset

Only a proportion of the balance of funds in the offset account works to offset the loan amount. So, if the loan is 400K, the offset account has $30,000, and it has a 50% offset capability, then the interest charged would be on a loan amount of 385K, so only half of the $30,000 is actually working for the borrower. This is better than no offset, but far less effective than a full offset account.

Line of Credit (LOC)

A line of credit is basically a loan facility with a variable interest rate. It can come with a higher limit than a credit card, because it is secured against a property. If funds are sitting in the LOC, no repayment is necessary on that amount. You would only pay interest on the amount of the loan facility that has been used (drawn down).

These facilities have a limit, like any other loan. It's like having money on demand once you set it up. You can use any of the funds as you see fit. It's cheaper than a credit card's ongoing interest rate (excluding these credit card schemes that allow you to transfer debt to them from another card for a zero or low interest rate for the first 12 months or so). It can be an additional loan split using a property as security, whether residential or commercial. Funds are easily accessible via internet banking, ATM cards, and phone banking.

It has its advantages for many people, particularly if the loan was interest-only. Those who are self-employed may use the savings as working capital, helping with their business cash flow; investors may use them as a deposit for another property or as a buffer for any vacancy, repair, or maintenance issue. Many use it just for daily living expenses.

The interest on the loan can be capitalised, so as long as you're under the limit on a loan facility that allows this, it is possible just to let the interest repayments accrue, without paying additional money into the facility (no fortnightly or monthly repayments are required in this instance). The interest rate is often 0.10% higher with an LOC than with a term loan; the term is often 25 years, and the loan can remain interest-only for the duration. It's vitally important not to blend the purpose of the funds if the intention is to claim any interest on the debt for tax purposes. In other words, don't mix home loan debt with investment debt.

Most lenders no longer offer these facilities, perhaps in part due to pressure from responsible lending rules.

Having a line of credit (LOC) also carries some problematic tax consequences, just as a redraw facility does. Having an offset account may equally be beneficial. With an offset account, you can be your own bank as well, you can access the redraw (monies you have accumulated in the offset account) as easily as with a LOC.

If you choose a line of credit to finance your property purchase, we recommend that you not use it for private purposes. If there is a fluctuating balance due to a variety of deposits and withdrawals, and if it is used for both private purposes and rental property purposes, it can quickly diminish the amount of interest that can be claimed as a tax deduction. The calculation of interest that can be included in the tax deductions is also quite involved and time-consuming.

Principal & Interest Versus Interest-Only Loans

Interest-Only (I/O)

For a period of time, usually 5 to 10 years, the borrower only has to make interest repayments on the mortgage and does not need to repay any of the principal during this period. Many, if not most, investors do this for all their investment properties to help build their portfolios.

It can assist first-time homebuyers with cash flow by reducing their monthly repayment commitments, helping them manage the costs of furniture and moving. A 1-year interest-only period may be suitable for some people, helping manage the cost of the loan. It provides more surplus for 'would-be' investors, which may make it easier to afford to hold a negatively geared property.

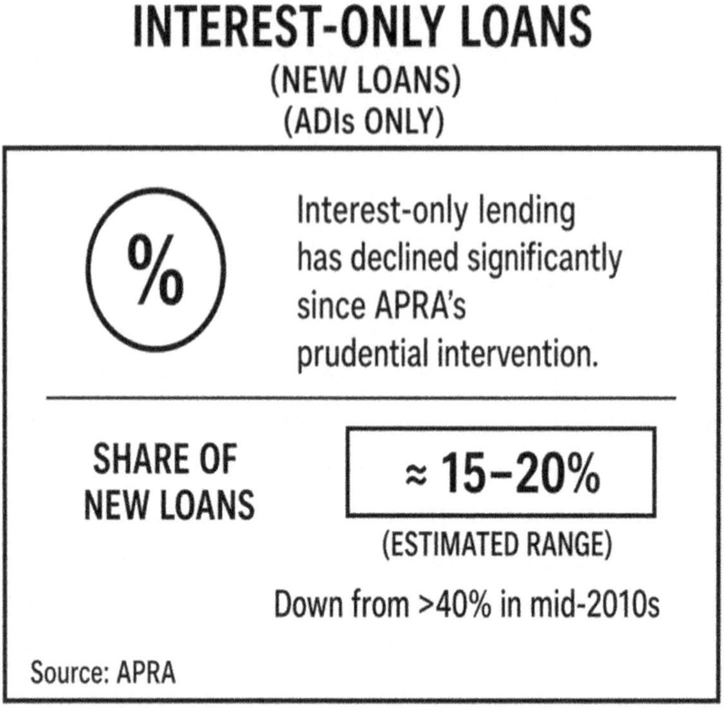

Note: ADIs = Authorised Deposit-taking Institutions.

It can assist in providing greater serviceability on a lender's calculator — perhaps 1.5–2 times more. Lenders used to assess interest-only repayments without adding a buffer in their serviceability calculators, but this has changed for most lenders. Most now service all existing debt, as they do new debt, at a qualifying rate equating to roughly 2% above the repayment rate.

A few lenders still assess existing debts at actual repayments rather than a higher qualifying repayment rate, so I/O loans can be very useful for calculating someone's borrowing capacity on serviceability calculators with these lenders, mitigating the reduction in borrowing capacity associated with servicing a debt on most lenders' calculators.

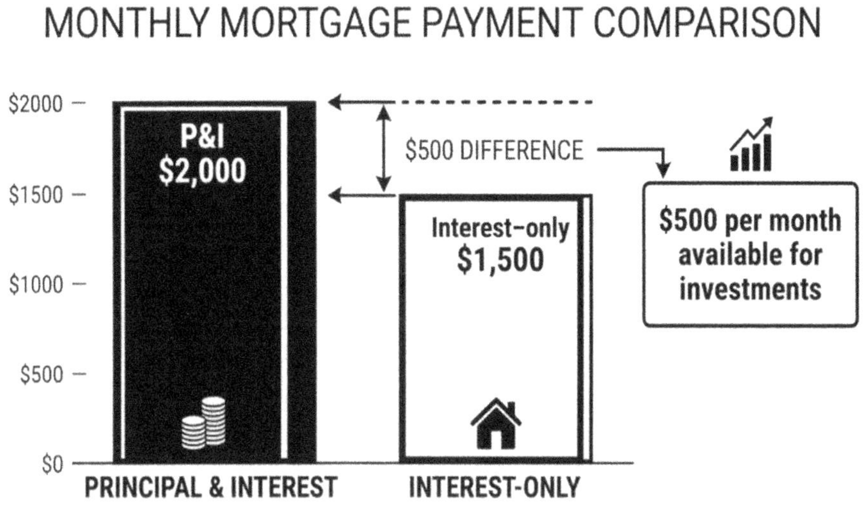

Regarding a bank's servicing calculator, your borrowing capacity will be reduced or increased depending on the lender chosen if you elect an I/O period. The particular lender may assume you will have to repay the entire loan in 25 years, not 30 (because the first 5 years of the 30-year loan term are an interest-only period, meaning the period over which principal is paid is only 25 years). This places pressure on servicing. It is a balancing act when working with these variations to provide the most suitable outcome for an individual borrower.

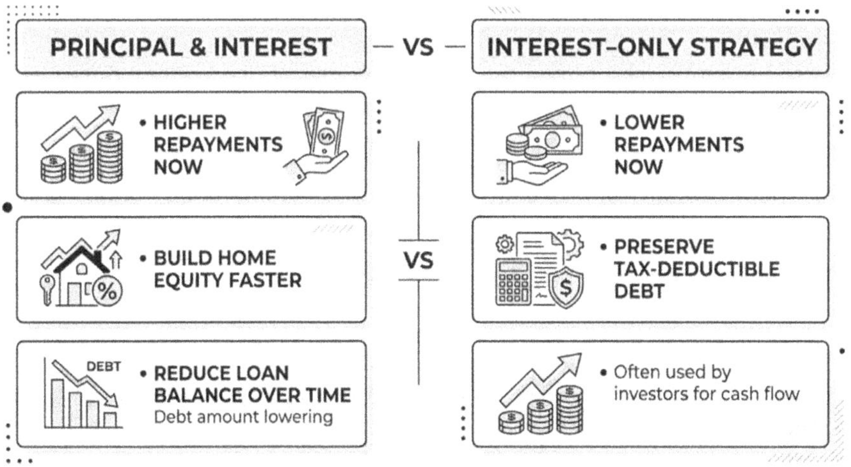

Wisely chosen lenders can often help overcome some of the above issues, or, as some say, impediments.

Borrowers risk being caught off guard if they have too many loans set up as interest-only. When the loan(s) convert to principal and interest (*P&I*), the repayments will jump up considerably for two reasons.

1. Previously, the borrower was only making interest-only repayments on the debt; now they're repaying the debt in instalments while still paying interest.
2. The debt increments now being repaid are compressed into the remaining life of the loan, say 20–25 years (the remaining life of the original 30-year loan, based on a 5–10-year interest-only period). This makes the weekly, fortnightly, or monthly debt increment much higher than it would have been if a P&I loan had been taken out to begin with and spread over the 30-year life of the loan.

Many investors, to avoid this higher, more condensed repayment schedule, refinance with another lender on a standard 30-year term, sometimes a 40-year term, just to make it easier to avoid the sudden jump in repayments associated with the more condensed time frame.

After ASIC completed a cost comparison, it found that a borrower could pay $32,000 more in interest repayments over the life of the loan if they chose a 5-year interest-only loan compared to a P&I loan (over $80,000 more in interest repayments) if the interest-only period was 10 years.

Many will argue that it is okay not to reduce investment debt because it allows you to borrow more for more properties and, therefore, create greater wealth. Until recently, it has been relatively straightforward for a borrower to refinance a loan every 5 years to continue with another 5-year loan term at

I/O. Property marketing companies (spruikers) will float in front of you wonderful-sounding capital growth figures, with a relatively low cost of holding the asset, by keeping your loans interest-only.

I want to be clear: it's becoming more difficult to find lenders that can meet all requirements, and if you keep accumulating debt without reducing it, your position becomes more precarious. Most importantly, pay off the home loan and consider not having an interest-only loan on it. By all means, consider keeping interest-only on an investment loan while the home loan debt is in place, but once the home loan debt is paid off, consider reducing the investment debt. Many lenders now offer better rates to borrowers who ask for P&I loans on investment debt anyway.

It is also worth distinguishing interest-only lending within traditional structures from capitalised interest arrangements often seen in private lending. In the latter, interest may not be paid monthly; instead, it is usually added to the loan balance and repaid at the end of the term. This structure is typically used where the loan is intended to be short-term and resolved through a defined exit.

Principal and Interest (P&I)

These loans have higher repayments than interest-only loans, as some of the repayment is going toward reducing the loan principal (debt amount) over the life of the loan.

If the borrower has a home loan and that loan was not taken out for investment purposes, no tax benefits apply. As a result, many borrowers prefer to focus on paying down their home loan before reducing any debt on an investment property.

In the early years of the loan term, the majority of each repayment is interest, with only a small amount applied to the principal. It's often better to make fortnightly repayments rather than monthly, because lenders compound interest daily — in other words, they charge interest not only on the loan amount but also on the interest charged on the loan amount 'every day', until the repayment is made.

So, if you pay fortnightly, the compounding interest is less costly. Because interest compounds, banks will charge you interest on your debt, as well as on the interest on that debt, daily. The more frequent the repayments, the sooner any accrued interest is paid and cleared, and the lower the cost to the borrower associated with the compounding effect of interest. This will be covered in more detail later in the book.

Over time, the principal component of the repayment starts to make up a large share of the regular payment on the loan. One of the main reasons the first several years of repayments consist mainly of interest (as a greater component of the repayment) is due to the fact that the bank is *not* a 'not-for-profit organisation'. They're a business, as mentioned earlier, and they only care about their shareholders and their profit margin.

Banks are not in the business of lending your money. They are in the business of making money from you by lending you money, and, given the average time a person remains with their lender is 3.5 years, it makes sense that the lenders want to make as much money as possible from you. Every time you refinance, you restart the 30-year loan term, effectively going backward and costing you much more in interest over the life of the loan.

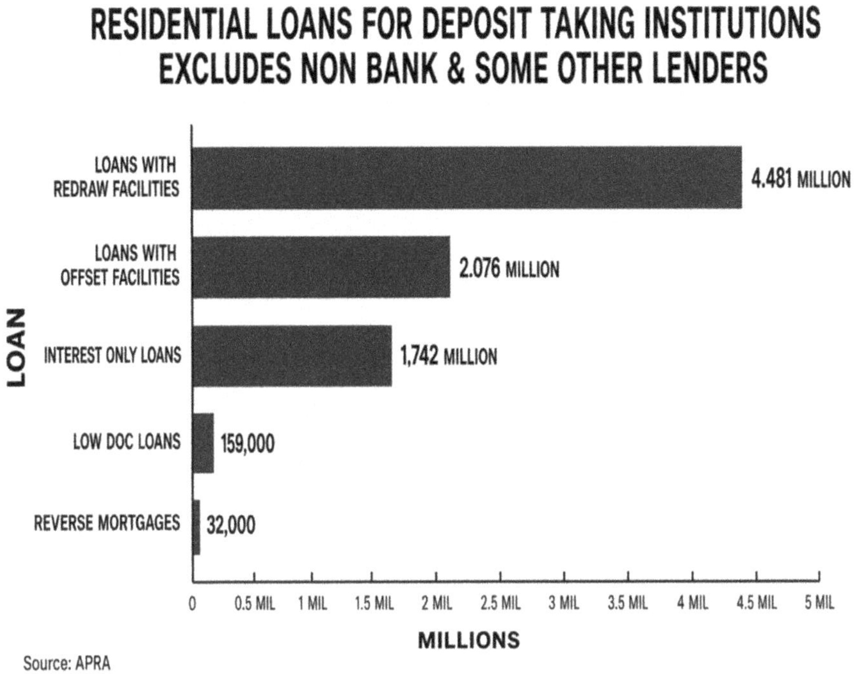
RESIDENTIAL LOANS FOR DEPOSIT TAKING INSTITUTIONS
EXCLUDES NON BANK & SOME OTHER LENDERS
LOAN
LOANS WITH REDRAW FACILITIES
4.481 MILLION
LOANS WITH OFFSET FACILITIES
2.076 MILLION
INTEREST ONLY LOANS
1,742 MILLION
LOW DOC LOANS
159,000
REVERSE MORTGAGES
32,000
0
0.5 MIL
1 MIL
1.5 MIL
2 MIL
2.5 MIL
3 MIL
3.5 MIL
4 MIL
4.5 MIL
5 MIL
MILLIONS

Source: APRA

6.

No Borrowing Capacity Lending

In order to apply for a loan without sufficient or any income, which in turn means less or no borrowing capacity, there are a few crucial points to understand, as to how it works.

Interest Capitalisation

Interest capitalisation is a simple concept with a practical purpose: instead of paying interest as it accrues, the interest is added to the loan balance and paid at the end of the loan term. In effect, the interest becomes part of the principal, and the borrower repays the entire amount in a single lump sum.

In straightforward terms, this means there are no monthly repayments. The loan runs for an agreed period—commonly between 1 and 36 months—and during that time, the interest is either set aside at the start or progressively added to the balance. At the end of the term, the borrower repays the total amount owing, which includes the original loan, the capitalised interest, and any agreed fees.

It is important to understand how the interest itself is calculated. These loans are structured on an interest-only basis, not principal and interest. That means the interest is calculated on the full amount borrowed, with no reduction in the underlying principal over the term. Because no repayments are made, the principal remains unchanged, and the interest accrues against that full amount before being capitalised—added to the balance rather than paid along the way.

This differs from a standard home loan, where each repayment typically reduces the principal and, over time, lowers the interest charged. However, not all standard home loans operate in this way. Many lenders offer interest-only periods, particularly for investment loans. During such a period, the borrower pays only the interest due each month, and the principal remains unchanged. The key distinction is that, in those arrangements, the interest is still being paid as it falls due, preventing it from increasing the loan balance. By contrast, with capitalised interest, those payments are deferred entirely, and the unpaid interest is added to the loan, increasing the total amount owing over time.

This structure is widely used in short-term lending, particularly in property transactions such as bridging finance, renovations, or development projects. It is designed for situations where income may not yet be available to service a loan, or where cash flow is better preserved for other purposes.

A key feature of these loans is the loan-to-value ratio (LVR). In most cases, lenders will cap the total exposure—being the loan amount plus capitalised interest and fees—at around 70% to 75% of the property's value. This is an important point: the interest is not "extra" on top of the limit; it is included within it. As a result, the initial amount advanced to the borrower may be slightly lower than the maximum LVR to allow for interest and costs over the term.

Repayment is typically made through a defined exit strategy. This might involve selling the property, refinancing with another lender, or using proceeds from a completed project. Because the entire debt comes due at once, it is essential that the borrower has a clear and realistic repayment plan within the agreed term.

LOAN-TO-VALUE RATIO
(OUTSTANDING LOANS)
(ADIs ONLY)

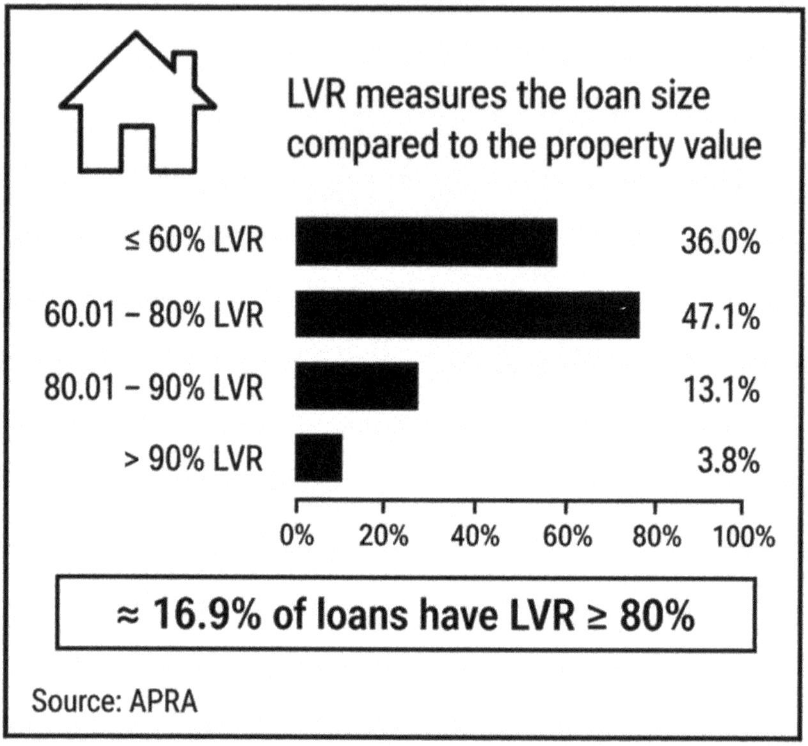

For example, consider a property valued at $1.5 million. At a maximum LVR of 70%, the total allowable exposure is $1,080,000. This figure must cover the loan, the capitalised interest, and any fees.

Assume the loan term is 12 months and the interest rate is 8% per annum. Because the loan is interest-only, the interest is calculated on the full loan amount for the entire term. If approximately $1,000,000 is advanced, around 80,000 in interest would accrue over 12 months. The lender may structure the facility so that this interest is included in the total limit. In practical terms, the borrower might receive slightly less than the full $1,080,000 to ensure that, once interest and fees are included, the total exposure remains within the 70% LVR cap. Note that for example purposes, simple interest has been used, but every lender uses compound interest. Compound interest will lead to a slightly higher figure.

It is also important to understand how pricing works in practice. While many fees in this type of lending tend to be relatively consistent—such as establishment or legal costs—the valuation fee can vary depending on the property and the complexity of the report required. More importantly, the interest rate itself is fixed across all scenarios. The rate depends on factors such as the property's location, zoning, land size, and the type of asset (for example, residential, commercial, or specialised use). A well-located metropolitan residential property in standard condition will generally attract a lower rate than a remote, irregular, or specialised asset.

A higher rate increases the amount of interest that must be allowed for within the capped LVR. Because the total exposure cannot exceed, say, 70%, a higher interest allocation reduces the amount of cash that can be advanced upfront. Conversely, a lower-risk property with a sharper rate may allow more funds to be released to the borrower, as less of the facility needs to be reserved for interest and costs.

Over the 12 months, the borrower makes no repayments. The principal does not reduce, and the interest is capitalised rather than paid monthly. At the end of the term, the borrower repays the full amount—say, approximately $1,050,000—through sale, refinance, inheritance, cash flow or some other means.

The primary benefit of interest capitalisation is cash flow. Removing the need for monthly repayments allows borrowers to direct funds towards completing a project or managing other expenses. It also provides simplicity, with a single repayment at the end, and flexibility for short-term opportunities. As there are no repayments, there is no need to service the loan if the exit is a sale.

In essence, interest capitalisation allows borrowers to defer payment obligations in the present, in exchange for a larger, structured repayment in the near future.

Exit Strategy

No borrowing capacity lending is often misunderstood. It is frequently described as a workaround, a last resort, or an exception to standard lending practice. In reality, it is none of those things. It is simply a different framework. Instead of relying on income to support ongoing repayments, it relies on structure and outcome. At the centre of that outcome sits one concept: the exit strategy. This type of lending is often a loan of first resort.

In a traditional loan, borrowing capacity determines the result. Income is measured, expenses are deducted, buffers are applied, and a figure is produced. That figure becomes the limit. If the numbers do not work, the loan does not proceed. Within that model, there is little flexibility because the structure assumes the loan will be repaid progressively through regular instalments.

No borrowing capacity lending operates on a different premise. The loan is not designed to be repaid over time through income. It is designed to be repaid at a point in time through an event. That event is the exit. Without that event, the structure has no foundation. With it, the structure becomes logical and, importantly, accessible.

Understanding the Shift in Assessment

When income is removed as the primary driver, the assessment does not disappear. It shifts. The lender is no longer asking, "Can this borrower make the repayments each month?" Instead, the lender is asking, "Will the loan be repaid in full when required?"

This is a more direct question, and often a simpler one. It requires a clear understanding of what will occur between the loan's commencement and its conclusion. It also requires confidence that the pathway to repayment is realistic.

As outlined earlier in the book, lending is not determined by a single factor. It is the interaction of multiple elements that creates a workable scenario. In no-borrowing-capacity lending, those elements still exist—property, structure, time, behaviour—but the weighting changes. The exit strategy moves from being one consideration among many to being the defining element.

Why the Exit Strategy Becomes Critical

In a standard loan, even if circumstances change, repayments continue. Income provides a buffer against uncertainty. In a no-borrowing capacity loan, that buffer does not exist in the same way. There are typically no ongoing repayments, particularly where interest is capitalised.

This makes the exit strategy critical. It is not a secondary plan; it is the primary method of repayment. If the exit does not occur as expected, the entire structure is affected. For this reason, lenders place significant emphasis on its clarity, feasibility, and alignment with the asset.

A vague intention is not sufficient. Saying a property "may be sold" is not a strategy. A strategy requires definition. It must identify how the debt will be cleared, within what timeframe, and on what basis that outcome is expected to occur. Of course, loan terms can be extended. Equally, if the loan is paid out early then any unused interest originally capitalised can be refunded.

CHOOSE THE RIGHT STRUCTURE

The right structure today creates options and protects tomorrow.

Sale as the Primary Exit

The most common and, in many cases, most effective exit strategy in this context is the sale of the property. This is particularly relevant in scenarios involving renovation, development, or repositioning of an asset.

A sale-based exit has several advantages. It provides a clear endpoint. It converts the asset into liquidity, which can then be used to discharge the debt in full. It also aligns naturally with short-term lending structures, where the objective is not long-term ownership, but the completion of a project or the realisation of value.

However, the strength of a sale-based exit depends on the quality of the underlying asset. Not all properties are equal in this regard. A property located in an area with consistent demand and transaction activity is more likely to support a timely and predictable sale. A property in a niche market or with limited appeal may introduce uncertainty.

This is where the assessment becomes more nuanced. The lender is not simply relying on a valuation. They are considering how that value can be realised. Liquidity, market depth, and buyer demand all become relevant.

The Importance of Realistic Value

One of the most common errors in structuring a sale-based exit is overestimating the end value. Optimism is not a strategy. A credible exit is based on evidence, not expectation.

Where the exit relies on a future sale, the anticipated price must be grounded in comparable sales, current market conditions, and the specific characteristics of the property. This is particularly important in renovation or development scenarios, where the projected end value may differ significantly from the current value.

Some lenders may consider the end value, rather than just the land and build together, when determining the loan, especially where works are being undertaken. For example, if the land is worth $1,000,000 and the build cost to construct 2 townhouses is $1,000,000, then, after subdividing the titles, the end value is $2,500,000, which then increases available funding and supports the project's completion. However, it also increases reliance on the exit. If the end value is not achieved, the margin for error reduces.

A disciplined approach involves allowing for variability. Markets do not move in straight lines. Pricing strategies may need to be adjusted. Timeframes may extend. A strong exit strategy accommodates these possibilities rather than ignoring them.

Timeframe and Execution

Time is inseparable from an exit strategy. Every loan has a term, and every exit must occur within that term. In no-borrowing-capacity lending, this relationship is direct. There are no ongoing repayments to manage the balance over time. The loan is made in anticipation of a defined outcome.

Shorter terms tend to provide greater certainty. There is less opportunity for external conditions to change. However, shorter terms also require efficient execution. Delays in preparing, marketing, or selling a property can compress the available timeframe and increase pressure.

Longer terms introduce flexibility but also more variables. Market conditions may shift, interest rates may change, and buyer behaviour may evolve. This does not make long-term plans unsuitable, but it does require a more considered approach to planning. As part of a long-term plan, using a private lender can serve as a stepping stone.

The key is alignment. The loan term must reflect the realistic timeframe required to achieve the exit. If the strategy involves renovation and sale, the term must allow for acquisition, works, marketing, and settlement. Each stage must be considered.

When Sale Is Not the Exit

While sale is the most common exit in no-borrowing-capacity lending, it is not the only one. Refinancing can also serve as an exit, particularly where the borrower's position is expected to improve.

For example, a borrower may not meet serviceability requirements at the outset but may do so once a project is completed, income increases, or financial circumstances stabilise. In such cases, the short-term loan acts as a bridge to a longer-term solution.

However, refinancing introduces its own requirements. The borrower must meet the criteria of the incoming lender at the time of refinance. This includes serviceability, credit profile, and policy considerations. If these conditions are not met, the exit may not be achievable.

For this reason, refinancing as an exit must be approached with caution. It requires forward planning and a clear understanding of what will change between the commencement and conclusion of the loan.

The Interaction with Structure

An exit strategy cannot be separated from structure. The two are interdependent. The structure must support the exit, and the exit must justify the structure.

In no-borrowing-capacity lending, the structure often involves interest-only arrangements with capitalised interest. This means the interest is added to the loan rather than paid periodically.

The loan balance remains the same over the loan term, and the full amount is repaid at exit.

This structure aligns with a sale-based exit of the property used as security or another property. There is no requirement for income to service the loan during the term. Instead, the focus is on the final outcome. However, it also increases the importance of the exit. The longer the term, the higher the accumulated interest, in turn, if the loan term is longer, more interest is capitalised, the less the net figure will be toward the purpose, and the greater the reliance on the final sale price.

This reinforces the need for precision. The structure must be designed with the exit in mind from the outset. It can be adjusted later without consequence, of course. If the exit was the primary stated plan, but the borrower repays the lender by some other means, such as a refinance, inheritance, a term deposit expiring, or the sale of shares or other assets, then no problem at all. The lender receives their money, and the borrower achieves their goal.

Risk and Lender Perspective

From a lender's perspective, no-borrowing-capacity lending is not about removing risk. It is about managing it differently. Instead of relying on income, the lender relies on the asset and the exit.

This shifts the focus to asset quality, loan-to-value ratio, and exit clarity. A lower LVR provides a buffer against market movements. A strong asset provides confidence in liquidity. A clear exit provides a pathway to repayment. This is why some borrowers can obtain funding despite having no demonstrable income, while others cannot. The difference lies not in the absence of income, but in the strength of the overall structure.

Where these elements align, the absence of borrowing capacity becomes less significant, and with a sale, it is insignificant. There is a caveat, which will be mentioned later, but it's worth highlighting now: if it is the borrower's only property and in their personal name. If they decide not to sell and their income is insufficient, the lender is left with the burden of the borrower. The lender then looks bad if the borrowers are stuck with them.

An ethical and responsible private lender will avoid this dilemma. The last thing an ethical private lender wants to do is repossess the only asset someone owns if it is in their personal name. If it is in a company or trust, then it is a non-code loan and no problem. Note: when mentioning a company or trust, I am referring to the ownership, not the borrower. The borrower is not the owner; the entity on title is the owner, and the borrower simply takes responsibility for the loan. This is the same for tax benefits for investors: some people assume the borrower determines any tax entitlements, but that is not correct; ownership determines them, in accordance with ATO rules.

EXIT COMMITTED OR PROPOSED?

**A committed exit is strong.
A proposed exit is uncertain
and much riskier.**

Behaviour and Responsibility

No borrowing capacity lending requires a disciplined approach. Without the structure of regular repayments, it is easy to lose sight of the end objective. The borrower must remain focused on the exit from the outset.

This includes making timely decisions, managing projects effectively, and responding to market conditions. It also involves being realistic about pricing and prepared to act when opportunities arise.

The absence of income-based servicing does not reduce responsibility. If anything, it increases it. The borrower is responsible for ensuring that the timing of the exit occurs as planned. The lender has structured the loan on that basis.

Bringing It Together

No borrowing capacity lending is not an exception to lending principles; it is an application of those principles in a different form. The same elements exist—property, structure, time, behaviour—but the emphasis changes.

At the centre of this model sits the exit strategy. It is the mechanism through which the loan is repaid. It determines the structure, influences the assessment, and defines the outcome.

A well-constructed exit strategy provides clarity. It aligns the elements of the scenario and creates a coherent pathway from borrowing to repayment. A poorly defined exit introduces uncertainty and undermines the structure.

Where the exit involves the sale of a property, its importance is heightened. The asset must support the strategy, the timeframe must be realistic, and the execution must be disciplined. When these factors come together, the absence of borrowing capacity ceases to be a barrier and becomes simply one aspect of a broader, workable solution.

In this context, the question is not whether a borrower has borrowing capacity. The question is whether the loan makes sense. When the exit is clear, supported, and aligned with the structure, the answer can be yes—even when traditional measures would suggest otherwise.

Sole Property, Sale as Exit, and Responsible Lending Risk

Introduction: When Exit Strategy Carries the Entire Loan

In no-borrowing-capacity lending, the loan is not sustained by income. It is sustained through outcome. That outcome is the exit strategy. Where a borrower cannot demonstrate sufficient income to meet ongoing repayments, the lender must instead be satisfied that the loan will be repaid in full at a defined point in time.

This shifts the entire assessment. The question is no longer whether the borrower can service the debt each month. The question becomes whether the loan can be repaid at the end of the term and how that repayment will be made.

In this framework, the exit strategy is not a supporting element. It is the foundation. If the exit fails, the structure fails. That is particularly important where the exit is the sale of property, and even more so where that property is the borrower's only asset.

The Sole Property Problem

In no-borrowing-capacity lending, the loan is not sustained by income. It is sustained through outcome. That outcome is the exit strategy. Where a borrower cannot demonstrate sufficient income to meet ongoing repayments, the lender must instead be satisfied that the loan will be repaid in full at a defined point in time.

This changes the entire assessment process. The question is no longer whether the borrower can comfortably service the debt each month. The question instead becomes whether the loan can be repaid at the end of the term and, if so, precisely how that repayment will occur.

In this type of lending, the exit strategy is not merely a supporting consideration. It is the foundation of the transaction. If the exit strategy fails, the entire loan structure can fail with it. This becomes particularly important where the proposed exit is the sale of property, and even more so where that property is the borrower's only asset.

Where a borrower owns only one property in their personal name, that property is often far more than a simple asset on a balance sheet. It may represent the borrower's entire position in the property market. In many cases, it may also become their future residence, even if they are currently renting, living with family or friends, or residing overseas. For that reason, where the proposed exit strategy relies upon the sale of that sole property, lenders must approach the matter with considerable caution and careful thought.

The issue is not simply whether the loan can technically be repaid. A sale may clear the debt in full, satisfy the lender, and achieve the proposed exit strategy on paper. However, the broader question is what position the borrower is left in once the transaction is complete. If the borrower moves from owning property to owning nothing, there is a legitimate question as to whether the lending arrangement was genuinely appropriate for that borrower's overall circumstances.

This is where responsible lending considerations become particularly important. A lender cannot focus only on the security position or the likelihood of repayment. Consideration must also be given to the practical consequences for the borrower. If the loan structure places the borrower on a path that could ultimately result in their being removed from property ownership altogether, many lenders will regard this as a serious concern.

Importantly, the borrower's willingness to proceed does not necessarily remove those concerns. Borrowers may initially agree to a strategy involving the sale of their only property, particularly where they are under financial pressure or seeking a short-term solution. However, circumstances and attitudes can change over time. A borrower who was comfortable with the arrangement at the outset may later argue that they did not fully appreciate the consequences of the transaction or that the lender should not have permitted the loan to proceed in the first place.

This is one reason why lenders, particularly traditional lenders subject to strict responsible lending obligations, are often reluctant to support transactions where the exit strategy relies upon the sale of a borrower's sole personally owned property. From the lender's perspective, the issue is not merely legal risk, but also reputational risk. Public criticism frequently overlooks the borrower's own decisions and instead focuses attention on the lender who provided the funds.

Examples of this are regularly seen in consumer-focused media reporting, where personal responsibility is sometimes overshadowed by attempts to portray the borrower as entirely blameless. In reality, lenders are increasingly aware that even when a borrower has willingly entered into a transaction, negative outcomes may later be publicly characterised as lender misconduct rather than poor personal decision-making.

For this reason, responsible private lenders often adopt a more conservative approach where only one personally owned property is involved. In contrast, the position may be different where the borrower owns multiple properties, where the property is held within a company or trust structure, or where the transaction clearly relates to a business or commercial purpose rather than personal home ownership. In those situations, the sale of one property may not entirely remove the borrower from the property market, and the overall risk profile may appear substantially different.

Similarly, borrowers will sometimes argue that they intend to downsize after the loan is completed or after the property is sold. On the surface, this may appear reasonable. However, from a lending perspective, this can still raise concerns because there is a clear gap in time between the borrower's current position and the proposed outcome. During that period, the borrower may still end up in a materially weaker position.

A lender cannot simply assume that a future downsizing strategy will occur exactly as planned. Circumstances can change. The borrower may later decide they no longer wish to sell; the property may not achieve the expected sale price; or market conditions may deteriorate, delaying the sale entirely. In some situations, the property may not sell within the required timeframe. This uncertainty creates risk not only for the lender but also for the borrower.

For this reason, many lenders take the view that if downsizing is genuinely necessary to improve affordability or reduce debt, it should occur immediately rather than at some uncertain point in the future. Otherwise, the borrower is still entering into a transaction that may temporarily, or even permanently, leave them in a less favourable financial and property position.

A commonly proposed exit strategy is therefore a future sale combined with downsizing. However, while this may sound sensible in theory, it remains inherently uncertain in practice.

The borrower may change their mind.

The property may not sell within the anticipated timeframe.

The achieved sale price may be lower than expected.

The borrower may not be able to locate suitable replacement accommodation.

If the loan is short-term, whether for one month or thirty-six months, the lender may ultimately be forced into enforcement proceedings if the sale does not occur. That outcome is rarely desirable for any party. It introduces legal risk, reputational damage, additional costs, and often public scrutiny.

A borrower may later claim they felt pressured, misunderstood the implications, or relied upon circumstances that ultimately did not occur. Regardless of the contractual position, the public perception can quickly become that the lender enabled the borrower to lose their only property.

For these reasons, a mere intention to sell at some future point is generally regarded as a weak exit strategy where the borrower's sole property is involved. Many lenders prefer to see a completed downsizing transaction underway or a much stronger, more immediate pathway to repayment before considering this loan structure appropriate.

From a practical perspective, if the genuine intention is to downsize to reduce debt and improve affordability, many lenders will consider whether the downsizing should occur immediately rather than at some uncertain point in the future. Otherwise, the borrower is still proceeding into a transaction that may temporarily, or even permanently, place them in a less favourable financial and property position.

This is particularly relevant where the borrower owns only one property. If the proposed strategy relies on selling that sole asset later, there remains a real possibility that the borrower could ultimately be left without any property ownership. For this reason, lenders often assess not only the proposed exit strategy itself, but also the realism, timing and reliability of that strategy.

Under the *National Consumer Credit Protection Act 2009 (Cth),* lenders must assess whether a loan is not unsuitable for the borrower. This involves making reasonable inquiries into the borrower's financial situation, requirements, and objectives, and taking reasonable steps to verify that information. The obligation is not limited to mathematical serviceability. It extends to suitability in a broader sense.

If a borrower's stated objective is to retain their home, but the loan structure makes that outcome unlikely, there is a disconnect. If the borrower states they may sell in the future, but that decision is uncertain and not committed, reliance on that future sale may be insufficient.

This is where complaint risk arises. The Australian Securities and Investments Commission (ASIC) oversees the regulation and enforcement of responsible lending obligations within Australia's financial services sector. ASIC monitors the conduct of lenders, brokers and other credit providers to ensure that lending practices comply with the requirements of the *National Consumer Credit Protection Act 2009 (Cth)* and related regulatory frameworks.

In practical terms, ASIC expects lenders to make reasonable inquiries into a borrower's financial circumstances, objectives and requirements before entering into a loan contract. This includes assessing whether a loan is unsuitable for the borrower and whether the borrower has the capacity to meet their obligations without experiencing substantial hardship.

ASIC's role extends beyond merely enforcing technical compliance. It also promotes broader standards of fairness, transparency and consumer protection within the lending industry. Where ASIC identifies systemic misconduct, misleading conduct, irresponsible lending practices, or failures in compliance systems, it has the authority to investigate, commence enforcement action, issue penalties, seek court orders, and impose licensing consequences on regulated entities.

Importantly, ASIC's oversight is generally strongest within the consumer lending space governed by the *National Consumer Credit Protection Act 2009 (Cth).* Certain business-purpose or non-code lending arrangements may fall outside that framework, although lenders operating in those areas remain conscious of reputational risk, general legal obligations, and broader expectations of fair conduct.

The Australian Financial Complaints Authority (AFCA) deals with borrower complaints and external dispute resolution between consumers and financial institutions. It provides borrowers with an avenue to raise concerns regarding lending conduct, hardship matters, fees, enforcement action and other disputes arising from financial products and services.

VIABLE POSITION AFTER LOAN?

Consider the borrower's position once the loan is repaid.

The Australian Prudential Regulation Authority (APRA), by contrast, focuses primarily on the prudential supervision and financial stability of banks, authorised deposit-taking institutions and other regulated financial entities. Its role is centred on ensuring that financial institutions remain financially sound and properly managed, rather than assessing the suitability of individual lending decisions or resolving borrower disputes.

The Exception: Unconditional Sale

The position changes considerably where the property has already been sold under an unconditional contract of sale.

In that situation, the decision to sell has already been made by the borrower independently of the proposed loan. The contract has been exchanged, the purchaser is legally committed, and the outcome is substantially determined, subject only to settlement occurring. The lender is therefore not funding a speculative future sale or relying upon the borrower deciding at some later point to place the property on the market.

Instead, the lender is simply providing short-term funding to bridge the period between exchange and settlement.

This distinction is extremely important from both a risk and a responsible lending perspective. The lender is not causing or encouraging the borrower to sell their only property. That decision was made prior to the loan being advanced. The lender is merely assisting the borrower through a temporary timing issue, such as a delayed settlement, a requirement for interim funds, or the need to complete another transaction before sale proceeds are received.

Importantly, this also removes substantial uncertainty from the exit strategy. The sale is no longer hypothetical. There is already a signed contract, an agreed purchase price, and a defined settlement date. This creates a far stronger and more reliable repayment pathway than a proposal that merely relies on the borrower intending to sell at some unknown point in the future.

For that reason, many lenders are significantly more comfortable when the exit strategy is supported by an unconditional contract of sale rather than a future intention to market the property. The risk profile is materially different because the repayment event is already in motion rather than dependent upon future decisions, market conditions, or borrower intentions changing over time.

Alternative Exit: Sale of Another Asset

A stronger structure arises where the borrower owns more than one property, and the exit is the sale of a different asset.

In this scenario, the lender is not relying on the borrower disposing of their only property. The borrower retains their primary asset while using another property to clear the debt.

This aligns more comfortably with responsible lending principles. The borrower's overall position is not necessarily diminished. The loan is repaid through asset realisation, but without forcing the borrower into a position of having no property at all.

Where such an exit is credible and sufficient, borrowing capacity may become less relevant, as the loan is not income-based.

Non-Code Lending and Structural Flexibility

The regulatory position changes where the loan falls outside the National Credit Code.

This may occur where the borrower is a company or trust, or where the loan is wholly or predominantly for business purposes, generally more than 50 per cent.

In these cases, the responsible lending obligations do not apply in the same way. The borrower may have greater flexibility in structuring the loan, including the option to rely on a property asset sale as an exit.

However, this does not eliminate risk. A business purpose declaration must reflect the true nature of the transaction. If the loan is in substance personal, the protections of the Code may still apply.

Equally, structuring a loan through a company purely to avoid regulatory oversight is not a sound practice. A responsible lender should not encourage artificial arrangements designed to bypass consumer protections.

The Role of Refinance as a Secondary Exit

Where a borrower's only property is involved, a responsible structure may include an alternative exit through refinancing.

If the borrower can demonstrate that they will have the capacity to refinance into a mainstream lender at the end of the term, the reliance on sale is reduced. Even if the borrower initially intends to sell, the presence of a refinance pathway provides a safety net.

Without this secondary exit, the loan may be overly reliant on a single uncertain outcome.

Enforcement Risk and Public Perception

If a borrower fails to execute the exit, the lender may have no choice but to enforce its security. Where that security is the borrower's only property, the consequences are significant.

Enforcement can lead to possession proceedings, forced sale, legal disputes, escalation of complaints, and potential media exposure.

Even where the lender acts within its legal rights, the perception can be damaging. The narrative often becomes one of imbalance: a lender enforcing against a borrower's home.

This is why lenders must consider not only the legal position but the broader context.

Extensions and Ongoing Responsibility

Short-term lending facilities often make available the option to extend the original loan term. In many situations, this flexibility can be beneficial for both the borrower and the lender. Delays can occur for legitimate reasons. A property sale may take longer than expected; refinancing may be delayed due to valuation or documentation issues; construction projects may experience setbacks; or broader market conditions may temporarily slow transactions. In those circumstances, a short extension can provide valuable breathing room and allow an otherwise sound exit strategy to be completed successfully.

However, while extensions can serve an important purpose, they also require discipline and careful assessment. An extension should not become an automatic solution each time the original repayment plan fails to materialise. Repeated extensions often indicate that the initial exit strategy was unrealistic, overly optimistic, or dependent on assumptions that did not eventuate.

This becomes particularly important in higher-cost lending environments. Short-term private lending facilities generally carry higher interest rates than traditional bank loans because they are designed to address short-term problems rather than serve as permanent long-term debt arrangements. The longer a borrower remains in that type of facility, the greater the risk that interest, fees, and holding costs will erode the borrower's equity position.

A borrower who originally entered the loan with a clear and achievable repayment pathway can gradually find themselves in a deteriorating position if extensions continue without meaningful progress toward repayment. Equity can reduce over time, refinancing options may narrow further, and the borrower may become increasingly dependent upon the lender continuing to extend the facility. This can create a cycle that benefits nobody.

For this reason, responsible lenders do not generally view extensions as a substitute for a genuine exit strategy. An extension should support an existing repayment pathway, not replace one. Before agreeing to extend a loan, prudent lenders will usually reassess the borrower's circumstances, review the current position of the proposed exit strategy, and determine whether there remains a realistic and credible pathway to repayment within the extended period.

For example, if a borrower intends to refinance to a traditional lender, there should usually be evidence that the refinance process is possible. If the strategy is the sale of property and the requested loan term is a matter of a few months, there should be genuine evidence of marketing activity, purchaser interest, or a realistic timeline toward settlement. Simply hoping that circumstances will improve over time is rarely sufficient.

This ongoing assessment is an important part of responsible lending conduct. A lender should not continue to extend a facility indefinitely where there is no clear improvement in the borrower's position or a realistic prospect of repayment. Doing so may simply postpone a larger problem while increasing costs and stress for the borrower.

In many respects, the discipline surrounding extensions is just as important as the original approval decision itself. A well-structured short-term loan should always begin with a realistic, clearly identifiable exit strategy, and every extension should move the borrower toward that outcome rather than further away from it.

Practical Lending Approach

A prudent lender will approach sole-property scenarios with caution and structure.

Key considerations include whether the property is the borrower's only asset, whether it is owner-occupied, whether the exit is already committed or merely proposed, whether alternative exits exist, and whether the borrower retains a viable position after the loan.

If the only exit is a future discretionary sale of the borrower's sole property, the lender should question whether the loan is appropriate at all.

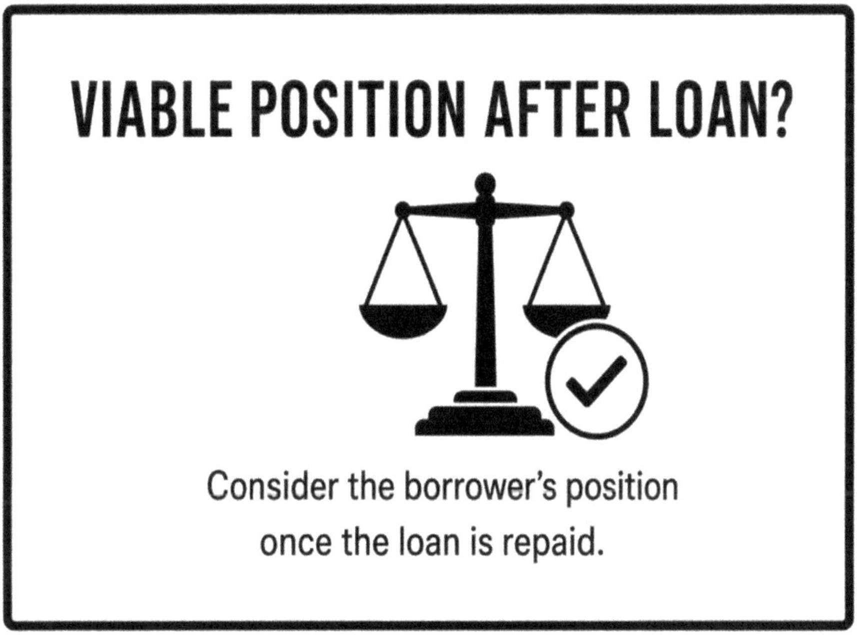

Conclusion: Exit Strategy Must Protect, Not Diminish

No-borrowing-capacity lending can provide effective solutions where traditional lending cannot. However, it requires a higher level of care, particularly where the borrower's only property is involved.

The central issue is not whether the lender will be repaid. The question is whether the loan structure places the borrower in a materially worse position.

A sale-based exit is valid in many circumstances. It becomes problematic when it results in the borrower losing their only property without a clear and deliberate plan.

A responsible lender does not simply accept an exit strategy. They assess its consequences. Where the exit preserves the borrower's position or reflects a decision already made, it may be appropriate. Where it leads to regression, it should be reconsidered.

In this context, the exit strategy is not merely a repayment mechanism. It is the test of whether the loan should exist at all.

7.

Requirements for A Mortgage Application

Credit Reporting Association of Australia (CRAA)

This has been discussed earlier, but a brief recap may be useful, because the borrower's credit score contributes to lending decisions.

One reason a deal may have to go to a different lender is a poor repayment history — that is, the client not living up to their responsibilities to repay the loan on time. Defaults on the CRAA are another problem. Many applicants/consumers do not consider a paid default from three years earlier much of a problem and often do not inform their broker of their default history.

Defaults and judgments can remain on the CRAA for typically five years and will not be removed unless paid. Some people offer to pay this to get the new loan they are after; in many instances, they are obliged to pay it anyway, so they are not doing themselves any favours by offering to pay it now. It should have been paid anyway. Please note on the CRAA whether the applicant was also aware of it. Maybe they applied for credit a few months earlier, in which case the lender would have informed them of the situation at the time — especially if their request for that loan was denied.

A person's CRAA report records all activity when applying for a loan, or debt, or even enquiring about debt (maybe via a credit card, store card at a shopping centre, personal loan, car loan, business loan, and mortgage) with a lender. Sometimes it is clear that people have been shopping around to different lenders, and if there are too many enquiries on the CRAA, lenders will not be happy.

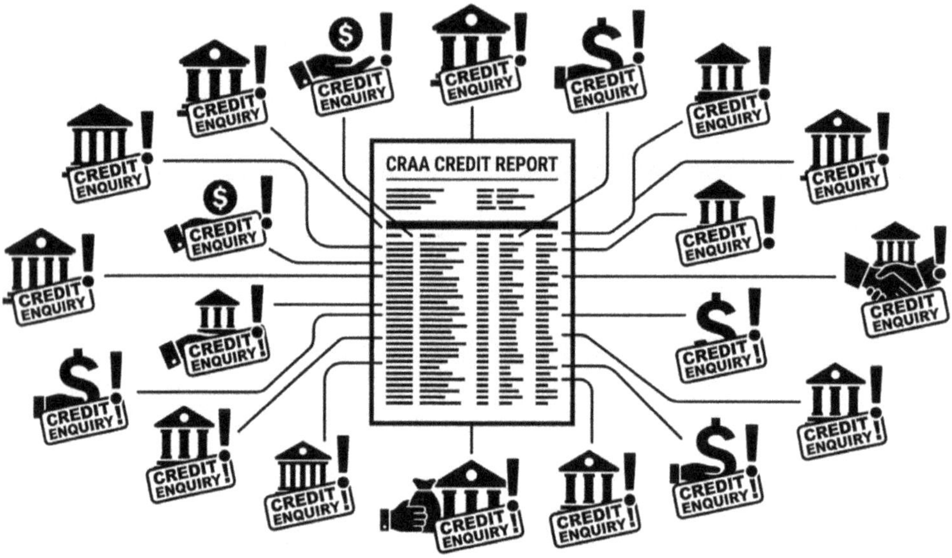

Most lenders have a credit scoring system, and both mortgage loan insurers do as well. This gives a person a score on the CRAA: the lower the score, the more unfavourable the CRAA is for lending purposes. This is another reason why it is important to choose the best broker — they will know who does 'credit score'. Sometimes it may be necessary to avoid lenders that 'credit score', and sometimes it's only possible to borrow 80% loan-to-value ratio as the deal may fail on the credit scoring software of LMI providers.

The Five Cs of Lending

Commitment

Collateral (Property — what the valuation says, zoning, density, postcode)

Character

Conditions (Policy)

Capacity (Servicing)

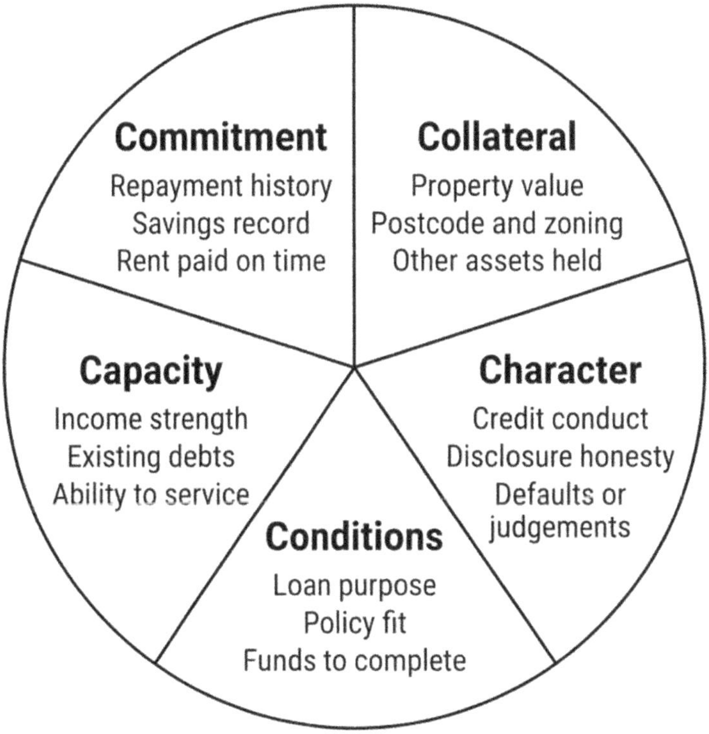

Commitment

Lenders want to see a track record of repaying debts before they're willing to trust someone to be responsible enough to take out a loan. A borrower may fail credit scoring because they have no debt and no history of making repayments on debt. It's therefore indeterminable whether that person has the inclination to repay the debt.

Applications where someone has 5% of their savings in a savings account are considered stronger by lenders, as they indicate the applicant has proven they can save money. More often, with the affordability crisis, first homebuyers may not have saved their 5%. They don't need the 5% as genuine savings, though, if using a lender that doesn't credit score. A gift, family pledge or borrowed funds can assist.

By the time the borrower receives the first homebuyers grant and the lender's mortgage insurance is capitalised, they may have avoided putting in any hurt money (their own money, leading them to be more motivated to make loan repayments, as their own money is at risk). Lenders don't like this, so a first homebuyer needs to consider all their options if they want to get onto the property ladder. Paying rent is a good indicator of commitment as well.

People with no genuine savings, or if they're not paying rent somewhere that can be sufficiently evidenced, usually end up with a specialist lender (or a 'non-conforming lender') who charges more, but can offer the person the loan they need.

Collateral

What the valuation says on the property is important, as is zoning,

density and postcode. Having other assets also provides support when applying for a mortgage. Whether it's your car, furniture, and other belongings that you have given a value to, or other property, shares, superannuation and cash — they all count toward painting a picture.

The older you get, the more assets the lenders would like to see. They don't like it when they see a 60-year-old person renting with friends and having no assets. They tend to consider the applicant as a significant lending risk. There are some circumstances that have led to someone near retirement age having limited or no assets. Most of the time, it's because of divorce, but lenders are simply not required to demonstrate empathy to someone who is not yet a client. If divorce is not the reason, then there would be even more concern. Perhaps a failed business, squandering money, who knows?

Lenders don't see things as 'a glass half-full'. They often put the burden of proof on the shoulders of the applicant to counter the immediate seeds of doubt that have grown in the minds of the credit assessors.

The type of security, besides servicing the debt, is the most important part of any transaction. Lenders categorise the suitability of security by postcode, the quality of the actual dwelling, and the associated risks.

See the Figure entitled 'Risk Analysis'.

If the proposed property is in a small town with 100 people, or even 1000 people, there would be few sales, little activity, and no appetite for a lender to lend; if they do, it would normally be no more than 70%.

There are exceptions, of course. A couple of lenders may not care at all. Some properties being offered are unliveable, so don't waste your time. If they don't have a certificate of occupancy, then almost all lenders will not lend against it; the same applies to a property in mid-construction.

Character

Character is of particular interest to a lender. Some things may be outside someone's control, of course. Other things are considered to be within someone's control, and it is these that lenders scrutinise to form an opinion on the applicant's character.

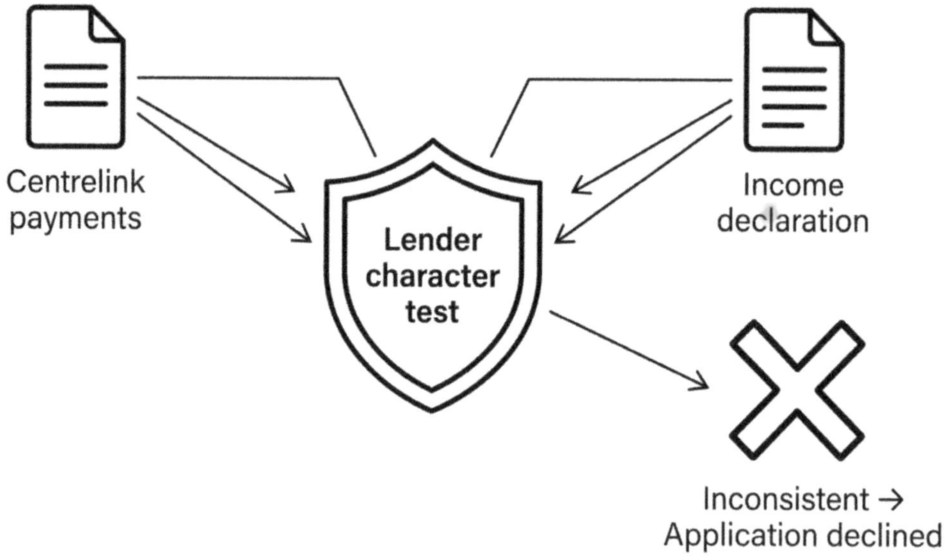

Is the borrower someone who has not paid their bills, credit cards, or loan repayments on time, and perhaps has defaults, tax debt, bankruptcy, judgments, and so on? This is often the type of individual lenders are concerned about. These borrowers end up on higher rates with specialist lenders. Some people are dishonest and don't disclose all of their liabilities (i.e. credit cards) on the application form, and lenders are unforgiving when this happens — and rightly so.

Sometimes, defaults do end up on someone's credit file without their knowledge, due to oversights or simple forgetfulness. Thousands of other excuses simply 'don't cut the mustard'.

A common excuse is that the individual 'went away and left a friend to take responsibility for paying the debt'. A default won't be recorded in as little as a week or three, though — it may take up to 60 days or longer.

Some people are debt junkies. They apply for short-term loans, or they apply for various credit cards and personal loans, or simply tyre-kick their way around the mortgage industry looking for the best rate. A tyre-kicker, as they are known in many circles within the financial services industry, is someone who wastes someone's time. They meet the broker, banker, or advisor, pretend to be interested in what the service provider has to say, but then do nothing about it. Others shop around, gathering and effectively stealing others' information (intellectual property), then try to do it themselves.

Lenders look upon these people unfavourably, and if they have too many enquiries on their CRAA (credit report), they are more likely to fail credit scoring. If the lender does not use a credit score, the credit assessors will probably still decline the application. No one likes these time wasters (or 'time vampires' — who suck valuable time from those they profess to want advice from).

Most of the time, credit hits on an individual's credit file occur because the individual is unaware that each time they apply for a mobile phone contract, change energy providers, or purchase a lounge suite or television on credit from a store, they incur a credit hit.

These types of 'hits' are generally acceptable, but when a lender sees three attempts to apply for a mortgage, at three different lenders, over a short period of time, they will usually fail that applicant — and the applicant ends up with a specialist lender, or sometimes without a loan at all.

Always tell the lender the truth. If you don't and get found out, that lender can notify the finance community of the attempt to defraud and that fraudster will be blacklisted. A fraud focus group meets regularly to combat financial services fraud.

Conditions

Policy governs how a deal is assessed. This is the more tangible method of assessing a loan and its creditworthiness. This is less about the borrower and more about the loan purpose, type, amount, valuation, security acceptability, exit strategy (if required), funds to complete, genuine savings, and the purpose of the loan or cash-out.

Many of these are determined prior to the borrower receiving conditional approval, and some are set as conditions on the approval that must be met before the loan is formally approved. Solicitors are instructed to prepare loan documents for the borrower to sign.

Each lender has a different policy manual, so it is important to use a broker rather than spend time calling around. Most scenarios will either pass or fail these pre-determined criteria. Some of the criteria allow exceptions, so the stronger the applicant, the more likely an exception to the normal policy is to be considered.

Capacity

Note that this is only applicable for non-private lenders, unless the exit strategy is a refinance.

What a person earns in the role they hold and how long they have been in that role both affect whether the loan is approved. A person must be able to service the debt they require, in conjunction with any other debts they already have.

This is another reason why a broker is better than a bank. A good broker is one who knows which calculators work better and which lenders are more forgiving. For a pay-as-you-earn (PAYE) borrower (an employee), their base wage is the primary factor in servicing the loan.

Should they also receive commissions and bonuses, these generally need to be evidenced over 2 years and averaged. Some lenders require only 6 months of evidence of commissions, while others need a letter from the employer stating it is ongoing and consistent. Other lenders require 12 months of evidence in addition to this letter.

All in the following list can be treated differently by different lenders. Some lenders will not factor certain sources of income into the borrower's ability to afford the loan. Other lenders will use only a portion of the total income attributable to these sources/benefits.

- Overtime
- Shift work
- Casual income
- Second job
- Rental
- Negative gearing, if any
- Salary sacrifice
- Maternity leave
- Pensions like the carers' pension and disability pension
- Centrelink support, like Family Tax Benefit Part A and B, and Parenting

The following are additional benefits/incomes and circumstances that no one's lender treats the same:

- Child maintenance payments
- Rental income
- Fringe benefits, like a car allowance
- Franked dividends
- Deductible interest
- Self-employed add-backs, including depreciation
- Salary packaging
- Overtime
- Shift work
- Probation
- One day of employment may be taken into account, provided there is evidence of 12 months in the same role, combined with industry experience. TAC, work cover and income protection insurance are not commonly used, but again, there are lenders who are exceptions to the rule.

Likewise, most lenders dislike lending to developers and sometimes builders, if builders, it's mainly builders who make a capital gain by selling properties. Lenders do not consider capital gains to be reliable, ongoing, and consistent income suitable for loan servicing. Builders who earn a fee-for-service are more commonly accepted.

The trend in these two professions is that many apply for low-documentation loans. Lenders often consider the reasons for this to be due to a borrower potentially being too lazy to complete tax returns, or being very good at minimising tax, and their tax returns don't support their income, or they're trying to disguise capital gains as income, and hope to get away with only using an accountant's letter to verify income.

It may also be that some other self-employed people make use of the availability of a low-documentation facility to lie to the lender about the true nature or amount of their income.

It could, of course, be that they simply have not had time to file their tax returns. I personally prefer to err on the side of optimism and would like to believe this to be the most common reason.

Even if they persist, developers should apply for commercial, not residential, interest rates, given the nature of their income and business model (this is the opinion of most lender representatives I have spoken to over the years). The exception is private lending, which will likely not require borrowing capacity.

When working for a family or a partner, wage slips are at risk of being doctored or fabricated. Likewise, the spouse of a business owner often doesn't receive regular, consistent payments into an account, even though they can provide pay slips suggesting otherwise. Many lenders ask for three months of bank statements to verify the receipt of that income. Blood can be thicker than water, they say, so can marriage, occasionally.

With regard to salary sacrifice, some lenders don't include the income as untaxed. This is because the income the person is not receiving directly cannot be used to service under the normal servicing calculation methods. It is not ignored, though and can be factored in.

Touched on earlier, given that most lenders sensitise the rate for a loan application, whatever the repayment rate, the lender adds perhaps 2% to the rate. This loading on the rate (buffer added, allowing for debt servicing if rates were to rise) is often applied to all debt, so it's not just what is being applied for, but also to existing debts.

It may be worthwhile to use a lender who services existing debt (not being refinanced) at the existing rate/repayments. This means that if they're 'interest-only loans', the lender factors in interest-only repayments; likewise for principal-and-interest loans. This type of calculator is quite advantageous to investors. Make sure the lender includes deductible debt, if applicable, on the calculator.

If a borrower owns a property with a friend, whether they have agreed to share the repayments or have agreed to have two separate splits (loans against the one property) so that they can each pay their respective payments, most lenders still deem them to be jointly and severally liable for their debt and their friend's debt. Lenders don't care about any private arrangement in place. Likewise, if one of them receives only half the rent due to being 50% on title, the lender will normally use only half of the total rental income to service another debt. This occurs even though they will allocate the entire liability to each. Some lenders do, however, look at things in a way that some may find fairer: they attribute half the debt and half the rent, or all the debt and all the rent.

Doctors tend to be provided something not many others are — up to a 90% LVR loan, with no LMI or an equivalent risk fee, saving what could be tens of thousands of dollars. We consider their capacity to repay the loan, given the security of their profession, to be better than anyone else's. Some lenders offer the same thing to lawyers and accountants.

Entering a Project Mid-Stream — The Defining Advantage (Expanded with Documentation Reality)

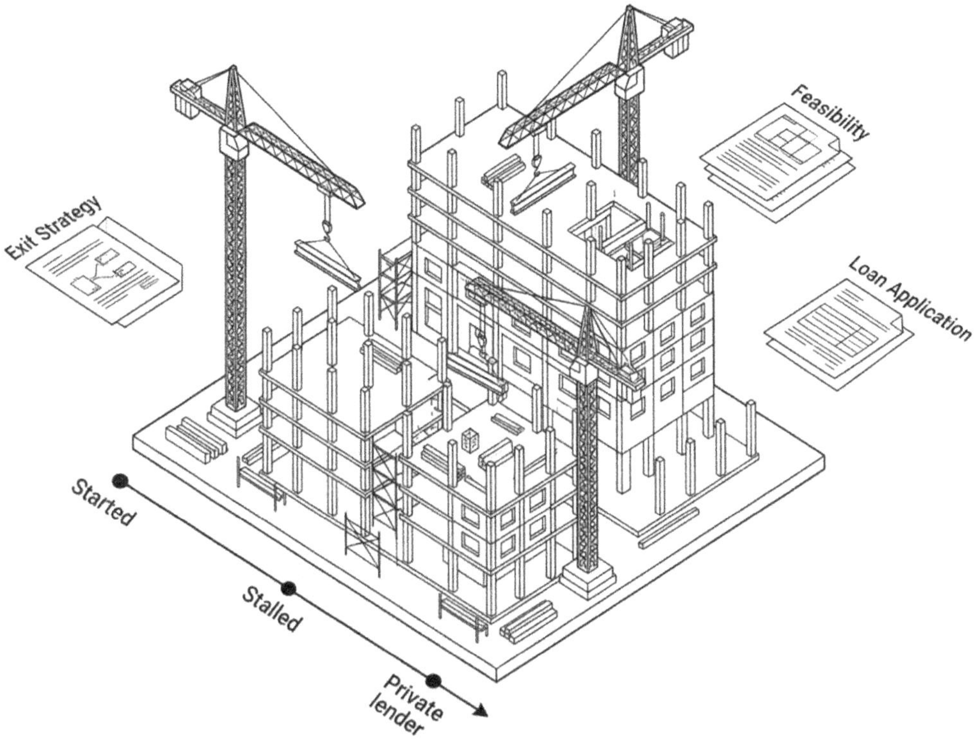

One of the most powerful aspects of private lending is its ability to step into a project after it has already begun. That statement alone is often repeated, but it is rarely understood in its full depth.

Because stepping into a project mid-stream is not simply about saying "yes" when others say "no." It is about having a framework that allows a lender to assess reality quickly, verify it properly, and fund it responsibly.

That is where documentation becomes critical.

Why Documentation Matters

Private lenders often require less documentation.

Traditional lenders collect documents to prove income and long-term serviceability.

Private lenders collect documents to answer a different question:

"Can this project be completed, and will the loan be repaid?"

The Foundation: Core Loan Documentation

Every transaction begins with the essentials. These are not optional—they are the baseline that allows the lender to even engage with the deal.

- Fully completed loan application (signed)
  This is not just a formality. It is the borrower's declaration of intent. It outlines the structure, purpose, security, and proposed exit. In private lending, clarity at the outset matters more than perfection.
- 100 points of identification
  This confirms the borrower's identity but, more importantly, ensures that the lender knows exactly who they are dealing with. In fast-moving transactions, certainty of identity is critical.
- Rates and water notices
  These confirm ownership, property details, and council alignment. They also provide insight into whether the property is current on obligations or already under stress.

These core documents form the starting point. Without them, nothing moves.

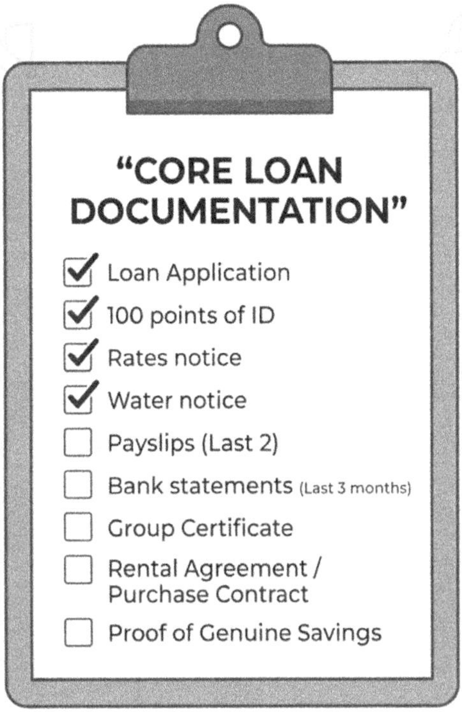

The Most Important Document in Private Lending: The Exit Strategy

Unlike traditional lending, where servicing is the primary concern, private lending revolves around one central document:

- **Exit strategy letter**

This is not a simple statement. It is the backbone of the entire loan.

It explains:

- How the loan will be repaid
- When will it be repaid

If the exit is a sale:

- Just the borrower's word is acceptable; the property need not be on the market.

If the exit is a refinance:

- Please provide payslips, or, if you are self-employed, BAS/bank statements or an accountant's declaration.

The exit strategy is where many deals succeed or fail. It is not about optimism. It is about responsible lending if in a personal name. If it's a company or trust, then it just has to make sense.

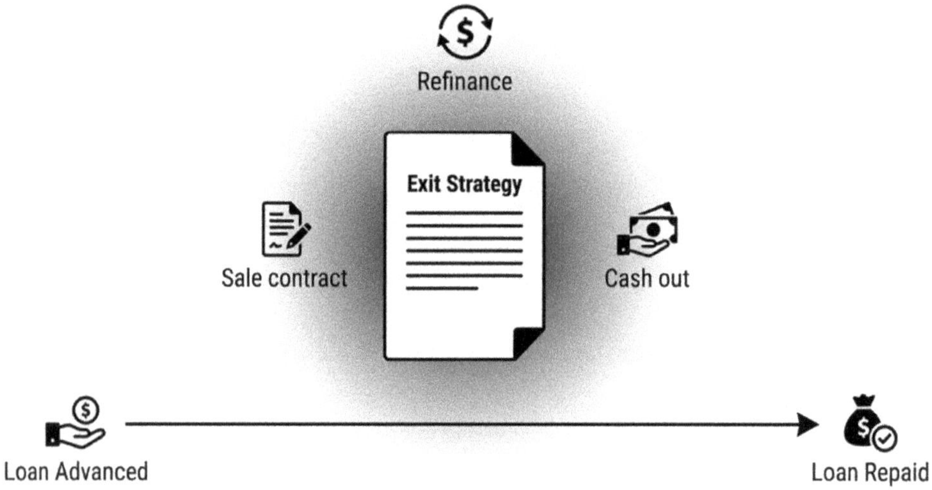

Complex Scenarios — Where Explanation Matters More Than Perfection

Private lending does not ignore issues, nor does it typically decline a loan application; however, it does require them to be explained.

- Credit defaults or arrears — written explanation.

This is required because the private lender requires transparency.

A borrower with a default who explains:

- What happened
- Why it happened
- With arrears, why will it not happen again

Ownership and other:

- **Trust deeds and structures**
  These define ownership and control. In development projects, complex structures are common, and clarity here avoids delays later.
- **Leases (if applicable)**
  These demonstrate income or future value, particularly in commercial or mixed-use assets.

Private lending is about embracing complexity. It is about understanding it, and not being afraid of it, unlike banks, which can often be.

Purchases and Equity — Proving the Position

Where a transaction involves acquisition or additional funding:

- **Purchase contract**
  This confirms price, terms, and timing.
- **Evidence of deposit and funds to complete**
  This shows commitment. It answers a critical question: *Has the borrower already invested in this project?*
- **Renovation schedules and cost breakdowns**
  These are essential in construction scenarios. They demonstrate planning, not guesswork.

Without this, a lender cannot determine whether the requested funds are sufficient.

Refinances — Understanding What Exists Today

For projects already underway:

- **Mortgage statements**
  These confirm the existing debt, the lender's position, and the repayment history.
- **Statements of liabilities being repaid**
  This shows where funds are going.

This is critical in mid-stream lending. The new lender must understand the current structure before replacing or supplementing it.

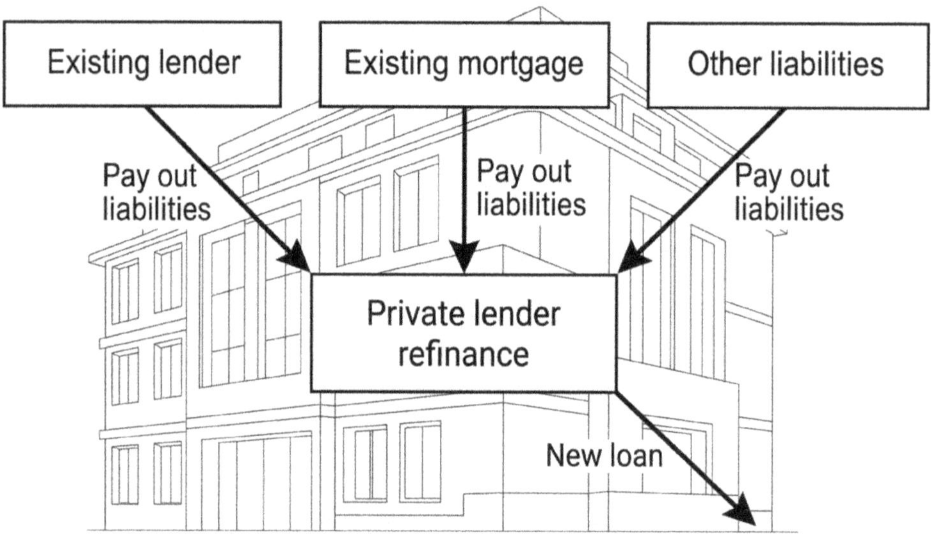

Construction Lending — Where Documentation Becomes Critical

This is where the checklist becomes most important.

Because in construction, documentation is not just verification. It is **control**.

Planning and Approvals

- **Planning permits and development approvals**

These confirm that the project is legally permitted. Without them, the project cannot proceed, regardless of funding.

Building Contracts and Plans

- **Approved plans and building contracts**

Even in cost-plus or owner-builder scenarios, plans are essential. They define what is being built and allow valuation of the completed project.

Builder's Insurance

- **Insurance documentation**

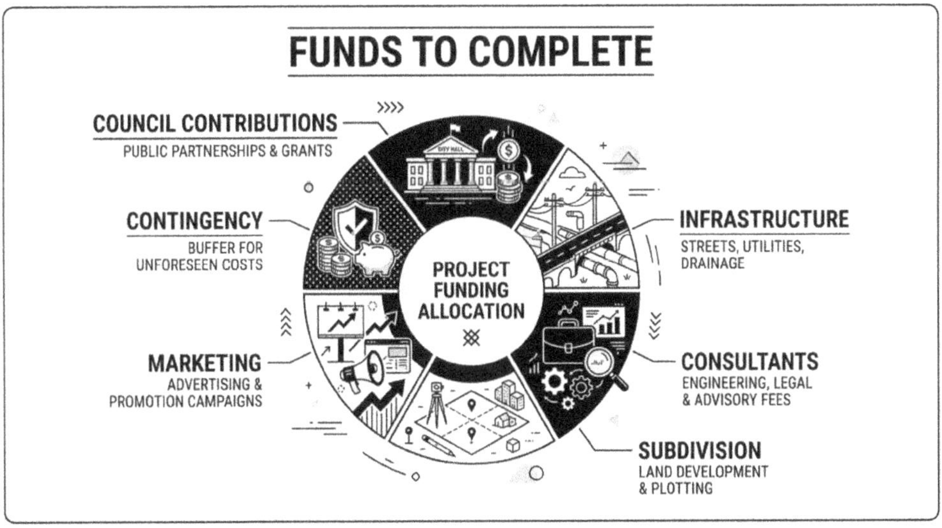

This protects both borrower and lender. Construction carries risk, and insurance ensures that unforeseen events do not destroy the project's viability.

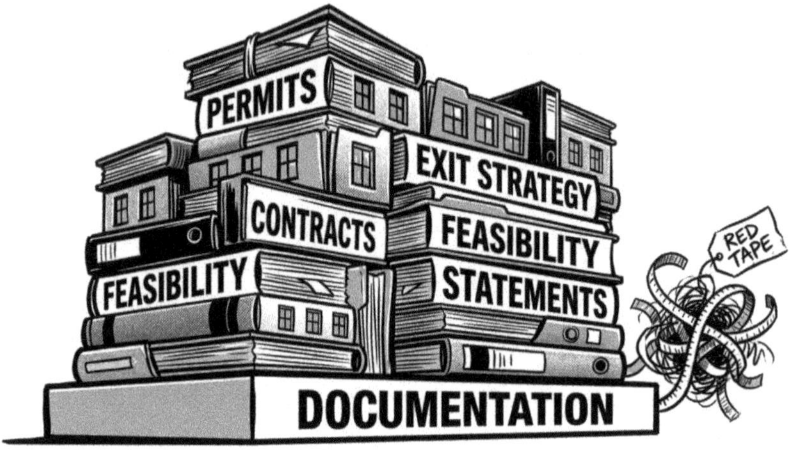

Developer Capability — Can This Be Delivered?

For larger projects:

- **Builder or developer capability statements** may strengthen the deal
- **Feasibility study**

These documents answer a key question:

"Can this borrower actually complete this project?"

Numbers alone are usually enough. Experience, track record, and planning can benefit the deal.

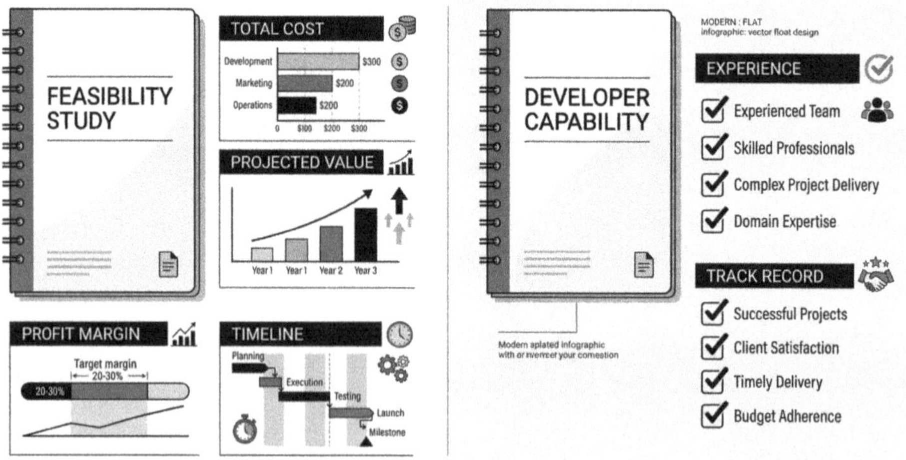

Feasibility — The Reality Check

A feasibility study is one of the most important documents in development lending.

It outlines:

- total cost
- projected value
- profit margin
- timeline

This is where optimism meets reality.

Private lenders rely on feasibility, particularly where:

- No fixed-price contract exists
- Cost-plus structures are used
- Multi-stage developments are involved

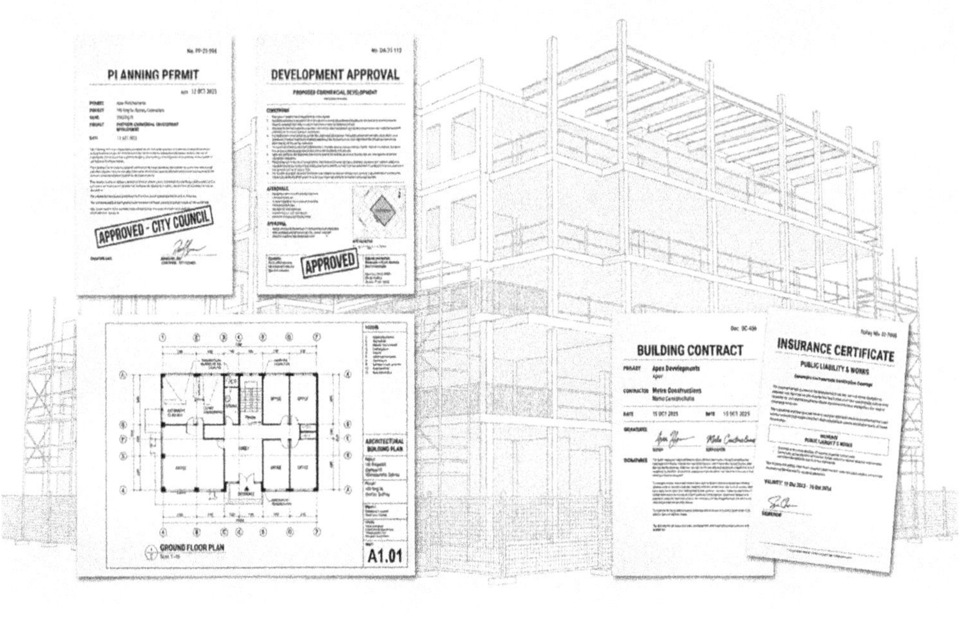

Presales — Optional

Private lenders do not require pre-sales.

- Presale schedules and contracts (if any)

These can provide additional comfort. They are not required, but they may strengthen the position.

This is an important distinction.

Banks require them.

Private lenders value them—but do not depend on them, it does not weaken the scenario.

Funds to Complete — The Most Overlooked Risk

One of the most critical documents in any construction deal is:

- Evidence of funds to complete non-contracted works

This includes:

- council contributions
- infrastructure costs
- consultant fees
- subdivision costs
- marketing

These are the costs often forgotten at the beginning—and the reason projects fail later.

Private lenders focus on this, as any lender would because they have seen what happens when it is ignored.

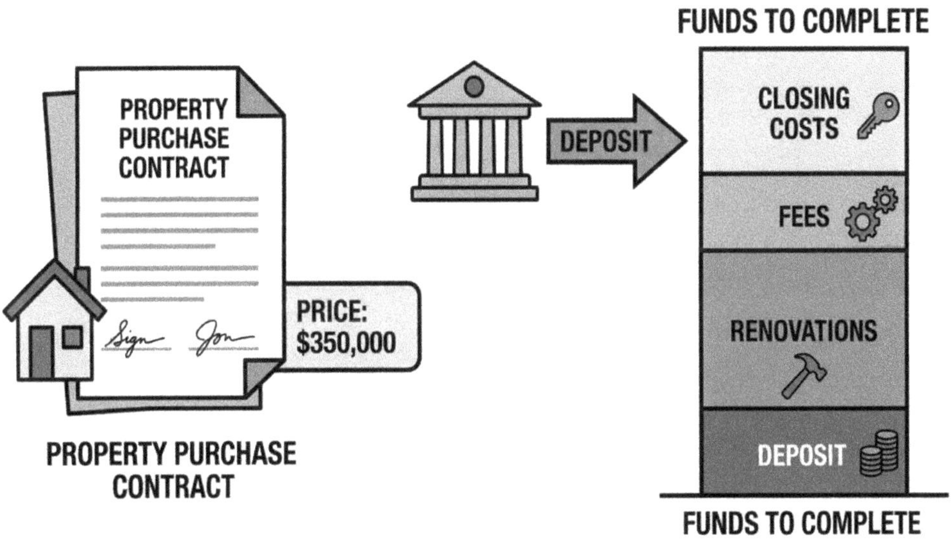

Why All of This Matters in a Mid-Stream Scenario

When a lender steps into a project midstream, they are not just funding what remains.

They are inheriting:

- Every decision made so far
- Every cost already incurred
- Every risk that remains

Documentation is what allows them to understand that position clearly.

Without it, the deal is uncertain.

With it, the deal becomes structured.

The Difference in Approach

Traditional lenders use documentation to confirm that a deal fits policy. Their policy is so often rigid and unforgiving.

Private lenders use documentation to understand whether a deal works.

That is the difference.

Final Thought — Documentation Is Not Red Tape, It Is the Structure

In a construction environment, documentation is always seen as important.

It is what allows:

- speed
- flexibility
- confidence

Private lending is fast, but it is not careless.

It works because it combines:

- real-time assessment
- practical understanding
- and the right documentation to support both

That is how a lender can step into a project halfway through, assess it properly, and move it forward with confidence. The irony is that banks make billions of dollars, yet they are afraid of simple out-of-the-box deals.

And that is what turns a stalled project into a completed one.

8.

Making Informed Property and Contract Decisions Within Lending

"Nothing would be done at all if a person waited until they could do it so well that no-one could find fault with it."

Cardinal Newman

When approaching any form of borrowing—whether for the acquisition of a residential or commercial dwelling, a construction project, vacant land, or a more specialised arrangement—it is necessary to understand that lending does not operate in isolation. It is not merely a financial transaction assessed by reference to income and expenses. Rather, lending is closely tied to the nature of the property, the structure of the contract, and the timing of the transaction. Each of these elements interacts in ways that shape how a lender evaluates a proposal.

The purpose of this discussion is not to suggest that one type of property or contractual arrangement is preferable to another. Instead, the intention is to clarify that each structure has its own characteristics, which influence how a lender approaches the assessment. A clear understanding of these relationships allows a borrower to proceed with greater certainty and to anticipate the considerations that may arise throughout the process.

Understanding Contract Types in a Lending Context

One of the first matters to appreciate is that not all property transactions are structured in the same way. The form of the contract has a direct bearing on how a lender assesses risk, timing, and certainty. While borrowers often focus on price and location, lenders tend to focus on structure and enforceability.

Contracts can broadly be categorised into immediate settlements, delayed settlements, and staged or conditional arrangements. Each presents a different lending profile, not because one is inherently superior, but because each introduces different variables.

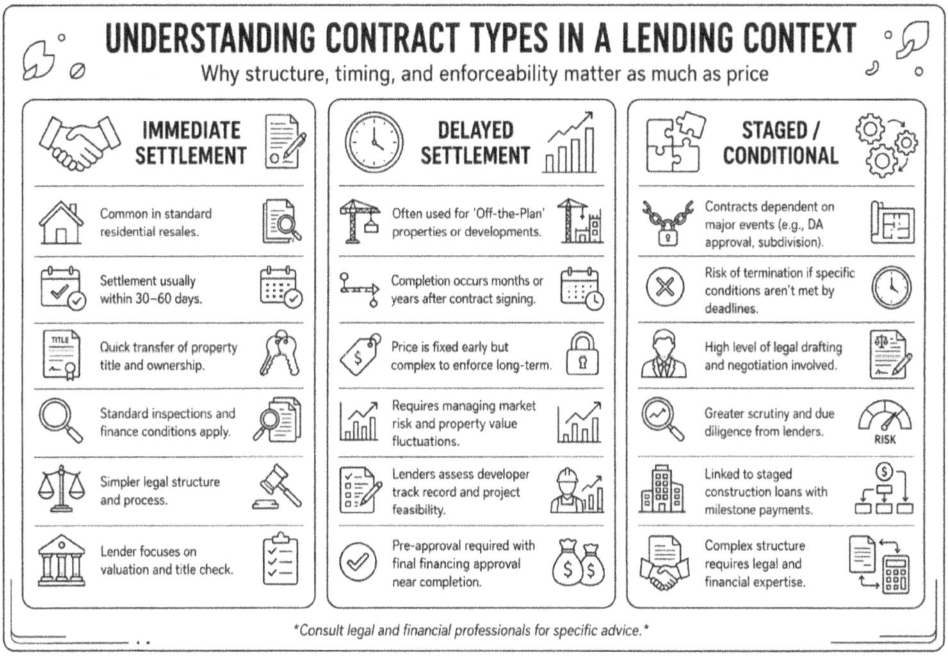

Off-the-Plan Arrangements

An off-the-plan purchase involves entering into a contract to acquire a property that has not yet been constructed. This commonly arises in apartment developments, townhouse projects, and certain house-and-land configurations. The defining feature of such arrangements is the delay between contract execution and settlement.

It is not uncommon for this period to extend from twelve months to several years. During this time, the borrower's personal circumstances may change. Income levels may fluctuate, employment arrangements may alter, and broader economic conditions may shift. In addition, lending policies themselves are not static. What is acceptable to a lender at the time of signing may not necessarily align with policy settings at the time of settlement.

This temporal gap introduces a degree of uncertainty. Importantly, any loan approval obtained at the outset is typically indicative only and subject to reassessment. Lenders assess the borrower's position at the time funds are required, not at the time the contract is signed. This distinction is often misunderstood.

That said, the delay is not without practical benefit. It provides an opportunity to accumulate savings, reduce other liabilities, and strengthen one's financial position. It may also allow for strategic planning in anticipation of settlement. However, these advantages must be balanced against the reality that the final valuation of the property may differ from the agreed purchase price. If market conditions soften, a property marketing company sold it, making 10's of thousands in referral fees (very common, almost guaranteed) the valuation may fall short, requiring the borrower to contribute additional funds.

Accordingly, off-the-plan arrangements should be approached with an understanding that flexibility is essential. The structure is neither advantageous nor disadvantageous in itself; rather, it requires a measured and informed approach.

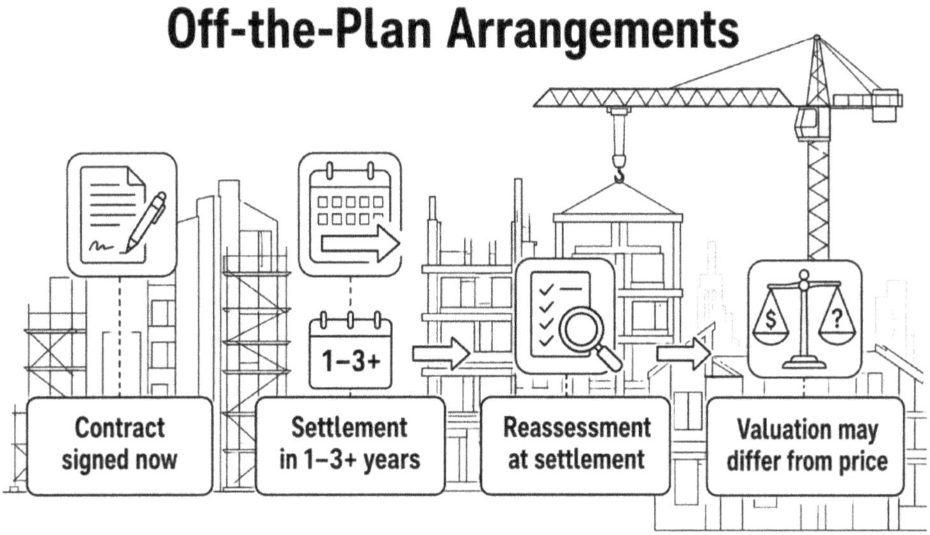

Market Dynamics and Supply Considerations

In developments where multiple similar properties are constructed concurrently, supply dynamics become relevant. Apartment complexes and townhouse estates often release a substantial number of comparable dwellings into the market at or around the same time.

This does not render such properties unsuitable. However, it does mean that market behaviour may differ from that of more unique or established properties. Increased supply can influence resale timing, rental demand, and valuation outcomes. From a lender's perspective, properties that are readily substitutable may be viewed differently from those with more distinct characteristics.

The key point is not that one type is preferable, but that certain property categories are more sensitive to supply-and-demand cycles. Recognising this helps align expectations with likely outcomes over time.

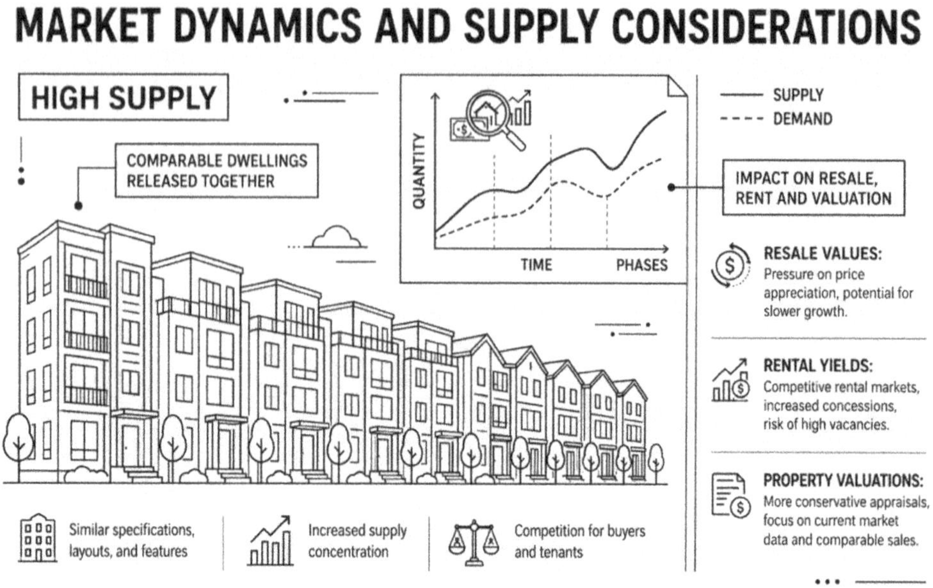

Construction and Progress-Based Contracts

Construction lending introduces an additional layer of structure. Rather than a single advance of funds at settlement, the loan is drawn progressively as the building works are completed. Payments are typically made at defined stages, such as the laying of the slab, completion of the frame, lock-up, fit-out, and final completion.

This staged approach reflects the practical realities of construction. It allows lenders to verify progress before releasing funds and ensures that the amount advanced corresponds with the value created at each stage. From a risk perspective, this provides a level of control and oversight.

However, it also introduces a holding period during which the borrower may incur costs without deriving immediate benefit. Interest may accrue on funds drawn, and there may be no rental income or utility from the property until completion. This period requires financial preparedness.

This is not a deficiency in the structure. Rather, it is an inherent feature of construction-based arrangements. Awareness of the timing and cash flow implications is sufficient to manage the process effectively.

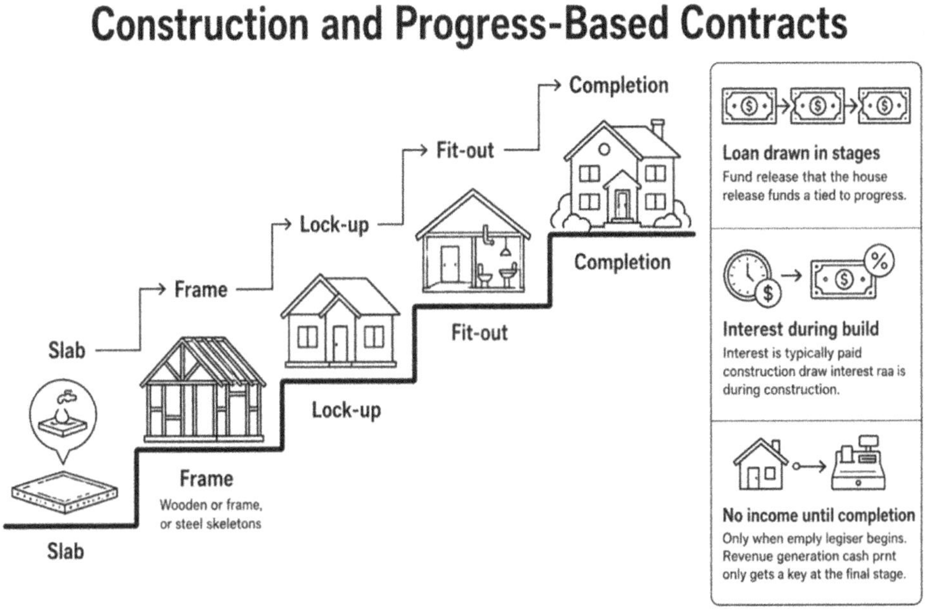

Split Contracts and Lending Complexity

In some developments, the acquisition of land and the construction of improvements are governed by separate contracts. This is commonly referred to as a split contract arrangement. While these structures can be appropriate in certain circumstances, they frequently introduce additional lending complexity and heightened risk considerations for lenders, valuers and mortgage insurers.

At a basic level, a lender prefers simplicity and certainty. The more straightforward and self-contained a property and construction arrangement is, the easier it generally is to assess, value and finance. Once a project involves interconnected dwellings, shared infrastructure, common walls, shared slabs, shared roofing systems, or mutual completion dependencies, the risk profile changes significantly.

This issue becomes particularly problematic in townhouse and medium-density developments where individual dwellings are legally separate but physically dependent upon one another. In these situations, one owner's property may depend on another owner's construction progressing correctly before the project can be completed as a whole.

For example, if Dwelling A shares a structural wall, slab, roofing system or services with Dwelling B, an obvious question arises: who ultimately controls responsibility for those interconnected components? If one owner delays construction, experiences funding difficulties, defaults, changes builders, or abandons the project entirely, neighbouring owners may be directly impacted.

This creates what lenders commonly view as counterparty risk. The completion of one property depends on the actions, financial position, and cooperation of another unrelated party.

From a lender's perspective, this creates substantial uncertainty. If a lender needs to enforce its security position, it may not be dealing with a clean, standalone asset capable of straightforward resale. Instead, it may be dealing with a partially completed structure tied to adjoining properties, shared infrastructure, body corporate obligations, planning restrictions or incomplete development works.

This is one reason why many lenders become uncomfortable with split-contract townhouse developments involving shared walls, shared slabs or interconnected construction dependencies. Industry commentary and lending guidance have increasingly recognised these concerns over time. Some lenders have specifically reduced or withdrawn their appetite for split-contract developments involving shared walls, roofs, footings, and common infrastructure because of concerns about valuation, saleability, and completion risk.

Importantly, the issue is not necessarily the mere existence of two contracts. Split contracts involving genuinely standalone dwellings on separate land parcels may still be acceptable to many lenders. The larger concern generally arises when the development cannot properly function or be completed independently of adjoining dwellings or owners.

In practical terms, lenders prefer projects where each dwelling can stand on its own. Where there are clear physical separations, independent slabs, separate structural walls, and minimal shared infrastructure, the property is easier to value, sell, and finance. The lender's security position becomes far cleaner.

By contrast, heavily interconnected projects introduce layers of complexity that many borrowers do not fully appreciate when signing contracts with developers or builders.

Unfortunately, some purchasers are drawn to these developments because they appear cheaper or are aggressively marketed as sophisticated investment opportunities. However, many buyers do not realise that securing finance approval can become difficult, or in most cases, impossible with every lender once the development's structure has been properly reviewed.

This is where purchasers must exercise caution. If a builder or developer is presenting a structure that large portions of the lending market are reluctant to finance, that fact alone should cause a prospective purchaser to ask serious questions. A buyer should always understand not only whether they can obtain finance today, but also whether future purchasers may encounter the same difficulties when it comes time to sell the property later.

That does not necessarily mean every split-contract development is problematic or improper. Also, if the private lender is lending to the builder rather than individual purchasers, the lender can control the build. Some developments are professionally structured, legally sound and entirely financeable. However, where developments involve interdependence among owners, shared structural elements, restricted building rights, or reliance on multiple parties completing construction simultaneously, the risk profile becomes unpalatable.

Industry discussions surrounding split-contract developments have repeatedly highlighted concerns about saleability, valuation difficulties, shared infrastructure obligations and incomplete construction risk. In particular, lenders and valuers have noted that where dwellings are interconnected, the standalone value and marketability of each lot can become difficult to assess independently.

This is why experienced brokers, lawyers and finance professionals often encourage borrowers to look beyond marketing brochures and headline pricing. The legal structure, construction arrangement and future financeability of the property can be just as important as the property itself.

Ultimately, the clearer, cleaner and more self-contained the project structure is, the more straightforward the lending assessment tends to become.

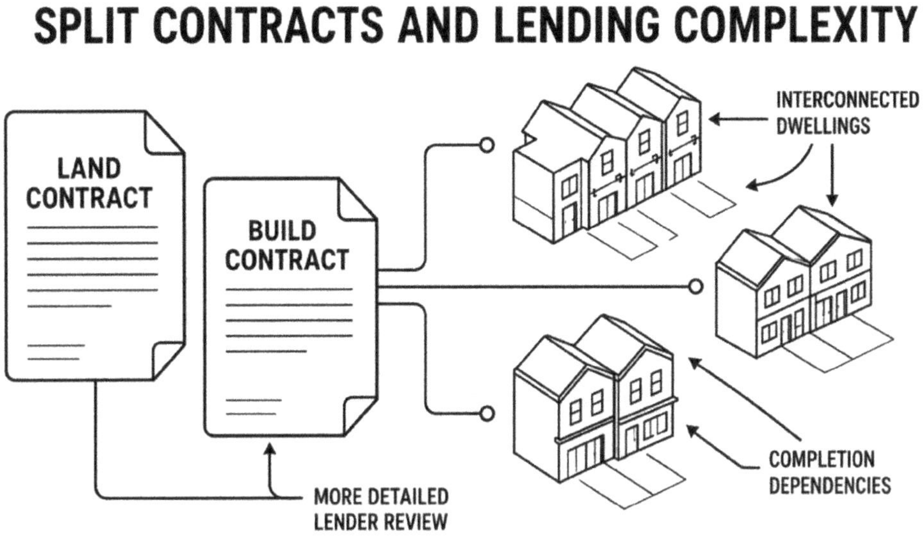

House and Land – A Structured Approach

House and land packages offer a more defined framework. They involve the purchase of land, accompanied by a construction agreement for a dwelling to be built on it. From a lending perspective, this provides a cohesive structure because both components are included in a single funding arrangement.

Once approved, the loan typically encompasses both the land acquisition and the construction costs. Funds are released in stages, consistent with the progress of the build. This allows for a degree of certainty in planning, as the process is established from the outset.

Nevertheless, the same considerations apply as with any construction arrangement. There may be a period during which the property does not generate income, and costs will be incurred progressively. Delays in construction can also affect timing.

Again, these are not shortcomings but features of the structure that must be understood and accounted for.

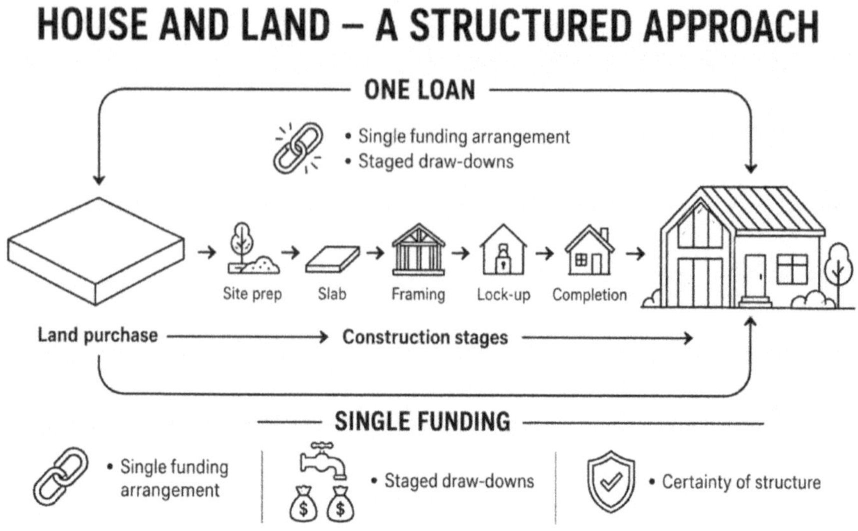

Additional Considerations Across All Property Types

Rather than focusing solely on specific categories of property, it is more instructive to consider the broader principles that apply universally.

Timing is a fundamental consideration. The longer the duration between contract and completion, the greater the potential for change. This applies equally to personal circumstances and external conditions.

Flexibility is equally important. A borrower who retains the capacity to adjust to changing circumstances is better positioned to manage delays, cost variations, or shifts in lending policy.

Liquidity refers to the ease with which a property can be sold or refinanced. Properties with broader market appeal tend to offer greater liquidity, which in turn provides lenders with greater comfort.

Simplicity facilitates assessment with private lenders in particular. Banks play in this space, also of course, but what will take many weeks to approve with a bank can take 3 days with a private lender. Straightforward arrangements with clear documentation are more readily understood and approved. Complexity is not inherently problematic, but it often requires additional explanation and verification.

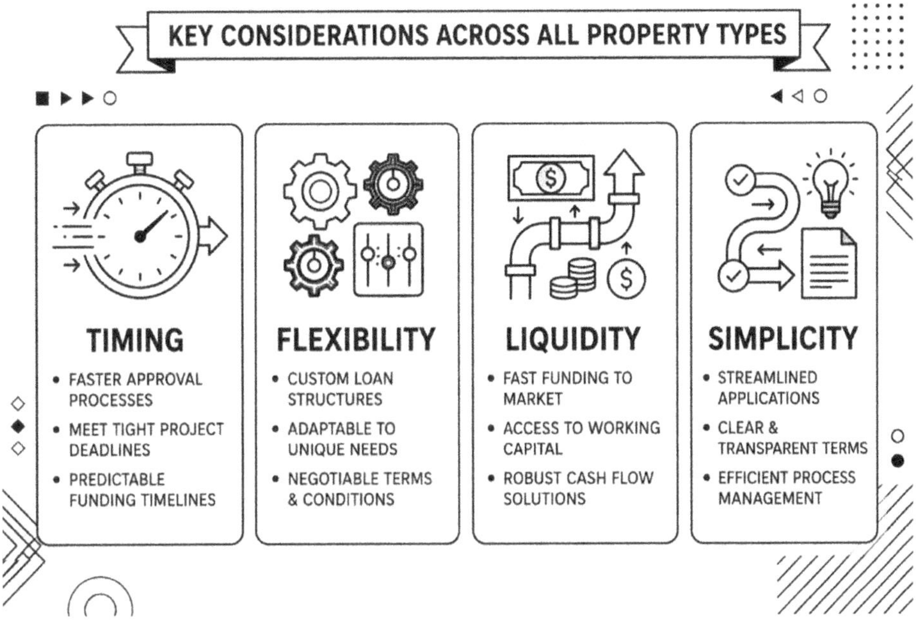

Established Properties – A Different Perspective

The acquisition of an existing property differs from new or uncompleted arrangements in several respects. The property can be inspected in its current condition, and there is typically a body of comparable sales data available to support valuation.

This provides a degree of immediacy and certainty. However, established properties may present other considerations, such as maintenance requirements or the need for refurbishment. There may also be legal or planning constraints affecting the property.

Matters such as zoning, heritage overlays, easements, and restrictive covenants can influence both the property's usability and the lender's assessment of it. These factors do not prevent lending, but they require careful examination.

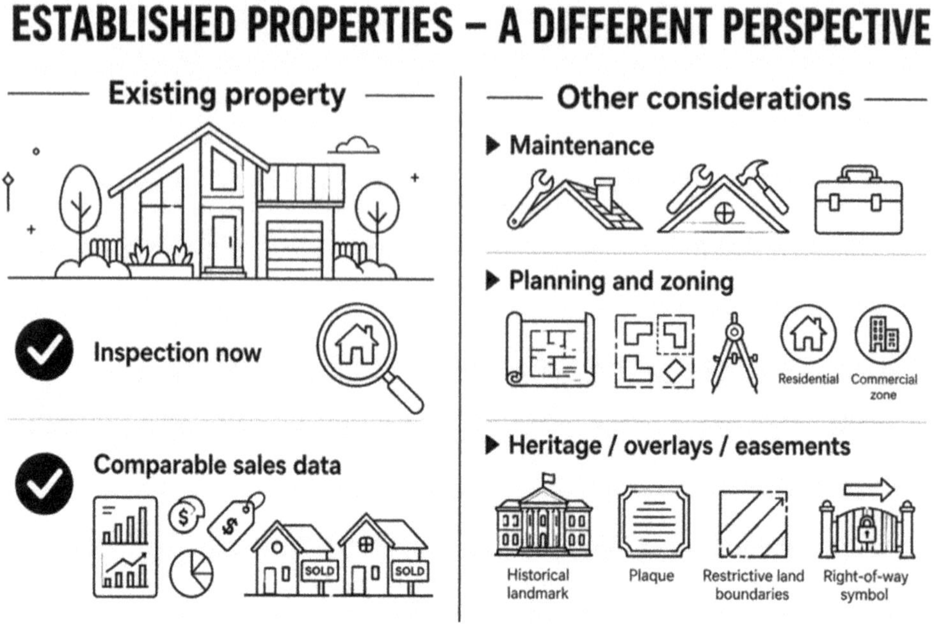

Due Diligence – A Universal Requirement

Regardless of the type of property or contract, due diligence remains essential. This involves a thorough review of contractual terms, an understanding of applicable regulations, and a clear appreciation of the financial commitments involved.

Informed decision-making is not a matter of avoiding risk entirely, but of understanding the nature and extent of that risk. A well-informed borrower is better equipped to proceed with confidence and to manage outcomes effectively.

The Role of Lending in Property Choice

A common misconception is that property selection can be made independently of lending considerations. In practice, the two are closely intertwined. Every property choice has implications for loan structure, borrowing capacity, and risk assessment.

Certain properties may attract a broader range of lenders, while others may be considered more specialised. This does not reflect a judgment on the quality of the property, but rather on how it fits within standard lending frameworks.

Understanding this relationship allows borrowers to align their property choices with realistic lending outcomes.

Supply, Demand, and Lending Comfort

Lenders consider not only the borrower's position, but also the characteristics of the property itself. One of the key considerations is how readily the property can be transacted in the open market.

Properties that appeal to a wide range of buyers are generally easier to sell and may be viewed more favourably. Conversely, properties with a narrower appeal may require more specific lending arrangements.

This is not a constraint, but a reflection of market behaviour. Recognising these dynamics helps set appropriate expectations.

The Importance of an Exit Strategy

Every lending arrangement must contemplate an exit. This may take the form of ongoing repayments, refinancing, the sale of the property, or completion of a project. Refer to earlier sections.

Holding Costs and Financial Awareness

All property transactions involve ongoing costs. These may include interest, rates, insurance, and maintenance. Even where income is anticipated, it may not commence immediately or remain consistent.

An awareness of these costs is essential. It enables accurate planning and reduces the likelihood of financial strain. Properly understood, these obligations form part of the overall structure rather than an unforeseen burden.

Lending and Property Diversity

There is no single model that applies universally. Borrowers have differing objectives, resources, and preferences. Lenders recognise this diversity and assess each proposal on its merits.

However, each type of property and contract will be considered through the lens of structure, marketability, and risk. This results in differing approaches to assessment, even where the underlying objective is similar.

A Balanced Approach

Ultimately, the question is not which property type is superior, but whether a particular arrangement is suitable in the context of the borrower's circumstances.

Considerations should include alignment with lending structures, clarity of risk, realism of timeframes, and overall financial position. By focusing on suitability rather than comparison, borrowers are better positioned to make decisions that are both informed and sustainable.

This expanded analysis reinforces a central proposition: lending and property decisions are inseparable. A clear understanding of how contract structures, property characteristics, and financial considerations interact allows for more effective decision-making. The objective is not to eliminate uncertainty, but to approach it with clarity and preparedness.

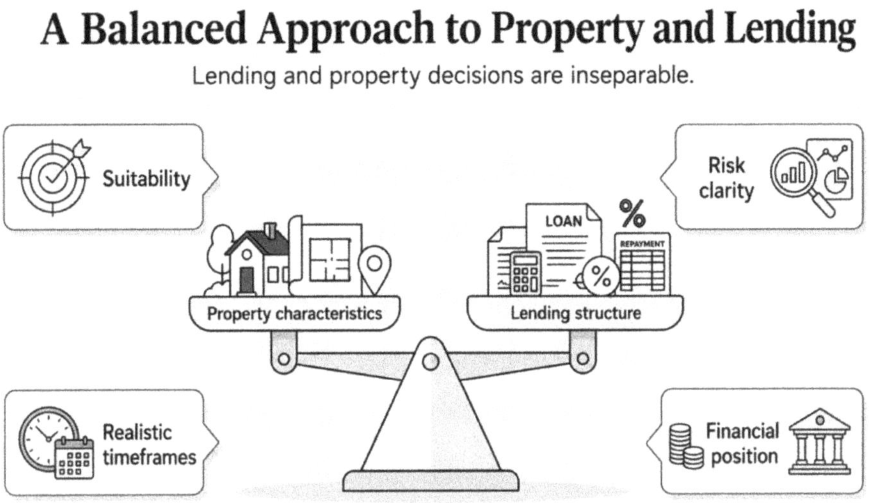

Overlay: Where the Earlier Structures Diverge in Practice (Private vs Traditional Lending)

What becomes clear when stepping back from the earlier sections is not that private and traditional lenders operate differently in theory—that has already been covered—but that they **react differently at the pressure points** within each structure.

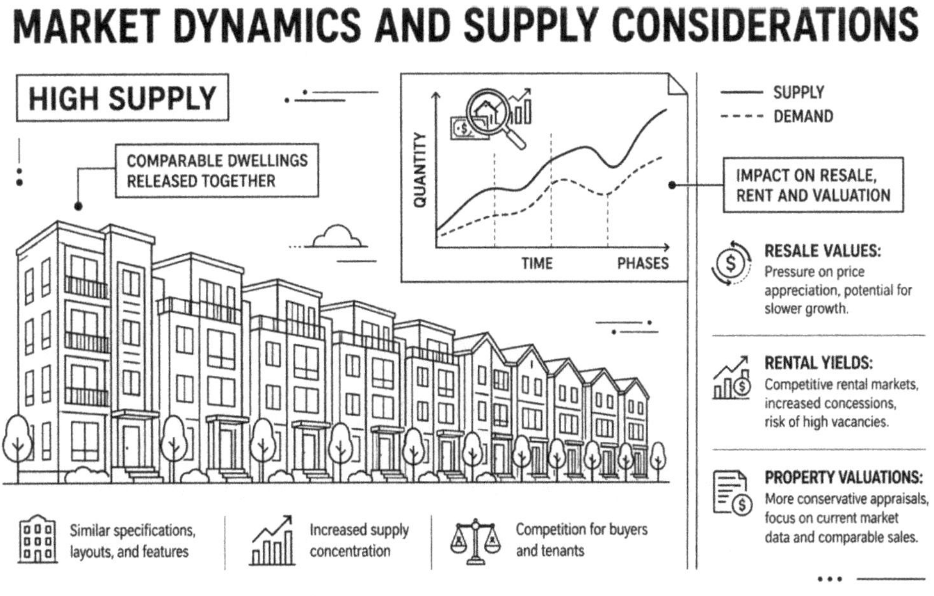

The distinction is most visible not only in straightforward transactions, but precisely where the earlier discussion identified **timing gaps, structural complexity, or uncertainty**.

Off-the-Plan and Delayed Settlement — The Reassessment Gap

Earlier, it was noted that off-the-plan purchases introduce a time delay between contract and settlement. The practical divergence lies in how that gap is treated.

For a traditional lender, the gap is a continuity problem. The borrower must effectively "requalify" at settlement. The approval at the contract stage carries little weight if policy, income, or macro conditions have shifted. The structure itself is acceptable, but the borrower must remain within policy at a future point that cannot be controlled.

The private lender does not attempt to solve that continuity problem. Instead, it reframes the issue entirely. The focus shifts to whether the property, at settlement, supports a **short-term position with a defined outcome**. The borrower's trajectory over several years is less relevant than whether the asset can sustain the loan within a compressed timeframe.

This is the first key divergence:

- Traditional lending attempts to **project forward stability**
- Private lending relies on **present value and near-term execution**

Construction — The Holding Period Problem

The earlier sections identified that construction introduces a holding period where costs accrue before income is realised.

Traditional lenders deal with this by requiring the borrower to demonstrate the capacity to **absorb the holding period**. This includes servicing buffers, contingency allowances, and strict adherence to timelines. Delays or cost overruns place pressure on the borrower's position and may trigger reassessment.

Private lenders do not eliminate the holding period, but they treat it differently. The question is not whether the borrower can carry the cost indefinitely, but whether the **end product resolves the position**. The holding period is accepted as a transitional phase rather than a stress test of long-term servicing.

This shifts the emphasis:

- Traditional lending tests **endurance through the process**
- Private lending tests **viability at completion**

Complex Contracts — Policy Friction vs Structural Acceptance

Where earlier sections discussed split contracts or multi-dwelling arrangements, the key issue identified was increased scrutiny.

In practice, this scrutiny arises because traditional lenders operate within **policy frameworks that favour uniformity**. Complexity introduces variables that cannot easily be standardised. As complexity increases, the transaction begins to fall outside predictable policy outcomes.

Private lenders are not immune to complexity, but they are less constrained by policy standardisation. Their assessment is not whether the structure fits a predefined model, but whether the structure can be **understood, valued, and exited**.

This produces a subtle but important difference:

- Traditional lenders ask: *Does this fit within policy?*
- Private lenders ask: *Can this be resolved if required?*

Market Supply and Property Type — Liquidity in Practice

Earlier, the discussion addressed supply dynamics and market behaviour, particularly in developments with multiple similar properties.

For traditional lenders, high supply can translate into **valuation conservatism** and tighter lending ratios. The concern is not merely current value, but how that value behaves under pressure.

Private lenders also consider liquidity, but often through the lens of **loan-to-value positioning**. Where sufficient equity exists, broader market concerns may be mitigated by the buffer between the loan amount and the asset value.

This reframes the same issue:

- Traditional lending manages risk through **selection and restriction**
- Private lending manages risk through **positioning and margin**

Exit Strategy — Not Just Important, but Decisive

An earlier section correctly identified the importance of an exit strategy. The distinction now is not its presence, but its **weight in the assessment**.

In traditional lending, the exit is secondary. Banks approve the loan, provided it is serviced over time. Sale or refinance is optional, not foundational, and, indeed, irrelevant. The lender knows the loan will be paid off in 30 years. This is one reason many banks and other major lenders discriminate against and will not lend to someone who is retired; sometimes, they will not lend to someone over 65. Why? The borrower will likely be dead before the loan ends.

In private lending, the exit is not simply relevant—it is **determinative**. The entire structure is built around it. Without a clear, evidenced exit, the transaction does not proceed. With one, many other constraints become less significant.

This leads to a different hierarchy of considerations:

- Traditional lending prioritises **income → stability → asset**
- Private lending prioritises **asset → exit → timeframe**

No End Debt — Where the Divide Becomes Most Pronounced

One area not expressly emphasised earlier but implicit across several sections is the concept of **no-end debt**.

In a traditional lending framework, transactions that do not lead to an ongoing loan relationship will likely be commercially unattractive. The effort required to assess, approve, and settle a loan is not offset by long-term interest income. As a result, scenarios in which the borrower intends to repay quickly—particularly through a sale—may receive less attention or a reduced appetite.

Private lending operates in the opposite direction. Short-term lending is not a limitation; it is the model. Where there is no ongoing debt requirement, the transaction aligns directly with the lender's objective. The absence of long-term servicing is not a weakness, but a feature.

This creates a practical reality:

- Traditional lenders may disengage where there is **no enduring loan**
- Private lenders may favour such scenarios, particularly where the exit is clear

Synthesis — Same Structures, Different Pressure Points

What emerges from this overlay is that the earlier property and contract structures do not vary by how they are understood by a lender. An off-the-plan purchase remains the same. A construction contract remains staged. A complex development remains complex.

What changes is **where the pressure is applied**.

Traditional lending applies pressure to:

- Consistency over time
- Income stability
- Policy alignment
- Predictability

Private lending applies pressure to:

- Asset sufficiency
- Exit certainty
- Timeframe clarity
- Equity position

The structures themselves are neutral. The outcome depends on which of these pressures is more easily satisfied in a given scenario.

Summary

The practical value in this comparison is not in preferring one model over the other, but in recognising when a transaction begins to move away from the strengths of one framework and toward the strengths of another.

Where timing is important, structures or property types are different or complex, or servicing is not the primary means of repayment, the transaction naturally aligns more closely with private lending principles.

Where income is stable, structures are straightforward, and long-term ownership is intended, traditional lending remains the more appropriate fit.

The earlier sections outlined the mechanics. This overlay clarifies the inflection point—where those mechanics begin to favour one lending approach over the other.

9.

Finance Strategies

For First-Time Homebuyers Wanting to Invest

This section combines much of what I have discussed throughout the book. It combines several ideas to forge a path forward. It brings to life many of the concepts covered, and whilst recapping them, I have incorporated the borrower's thinking process and the course of action considered and implemented. What they chose does not and will not suit everyone.

Getting your financial structure right for investing and choosing the right lender in real estate are absolutely critical. Getting it right can enable you to more easily purchase your first property and lead you on a path of achieving your property investment goals. On the other hand, if it's not set up correctly it almost certainly will result in placing premature limitations on what you will be able to do, resulting in frustration and missed opportunities.

Your finance structure and strategy need to work for you. It must be sustainable given your circumstances and flexible enough to let you manage it on your terms. Understanding structural differences in potential paths forward will help in the future, not just the next 12 months or 3 years.

Scenario

This particular client considered the following: lines of credit and interest-only loan types, since they can be very useful for investors, if managed correctly. With these types of facilities, they (the client) would only be required to make interest-only repayments based on the outstanding balance, whilst also providing the option to make principal reductions should they choose.

An offset account was also considered, as it would allow them to save interest on the loan without actually reducing the loan balance. The loan if interest-only, would allow them to enjoy the benefits of lower repayments as they grow their savings while not eroding the tax-deductible nature of the debt for the future.

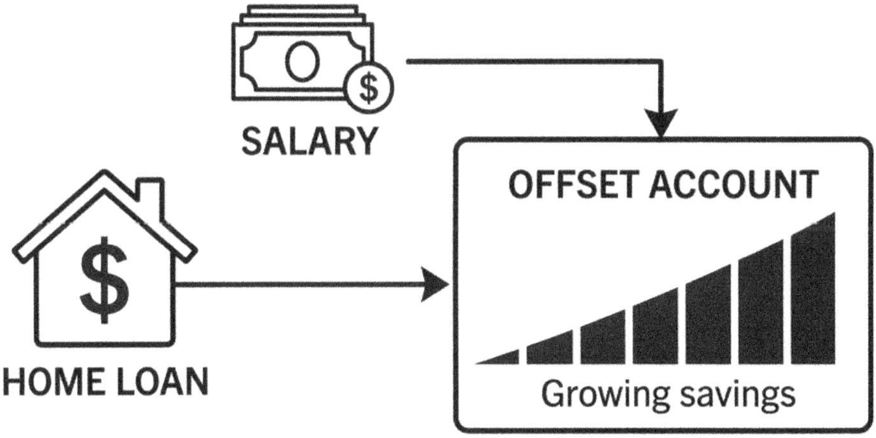

Interest calculated on loan minus savings

They decided that interest-only loans should be considered not only for their investment properties but also for their owner-occupied loan, because they were growing their own business and wanted to build an investment portfolio. For people who take money management seriously and are financially disciplined, it can be a highly strategic decision with significant benefits.

Some people purchase their first home to live in, knowing it's a stepping stone to another property they'll buy and live in at some point in the future. They could take out a principal-and-interest loan and set about paying off the debt as soon as they can. Without giving it much thought, they could conclude that this is really the most financially responsible thing to do.

Although debt reduction is usually the better option, particularly for an owner-occupied loan, the client in this scenario chose a different strategy, believing it would achieve the same result while providing greater flexibility now and in the future.

Instead of reducing debt, the strategy chosen for their owner-occupied loan was to grow their savings. By growing those savings in an offset account, or a series of offset accounts, their interest obligation on the loan will continually decrease, leaving more available funds to add to the offset account(s) each month. They will grow their savings much more quickly while enjoying lower loan repayments.

It's important to bear in mind that although the loan balance isn't reducing, it's possible to calculate roughly what it would be by subtracting savings from the loan balance, remembering that when principal and interest payments kick in, unless it's refinanced to another 30-year loan term lengthening the interest-only period for another 5–10 years, the repayments will go up dramatically, as there would be less time remaining on the term of the loan they are currently in.

The idea of not reducing an owner-occupied loan for several years may challenge many, but for some people, there are benefits. Your entry into the investment space may involve converting your first or current home into an investment property. If you have used the interest-only strategy, you have preserved the amount of debt, which will most likely be a significant factor when deciding whether your current property makes sense to keep as an investment, since it could then become tax-deductible.

I have seen many situations where people decide to sell a property because, from a tax standpoint, it makes no sense to keep it. Paying down the debt when first purchasing a property can be the right thing to do for most borrowers, but for some, doing so can make the property not a viable option to keep as an investment going forward and by structuring the loan interest-only upfront will leave all options on the table.

Having an interest-only home loan can also make investing in other property a more viable option from a cash flow management perspective. In the earlier scenario, keeping their commitments at home to a minimum meant there was more income available to invest. For example, the monthly difference between a principal-and-interest loan and an interest-only loan might have been $500, which means that money could go toward covering the financial commitments on one or more investment properties.

The goal for this client was to control as much of the property's asset value as was practical and appropriate given their circumstances. The greater the asset base at the beginning, the greater the value in the future as compounding growth occurs over time. For example, you could buy an owner-occupied home with a principal and interest payment of $2,000 per month, depending on the loan amount, and it may be the only property the borrower could afford if that was their monthly budget. Let's say the interest-only commitment on the same loan was $ 1,500 per month, which would leave $500 per month available to help fund the holding costs of one or more additional properties.

Wealth creation comes from controlling assets that produce income and grow over time. As a property buyer, your role is to do this within our financial means and then hold on to them for as long as we can to achieve the desired results. Choosing the right financial structure and strategy will have a huge influence on what can and cannot be achieved. Managing your finances correctly can lay the foundation for prosperity, whereas being structured inappropriately could mean you miss a whole lot of opportunity!

Strategies for Buying Multiple Investment Properties

How do you build a large property investment portfolio? It's a great question, and there are many topics that could be discussed to answer that question. I'm going to focus here on financing strategies to help make multiple property purchases possible.

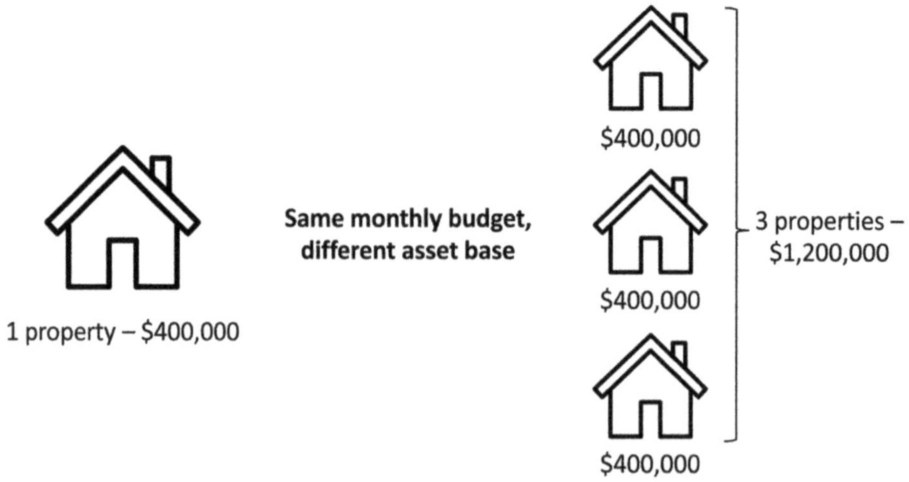

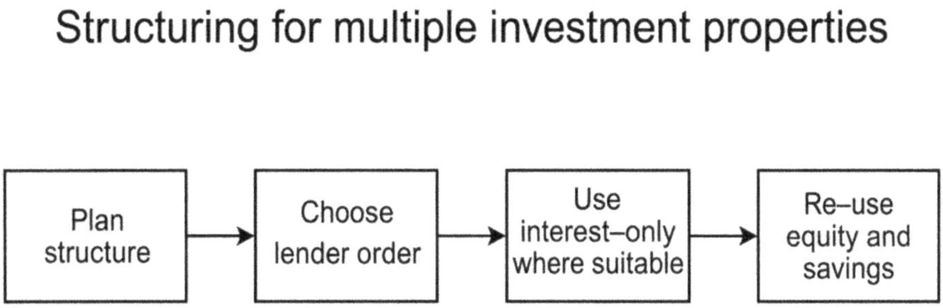

Let's recap and combine more topics and put the pieces together. It's all about being prepared and in the best position.

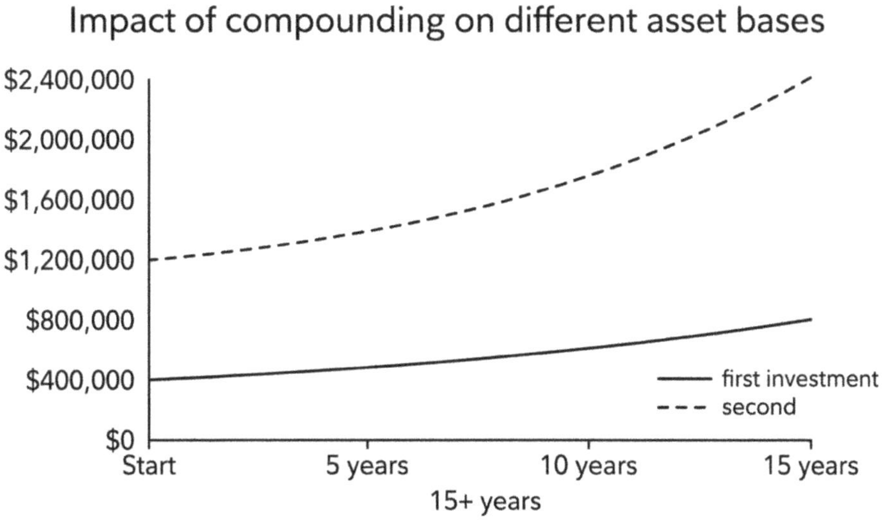

Criteria to Borrow Money

When it comes to obtaining finance to purchase property, there are three main criteria we need to meet to get the green light. The first is that you need a good credit rating (or at least not a bad one), so make sure you're always on top of your financial commitments and pay your bills on time so you never end up with any black marks on your credit file.

The second is that you need sufficient cash/equity to cover the gap between what the lender will lend you and the total cost of acquiring the property (including the deposit).

The third is that you need to show sufficient income to service the debt you're requesting, or consider using a private lender. If using a traditional lender, this will be based on your income from your job, Centrelink, and the rent from your property or properties. If you continue to be able to tick all three boxes, then there really should be no reason why the lender wouldn't be keen to advance further funds to expand on a portfolio, but it would be unreasonable to perceive a blanket statement is being made here, though. There are many other assessment criteria that a loan application will be subject to— this is simply a good start.

Self-Employed Loans

According to data from the Australian Bureau of Statistics, there are approximately 2 million self-employed people, which equates to approximately 17% of the working population. Over 60% of these have no employees, and over 980,000 are independent contractors.

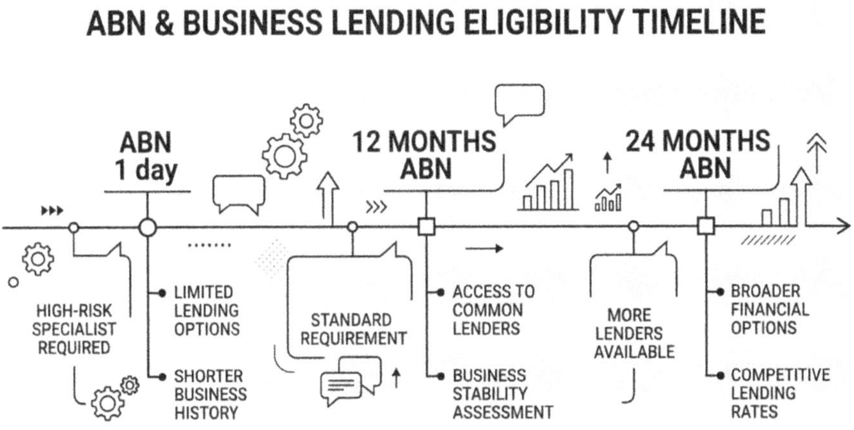

Low Doc, Alternative Documentation Loans

When this was established as a lending product, the intention was to assist those self-employed people who legitimately had not had the time to complete their tax returns to apply for a loan. The more acceptable excuse was that their company structure was too complex. In the years since, lazy sole traders, and more simply structured companies that have little excuse not to get their tax returns done on time, and those that have just had a lower profit year, or have just started out, have used this type of product to obtain finance. Some people that are outright tax dodgers (i.e. operating a 'cash' business) have also used this type of product.

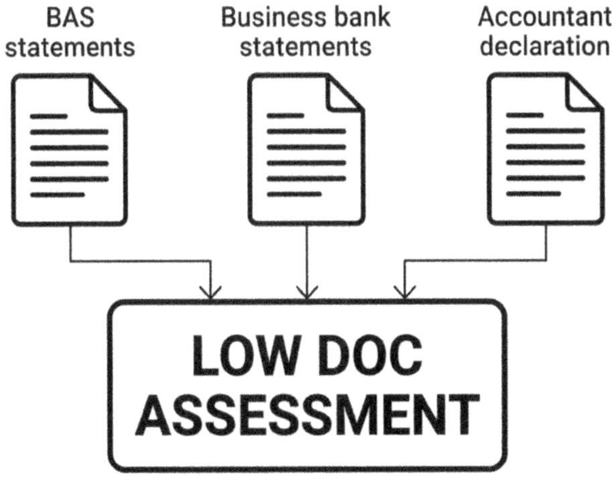

Some borrowers have a very good accountant and prefer to reduce tax rather than increase their borrowing capacity on paper for servicing purposes. Those that have been well-structured, with a focus on legitimate tax minimisation, may find it too difficult to provide all documentation to a lender by the applicable time. This is all perfectly acceptable to some lenders. Some borrowers may have had a lower-profit year or just started out, so this should also be considered. Commonly, self-employed people may be advised by their legal advisor not to get their tax returns done if they're going through a divorce — this way, the true extent of income is hidden from or unclear to the ex-wife/ ex-husband.

In fact, lenders don't care why the borrower is seeking a low-documentation loan; any of the above are, by default, acceptable, because a lender doesn't ask the reason the borrower cannot provide tax returns.

EMPLOYEE – FULL DOC	SELF-EMPLOYED – FULL DOC / LOW DOC
• Payslips, PAYG payment summaries • Verification of income and employment history • Often eligible for standard interest rates	• ABN history and business registration details • BAS (Business Activity Statements) or business bank statements • Potential for higher interest rates or fees

Banks used to even provide pay-as-you-go and/or pay-as-you-earn (PAYG/PAYE) borrowers with low doc loans based on certain criteria, such as not being able to prove alleged commissions and bonuses. There, of course, was some dodgy behaviour that went on, and these few ruined it for the many. Post global financial crisis (GFC), this type of low doc loan has been removed from lender offerings, as has what was called a 'no doc loan', where nothing needs to be provided regarding income, and someone could get a loan on the back of their word. Private lenders often offer 'no doc' loans; still, it is very common and very helpful to many borrowers. Someone's word, when it comes to lending, holds less weight these days with regard to income being earned.

Alt (alternative)-doc, lo doc, low doc and low documentation are all labels used for this type of loan.

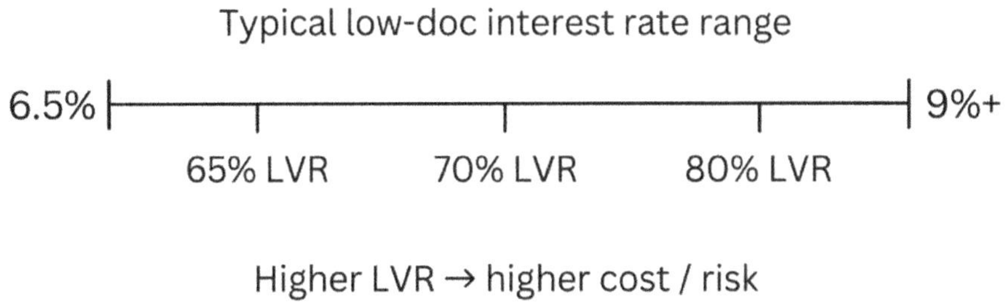

Case Study

A recent example of a tax dodger applying for a loan was a self-employed cleaner. A broker submitted a deal to a particular lender. The borrower self-declared he earned 82K p.a. The deal looked okay on the surface; however, the broker was complacent and provided a Centrelink statement confirming that the borrower (a single male with two kids) was receiving parenting payments and Family Tax Benefit (FTB) Parts A and B. Now, while the FTB Parts A & B are okay, some lenders also accept parenting payments, but these government entitlements are based on earnings. The more someone earns, the less parenting payments they're entitled to.

Looking at the parenting payments, this applicant was receiving, the amount was close to the maximum allowable entitlement payable by Centrelink, indicating he had informed Centrelink that he was earning very little (like under 30K p.a.). The self-declaration he provided stated that he earned 82K p.a., a figure supported by an accountant's letter. It was determined that he was either lying to the lender or to Centrelink, or both.

It later became obvious he was, in fact, lying to the government, as the broker later offered BAS statements to support the income. The broker told the lender not to act as the tax police. The lender informed the broker that one of the assessment criteria for a borrower is the five Cs of lending, one of which is 'character'. This applicant clearly was a liar and was committing fraud. The deal was declined, much to the broker's disgust. I was surprised that the broker was upset. Surely, I thought, the broker should not have wanted to jeopardise his licence by supporting a fraudster. Obviously not!

Requirements for Low Doc Loans

The requirements for low-documentation loans can vary greatly. I will talk about the most common here and then point out the more left-field possibilities still available in the market.

Normally, a self-employed applicant must have held an ABN for at least 2 years. This ABN can be used by a sole trader, a trading trust, or an incorporated entity. Sometimes a sole trader is advised by their accountant to set up a company or trust after some time, and even if the new ABN is just a few days old, as long as there is continuity in operation for the same business, then a few traditional lenders may accept this continuity in ABN, and a private lender will usually accept this.

There are some lenders who will accept having had an ABN for only 12 months, and even one or two who accept down to having an ABN for only 1 day. 'Would-be' borrowers have also made some poor decisions; for example, they had a good job, loads of opportunity to apply for finance in preparation for becoming self-employed, but instead they waited until they left their cushy job, and suddenly had no income, a great deal of outgoing expenses and then they applied for a loan a week after registering an ABN.

Income requirements can include one of the following options: either 6–12 months BAS statements, and/or 6–12 months business bank account statements and/or an accountant declaration.

Some of these declarations ask the accountant to verify the income being earned, and a couple of them just ask the accountant to verify that the applicant can afford the loan, with no specified income figure. This last method seems a bit wishy washy, and does not go to support a specified income, but some accountants like it since it does not put them in a difficult situation of verifying an income that they have not necessarily fully confirmed, given also the applicant may not have provided all their paperwork to the accountant.

The method of just confirming that the borrower can afford the loan seems difficult; how could the accountant know that person's living expenses? It could be more unreliable than specifying a figure.

When providing BAS or trading statements, the methods used to assess income vary.

Many lenders don't offer low-documentation loans, but those that do will often use only 40% of sales (revenue) on the BAS (annualised). This includes LMI providers; some lenders use up to 80% of turnover/ sales (and one lender I'm aware of uses 90% of turnover). The same percentages apply to trading account/ bank statements. Sometimes, the borrower's industry will be taken into account. For example, a builder will have more expenses than a stay-at-home hairdresser or IT consultant. Lenders will sometimes consider what is normally appropriate in the industry to apply some due diligence regarding the accuracy of the declared income.

Some banks also ignore whether a business is solvent or profitable. They ignore what is actually on the BAS, even though it has been requested, and instead use 40% of sales.

Case Study

A builder provided BAS statements — sales were $4 million over 12 months, and non-capital expenses were also $4 million. What this means is that, based on the BAS, the business made zero (yes, zero) profit during that financial year, but the lender ignored this and accepted that the builder was making a taxable profit/income of 400K per annum.

Sometimes the person may not be GST-registered, so BAS is not an option; perhaps they only submit a yearly BAS or have not even completed their BAS. No problem! Bank statements should be provided, and would provide a clear figure of money in and money out. The reality of providing bank statements is often quite different.

There are many businesses that operate on a cash basis. They don't run all their income through the books. Their goal may be to dodge taxes, and this will naturally negatively impact their ability to obtain financing. Often, a decision needs to be made — do you avoid/minimise or dodge tax, or does the person show more income over a couple of financial years to get a better rate, or even get a loan?

Lenders do scrutinise certain endeavours that traditionally have cash income and are more likely to potentially be dodging tax. Note: this is not necessarily most or all of them, but rather the perception many lenders have of them. They can include cafés, taxi drivers, hairdressers and small-scale builders, among many others. There are an inordinate number of borrowers who don't want to or simply cannot provide bank statements to a lender.

Other methods include deducting non-capital expenses, GST and wages from sales, and ignoring capital expenses, then annualising BAS for the income to be used for servicing. On bank statements, they add up the credits (income) and subtract the debits (expenses), then use the net figure, which is a more accurate way to determine taxable income before paper losses like depreciation. The personal expenses that many self-employed people run through their bank account can often be stripped out and ignored. Personal expenses would be accounted for under living expenses. It's wise not to run personal expenses through a business account, of course, but many do.

On this note, lenders are surprised that self-employed individuals, even if they are skilled in their trade, service, or product, are not necessarily good at running a business or managing their accounts. It is unwise for a self-employed person to use the business account for personal expenses; it muddies the books, creates a headache for their accountant, and increases the risk of an ATO audit.

Interest rates for low-documentation self-employed borrowers/applicants are higher than those for a normal term loan offered to an employee and higher than the rate on a full-documentation loan offered to a self-employed borrower. They can range from 6.5% to 9% or more, depending on the situation. The loan-to-valuation ratio (LVR) for a 'low doc' loan is normally 80%. Some lenders go up to an incredible 90% LVR, almost the same as a normal loan, and, in this case, the ABN only needs to be 12 months old. 85% LVR is possible with only 6 months ABN. Accompanying income verification is only a letter from the borrower's accountant. With a private lender, ABN may not matter.

Loan amounts can reach several million at 70% LVR. LMI normally kicks in at 60% LVR; some lenders will go to 70% with no LMI, and some lenders avoid LMI entirely and charge a risk fee (self-insurance) fee. This further helps the borrower avoid the potential hassle and scrutiny of dealing with a mortgage insurer. It avoids credit scoring against their CRAA file.

Genuine savings are often required for an LVR in mortgage insurance territory. It does seem odd when a self-employed person needs to borrow money from their parents. Lenders prefer to lend to more independent and successful self-employed people, especially if the borrower cannot provide tax returns.

GST Registration

Almost all lenders will require the borrower to be GST registered if the suspected or evidenced turnover is ≥75K. That's the law. It surprises me that the number of borrowers who don't understand the basic principle of turnover and taxable income.

It is turnover that determines the requirement for GST registration, not taxable income. Taxable income is derived by naturally deducting all business-related expenses from revenue.

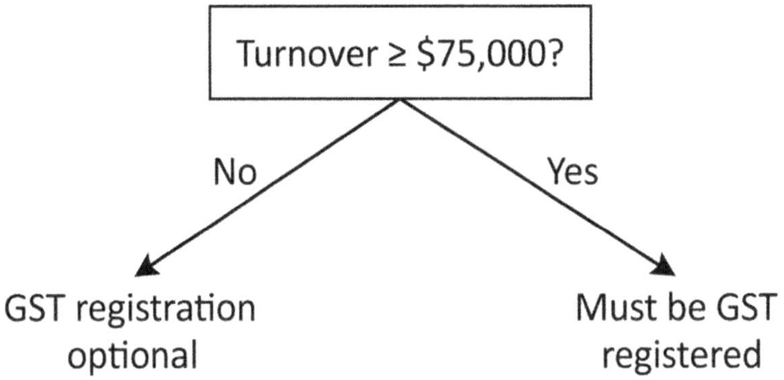

Taxable income ≠ Turnover

One of the most misunderstood aspects of self-employed lending is the difference between turnover and taxable income. The distinction may seem simple, yet it causes enormous confusion in loan applications, particularly when borrowers complete self-declaration forms.

Every self-employed borrower who completes a self-declaration form for a lender is declaring taxable income, not gross turnover or revenue. This is a critical distinction. Taxable income is the amount remaining after business expenses, deductions and depreciation have already been taken into account. It is not the total money flowing through the business bank account.

Surprisingly, this confusion is not limited to borrowers. At times, even brokers appear to misunderstand the distinction, particularly when trying to reassure a borrower that "the deal should be fine" before properly analysing the numbers.

Consider a common example. A borrower self-declares taxable income of approximately $74,000, yet they are not registered for Goods and Services Tax (GST). At first glance, some may not see a problem. However, once the figures are analysed properly, the issue quickly becomes obvious.

If taxable income is $74,000 after expenses have already been deducted, then the business turnover before expenses would almost certainly exceed the GST registration threshold of $75,000. In practical terms, very few genuine businesses operate with almost no expenses whatsoever. Even the smallest business generally incurs costs such as fuel, software subscriptions, phone expenses, accounting fees, equipment purchases, advertising, vehicle costs, insurance, internet access, tools, office supplies, or depreciation.

Yet occasionally, applications are presented in a manner that would require the lender to believe the business somehow generated nearly pure profit with virtually no deductions. At that point, the numbers stop looking commercial and start looking creative.

Lenders are not merely assessing whether the borrower earns income. They are assessing whether the declared figures make logical, commercial and regulatory sense when viewed as a whole.

In situations like this, there are generally only a few possible explanations, and unfortunately, none of them is particularly attractive from a lending perspective.

The first possibility is deliberate inflation of income. In other words, the borrower is overstating their earnings to qualify for a larger loan. This is obviously a serious issue. Providing false or misleading financial information to obtain finance is not simply "stretching the truth"; it can amount to fraud.

The second possibility is that the income figure is accurate, but the borrower should legally be registered for GST and is not. If taxable income is approaching the GST threshold after deductions have already been taken into account, then common sense suggests turnover itself is likely well beyond the registration threshold. From a lender's perspective, this raises concerns not only about compliance but also about the overall reliability of the borrower's financial affairs.

The third possibility is theoretically possible, although often commercially improbable. The borrower may genuinely have extremely low expenses. Perhaps they operate a business with almost no overheads, minimal depreciation and very few deductible costs. While this can occur in limited circumstances, lenders will often view such claims cautiously, particularly where the taxable income sits suspiciously close to the GST threshold. It may also suggest the borrower is failing to claim legitimate deductions to which they are entitled, in which case they may need a better accountant rather than a larger loan.

The fourth possibility is a simple misunderstanding. Many self-employed borrowers genuinely do not understand the distinction between turnover and taxable income. Some assume that because their business generated a certain amount in revenue, that figure represents their usable income for lending purposes. Others believe lenders assess "money coming in" rather than profit after expenses. In reality, lender servicing calculators are generally based on taxable income, not turnover. A business can generate substantial revenue while producing relatively modest taxable income once costs are deducted.

This misunderstanding can create uncomfortable conversations. A borrower may proudly announce that their business "turns over" several hundred thousand dollars per year, only to discover that their actual taxable income is a fraction of that amount. Turnover may impress people at barbecues, but lenders are far more interested in what remains after the bills are paid.

Equally concerning is where brokers fail to identify the issue before submitting the application. A competent broker dealing with self-employed borrowers should immediately recognise the relationship between turnover, taxable income and GST registration thresholds. If the numbers do not align logically, the issue should be addressed before the application reaches a lender's desk.

From a lender's perspective, inconsistencies like these are not minor technicalities. They go directly to credibility. Lending is heavily reliant on trust, the accuracy, and the consistency of financial information. Once the numbers no longer make commercial sense, the lender begins questioning everything else in the application as well.

This does not mean every inconsistency is dishonest. Sometimes borrowers are simply inexperienced in business, poorly advised, or unfamiliar with tax concepts. However, self-employment carries responsibilities. Understanding the difference between turnover, profit and taxable income is fairly fundamental to operating a business. If a borrower does not understand those concepts, it may indicate they require stronger accounting support or greater financial education before taking on significant debt obligations.

Ultimately, lenders are not expecting perfection. They are expecting figures that are realistic, internally consistent and commercially credible. If the financial story being presented requires the lender to suspend basic arithmetic and common sense, the application is unlikely to end well.

Full Documentation Loans for Self-Employed

For those who are self-employed, full-documentation loans normally require 2 years of tax returns with assessment notices for the individual and 2 years of tax returns for the company and/or trust, though some lenders only require 1 year of tax returns.

Often, traditional lenders will use the most recent of the 2 years' tax returns; the two most recent returns would be the two previous years to the financial year just ended, if after June 30, and after March the following year, if prior to March, then the prior to the most recently completed financial year is normally ok. Tax returns for the self-employed may not need to be completed until March the following year.

Lenders will normally use the lower of the most recent year or the previous year plus 20%. Others will average the 2 years. The previous section on the self-employed is a bit of a minefield, and it's so important not to go to a bank, but rather a good broker experienced with these situations.

Deposit Bonds — An Often-Overlooked Property Finance Tool

A deposit bond is one of the most misunderstood tools in Australian property transactions. Many purchasers, particularly first-home buyers and inexperienced investors, assume that a full cash deposit must always be paid immediately when signing a Contract of Sale. In reality, there are circumstances where a deposit bond can replace the traditional cash deposit and allow the purchaser to preserve liquidity until settlement.

In simple terms, a deposit bond is a guarantee issued by an insurer or approved provider on behalf of the purchaser.

Instead of handing over cash up front, the purchaser provides the vendor with a certificate confirming that, if the purchaser defaults, the issuer will pay the deposit amount to the vendor. The purchaser then reimburses the issuer. The bond therefore operates as security for the seller while allowing the buyer to retain access to their own funds for a period of time.

The concept sounds straightforward, yet many purchasers are unaware deposit bonds even exist until introduced to them by a broker, solicitor, conveyancer, or real estate professional. For some buyers, particularly those purchasing higher-value property, deposit bonds can provide a significant cash-flow advantage.

Deposit bonds are generally available for up to 10% of the purchase price, may be short-term or long-term, and are commonly used where settlement periods are extended. However, there are additional practical and legal considerations worth understanding in greater depth.

Why Deposit Bonds Exist

The traditional property purchase process assumes a purchaser has immediate access to a cash deposit, often 10% of the purchase price. On a $1,500,000 property, that could mean finding $150,000 immediately upon exchange of contracts. Many purchasers may ultimately have the money available but simply cannot access it immediately.

This commonly occurs where:

- funds are tied up in another property sale;
- money is held in investments or term deposits;

- the purchaser is awaiting settlement proceeds;
- the purchaser is buying off-the-plan years before settlement;
- the purchaser wants to preserve liquidity;
- the purchaser is using funds elsewhere in a business or development project.

Without a deposit bond, the purchaser may need to liquidate investments prematurely, borrow money short-term, or delay the purchase entirely.

Deposit bonds were effectively created to solve this timing problem.

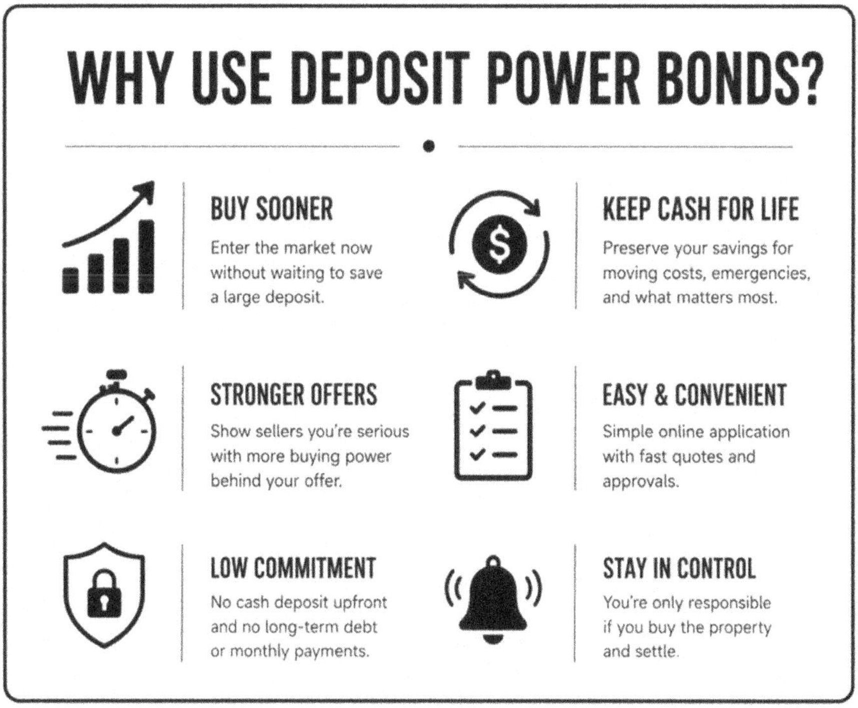

How a Deposit Bond Works in Practice

The purchaser applies to a deposit bond provider, usually through an online platform or broker. The provider then assesses whether the purchaser appears capable of completing the purchase at settlement. This assessment may include:

- equity in existing property;
- loan approvals;
- evidence of savings;
- sale contracts for existing property;
- asset and liability position;
- income evidence;
- identification and verification checks.

If approved, the provider issues a digital certificate or bond document which is then provided to the vendor or real estate agent in place of cash. The vendor accepts that certificate as security.

Importantly, the purchaser does not "borrow" the deposit amount. This is one of the largest misconceptions surrounding deposit bonds. Instead, the purchaser pays a relatively small one-off fee for the guarantee itself.

At settlement, the purchaser simply pays the full purchase price, including the deposit portion, as part of the normal settlement funds.

If settlement proceeds successfully, the bond expires automatically.

Deposit Bonds Are Not a Home Loan

Another important clarification is that a deposit bond is not a replacement for finance approval.

A purchaser still requires the ability to complete settlement. The bond simply deals with the deposit component during the period between exchange and settlement.

This distinction is critical because inexperienced purchasers sometimes incorrectly assume that obtaining a deposit bond means they are financially approved for the entire purchase. It does not.

The issuer merely assesses whether the purchaser appears capable of settling later.

Short-Term vs Long-Term Deposit Bonds

Short-term deposit bonds are generally used for standard residential purchases where settlement may occur within three to six months. These are commonly used where:

- the purchaser is awaiting settlement of another property;
- refinance proceeds are pending;
- temporary liquidity issues exist;
- the purchaser wants to retain funds in offset accounts or investments until settlement.

Long-term deposit bonds are more commonly associated with off-the-plan purchases and developments.

In some off-the-plan projects, settlement may not occur for several years. Rather than having a purchaser's deposit sitting in a trust account for three, four, or even five years, a deposit bond allows the purchaser to preserve those funds until settlement becomes due.

This can create substantial financial advantages.

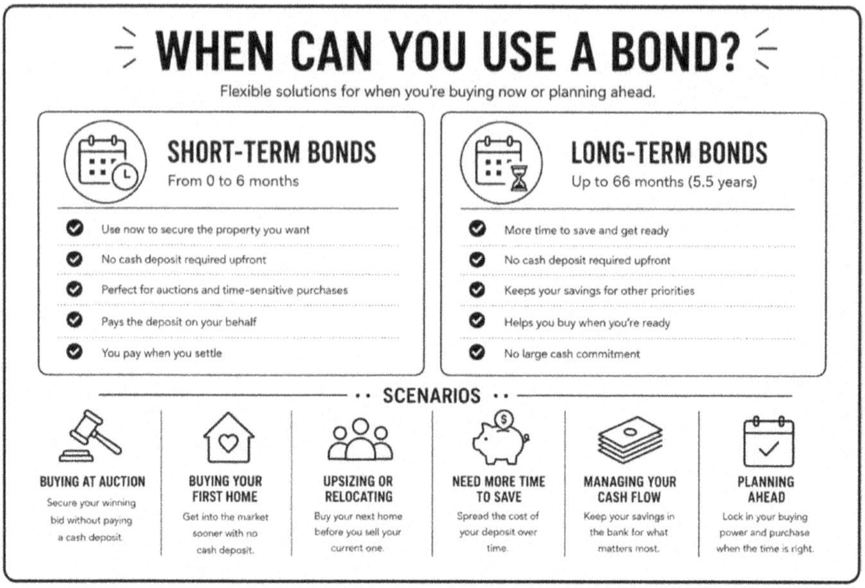

Off-the-Plan Purchases and Liquidity Preservation

One of the strongest uses for deposit bonds is in off-the-plan transactions.

When buying off-the-plan, purchasers often exchange contracts years before the property is completed. A traditional cash deposit may therefore remain locked away for an extended period.

This creates what banks and finance professionals refer to as a liquidity issue.

Liquidity simply means access to available cash.

If a purchaser locks away $200,000 for four years into a trust account, those funds cannot easily be used elsewhere. The purchaser loses flexibility, opportunity, and potentially investment returns.

Deposit bonds allow the purchaser to retain access to those funds while still securing the property purchase.

- For investors, this may allow:
- retention of funds in offset accounts;
- continued investment earnings;
- business working capital preservation;
- flexibility for renovations or developments;
- ability to secure additional investments.

This is one reason deposit bonds are particularly popular among sophisticated investors and developers.

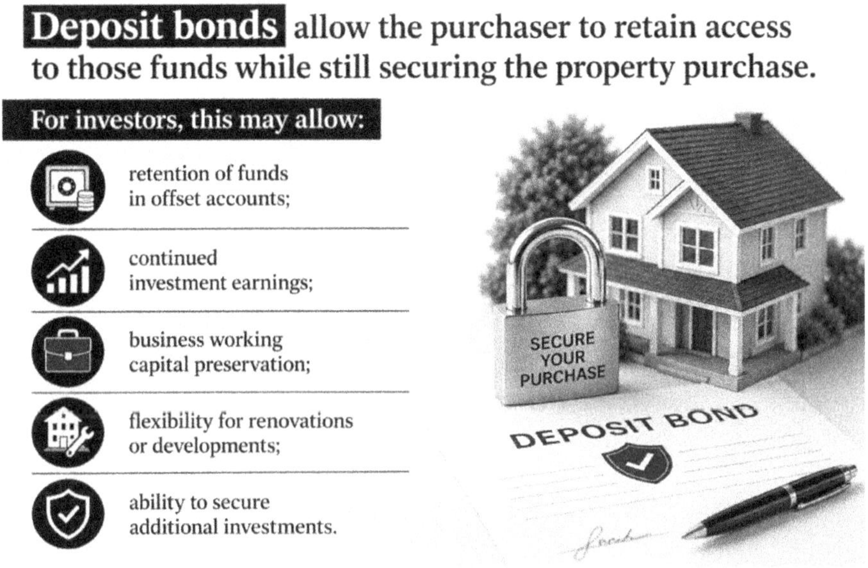

Deposit Bonds Compared to Bridging Finance

Deposit bonds can sometimes avoid the need for short-term borrowing.

Without a deposit bond, some purchasers may seek bridging finance simply to raise deposit funds. Bridging finance can be more expensive and often carries interest costs, establishment fees, and additional lending assessments.

By contrast, a deposit bond generally involves a one-off fee only.

For this reason, deposit bonds can sometimes be substantially cheaper than borrowing money solely for a deposit requirement.

However, purchasers must remember that the full purchase still needs to settle eventually.

Auction Purchases and Deposit Bonds

Deposit bonds can also be used at auctions, although this requires careful preparation.

Auction contracts are unconditional immediately upon acceptance of the winning bid. This means the purchaser must satisfy the deposit requirement instantly.

If intending to use a deposit bond at auction, the purchaser should:

- obtain approval beforehand;
- ensure the vendor agrees to accept the bond;
- confirm the bond wording satisfies the contract conditions;
- advise the auctioneer in advance.

Failing to do so could create serious legal issues.

Some vendors refuse deposit bonds entirely, particularly where they want immediate access to cash or where their own purchase depends on receiving deposit proceeds quickly.

Risks and Limitations

Although deposit bonds provide flexibility, they are not risk-free.

One major issue is that vendors are not obligated to accept them unless the contract permits their use.

These are convenient and quick in relation to modern digital bond systems. However, legal enforceability and acceptance remain critical.

From a vendor's perspective, a cash deposit is simple and immediate. A deposit bond introduces another party into the transaction — namely the insurer or issuer.

This means the vendor becomes reliant upon the strength and solvency of that issuer.

Accordingly, reputable underwriters and insurers are extremely important. Some providers emphasise their insurance backing and credit strength specifically to reassure vendors and conveyancers.

There are also timing risks.

If a bond expires before settlement, or contains errors in names, addresses, or contract details, enforcement complications may arise. Legal practitioners therefore need to carefully review bond wording and expiry dates.

Financial Assessments Still Apply

Another misconception is that deposit bonds are "easy approvals".

Although they are generally simpler than full mortgage applications, issuers still undertake financial assessments. Some providers require evidence of:

- sufficient equity;
- genuine savings;

- loan approval;
- asset backing;
- income position;
- sale proceeds.

In this sense, the issuer still needs confidence the purchaser can complete settlement.

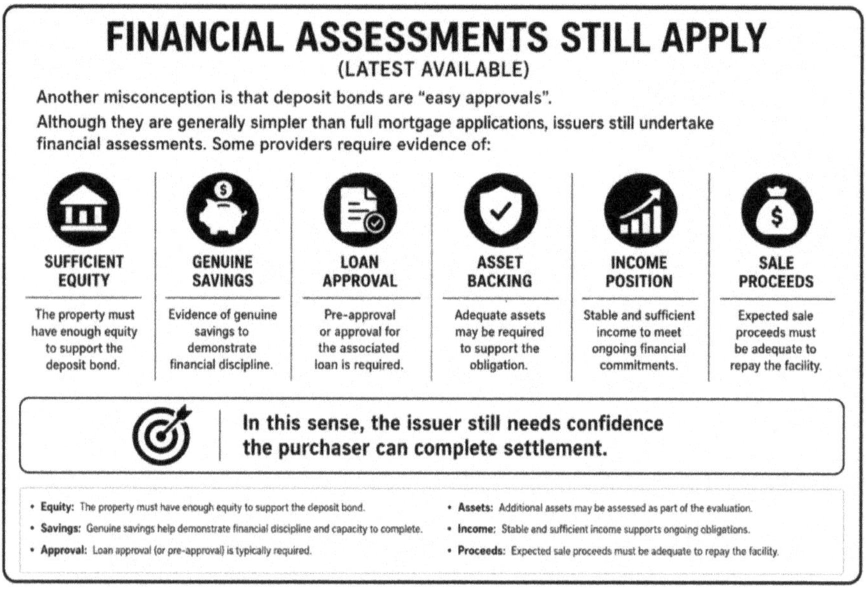

Relationship With Responsible Lending

Deposit bonds also indirectly intersect with broader responsible lending considerations.

Financial institutions and insurers cannot simply issue guarantees recklessly. They still need comfort that the purchaser is not entering into a transaction they are incapable of completing.

This aligns broadly with the broader Australian credit environment where lenders, insurers, and financial providers assess risk exposure, liquidity, repayment ability, and financial stability. Prudential regulation in Australia places significant emphasis on liquidity management and risk controls across financial institutions.

Although a deposit bond is not a traditional mortgage product, the issuer still assumes contingent financial exposure.

Why Sophisticated Investors Use Deposit Bonds

Sophisticated investors often view cash differently from owner-occupiers.

Rather than seeing cash as something to sit idle, investors generally prefer funds to remain productive.

For example, an investor may prefer to:

- retain funds in an offset account reducing interest;
- continue earning investment returns;
- preserve liquidity for future acquisitions;
- maintain business cash reserves;
- avoid unnecessary liquidation of assets.

From that perspective, paying a relatively modest bond fee to preserve six figures in liquidity can make commercial sense.

Example Scenario

Consider a purchaser buying an off-the-plan apartment for $1,500,000 with settlement expected in three years.

A traditional 10% cash deposit would require $150,000 immediately.

If those funds were instead retained in an offset account against a mortgage charging 6.5% interest, the purchaser could potentially save substantial interest over the three-year period.

Rather than locking away that money in a trust account, a deposit bond may allow the purchaser to preserve that financial flexibility.

This is why many financially experienced purchasers use deposit bonds strategically rather than simply because they lack funds.

Final Thoughts

Deposit bonds are not a loophole, nor are they "free money". They are a financial guarantee designed to solve a timing and liquidity issue in property transactions.

Used appropriately, they can:

- preserve cash flow;
- improve liquidity;
- assist with simultaneous property transactions;
- reduce reliance on bridging finance;
- support off-the-plan purchases;
- improve investment flexibility.

However, they also require careful consideration of:

- vendor acceptance;
- settlement timing;
- expiry dates;
- financial capacity;

- legal documentation;
- issuer strength.

For purchasers, brokers, lawyers, and conveyancers, understanding how deposit bonds operate can create additional flexibility in structuring property transactions while preserving liquidity and financial efficiency.

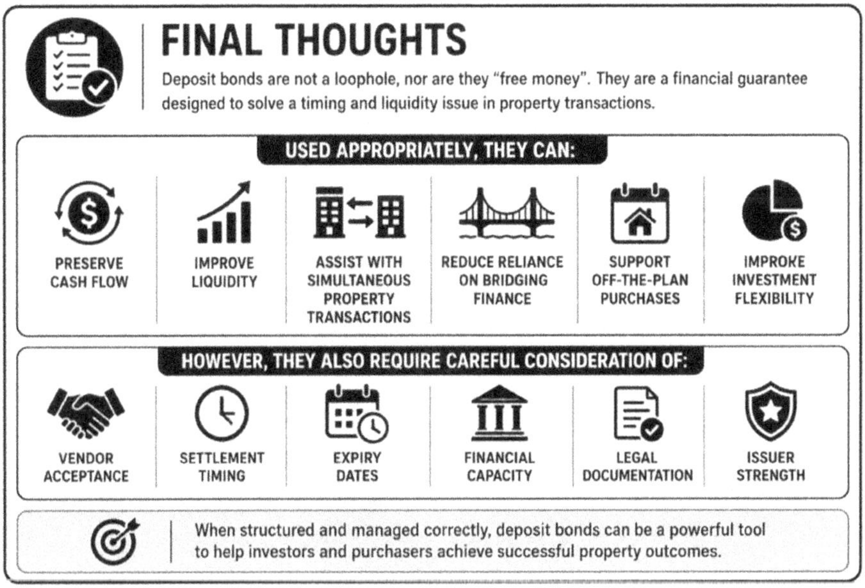

Structuring Your Finances

Have a plan. Traditional lenders need to be confident that you have sufficient income to service the new funds you are requesting and your existing loans. Because different lenders use different servicing rates, choose lenders based on which will suit your needs now and later (there is a big difference). Brokers can maximise borrowing capacity by choosing one lender over another.

Remember, most lenders will test your capacity to borrow money using a sensitised interest rate (higher than the actual rate) and apply principal and interest repayments to the new money you are requesting over the term of the loan (i.e., if the loan is 30 years with the first 5 years interest-only, they will assess the principal and interest repayments over 25 years).

Some lenders will use the actual repayments you're making on your loans and buffer those payments by 30%. This is still well below a qualifying rate, so interest-only repayments can be beneficial, as the 30% buffer is added to the interest-only repayment. If it were a principal-and-interest repayment, 30% would be added to it. Some lenders will assess existing mortgage payments at the actual repayment you are making, even if it is interest-only. Some lenders will assess existing mortgage payments the same way they assess new money if the existing loan is with them, as they are already exposed to it. Otherwise, they'll assess it more leniently if the existing mortgage is with a different bank.

To overcome the many hurdles, you need to be selective about the lenders you use and the stage at which you use them in your purchasing cycle. A borrower could consider using a lender that sensitised debt at a normal rate for the first couple of properties, then move to lenders that assess existing debt based on actual repayments. This way, you reduce the risk of exhausting your borrowing capacity with these better-servicing calculators.

If a borrower wants to expand and become an investor, like in the earlier scenario, keeping their mortgage commitments to a minimum will really maximise their borrowing capacity, so a borrower should think about and seek advice on whether keeping all of their loans on an interest-only repayment basis will suit their needs, and only if it suits their circumstances should they have interest-only. For many, principal and interest at least on the home loan is better; a broker can determine this.

Involving LMI in a Deal

To remain eligible for financing, the borrower will need to continue building their savings or have their existing properties appreciate in value so they can use the equity as the contribution toward the next purchase and the one after that. LMI is available to help you make your capital stretch a little further. Given the additional leverage LMI can provide, a borrower can do more with their existing funds. LMI is fantastic when the borrower is in expansion mode because it can allow them to make more purchases with smaller deposits and less equity. Remember, it's a tool, and it should be used when you feel it is appropriate and responsible to do so.

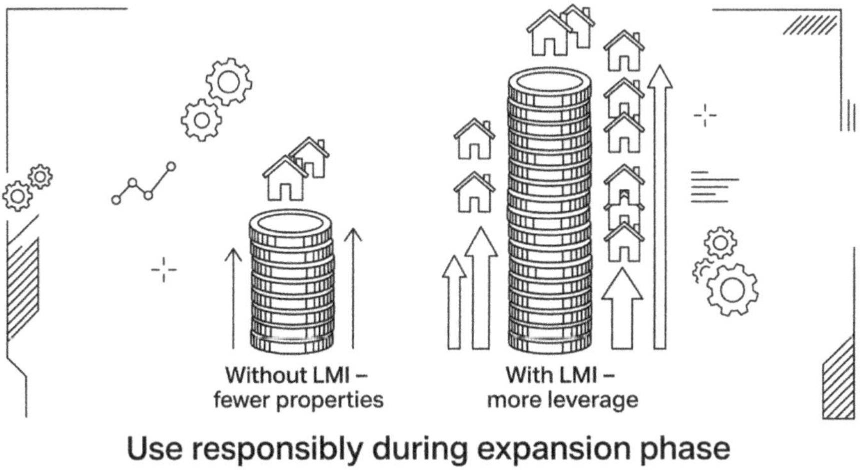

You also need to consider how much against a property's value you should be borrowing, whether it's 85%, 90% or 95%? This decision should be based on the merits of each transaction, an assessment of the risks and benefits, and ensuring you remain in a strong financial position without overcommitting. I have personally found an 88% LVR to work out better than an LVR above that, due to the higher premium that kicks in at higher LVRs.

Vendor Finance

Vendor finance is a form of private finance in which the owner of a property (the vendor) agrees to sell the property under the terms of a contract. The terms of the contract will outline all the particulars of the sale agreement (including the purchase price and the period over which payments will schedule), as well as the payment amounts required to complete the purchase of the property. In layman's terms, the owner of the property finances the purchaser.

These agreements are typically drawn up over a thirty-year term, although the intention is, in most instances, for the contract to be paid out much sooner, when the purchaser can refinance the debt through a conventional home or investment loan. This type of financing arrangement would appeal to a purchaser who, for whatever reason, can't qualify for a conventional loan at the time of purchase.

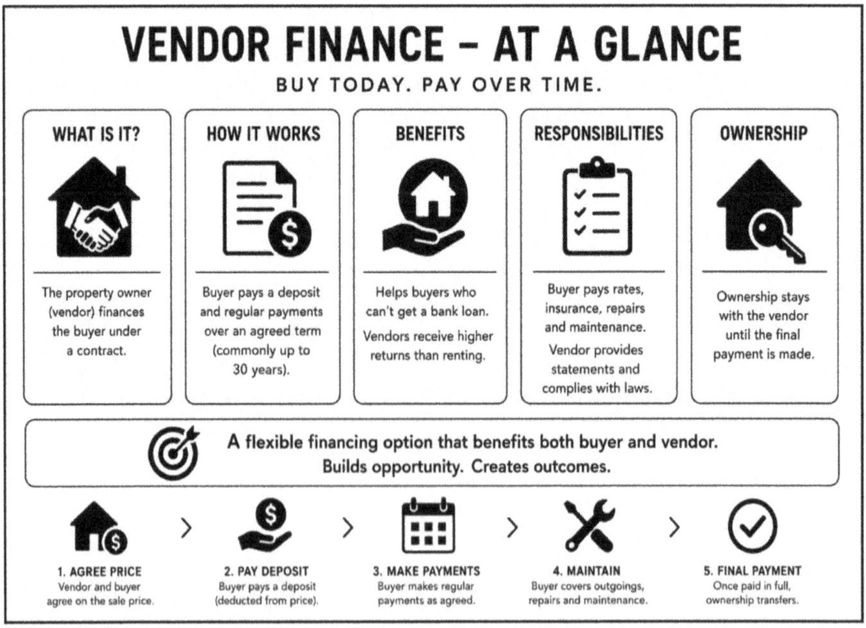

Structuring the Agreement

The vendor and the purchaser agree on a sale price for the property. The purchaser should, and in most cases will, pay a deposit, which will then be deducted from the sale price of the property. So, let's say the sale price of the property is $250,000 and the purchaser pays a deposit of $25,000. The remaining balance owed, under the terms of the contract, will be $225,000. It is on this remaining balance figure that the repayments, under the terms of the contract, will be calculated.

An interest rate will be agreed upon between the two parties, say 7%, and the repayments can be determined. On a thirty-year loan agreement, $225,000 at 7% means a weekly payment of $374.23. The purchaser is also responsible for paying the outgoings on the property — such as council and water rates and insurance. These additional costs are then calculated and added to the weekly payment. For example, they may total $40 per week, resulting in a vendor payment of $414.23.

The interest rate under a term contract is likely to change over the term of the agreement, just as it would under a conventional property loan arrangement. If it is a variable rate, which most are under these agreements, it will likely track changes in the Reserve Bank rate, or, if the vendor has a mortgage over the property, it may track changes in that interest rate. Fixed rates can be agreed to under a terms contract, but, like conventional fixed-rate property loans, they can be subject to break costs if the loan is paid out or significantly reduced during the fixed-rate term.

Whilst under a terms contract agreement, the title of the property remains in the vendor's name. This will also mean that the council and water rates, as well as insurance, will also be in the vendor's name: paid by the vendor, and recouped each week via the weekly payment, under the terms of the contract agreement. Title to the property transfers to the purchaser when the final payment *and* stamp duty is paid, to complete the property transfer.

The purchaser will also be responsible for any other costs that arise in relation to the property, like maintenance and repairs. This is because the rights to ownership of the property belong to the purchaser — from the date of signing the terms of the contract — meaning the purchaser is entitled to all future capital growth in the property and is therefore responsible for all costs associated with the property, just like any property owner.

Vendors Obligations

As the vendor is providing finance, it will need to comply with any legislative requirements applicable to a finance provider. These will include (but are not limited to):

- Ensuring the finance is not unsuitable to the purchaser
- Making sure the council and water rates, and insurance, are paid and up to date
- Confirming and verifying that the borrowers can meet their financial obligations under the terms of the contract agreement
- Ensuring the vendor provides regular loan statements to the purchaser
- Meeting its financial obligations — if there is a mortgage on the property
- Ensuring there are no changes to any mortgage over the property, after the terms
- The contract agreement has been signed, including (but not limited to) increasing the debt or refinancing

- Ensuring the property is not cross-collateralised with any other properties
- Having a dispute resolution mechanism in place
- Ensuring proper process is followed, and appropriate action is taken if the purchaser falls into arrears, or they develop poor conduct on the loan facility.

I would just like to elaborate a little further on the point about ensuring the finance is not unsuitable for the purchaser. It is critical that the vendor takes appropriate steps to understand the purchaser's objectives and assess whether entering a terms contract will, in fact, address and meet those objectives. By entering into the agreement, is the purchaser likely to be able to complete the agreement at some point in the future? Is their income sufficient to meet their loan repayment commitments? Are there any foreseeable changes that may affect their capacity to meet their obligations under the agreement? If all reasonable steps have been taken to satisfy these points, then a vendor terms contract can be considered as a viable option for the purchaser to buy a home.

Benefits for the Vendor

Offering a property for sale under a terms contract can have many benefits for a vendor, particularly for vendors where the property is an investment. It is a great way for an investor to receive more income from the property than would normally be achieved if the property was rented out. This additional income will certainly mean this investment is making money each year, which can be used as a supplementary income for the vendor, or used to boost the overall cash flow of the vendor's property investment portfolio.

This additional cash flow is a powerful factor for investors looking to expand their property portfolios. When applying for finance to purchase a property, you need to demonstrate to the lender that you have enough income to service the debt you are requesting. Having property/properties where you have significant surplus income, over and above all costs, means you have additional income that you can evidence to demonstrate your capacity to take on more debt. In most instances, having a terms contract in place will increase your borrowing capacity, so the more of these you have in your portfolio, (potentially) the more property you can buy.

You will also have an occupant of the property, who is planning on staying there for an extended period of time, providing the vendor with more revenue certainty. The occupant will also be more likely to take care of the property, and it is also very common for the purchaser to make improvements to the property. After all, they are purchasing it.

In some instances, under a terms contract, the purchaser will not complete the contract and may request to be released from the contract. This can have huge benefits for the vendor. The vendor was collecting substantial income during the time the agreement was in place, and now that the purchaser has been released from the contract the vendor is again the only person with an interest in the property, and is therefore entitled to all future capital growth in the property (from the date of the release letter being signed.) The vendor will be obligated, though, to pay the outgoing purchaser any equity they have built up in the property during the time the terms contract was in place.

Having just outlined the benefits to the vendor, assuming the purchaser does not request a release from the contract and does go on to complete the purchase, the vendor has traded the additional income for not receiving any capital growth in the property over and above the agreed sale price. It certainly doesn't detract from the benefits that can be gained from the terms contract, but it does highlight that this arrangement is an income generating strategy, and a far less capital appreciation strategy.

Benefits for the Purchaser

As with the vendor, the purchaser gains many benefits by purchasing a property under a terms contract. It's great for purchasers who have a small deposit, which wouldn't meet the minimum amount required if applying for a loan through a conventional mortgage provider. This enables purchasers, in this position, to enter the property market sooner than they otherwise could have.

Vendors will also consider purchasers that may have a less than perfect credit history, which, again, can be a barrier to obtaining finance the conventional way. This by no means suggests that vendors will provide this opportunity to everyone, but a personalised solution can be assessed, based on the credit history of the purchaser.

Purchasers that have varied income streams can also be considered as suitable purchasers under terms contracts. This can include people starting a new job, changing industries, starting a business, reliant on commission or bonuses, or self-employed people who don't have their financial records up-to-date. Purchasers, in these categories, can often be overlooked in the conventional financing arena as unsuitable borrowers. Diligent assessment will need to be undertaken for people in these categories, but solutions can often be found to assist purchasers who find themselves in this position.

The purchaser really does have control over the property, which provides comfort and certainty. Changes and improvements to the property can and often are undertaken, which can help increase the rate at which equity is built in the property. The purchaser can also sell the property on the open market or negotiate with the vendor to pay them out of their equity, should their circumstances change and they need to move on.

Interest rates and fees that may apply to term contracts are often in line with (if not more competitive than) a non-conforming lender that provides finance solutions to purchasers who fall into some of the categories I mentioned earlier. Terms contracts really are a genuine alternative for purchasers seeking a solution to enter the property market.

The Risks

Although vendor finance really is a win/win for both parties, like all investments/opportunities, there are risks that need to be understood and considered before either party enters into an agreement. The vendor needs to ensure they are compliant with their obligations under the agreement and complete their due diligence on the purchaser to ensure they are credit-worthy applicants (who can fulfil their obligations under the agreement as well) The vendor can face significant disruption to the performance of the terms contract if the purchaser fails to meet their obligation, and it can take time and financial resources to bring the purchaser back in line, or move them on.

From the purchaser's position, they need to be dealing with a credible vendor who agrees to fair and reasonable terms in the agreement, particularly with the sale price, interest rate, and fees, to ensure there is real opportunity for the purchaser to complete the contract at some point in the future. The vendor also needs to meet their obligation under the agreement and, in particular, meet their financial commitments to the property outgoings and any mortgage that may be on the property.

Seeking the right professional advice is critical for both parties to ensure the agreement is compliant in every way, and that it meets the needs of both the vendor and purchaser. Risk shouldn't be a barrier to either party entering into a contract: they just need to be understood, and appropriate action taken to mitigate and minimise them.

Private lenders can accommodate this situation, whereas other standard lenders often may not.

Case Study

'Starting out as a property investor, I was very much aware of the importance of cash flow. I knew that it would be an integral part of my investment strategy to build and maintain a strong cash flow position. It was a strong focus of mine from the outset, particularly given my financial position at the time I was building my portfolio — with limited capital and a very modest income.

'My personal property investment strategy was quite heavily weighted on purchasing properties that were generating good income, in part given my personal circumstances, but also because it just made a lot of sense to me to purchase assets that produced income, over and above the costs associated with holding that asset. This wasn't always achievable with the properties I was buying, and I was finding I needed to contribute funds to the portfolio to support it on a monthly basis.

'Despite having some properties that were making money each month, albeit only by a hand full of dollars, it only took some small unanticipated expenses to enter into negative cash flow territory. I was also finding the

more properties I was buying, the more exaggerated the issue became. If I was going to continue to grow and expand my property portfolio, I needed to find a solid cash flow solution that would turn this situation around.

'I was introduced to vendor financing, in around 2006, and became very interested in the concept immediately. I tried to find out as much as I could about how it worked, and search for people who could help me implement it. My initial experiences were less than ideal, and the people I entrusted to help me had a lot of fundamental issues with their implementation of the strategy. A key aspect to a successful terms contract agreement is to have a credible purchaser, and this was the area in which the people I engaged to help got it horribly wrong.

'As the first three properties I purchased (specifically to use a terms contract strategy on) slowly started to unravel, it became clear to me that the purchasers I had been advised to sell my properties to were unsuitable for this type of transaction. Failings in two key areas became apparent: lack of deposit put down by the purchaser, as well as very unstable employment history (in conjunction with the use of Government benefits to demonstrate capacity to service debt.) Looking back now, those first three attempts at making this strategy work were destined to fail from the outset.

'Believing in the concept and accepting my failed attempts to make this strategy work were due to getting the fundamentals wrong, I set out to better educate myself and find the right people to help me execute this correctly. It wasn't long before I was surrounded by experienced people who were having success with the strategy. With their help and guidance, I was able to turn a quite unsuccessful moment in my property investing journey into a very successful and important one, for my growth going forward.

'At one point, I had just over ten of these deals in place, making anywhere from $600-$1000 a month positive cash flow, after all expenses. This couldn't have come at a better time as, unbeknown to me at the time, we were heading for the GFC and interest rates were rising, putting my

portfolio under the most extreme cash flow pressure I had experienced. This surplus cash flow I had created not only ensured I survived the GFC well but also strengthened my portfolio to enable me to expand it at the rate I wanted to.

'Seven years on, from when I first came across the terms contract concept, I am now able to reflect back on how this strategy has played out, and how the agreements reach a conclusion. I've had a number of purchasers fall behind with their financial obligations (of the agreement) and I have been required to move them on from the property. On the surface this may not appear to be a desired outcome, but it's actually not as bad as it sounds. Some people will fall behind. It happens on conventional contracts as well, and they need to take responsibility for that situation. In this instance, the purchaser moves out of the property and no longer has any entitlement to the property. If there is equity that has been built up over the time the purchaser has been there, then that is theirs, and as the vendor I am obligated, and do, pay that to them. I can then enter into another terms contract agreement, rent the property out, or sell it.

'In my experience, most purchasers will meet their obligations under the agreement, and the terms contract works well for both parties. Most of the terms contracts I have entered into are still in place and are working well for both the purchaser and me. The longest has been going for around five years, I'd say; it won't be many more years now before there has been adequate growth in the properties for the purchasers to then seriously consider refinancing and completing the agreement. I look forward to these coming to successful conclusions, where both parties have achieved their objectives and benefited accordingly.

'Deciding on what to do with a property, when I take back full control of it, will depend on what my property portfolio needs at the time. If it needs additional cash flow, I will resell it again on a terms contract. If the cash flow position of the portfolio is sound, then I will most likely rent the property out, which really is a fabulous outcome for the vendor/

investor. If my portfolio is in this strong cash flow position, I will be able to change strategy with the property and benefit from the capital growth in the future.

'For me personally, terms contracts played a significant role in allowing me to build a reasonably large property portfolio and manage the cash flow in a way that required very little financial input from me. I made this very strategic decision, as I didn't want to be a slave to my investments, and truly wanted them to work for me. For some, term contracts are the primary investment strategy delivering great cash flow, which results in financial flexibility by providing an alternative to working a regular job. For me, it added strength and diversity to my portfolio and, looking back now, even after a rocky start, was one of the best decisions that I would repeat again if starting over.' — Garry Harvey

10.
Bridging Finance

Bridging Finance: When Banks Say No, and Private Lenders Say "Yes"

Bridging finance exists because property transactions do not occur in a perfectly sequenced or predictable manner. In an ideal scenario, a borrower would sell their existing property, receive the proceeds, and then purchase the next property with complete financial clarity. In reality, however, the market does not operate this way. Opportunities arise unexpectedly, i.e., a suitable property becomes available before a sale is finalised. A builder is ready to commence construction while the current property is still being prepared for the market. A retirement village or downsizing option becomes available within a specific timeframe that cannot be delayed. In each of these cases, the borrower is financially capable of making the move, but their equity remains tied up in a property that has not yet been converted into cash.

Bridging finance is designed to solve this problem. It allows a borrower to proceed with the purchase of a new property while retaining the existing one, effectively bridging the gap between the two transactions. It is, at its core, a timing solution rather than a traditional long-term debt structure. It enables action in situations where waiting would result in lost opportunity or unnecessary disruption.

Traditional lenders rarely offer bridging finance, and the one that does, does so within defined and restrictive parameters. Private lenders, by contrast, approach bridging finance as a core lending activity and therefore offer a broader, more flexible range of solutions. The differences between these approaches are significant, not only in terms of policy and structure but also in the underlying philosophy of how risk is assessed and managed. This chapter explores those differences in detail, examining how standard bank bridging operates, the limitations that borrowers frequently encounter, and how private bridging finance can provide an alternative pathway where traditional lending falls very short.

At a structural level, bridging finance allows a borrower to temporarily hold two properties: the one they currently own and the one they intend to acquire. During this period, the borrower effectively carries two loans. The total of these loans is referred to as the peak debt. This is the highest level of exposure at any point in the transaction and represents the figure that lenders focus on when assessing risk.

Once the existing property is sold, the net proceeds—after agent commissions, legal costs, and other associated expenses—are applied to reduce the peak debt. The remaining balance is referred to as the end debt. This is the amount that continues as the ongoing loan secured against the new property and is repaid over time in the usual manner.

In some scenarios, there is no end debt at all. The proceeds from the sale of the existing property are sufficient to repay the entire bridging facility, including any accrued interest during the bridging period. The borrower transitions into the new property completely debt-free. This outcome is particularly common among downsizers and retirees who have accumulated significant equity over time. It represents a logical and conservative financial outcome from the borrower's perspective. However, it also highlights the divergence between traditional and private lending models.

The one major bank in Australia that does offer bridging, structure bridging loans in broadly similar ways. While the specific policy varies, the core features are consistent. Bridging facilities are typically offered for a short duration, usually up to six months for the purchase of an established property and up to twelve months where construction is involved. During this period, the loan is generally interest-only. In some cases, the interest is capitalised and added to the loan balance, allowing the borrower to defer repayments until the bridging period concludes. In other cases, the borrower may be required to service interest payments on one or both loans.

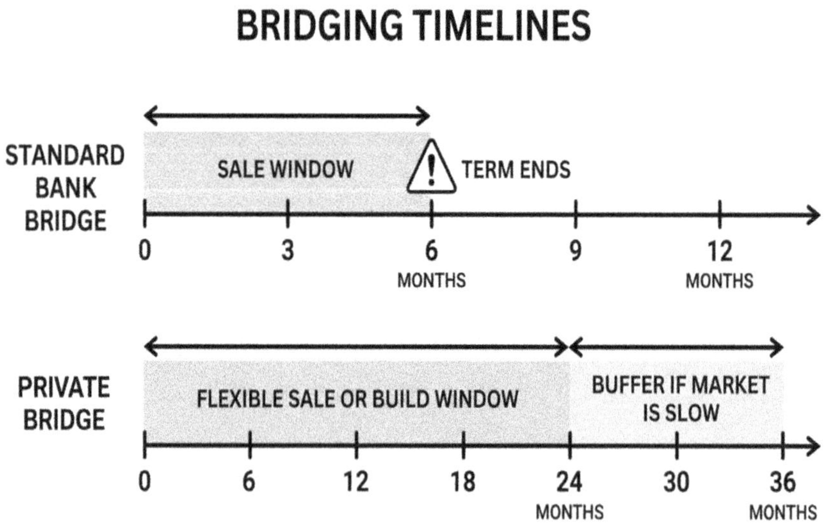

Bank vs Private Bridging

Bank	Private
6–12 months	Up to 36 months
Full doc income, age limits	Low doc, no age restriction
Owner-occupied only	PPR, investment, commercial, land
LVR to 80–85% using reduced valuations	LVR to 70% of full valuation

Servicing is typically assessed based on the end debt. This means that the lender evaluates whether the borrower can afford the loan once the bridging period has ended and the existing property has been sold. Loan-to-value ratios are calculated based on the peak debt, often allowing up to approximately eighty to eighty-five per cent of the combined value of both properties. This calculation includes any capitalised interest and, where applicable, lender's mortgage insurance.

Banks are most comfortable operating within a clearly defined set of conditions. These include transactions involving owner-occupied/ principle place of residence (PPR) residential properties in established areas, borrowers with stable and verifiable income, and situations where the end debt can be comfortably serviced. Where these conditions are met, bridging finance can be relatively straightforward.

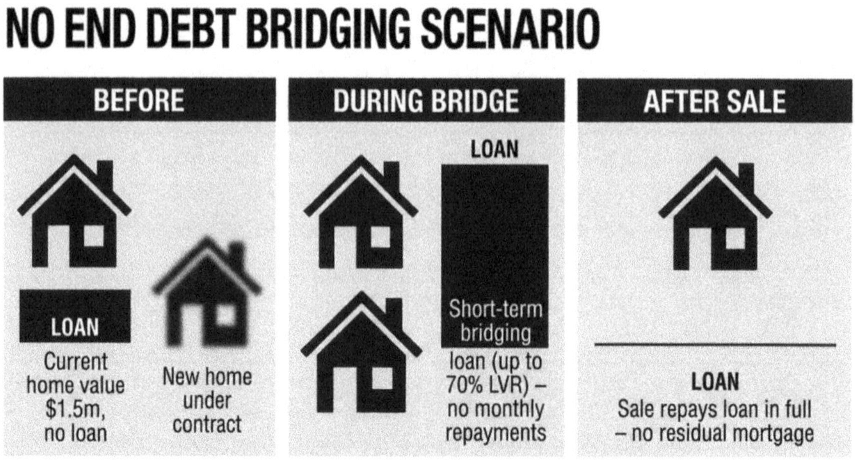

Age and income less important when there is no residual debt and strong equity

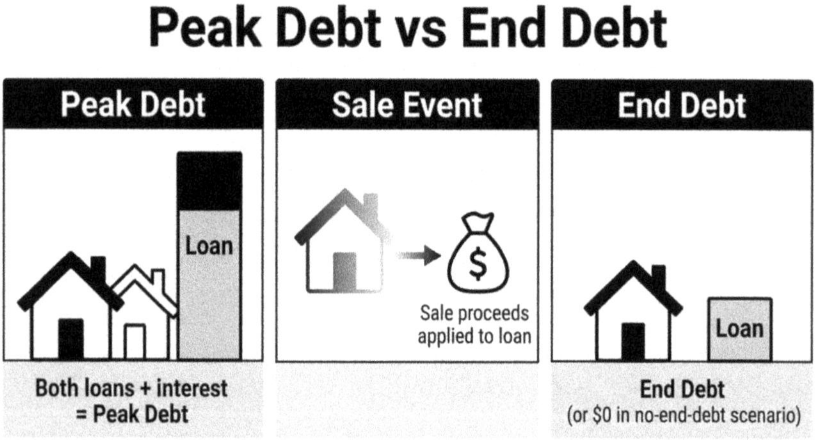

Lenders assess risk at peak debt, not just at the end position.

However, once a transaction moves outside this framework, limitations begin to emerge. The relatively short bridging period can create pressure in slower market conditions or where the property being sold is more specialised. Construction introduces additional uncertainty, and almost all lenders impose strict conditions or decline such scenarios altogether. Age-related considerations can also be a factor, particularly for borrowers approaching or already in retirement, even if their intention is to have no residual debt after the sale.

Traditional lenders (the only one that offers bridging) also favour owner-occupied scenarios. Bridging involving commercial property, vacant land, or purely investment-driven strategies is often restricted or excluded. In many cases, borrowers are required to have already listed their property for sale or even to have secured a contract before the bridging facility is approved. Valuations are often treated conservatively, with internal buffers applied to reduce effective lending capacity. While servicing is assessed on the end debt, applying strict assessment rates and living expense assumptions can make approval difficult for borrowers with non-standard income profiles.

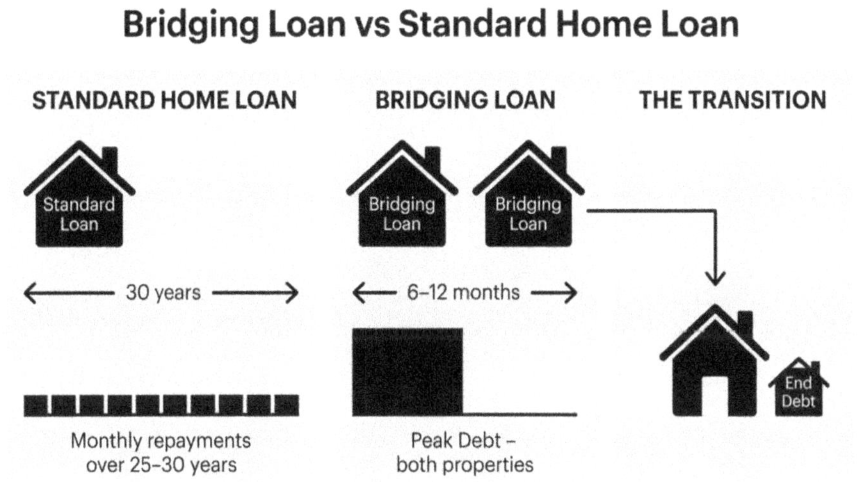

These constraints reflect the broader commercial reality of banking. Banks are structured to generate long-term income through sustained lending relationships. A standard home loan provides predictable repayments over decades, allowing the lender to recover costs, generate margin, and build a relationship with the borrower, albeit superficially. Bridging finance, particularly where there is no end date for the debt, does not align with this model.

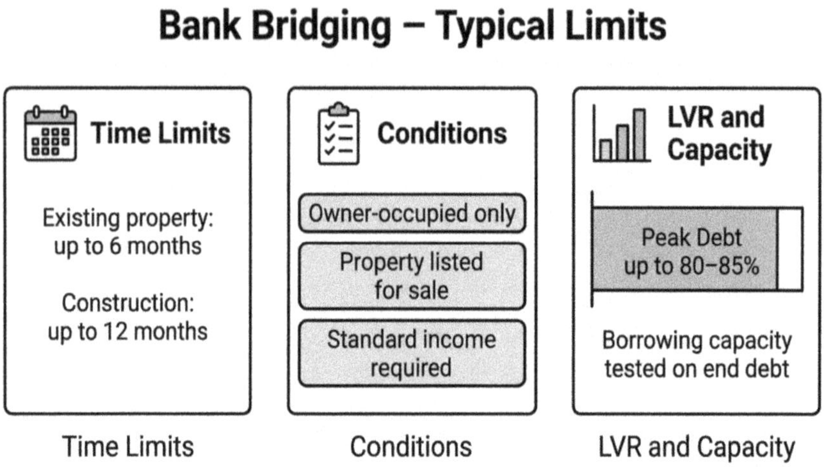

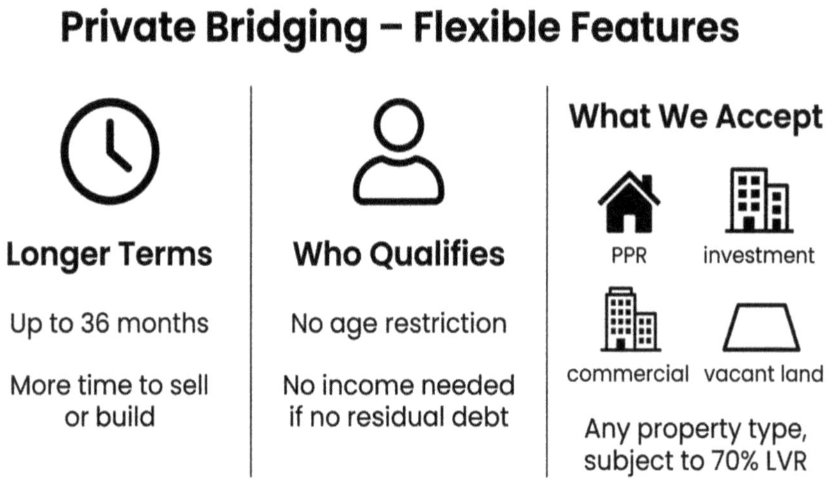

Where a bridging loan is repaid in full within a short period, the lender receives limited interest income and does not establish an ongoing relationship. The administrative effort required to originate and manage the loan remains substantial, but the financial return is constrained by the short duration. As a result, such transactions may be viewed as commercially inefficient, even if they are relatively low risk from a borrower's perspective.

This explains why only one traditional lender actively offers bridging finance and why they may be unwilling to engage in scenarios with no residual debt. The issue is not simply one of risk, but of alignment with the lender's business model.

Private lenders operate under a different set of assumptions. Their model is built around short-term lending, where capital is deployed for a defined period and then returned. They do not rely on long-term income streams or ongoing customer relationships in the same way that banks do. Instead, they focus on the quality of the asset, the strength of the borrower's equity position, and the credibility of the exit strategy.

This approach allows for a much greater degree of flexibility. Bridging facilities may extend up to thirty-six months, providing borrowers with additional time to complete construction, manage renovations, or achieve an optimal sale outcome. Sale contracts are not required at the outset, allowing borrowers to structure their transactions without being forced into premature commitments. Age is not treated as a limiting factor, enabling older borrowers to access bridging finance where traditional lenders may be unable to assist.

Full-Doc vs Low-Doc Bridging

Full-Doc (Bank)	Low-Doc (Private)
Tax returns	Accountant declaration (investment)
Payslips	BAS statements (owner-occ)
Detailed expenses	No income if no residual debt
Strict serviceability test	Servicing only on final debt

Both options still assess equity and exit strategy

One of the most significant differences lies in how income is treated. Where there is no residual debt, private lenders will not require income verification at all. The focus shifts entirely to the asset and the exit strategy. If the property being sold is expected to generate sufficient proceeds to repay the loan in full, the borrower's long-term income becomes irrelevant.

Security is also treated more flexibly. Private lenders may accept a wide range of property types, including commercial assets, vacant land, and investment properties, as well as owner-occupied residences. Valuations are generally taken at face value, without internal reductions, although maximum loan-to-value ratios are typically capped at around 70%. This lower LVR provides a buffer against market fluctuations and allows the lender to be more flexible in other areas.

Servicing, where applicable, is assessed only on the residual debt. This represents a fundamental shift from traditional lending, where income and affordability are central to the assessment process.

The result is a different set of incentives. Where banks may view short-term, self-liquidating loans as commercially unattractive, private lenders see them as aligned with their core business model. The absence of end debt is not a disadvantage; it is often the preferred outcome. It provides a clear and predictable exit, allowing capital to be redeployed efficiently.

Despite these advantages, bridging finance carries inherent risks regardless of the lender. The most significant risk is that the existing property does not sell within the expected timeframe or at the anticipated price. If this occurs, the borrower may be required to commence repayments on the full peak debt, which may not be sustainable. In extreme cases, this can lead to enforcement action and the forced sale of one or both properties.

Market conditions play a critical role in this risk. In strong markets, properties may sell quickly and at favourable prices. In weaker markets, sales periods may extend, and prices may be lower than expected. Borrowers must therefore approach bridging finance with realistic assumptions and a clear understanding of the potential outcomes.

Ultimately, bridging finance is not simply a loan product. It is a strategic tool that allows borrowers to navigate the timing complexities of property transactions. Its effectiveness depends on the alignment between the borrower's objectives and the lender's model. Traditional lenders provide a structured, policy-driven approach suitable for standard scenarios. Private lenders offer flexibility and adaptability in more complex situations.

Understanding this distinction allows borrowers to make informed decisions and structure their transactions to maximise the likelihood of success.

11.
Business Loans

Business Lending Secured by Property: Practical Use, Structure, and Lender Approach

Business lending occupies a distinct position within the broader lending landscape. While residential borrowing is generally assessed based on personal income and long-term servicing capacity, business lending often introduces additional variables—cash flow variability, trading history, tax position, and commercial risk. When these variables do not align neatly with conventional lending policy, the use of property—whether residential or commercial—as security becomes a central mechanism for obtaining funding.

This chapter examines how property can be used to support business lending, and how the same transaction may be treated differently depending on whether the lender is a traditional institution or a private lender. The focus is not on abstract comparison, but on the practical realities of how transactions are structured, approved, and executed.

The Role of Property in Business Lending

At its core, property-backed business lending is a reallocation of risk. Rather than relying solely on the business's performance, the lender relies on the value of the secured asset. This shifts the assessment away from speculative projections and toward something more tangible.

Where a borrower owns real property—whether a residential investment property, a principal place of residence, or a commercial asset—that property can be leveraged to obtain funds for business purposes. These purposes may include working capital, acquisition of a business, settlement of liabilities such as tax debts, or bridging short-term financial gaps.

The key distinction is that the loan is not advanced solely on the strength of the business. It is advanced because the property provides a level of security that supports the transaction.

Traditional Lending Constraints in Business Contexts

Traditional lenders approach business lending through a structured and policy-driven framework. This typically requires:

- Verified income, often through financial statements or tax returns
- Evidence of trading history, commonly a minimum of two years

- A registered and active business structure (such as an ABN)
- Demonstrated capacity to service the loan over time

Where these elements are present and stable, traditional lending can offer competitive rates and long-term funding solutions. However, where any of these elements are absent or insufficient, the transaction may not proceed.

In practical terms, this means that scenarios such as:

- A newly established business with limited trading history
- A borrower seeking to acquire a business without an existing ABN
- A requirement for funds to pay a tax liability
- A need for working capital without clear income evidence

may fall outside standard lending policy. This is not a reflection of the borrower's overall position, but rather the limitations of a system designed for consistency and predictability.

Private Lending as a Property-Based Alternative

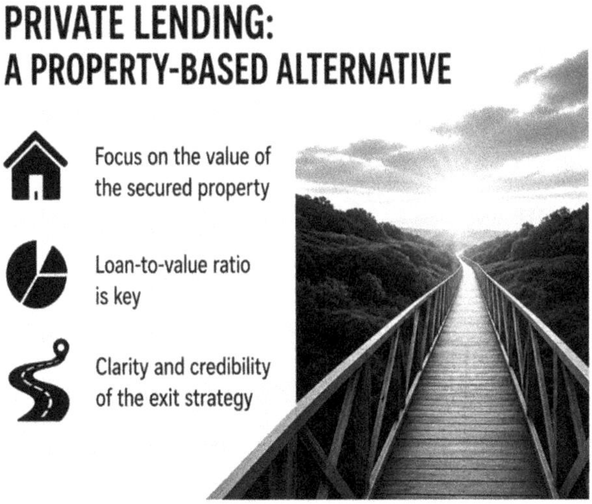

Private lending addresses these same scenarios through a different framework. Rather than requiring full alignment with income-based servicing metrics, private lenders assess the transaction primarily by reference to:

- The value of the secured property
- The loan-to-value ratio
- The clarity and credibility of the exit strategy

This allows funding to be considered in circumstances where traditional criteria are not met. Importantly, this does not imply a relaxation of standards. The assessment remains rigorous, but the focus shifts.

Where a borrower seeks funds for working capital, a tax debt, or the acquisition of a business without an established trading history, a private lender may consider the application provided that the property position supports the loan and the exit is defined.

Working Capital and Business Liquidity

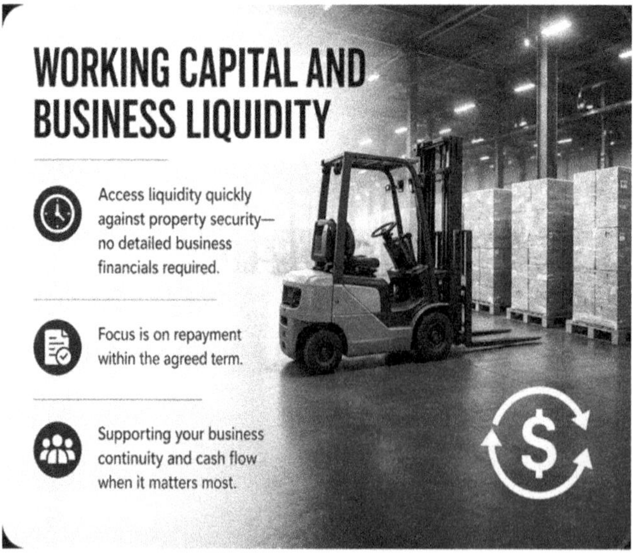

Working capital is often the most immediate need within a business. It may be required to fund operations, manage cash flow gaps, or respond to opportunities. Traditional lenders typically require evidence that the business can service additional debt, which may limit access when financials are incomplete or the business is newly established.

Private lenders, by contrast, may advance funds against property security without requiring detailed business financials, provided the loan is appropriately structured. The focus is not on the day-to-day cash flow of the business, but on whether the loan can be repaid within the agreed term.

This allows businesses to access liquidity when timing is critical and conventional pathways are unavailable.

Tax Debts and Financial Restructuring

Tax liabilities present a particular challenge in traditional lending. Many lenders are unwilling to advance funds to pay tax debts, particularly when such a liability indicates financial stress.

Private lenders approach this differently. A tax debt is treated as a liability to be resolved, rather than a barrier to lending. Where the secured property provides sufficient coverage, funds may be advanced to clear the debt, allowing the borrower to stabilise their position.

This can form part of a broader financial restructuring, with the expectation that the position will later transition into a more conventional arrangement.

Acquiring a Business Without an Established Structure

The acquisition of a business without an existing ABN or trading history is another area where traditional lending is often constrained. Without historical financials, lenders cannot apply their standard assessment models.

Private lenders, however, may consider such transactions where the property security is sufficient and the exit is clear. The absence of a trading history does not preclude lending if the repayment pathway is not dependent on long-term business performance.

This enables transactions to proceed where the opportunity exists, but the structure has not yet been formalised.

Cost Considerations: Secured vs Unsecured Business Lending

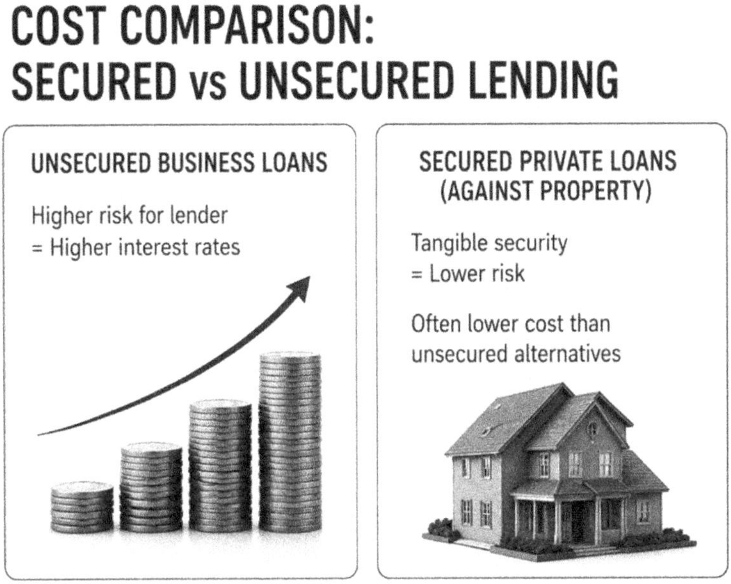

A common misconception is that private lending is invariably more expensive than traditional lending. While this may be true for long-term, fully verified residential loans, it is not necessarily the case for unsecured business lending.

Unsecured business loans often carry higher interest rates due to the lack of collateral. The lender bears greater risk, which is reflected in pricing.

By contrast, a private loan secured against property—whether residential or commercial—benefits from the presence of tangible security. This can result in pricing that is, in many cases, lower than unsecured alternatives, despite the shorter term and flexible structure.

The relevant comparison, therefore, is not between private lending and standard home loans, but between secured and unsecured business funding.

Speed of Execution and Commercial Timing

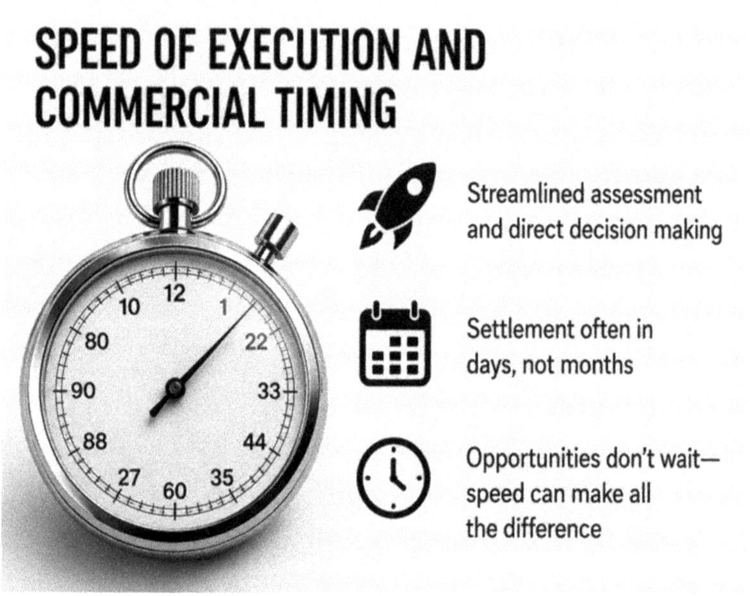

One of the most significant practical differences lies in the timeframe for approval and settlement. Traditional lenders may require extensive documentation, multiple levels of assessment, and compliance processes that extend over several weeks or months.

Private lenders, operating with a more direct assessment model, can often settle transactions within a matter of days. In some cases, funding may be available within as little as three days from formal approval.

This speed is not merely a convenience. In a business context, timing can determine whether an opportunity is realised or lost. The ability to act quickly can be critical.

Residential vs Commercial Property as Security

Both residential and commercial properties can serve as collateral for business lending. Each has its own characteristics, but the underlying principle remains the same: the property provides the foundation for the loan.

Residential property is often more readily accepted due to its broader market appeal and established valuation benchmarks. Commercial property, while equally viable, may be assessed with greater attention to tenancy, location, and use. The tenancy is often irrelevant for private lending.

Private lenders generally consider both categories, provided the loan-to-value ratio and exit strategy are appropriate.

Exit Strategy and the Absence of Servicing Requirements

Where a property—particularly an investment property—is intended to be sold as part of the exit strategy, the need to demonstrate ongoing servicing capacity may be reduced or removed entirely within a private lending framework, removed entirely when there will be no end debt.

The lender's assessment focuses on whether the sale of the property will satisfy the loan within the agreed term. If the equity position is sufficient, the borrower's income becomes less central to the decision.

This is a defining feature of property-backed private lending. It allows transactions to proceed where traditional servicing metrics are not met, provided that the exit is realistic and supported by the asset.

Transition and Refinancing

While private lending often serves as a short-term solution, it does not preclude a longer-term outcome. Once the immediate objective has been achieved—whether stabilising a business, resolving a liability, or completing an acquisition—the borrower may seek to refinance into a traditional facility.

The key factor is alignment between the transaction's initial representation and its execution. What is presented to the lender at the outset—particularly regarding the exit—will determine the loan's structure and the expectations attached to it.

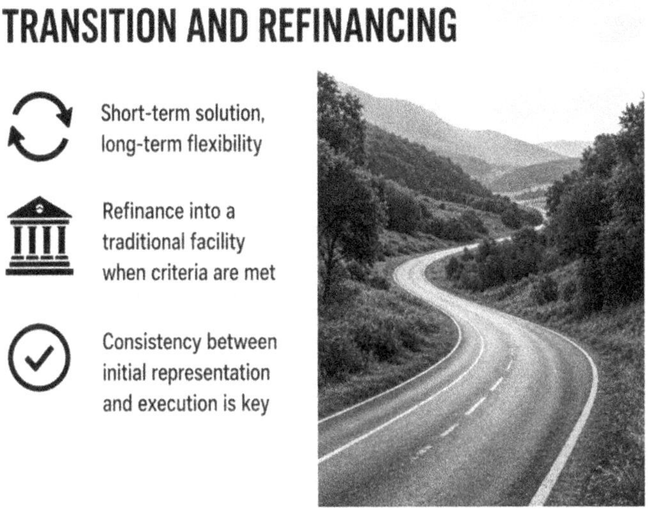

Where circumstances change, the borrower retains the ability to reassess and transition, provided the underlying position supports such a move.

Summary

Business lending secured by property provides a mechanism for obtaining funding in circumstances that fall outside conventional parameters. The distinction between private and traditional lending is not simply one of cost or preference, but of structure and assessment.

Traditional lenders prioritise income verification, trading history, and long-term servicing. Private lenders prioritise asset value, timing, and exit strategy.

When a transaction is urgent, complex, or lacks conventional income evidence, property-backed private lending offers a structured, viable option. Where stability and long-term servicing are established, traditional lending remains appropriate.

The critical point is not to view these approaches as competing, but as complementary—each suited to different stages and different circumstances within the broader business lifecycle.

12.
Accounting "The Money"

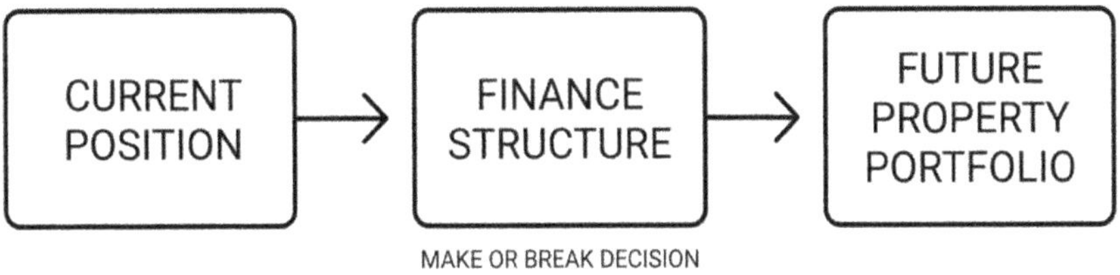

Tax laws are complicated and always changing. An accountant may address a particular issue, and then find this opens a whole 'can of worms'. For instance, you can structure the ownership to take advantage of the 'now', but where does this position put you, the taxpayer, for capital gains tax in the future? There are many 'grey areas' where the law is unclear and open to misinterpretation, and it takes knowledge and experience to make the best decision.

When entering the property investment arena, it is essential to set the correct foundations. This includes selecting good property that will appreciate in value, financing it correctly, ensuring the ownership is as advantageous as possible, and then taking advantage of every means available to make the property affordable to hold.

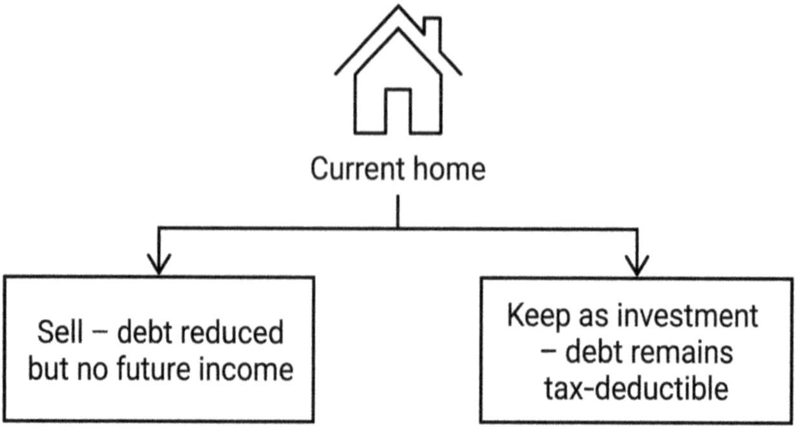

Affordability

An accountant's role is to help you look after your money: they want to minimise the holding costs of the investment and ensure the property is as affordable as possible.

First, it is essential to purchase the right property and ensure there is no likelihood of extended vacancies.

A client's financial situation should be assessed before purchasing a property. An accountant or property advisor can give an estimate of the weekly out-of-pocket cost you can expect to incur. Clients are often amazed at how affordable it can be to hold a property in their particular situation. On the other hand, it may be out of their reach at present, and they have to save or earn a little more.

It is important not to suffer from interest rate rises. Accountants and brokers can factor in scenarios of 1% or 2% interest rate increases to show the likely additional cost, bring it to your attention, and help you determine whether you can accommodate this rise.

When the investor has set their sights on a particular property and has received some detailed information, a good accountant and property advisor can provide cash flow that shows the real out-of-pocket expenses and the after-tax cost per week, not what spruikers and developers are telling you.

A combination of the correct ownership structure, financing, depreciation reports, and variations in tax instalment deductions works together to ensure that the cost of holding the property is minimised.

Some of the key areas that you can ask your accountant to address are:

Structuring
Financing
Tax Depreciation Report — existing property versus new property
Tax instalment deduction variation

Structuring

Establishing the correct foundation through structuring is vital, and it is very important to receive sound advice from an expert in this field—not a mate, some random person at the pub, or the real estate agent.

Generally, the capital gains, losses on sale, and profits and losses incurred each year must be apportioned according to the ownership on the title, not who is on the loan.

There is no one ideal structure for holding investment property, but it is important to take into account the personal goals, work goals, and how long the property is likely to be held for. If a couple is purchasing the property, is one party likely to cease work in the short term or return to work? What are the projected incomes?

Does the client wish to build a property portfolio? Are the properties likely to become positively geared within the next few years, or is the investor in a position to positively gear some property?

What about asset protection? Maybe one of the parties owns a business, and it is important not to have valuable assets in their name.

Ownership as an Individual or a Partnership

If a couple purchases a property under joint ownership, the ownership defaults to 50:50.

However, if two or more people are purchasing a property and wish to vary the ownership to suit their situation, the property may need to be purchased as 'tenants in common'. This not only allows flexibility in ownership percentages but also allows each party to will their share of the property to a beneficiary of their choice, which is not the case with joint ownership.

If the property is expected to be negatively geared for a number of years and the negative-gearing benefits are likely to be substantial, it makes sense for the higher-income earner to own more of the asset and offset the tax deduction against their higher income.

A disadvantage of this strategy is that if the asset becomes positively geared or is sold, any net profit or capital gain will be taxed at the individual's high marginal tax rate.

Company or Trust

A significant disadvantage of holding a negatively geared property in a company or trust is that excess losses are 'trapped' in the company or trust. They cannot be used to offset the investor's taxable income with the intention to deliver an attractive refund to assist with the costs of holding the property.

The losses are carried forward in the trust and can be used to offset future profits generated in the company or trust. However, these losses do not offset future capital gains, much to the disappointment of many investors. Capital gains can only be offset by capital losses.

Accountants may generally advise against using a company to hold an investment property. A company could be used to hold a property if it is positively geared and the investor wishes to use the lower company tax rate or help with asset protection.

However, a company does not provide the same level of asset protection as a discretionary trust because the shares a taxpayer owns can be sold to satisfy the taxpayer's debts.

The most significant disadvantage of holding property in a company is that it is not eligible for the 50% discount on capital gains that an individual taxpayer is. Being unable to access the CGT discount is a disincentive to holding assets in companies.

A discretionary trust, however, provides superior asset protection because even if an individual taxpayer is bankrupted, the assets in the trust may be protected, as the individual owns no interest in a discretionary trust.

A discretionary trust can be used to distribute capital gains to beneficiaries in an effective manner, and the individual beneficiary is also able to obtain a 50% discount on capital gains tax in their own individual returns.

Tax Depreciation Report

Investors who purchased a property built after 16 September 1987 are entitled to claim a 2.5% depreciation rate on the building's cost. This claim for construction costs can make a property much more affordable for the investor, as a significant deduction can be claimed without requiring a cash outlay.

There is an important but often overlooked point: the 2.5% building write-off reduces the property's cost base and will increase capital gains tax when you sell it. However, it can be twice as effective to claim the 2.5% deduction due to the 50% capital gains tax discount.

It can work well for an investor with a high income to provide a tax deduction, even more so if they don't plan to sell the property until they retire or until their income reduces.

As mentioned earlier, you can obtain this report from a quantity surveyor for approximately $600 to $700. This cost is likely covered in the first year through tax savings, and the report's cost is also tax-deductible.

Federal Budget announcement: There are some proposed changes to negative gearing and capital gains tax that may affect borrowers.

Properties held before **7:30 pm AEST on 12 May 2026** will be exempt from the negative gearing changes, and the CGT reforms will only apply to gains accruing after **1 July 2027**.

From what has been announced, the proposed changes would limit negative gearing for established residential properties, replace the current 50% CGT discount with a cost-base indexation model, and introduce a 30% minimum tax on real capital gains. However, new builds are exempt from these changes and are expected to receive favourable treatment under the proposed rules.

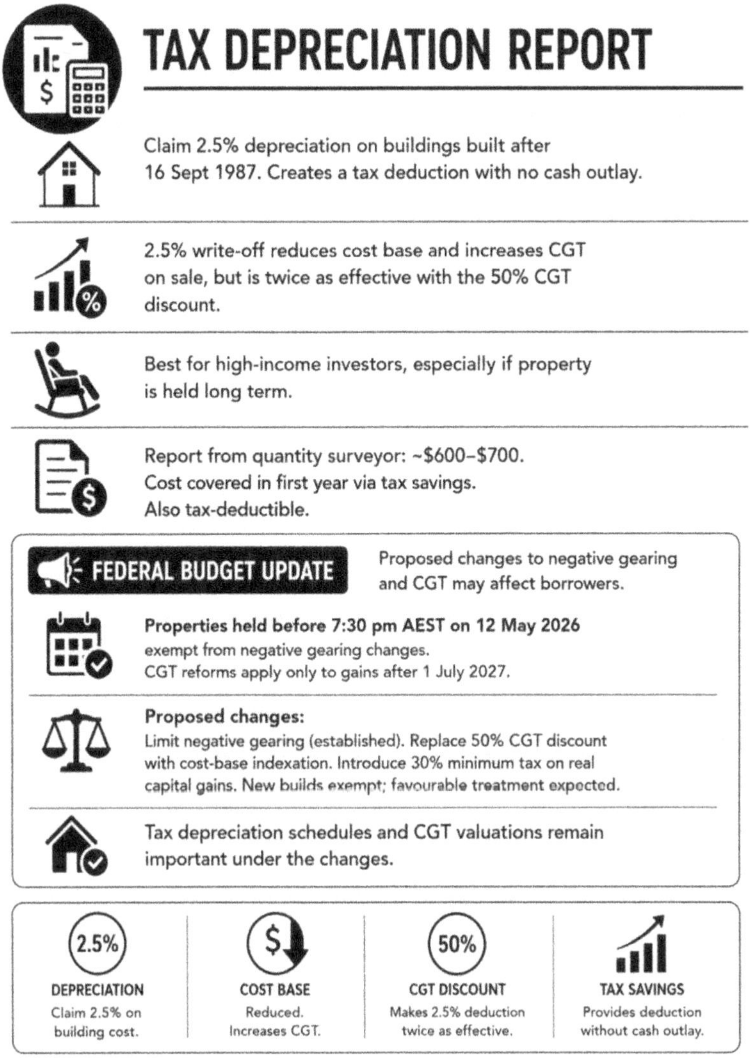

Potential Negative Gearing Changes and the Likely Shift Toward New Housing

The proposed Federal Budget changes to negative gearing and capital gains tax have the potential to significantly reshape Australian property investment behaviour, particularly if tax benefits become largely restricted to newly constructed housing. While the proposals are still subject to political and legislative processes, the direction under discussion may create unintended consequences for both investors and first-home buyers, especially in outer-suburban growth corridors, where affordable new housing is most commonly located.

Under the proposals announced, established residential properties purchased after the nominated date may no longer attract the same negative gearing benefits currently available to investors. At the same time, the existing 50% capital gains tax discount may be replaced with a cost-base indexation model, alongside a proposed minimum tax on real capital gains. Importantly, newly constructed properties appear likely to retain more favourable tax treatment, including continued access to negative gearing benefits.

At first glance, the policy objective appears straightforward: encourage investment into housing supply rather than established dwellings. In theory, directing investors toward new construction may increase housing stock and stimulate the construction sector. However, the practical market consequences may be far more complex.

One of the most obvious outcomes may be a substantial increase in investor demand for new properties. Investors are highly responsive to tax incentives, particularly when negative gearing benefits improve cash flow and reduce taxable income. If tax advantages become largely restricted to new dwellings, many investors may simply redirect their purchasing activity away from established homes and toward house-and-land packages, apartments, and new developments.

The issue is that these are often the same properties that first-home buyers' target.

In many Australian cities, particularly Melbourne, Brisbane, and Perth, and in parts of Sydney's outer suburbs, newly built homes in developing estates are frequently more affordable than established homes closer to the CBD. First home buyers often gravitate toward these outer suburban locations because they offer lower entry prices, government grants, and modern housing stock. These markets are already heavily reliant on demand from younger owner-occupiers entering the property market for the first time.

If investors suddenly receive preferential tax treatment for purchasing these same properties, competition in these markets may intensify significantly. Investors generally possess stronger borrowing power than many first home buyers because they may already own property, have existing equity, higher incomes, or broader access to lending solutions. As investor demand increases, property prices in these outer suburban growth areas may rise accordingly.

This creates what many critics would describe as a policy contradiction. A scheme intended to improve housing affordability may instead place additional pressure on the very segment of the market that first-home buyers rely on most.

There is also the risk that developers and builders respond by pricing new housing stock more aggressively once they recognise investors are being funnelled toward these properties for taxation reasons. Historically, government incentives tied to particular property segments have often resulted in at least part of the benefit being absorbed into higher sale prices rather than benefiting purchasers in full.

Another issue is that not all new properties perform equally well from an investment perspective. Investors chasing tax benefits may overlook fundamental investment considerations, including location quality, infrastructure, rental demand, oversupply risks, and long-term capital growth potential. Australia has previously seen examples of heavily marketed investor-focused apartment developments underperforming due to oversupply and inflated pricing.

One area likely to become even more important under these proposed changes is the use of tax depreciation schedules and capital gains tax valuations. Although treated differently by the Australian Taxation Office, both become increasingly significant where taxation outcomes are more closely scrutinised. Depreciation schedules remain highly valuable for new properties because construction cost write-offs and plant and equipment deductions may materially improve after-tax cash flow outcomes for investors. Similarly, accurate CGT valuations become critical where different taxation rules apply to gains accruing before and after legislative commencement dates.

The proposals may also create a two-tier property market, where established dwellings become less attractive to investors while new properties receive disproportionately strong demand. Over time, this may distort pricing behaviour across different market segments and potentially reduce liquidity in some established housing markets.

Ultimately, while encouraging new housing construction is a reasonable policy objective, restricting negative gearing primarily to new properties may create substantial unintended consequences. Investors are likely to follow tax incentives, and if this leads to increased competition for affordable new housing stock, first home buyers may find themselves competing even more aggressively against seasoned investors in the outer suburban markets they traditionally rely on to enter the property market.

Tax Instalment Deduction Form (TID)

Instead of waiting for the nice big refund when the tax return is lodged at the end of the financial year, the tax office can allow the investor to submit a 'tax variation form', which authorises an employer to deduct a reduced amount of tax from the employee's regular pay. This gives the investor extra money in their pocket throughout the year; do remember that the year-end refund will be reduced.

So, instead of waiting for a refund cheque of, say, $5000 after 30 June, the investor can receive an extra $100 or so per week in their pay packet throughout the year. The Australian Tax Office (ATO) doesn't pay interest on delayed refunds, so it is better for the taxpayer to have the money working to earn interest throughout the year.

It is important to stress that care is needed when lodging a TID variation. It is a provisional tax return based on estimates for the upcoming financial year. It is important to err on the side of conservatism when calculating expenses, rather than finding that not enough tax has been paid throughout the year.

What Expenses Can Be Claimed?

Typically, there are four categories that accountants work with.

Is the expense not deductible because it is private in nature? (e.g. holiday house)

Can an immediate deduction be claimed in this year?

Does the expense need to be claimed over a number of years? (i.e. depreciation of fixtures & fittings). Can it be?

Does the expense need to be included in the capital cost?

If so, is it part of the building and therefore can be written off at 2.5% pa?

Is it not part of the building (e.g. landscaping) and can only be included in the capital cost written off over a different time frame?

Not Deductible

If an investment property is not earning rental income, then expenses cannot be deducted. For instance, expenses on a vacant block of land need to be capitalised and included in the cost base for the capital gains tax calculation, unless the property is earning, for example, agistment income.

If a holiday home is let for part of the year, then expenses must be apportioned between the rental period and private use.

Immediate Deductions

To claim these expenses, the property must be available for rent. The borrower would need to show that the property is listed for rent with an agent and that the requested rent is consistent with the market. This list is not exhaustive but outlines the typical deductions that can be claimed in the annual rental property return.

Further information for items marked with an asterisk (*) is provided below this list.

Council and water rates

Insurance, such as building and contents, and public liability

Land tax

Repairs and maintenance *

Gardening and lawn mowing

Interest on loans *

Agents' fees and commissions

Body corporate fees *

Advertising for tenants

Travel to collect rent, inspect or maintain the property *

Stationery, telephone and postage

Legal expenses (incurred in relation to tenant, not acquisition or disposal)

Borrowing expenses*

Repairs and Maintenance

The deductibility of repairs and maintenance can be a grey area. For instance, painting is normally considered maintenance and is fully deductible in the year the expense is incurred. However, if the home was newly acquired and needed to be painted at that time, the painting is considered part of 'initial repairs' and forms part of the capital cost. Judgment is required to determine at which point the painting is no longer classified as 'initial repairs'.

Repairs generally relate directly to wear and tear or other damage that occurred as a result of renting out the property. For example, if tenants have damaged the property in the early years, then painting becomes a repair. If this occurs, please take photos as evidence of any damage caused by tenants.

However, if you are planning to rent out your main residence, or even a property you have inherited, and painting is needed to get the property ready for rental, the painting may be eligible for the first-year claim.

Interest on Loans

Should a loan be taken out to purchase a rental property, the interest charged on that loan can be claimed as a deduction. However, the property must be rented, or available for rental, in the income year for which you claim a deduction. If not, then the income is not deductible or must be apportioned.

If you choose a line of credit to finance your property purchase, we recommend that you not use the loan for private purposes. If there is a fluctuating balance due to a variety of deposits and withdrawals, and it is used for both private purposes and rental property purposes, it can quickly diminish the amount of interest that can be claimed as a tax deduction. Calculating interest that can be included in rental deductions is also quite involved and time-consuming.

Travel to Collect Rent, Inspect or Maintain the Property

There is a misconception that you are allowed two trips to inspect a property per year. This may have arisen from the belief that it is reasonable from the tax department's perspective. However, claiming two interstate trips per annum to 'inspect rental properties' is likely to be considered very unusual.

On the other hand, if you have decided to collect the rent yourself or handle the garden maintenance for your property, then twelve visits per year (monthly visits) would be reasonable.

With interstate property, if you fly to inspect the property, stay overnight, and return home the following day, the airfare and accommodation expenses would be allowed, provided the whole purpose of the trip was to inspect the rental property.

However, if the trip is combined with a holiday, the expenses may need to be apportioned, taking into account the main purpose of the trip. Was the holiday incidental to the trip, or was the inspection of the property incidental to the trip?

Body corporate fees covering general maintenance and administration are deductible in the year incurred, but if funds are set aside in a special purpose fund and used for capital expenditure, the expense must be capitalised.

Expenses Deductible Over a Number of Income Years

There are three types of expenses you may incur for your rental property that may be claimed over a number of income years:

- Borrowing expenses
- Amounts for the decline in value of eligible depreciating assets
- Capital works deductions.

Borrowing Expenses

These are expenses directly incurred in taking out a loan. If total expenses are less than $100, the expense can be written off in the same year, the expenses are claimed over a period of five years or the period of the loan.

Decline in the Value of Depreciating Assets

Depreciating assets are generally items that can be easily removed and replaced and are not part of the building structure. For example, a free-standing bookcase can be depreciated at the higher depreciation rates, but a built-in bookshelf must be claimed at just 2.5% as part of the cost of construction or special building write-off.

The types of fixtures and fittings (plant and equipment) that the tax office allows you to claim deductions for include stoves, dishwashers, curtains, heaters, air conditioners, and carpet. Depreciation rates typically range from 10% to 25% of the cost per item; this can be claimed annually. If items are less than $ 1,000 in value, they can be added to a 'low value pool' and written off at 18.75% in the first year and 37.5% thereafter.

Plant and equipment costing less than $300 per owner can be written off each year. For example, for joint owners, items under $600 can be written off, as the cost is split between the owners, resulting in $300 each.

Capital Costs

I referred earlier to gaining a building surveyor's report, and it is in this that the capital cost of constructing the building can be written off at 2.5% for normal residential property over the next forty years. This applies to property built after 16 September 1987 and is often referred to as 'special building write-off'.

It is calculated based on the original cost of constructing the building, plus the original cost of improvements. It has nothing to do with the purchase price of the home.

Until May 1997, this building write-off was of significant benefit because the capital cost claimed did not reduce the building's cost base, and therefore the capital gain was not increased. However, the building write-off for properties built after this date reduces the property's original cost, thereby increasing the capital gain.

Capital Gains Tax

If you acquired a property after 19 September 1985, you may make a capital gain or capital loss when you sell the property or your share in the property.

You will make a capital gain from the sale of your rental property to the extent that the capital proceeds received are more than the cost base of the property. You will make a capital loss to the extent that the property's reduced cost base exceeds those capital proceeds. If you are a co-owner of an investment property, you will make a capital gain or loss according to your ownership interest in the property.

The cost base and reduced cost base of a property include the amount you paid for it together with certain incidental costs associated with acquiring, holding, and disposing of it (for example, legal fees, stamp duty, and real estate agent's commissions). Certain amounts that you have deducted or which you can deduct are excluded from the property's cost base or reduced cost base.

You may then qualify for a 50% discount on the capital gain, provided you hold the property for more than twelve months.

Your capital gain or capital loss may be disregarded if a rollover applies (e.g. if your property was destroyed or compulsorily acquired, or you transferred it to your former spouse under a court order following the breakdown of your marriage)

Often, investors become very worried about capital gains tax; keep in mind that because of the 50% discount, you will generally not pay more than 15% tax on your gain. This means that you can keep up to 85% of the gain.

What Do You Give Your Accountant at Tax Time?

Your investment property should be a passive investment (one that takes very little of your time) that makes money for you without being a burden. If you get your real estate agent to pay for everything, it will minimise your workload. If you have to pay for something yourself, please keep a record and take it to your accountant at tax time. The accountant does not need the receipt, but it is important that you keep it.

In the first year of purchase, you need to bring the following with you:

1. Quantity surveyor's depreciation report (if relevant)
2. The conveyancing settlement letter and notice of adjustments
3. Real estate rental property summary
4. Bank statements for the loan
5. Summarise extra payments made that were excluded from the statement from the real estate agent. It is important to never throw away receipts, even after 5 years, as they are essential in the event of an ATO audit and to assist with calculating capital gains in the future.

In your second year, and all subsequent years, you must bring everything included in the above list, except for items (a) and (b).

It is always wise to seek advice. Also, seek advice on all the previously mentioned points; this is not a substitute for advice, and as the law can change, the information herein can change.

13.

Loans for Different Property Types and Structures

There are so many scenarios that people find themselves in. Properties they are interested in buying, and often confusion surrounds what the perfect type of loan is. Everyone is different, and one loan does not fit all. This chapter should make it easier for you to understand what may be more suitable or in fact, unsuitable and hazardous for your needs.

Owner-Builder Loans/Incomplete Dwellings

Some people still think they can and should get a loan to build their own dwelling on their land. The reality is that, whether the individual is a builder or not, more emotion is involved when it's your own home. Cost overruns are common due to changes, upgrades, and so on. Traditional lenders do not want to be stuck with a block of land with an incomplete, unmarketable structure. This is why lenders, on the whole, tend to avoid owner-builder loans. This type of loan is the bread-and-butter type of lending for a private lender and is relatively easy to finance.

Incomplete Construction

Incomplete construction on a property is common. The builder has run out of money, or the borrower no longer likes the builder they engaged; maybe it's a purchase where it was an owner-builder situation, and the owner ran out of money, and the purchaser can make some money. Finally, there may be a fixed-price contract, but before finance is approved, the borrower decides to have the builder commence construction and pay the first couple of invoices themselves, then ask the lender to take over when the finance is approved. No matter how you slice it, traditional lenders hate these things. Private lenders offer financing for these situations regularly.

Lenders like to manage the construction process and arrange for valuations to be undertaken at different stages; for example, at the frame stage and the certificate of occupancy issuance stage. It gives the lender greater confidence that an acceptable standard of work is being complied with. In rare cases, if the borrower already owns the land (not purchasing it) and has engaged a builder to commence construction, private lenders may consider funding the remainder of the construction.

Kit/Modular and Transportable Homes

This type of dwelling is constructed in a and then transported to the land where it will be connected to services such as water and electricity. Again, there is always a lender out there who may consider this. Most lenders don't like it because the dwelling isn't being built on the land. Lenders do not like to blindly trust or rely on the authenticity or solvency of the firms that build these types of properties. There are too many examples where the dwelling never made it to the land, or the firm ended up in administration. Consider if it is on the way to the borrower's land, and the truck driver crashes, and is discovered to be under the influence of drugs or alcohol, it's unlikely the dwelling will be insured. Lenders will more likely lend against these once the dwelling is on the land and all services are connected. Private lenders may consider this if they fund only the construction drawdowns once the dwelling is on the land, albeit as a shell.

KIT/MODULAR AND TRANSPORTABLE HOMES

This type of dwelling is constructed in a factory and then transported to the land where it will be connected to services such as water and electricity.

Most lenders don't like it because the dwelling isn't being built on the land. Lenders do not like to blindly trust or rely on the authenticity or solvency of the firms that build these types of properties.

There are too many examples where the dwelling never made it to the land, or the firm ended up in administration.

Lenders will more likely lend against these once the dwelling is on the land and all services are connected.

Private lenders may consider this if they fund only the construction drawdowns once the dwelling is on the land, albeit as a shell.

Tiny Homes

Tiny homes in Australia — practical overview

Tiny homes can be a good option, to save money on building a normal home. Perhaps they can be put onto a parent's property as well, if they have sufficient land, saving the first home buyer the cost of buying land, but they are not as simple as "buy it, park it, live in it". The key issue is whether it is treated as a dwelling, caravan/moveable dwelling, small second dwelling, granny flat, studio, or temporary structure. That classification affects council approval, insurance, finance, resale value and whether someone can lawfully live in it full-time.

Where to buy

You can buy through Australian tiny-home builders, modular-home companies, portable-cabin suppliers, caravan-style tiny-home builders, or flat-pack/pod retailers. Prices may range from $26,000 (studio/pod style and may not be complete lawful residences) to $200,000+ as a general range as at 2026.

A practical Australian budget is usually:

Basic pod/studio: about **$26,000–$60,000,** but often not a complete home.

Tiny house on wheels: often **$75,000–$160,000+**.

Premium turn-key tiny home: roughly **$150,000–$200,000+.**

Modular granny flat/small dwelling: can start around

$150,000–$170,000+, often more once site works are included.

Add delivery, crane, footings, plumbing, electrical connection, water tanks, septic, solar, decks, permits, BAL/fire requirements, engineering, insurance and council costs. The cheap sticker price is rarely the final cost.

Approvals and where you can put one

In Victoria, a small second home can be easier to approve because planning changes from December 2023 allow some small second dwellings without a planning permit, but a building permit is still required (why? councils need something to do, they love red tape, no wonder there is a housing supply shortage), and the dwelling generally cannot be separately subdivided or sold from the main home.

For tiny homes on wheels, the position is more complicated. Some seller's market them as "caravans", but councils may still regulate use, health, safety, waste, setbacks and long-term occupation. One Council states that tiny houses in Victoria are not automatically exempt from planning or building controls merely because they are small or moveable.

In Queensland, the State planning guidance says temporary tiny homes may not need planning approval or Building Code approval, but a tiny home without proper dwelling approvals is not suitable for permanent living.

In NSW, moveable dwellings, caravans, manufactured homes and caravan parks are governed by specific local government regulation, and councils may still have a role even where the structure is on wheels.

Finance issues

Finance is often harder than buyers expect. A normal home loan usually needs land and a fixed dwelling that gives the bank acceptable mortgage security. A tiny home on wheels may be treated more like a caravan, vehicle, personal asset or chattel, so finance may come through a personal loan, asset finance, chattel mortgage, business loan, or equity release against existing property. Personal-loan style tiny-home finance is marketed in Australia, but loan amounts and terms may be lower than a normal mortgage.

If the tiny home is for business use, such as farm stay, Airbnb, worker accommodation or tourism, a chattel mortgage or business loan may be possible. Current chattel mortgage rate guides show broad ranges, with some starting around circa 1% p.a. higher than a mortgage rate, with higher-risk borrowers paying much more. A private lender is more likely to be more helpful in my experience, than a traditional lender.

Main things to check before buying

Check the council position before paying a deposit. Ask whether the home can be lived in full-time, whether it needs a planning permit, building permit, occupancy certificate, septic approval, driveway approval, bushfire report, or connection approval.

Check whether the builder provides engineering certificates, road registration details, warranties, insurance certificates, weight certificates and Australian compliance documents. A tiny home on wheels should usually stay within road limits such as about 2.5 m wide, 4.3 m high and 12.5 m long, unless special transport permits are used.

Also check insurance. Unapproved structures can create major problems, including fines, demolition orders and denied insurance claims. Recent reporting has highlighted that illegal or unapproved structures can cause serious financial exposure for owners and buyers.

Best buying strategy

For personal living, the safest pathway is usually a council-compliant small second dwelling/granny flat/modular dwelling on land already owned by the family. Why? Councils often create enough headaches as it is, why give yourself a migraine (worse than a headache) which you will risk in dealing with council with anything involving thinking outside the square.

For lower cost and flexibility, a tiny home on wheels may work, but only if council use, insurance, waste, access and finance are checked first.

For investment, the numbers can work in tourist locations, but approvals, short-stay rules, cleaning, management, insurance and tax need to be priced in.

The biggest mistake is buying the tiny home first and looking for land later. The better order is: land/use approval first, then finance approval, then builder contract, then delivery and connection costs.

Acreage, Farms, Hobby Farms, Rural Zoned Properties, Environmental zoning, Green wedge

A private lender can often consider these. Traditional lenders don't like someone running their business from the property because, if they ever had to repossess, they would not only take the property away from the borrower but also negatively impact the borrower's income by removing the location from which the income is generated. Normally, for traditional lenders, up to 25 acres with a dwelling on the land is the maximum size; some lenders go into the 100s of acres. No vineyards, manufacturing facilities, or commercial offices should be on the property.

With rural properties, traditional lenders have issues with unpaved roads leading to the property or with no council-supplied electricity or water connected to it. Private lenders can consider this.

Display Homes

It is not unusual for a builder to construct a home for advertising/ display purposes and subsequently offer the home for sale to a property investor on a leaseback arrangement, often at above market rental rates.

In some cases, Genworth LMI and traditional lenders will consider this as a standard situation. Bear in mind that builders often offer rental guarantees on these properties, and on 'off-the-plan' sometimes. Remember: this is almost always built into the price, and it is not a free handout. Lenders will not use a rental guarantee. They will use market rent for servicing the debt. The reason is that the guarantee may run for only typically 2 years, if after that time the loan will not service, based on the applicant's income or be affordable to the borrower according to the borrowing/servicing capacity calculator, then it would be irresponsible of the lender to have provided the loan, and irresponsible for the borrower to apply for the loan in the first place for that matter. Private lenders usually have no issue.

LMI rules do change slightly if the display home is in an 'exhibition village' with an active life of being a display home for more than 6 months. The lender may not use the rental income at all.

Private lenders often have no problem for these.

DISPLAY HOMES

It is not unusual for a builder to construct a home for advertising/ display purposes and subsequently offer the home for sale to a property investor on a leaseback arrangement, often at above market rental rates.

In some cases, Genworth LMI and traditional lenders will consider this as a standard situation. Bear in mind that builders often offer rental guarantees on these properties, and on 'off-the-plan' sometimes. Remember: this is almost always built into the price, and it is not a free handout. Lenders will not use a rental guarantee. They will use market rent for servicing the debt. The reason is that the guarantee may run for only typically 2 years, if after that time the loan will not service, based on the applicant's income or be affordable to the borrower according to the borrowing/servicing capacity calculator, then it would be irresponsible of the lender to have provided the loan, and **irresponsible** for the borrower to apply for the loan in the first place for that matter. Private lenders usually have no issue.

Lenders will not use a rental guarantee. They will use market rent for servicing the debt because rental guarantees are time-limited (typically 2 years) and may not be reliable for the full loan term.

LMI rules do change slightly if the display home is in an **'exhibition village'** with an active life of being a display home for **more than 6 months.** The lender may not use the rental income at all.

Multiple Dwellings on One Title

These are becoming more common in the Australian landscape. A house is knocked down on a 600 sqm block of land in suburbia, then a couple, many units, or townhouses are built on the land, subdivided, and sold off, often for much more than the original cost of the land.

Traditional lenders will typically lend on these scenarios if there are two dwellings on one land title. More than two, and traditional lenders start requiring pre-sales, and they label it commercial, when it is not commercial. Traditional lenders prefer not to lend to developers on a residential lending basis.

The borrower may incur a valuation expense, which may be $1500–2000; the valuation can often be based on the land value (pre-subdivision) plus the fixed-priced building contract, plus 'post-subdivision' combined land values. A traditional lender may not use the end value; they may just use land plus build. The weak argument here is that it is speculative, as any valuation is not based on the current state, but rather the future state; there may be no guarantee the land ends up subdivided (i.e. application submitted to council, council approval provided, then new titles registered at the titles office), and so the loan ends up being too high based on the LVR.

With private lenders, the end value can be used, providing much more lending capacity.

Serviced Apartments and Student Accommodation

There are many strategies available for investors. Some strategies can be considered opportunities and generate strong cash flow or capital growth, while others can be detrimental to an investor's property objectives. Student accommodation and serviced apartments are considered by many to fall into the latter category of challenging investments.

Consideration 1: Banks generally do not lend more than 60% of the value of either type of property as debt. The underlying reason is it is considered one of the riskiest residential investment property decisions that an investor can make, and traditional lenders don't wish to expose themselves to such risk. Private lenders are more flexible.

Consideration 2: As lenders generally consider only 60% LVR (loan-to-value ratio), with a rare exception of 70% LVR, an investor must contribute 40% plus costs to the deal. This is a waste of equity/ cash. These monies could have been allocated to other investment properties with greater capital growth potential.

For example (excluding costs and lenders' mortgage insurance): an 800K serviced apartment with a 60% LVR loan would require the investor to contribute 320K. Consider a normal residential investment property type, assuming a 90% LVR, the borrower would only need to contribute 80K toward the 800K purchase, plus stamp duty. The difference is a large amount that could potentially be used as a deposit and cover the costs of two to three more properties, providing the investor with a portfolio much more quickly and easily than if they purchase a student accommodation property or a serviced apartment property.

Consideration 3: When the investor wishes to sell a property, there may not have been much capital growth, which is bad enough, but the resale market is considerably smaller than the normal property market. There would be far fewer buyers willing to put in 40% themselves. They would also find it difficult to obtain finance, as the original investor would have. The incoming purchaser may not be aware of private lenders either, so they will then struggle to obtain finance.

Few investors want to plough in 30–40% of their own money, and many won't have that much money anyway. So don't think about it in terms of whether you can afford to do it; think of it in terms of how many others can financially do it — the answer is not very many.

Capital growth potential for serviced apartments is limited and linked to the property's rental increases. Some serviced apartment contracts have built-in rental increases over a set period. The rental increase directly affects the capital growth. The increase is, effectively, the capital gain.

Please note that the value may not increase at the same rate or in the same time as a normal apartment. The added risks with serviced apartments, over and above those for normal apartments, are the quality of the management service provider, the use of the dwelling, whether it can be owner-occupied, and the exit strategy. They are very onerous, limiting, controlling, and expensive (more reasons lenders don't like them). Investors, depending on the type of serviced apartment provider, are required to spend $5,000 every 5 years to upgrade the internal appeal (refurbishment). What a burden!

Serviced apartments can be good cashflow vehicles on the surface, but after management fees/body corporate fees, and forced 5-yearly upgrades, the true value of the higher cashflow can be quickly eroded. It is always recommended that thorough research and due diligence regarding where they are, how many there are at that location, and their proximity to amenities be undertaken and considered. The fees can kill not only the deal but also the motivation for buying such an investment property.

Sometimes the management contract reverts to the owner after 5 to 10 years, which can eliminate the enforced requirement to refurbish (after this period), but, on the other hand, you then have to spend time and effort finding someone to manage the property on your behalf. This may prove difficult if the dwelling is in a building with other dwellings that still function as serviced apartments. The fact that the dwelling itself may have reverted to a normal apartment may not reduce the difficulty of obtaining finance, since it may still be in a building with other serviced apartments, which remains a deterrent for lenders.

Student accommodation can be a good income earner, but is often a much smaller property (usually under 50 square metres), and these property investments involve greater risk as well.

Student accommodation may have less onerous contracts, depending on where it is located. Some investors turn a house into a room-by-room lease, but structurally, the dwelling is still a suburban house. This is better than a designated student accommodation scenario, as it allows the flexibility to borrow at normal debt levels if the valuer values the dwelling before locks are fitted on each bedroom door. This way, lenders see it as a house, and are not aware, at the time of lending, that the purpose of purchasing the property may be to lease it out to students.

Furthermore, specifically designed student accommodation properties are often not in short supply — there's no uniqueness or scarcity factor to assist with capital growth. They are often the same as all of the others in the building. There's often a large supply of these and strong competition from other investors all wanting to rent them out around the same time, which forces the investor to lower the rent to attract a tenant. It's the same when selling them — you'll be competing against others — it may always be a monkey on the investor's back, a perennial hindrance to obtaining a loan, renting it out, and selling it. If someone was considered crazy to purchase a high-rise off-the-plan 55 sqm apartment, then someone doing the same (i.e., buying a high-rise, off-the-plan, small student-accommodation-type dwelling) is not only crazy but also incredibly foolish.

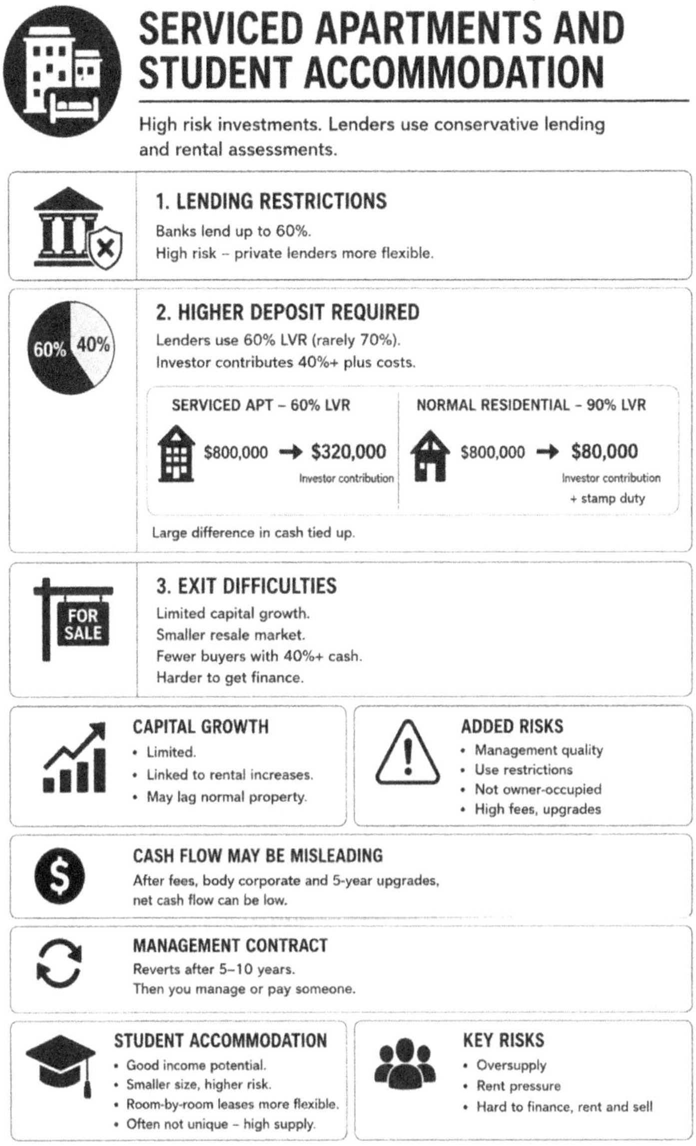

Vacant Land

Many lenders will only lend up to 90% plus LMI when there's no construction contract for land less than 5 acres. A loan increase later on can allow for construction, up to 95% LVR. Often, lenders want water and electricity to be connected to the land to make it more marketable. Private lenders are more flexible.

Off-the-Plan

If you sign an off-the-plan contract today for a property that may be 12 months (or more likely 2 to 4 years) away from being completed, you will normally put down a 10% deposit and the rest of the money when it's built. You can apply for finance when you sign the contract (i.e., now). This provides the borrower with confidence that, at that moment, there is little reason they are not eligible for finance.

The comfort gained by applying for finance now, when signing an off-the-plan contract, is unequivocally superficial, meaningless and ultimately absolutely and utterly *useless*. Beyond the borrower knowing their credit history by paying about $30 to obtain a copy of their own CRAA report, it is a waste of the lenders' and borrowers' time to apply for a loan, knowing full well that the approval will expire well *before* settlement. The approval will expire 3–6 months after it was issued.

Every off-the-plan contract contains a sunset clause, which entitles a developer to void the contract if certain milestones have not been met, such as the completion of the development. A sunset clause is a statement in the purchase contract that sets the date by which the developer must complete the project (build the apartment and have it ready for occupancy). If the apartment is not completed by this agreed-upon date, the buyer can walk away and receive their deposit back. Likewise, the developer can rescind the contract, return the buyer's deposit, and then market the property to someone else at a higher price.

Some developers in Sydney were exercising their right to void contracts that many buyers had signed 4 years earlier because prices had risen so much that they wanted to relist the same properties at 60% higher prices. Investors believe that by signing a contract 3–4 years before the apartment's completion, they can achieve significant capital growth.

The main problem is that, in addition to a finance clause that provides no protection, in a rising-rate market, what a borrower could borrow 3 years earlier can be light-years apart from what they can borrow now. There can be an oversupply of these.

Most off-the-plan properties are inner-city or in high-density buildings in good suburbs within 20 km of a CBD. These locations can have a large supply.

The other prevalent problem with off-the-plan contracts is that the chosen purchase is often part of a complex building or development zone: one of many, largely the same in design. The buyer then ends up competing against all of the other people wishing to rent them out

— with many attempting to do so at the same time.

There would also be no transparency into how many investors, versus owner-occupiers, are buying into the building.

Additionally, please keep in mind that in the future you may want to sell the property, and by then the apartments/units would have been completed, with competition from others in the same building who are trying to sell their property. This competition will then put pressure on the buyer to lower their asking price to compete with their fellow property investor neighbours, and may be forced to accept a reduction in any perceived profit.

Developers allow only 14 days for settlement once the title has been registered. If the borrower cannot obtain finance within that time, then that is unfortunate. They will start paying penalty interest. Traditional lenders can take a month to pick up an application, then an unknown amount of time to review it, and potentially an excessive amount of time to settle the loan. A private lender can provide finance in as little as 3 days. If the borrower cannot obtain finance to settle, then again, this is unfortunate; they will lose their original 10% deposit and could end up in court.

On the finance side of things, let's say for a 600K apartment: the deposit paid 3 years earlier was 60K (10%). The buyer would typically rely on the bank to provide the remaining 90% of the contract price, 600K. Now, let's say the valuation comes in at 540K, then the borrower can only borrow 90% of 540K, equalling 486 K. The bank will no longer lend 90% of 600K, so now another 60K must be paid out of the borrower's pocket. If the borrower cannot get the money, this is unfortunate again. Conversely, if the value has increased between signing the purchase contract and settling on the loan some years later, traditional lenders may typically still only use the original purchase price, not the current valuation. A private lender may typically use the valuation now to base the LVR on, which could mean potentially that the borrower could borrow more than they need, maybe to use for other things. Alternatively, they won't need to borrow as much, and so the interest rate may be lower.

With off-the-plan, it's not all bad. On the contrary, many opportunities can be had with low-density projects, with perhaps less than 20–30 in the building.

Self-Managed Super Fund (SMSF) Loans

Residential

This section is not advice, but rather designed to provide insight into how lenders treat this type of ownership structure.

Very few lenders offer these types of loans. The LVR is normally 70%, sometimes 80%. Some lenders offer an offset account. Often, all members of the SMSF must be guarantors of the loan.

While there is just one or two lenders out there who will lend on a just-completed 'off-the-plan' property or other new property, within an SMSF, most will not. One of the reasons is the involvement of a developer in the sale and a property marketing company (spruiker), with the risk that the spruiker has overcharged the person and provided advice to set up an SMSF when this advice could not legally be provided to the purchaser.

Most lenders require the SMSF to have at least 200K in the fund; many would argue that having less than 150K is unwise when setting up an SMSF (auditing fees alone would quickly erode some of the intended benefit).

Further, on a lending front, a minimum of 10% of any debt in the SMSF must remain as liquid assets, such as shares or cash, as a buffer in case the property is ever untenanted. Any equity in the property is trapped forever (until the property is sold). Lenders will not touch it, will not lend against it, will not leverage it — it's considered inaccessible and useless for any future property purchase while the property is still owned by the SMSF. Unlike a property outside an SMSF, you cannot access any of the growing equity in the property in an SMSF.

Many lenders will only lend to Australian residents, and often only to postcodes in category 1 and, in case-by-case, category 2 locations.

Category 1 locations are often considered the safest or best places to buy, such as capital cities, suburbs within a metropolitan area of a CBD, and major regional cities with frequent sales, diverse industries, and large populations.

Category 2 locations include some outer suburbs, outside the metropolitan suburbs surrounding a capital city, or a medium-sized regional town or city. Outside these categories, traditional lenders have a reduced appetite for larger loan amounts and LVRs across all loan types, not just SMSF structures.

The trustee of the bare trust and the super fund may, from a financial perspective, be either an individual or a corporate entity, depending on the funder.

Restrictions on Security

The following scenarios are unacceptable for lenders to finance: owner-occupied property, construction, second mortgages, properties over 5 hectares, and vacant land. Other problematic property types were mentioned a few pages earlier.

Credit impairment is unacceptable, as are low-documentation loans with traditional lenders. Interest rates are higher as well, roughly 1.6–2% above a standard home loan variable interest rate.

Family Pledge and Guarantor Loans

Family Pledge

A limited guarantee that helps family, but comes with legal responsibility.

This is used for the purchase or construction of a principal place of residence or, very occasionally, an investment property, whereby a relative (normally the parents) would use their property as security for the lender, in conjunction with the child purchasing the property. Normally, repayments must be principal and interest. LVR can be up to 110% of the purchase price.

Example: if purchasing a property for 600K, one can borrow 80% of the purchase price against the property and 20% plus costs against the parents' security, which is pledged. Some lenders have allowed the parents' income to assist with servicing the debt as well, but most will require that the pledge receiver be able to service the entire debt (i.e., have enough income to afford the entire loan). Naturally, the pledgee must have sufficient equity in their property to allow the pledge.

The benefits of this is that it avoids the need to have genuine savings, overcomes the fact the child has not saved or does not have the funds to complete the purchase of their first property, and best of all for some families, gets the child out of the parents' home (so parents can have the option of enjoying some personal space and the child can have their freedom). Some parents may never want their child to leave the nest, but given the choice, they would rather their child not live at home well into their late 20s or 30s if they can help it, in Australian culture anyway.

I have seen situations where cousins and other remotely related people have tried to help someone in the family, but the more distant the pledge provider is from the receiver, the more lacking in common sense it appears to be to the lender (i.e. that they would want to risk their house for the person receiving this help). It should normally be an immediate family member, such as a sibling, parent, or child, who provides the pledge.

The pledge provider is legally responsible for their portion of the debt, a limited guarantee in many circumstances. The pledge provider must be able to afford the portion of the debt against their property. Sometimes the guarantee may not be limited, in this instance, and if the child leaves the country and stops making repayments, the parents (assuming they are the guarantor) will be liable for the entire repayment on the debt, and if they cannot afford this responsibility, they can potentially risk losing their home.

Strengths that may support a family pledge loan application include: the parents are under 55 years old, have a high income, and offer an investment property to the lender as collateral instead of their own home. Any debt already against the property would need to be refinanced across to the new lender. As with most loans, where all people on title need to be applicants (and all people on title in a family pledge situation need to be guarantors), we recommend that the pledge provider seek legal and financial advice. A lender will normally provide a pro forma (a pre-prepared template) for a lawyer to sign. Bear in mind that most lawyers will advise against a family pledge, but the pro forma does not represent advice that the guarantor should enter into this situation, merely that they have sought advice.

3 popular strategies that first homebuyers use to save money, in this order, include:

1. Being frugal with household expenses
2. Cutting back on eating out, entertainment, shopping and holidays
3. Living with family

Many professionals in the property industry advise that you should carefully consider whether you should be a co-borrower or guarantor on a loan or enter into a family pledge arrangement. Liability may not be limited; the guarantor risks losing their house. However, this is becoming increasingly popular as a way for a parent to help their 20-something-year-old child get into property.

The security guarantee allows borrowers with limited deposits to enter the housing market. In this situation, a relative or friend (usually the borrower's parents) is prepared to use the equity in their home to guarantee the borrower's deposit.

If this is something you wish to consider, this section is a 'must-read'.

If a borrower wants to assist someone else, then, from a risk-mitigation point of view, they could consider applying for a loan in their own right, and apply for cash out; this way, the property is not used as a joint security with the purchase property. Additionally, going on the title of the purchase property to at least have a legal benefit to the property.

If it is just a loan against the property of the gift provider, then when the lender settles on the loan (*reminder:* 'settle' refers to you now owning the property, or in the case of a refinance, you are now officially in the loan and responsible for the repayments on it), those funds could transfer to the child being assisted. Whilst this may be far less risky than going guarantor on a loan, the odds of receiving the money back may be low, and the law of averages of receiving it back are against the gift provider. It is very emotionally difficult to commit to pursuing a family member or friend, and it can kill the relationship in doing so.

Being a guarantor is, in most instances, tantamount to being on the loan itself and exposes the guarantor to the same risks as if they were the actual borrower and owner of the property, without any financial benefit. Should repayments on the loan be defaulted on, and/or being a guarantor, **will** negatively impact the guarantor's ability to get another loan, or as large a loan as they may otherwise be eligible for.

What Is a Guarantor or Co-Borrower?

Guarantor

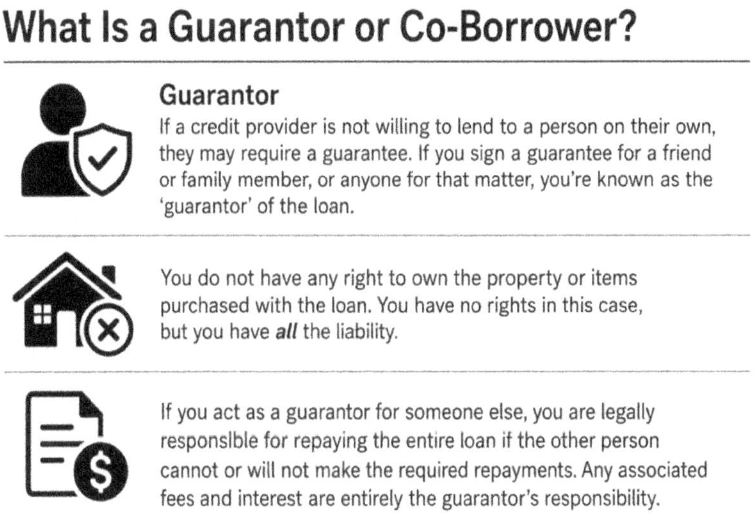

If a credit provider is not willing to lend to a person on their own, they may require a guarantee. If you sign a guarantee for a friend or family member, or anyone for that matter, you're known as the 'guarantor' of the loan.

You do not have any right to own the property or items purchased with the loan. You have no rights in this case, but you have *all* the liability.

If you act as a guarantor for someone else, you are legally responsible for repaying the *entire* loan if the other person cannot or will not make the required repayments. Any associated fees and interest are entirely the guarantor's responsibility.

Co-Borrower

Someone is a co-borrower if they sign a loan with someone else. In most instances, both co-borrowers are jointly and severally liable for the *entire* debt. If the borrower assisted by the co-borrower is unable to pay their share of the loan, the other will typically be responsible for repaying the full outstanding balance for both. There is one lender that will allocate a percentage of responsibility to each borrower, but this may not prevent the property from being repossessed if one of the borrowers fails to make their repayments.

Guaranteeing a loan will affect your credit file (CRAA report) and your ability to get a loan in the future.

Just as if you're the applicant on a loan, when you apply for a loan, you'll need to disclose to your finance provider any loans you're a guarantor for. I have seen cases of borrowers applying for a loan for themselves and not disclosing to the lender that they were a guarantor on another loan. Whether it was due to ignorance or forgetfulness, the lender declined to offer them a loan because of non-disclosure.

Normally, a lender will factor in all repayments on any loan you are taking out, guaranteeing or acting as a co-borrower for. With positive credit reporting picking up steam, it could very soon be the case that payments on the loan the guarantor has guaranteed will appear on the guarantor's credit file, as will the conduct of the loan. So, in other words, the guarantor will be held accountable for the borrower's conduct on the loan.

The guarantor may end up with a bad credit record if the borrower can't pay back the loan. The loan will be listed as a default or nonpayment on the guarantor's and borrower's credit files, making it harder and more expensive to obtain credit for at least 5 years.

Think Carefully Before Guaranteeing Anything

Seek advice on another solution, as mentioned earlier. I recommend that anyone considering being a guarantor consider how they will be able to afford to repay the loan or make the repayments. If a guarantor had to make repayments on a loan they had guaranteed, it could lead to their financial downfall. See the section on credit impairment and bankruptcy in this book.

An alternative is a *gift* accompanied by a statutory declaration stating that it's non-refundable (if, in fact, it is non-refundable).

Some financial planners have advocated using margin loans as leverage to grow first-homebuyers' finances from a lower base (i.e., a lower level of assets/wealth). Beware of risks associated with margin calls, of course.

Borrowers need to factor in any government assistance they may receive.

Reverse Mortgage

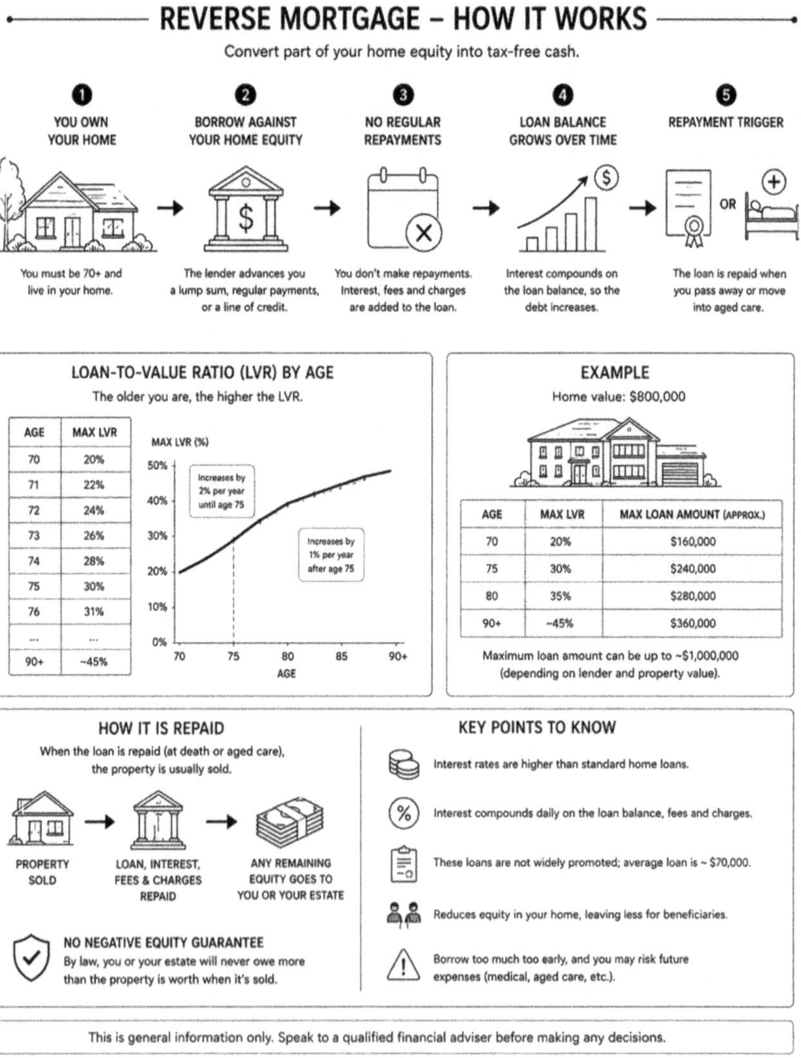

In some ways, a reverse mortgage is similar to a normal loan. There is a debt, and interest is charged on the debt. The main difference is that the interest does not need to be paid through normal repayments. Interest accrues and is added to the loan. Interest is charged on the interest and on fees and charges — the loan just gets bigger over time. These loans normally have to be paid at death or upon moving into aged care, for example, by selling the property.

Some lenders only offer this type of facility to borrowers over 70. Age also determines the loan-to-value ratio (LVR). At 70 years old, for example, the LVR offered may not exceed 20%. It can increase by 2% per year until age 75, then by 1% per year thereafter. The older the borrower, the higher the LVR can be, up to roughly 45%. The borrower can even be over 90 years old and apply for one of these.

The reason why the LVR offered is higher as the person becomes older is for a couple of reasons:

- Because the interest capitalises on the loan and generally does not need to be paid back until death or aged care, the property is sold in the process. If too much is borrowed against the property at too early an age, the borrower may be unable to afford future costs, such as medical expenses or moving into aged care.
- The older they are, the sooner they will die. So, the less likely it is that the interest on the debt will compound to the point of being worth more than their home. By law, lenders must guarantee that, when the property is sold, the borrower will not have to repay more than the property is worth (known as a 'no negative equity guarantee').
- These reverse mortgage loans are not widely promoted either; the average loan is around 70K. Interest rates are much higher, and the maximum loan amount can be up to

1 million, with no fixed loan term. It also reduces the equity in the property of course, so there could be little available for the kids.

Example

An older person, 75 years old, wants to purchase a home, they have $600,000 in savings, and require $150,000 to purchase an owner-occupied home worth $710,000. They require a deposit, so they could apply for a deposit bond to preserve their funds, and a reverse mortgage to settle. Their remaining funds can then pay the stamp duty.

14.

Non-Real-Estate Asset Finance and Unsecured Loans

Finance Beyond Property – Borrowing Against Assets That Move

Why This Chapter Matters

Here is a truth: the finance industry is not particularly keen to advertise: most Australians are sitting on borrowing power they have absolutely no idea exists.

Not in their property. Not in some secret government scheme requiring a form with seventeen sections and a statutory declaration from someone who knew you before you made any mistakes. In the stuff they already own. The truck in the yard. The equipment in the shed. The machinery that gets up and goes to work every single day — and yet never gets invited to the conversation when it is time to raise capital.

The average Australian's approach to borrowing looks something like this: need money, use house. Need more money, use house again. Hit the limit on the house, feel stuck. Apply to a bank that requires a blood sample, a ten-year trading history, and a therapist's note confirming emotional stability — then wait six weeks to be told no.

And somewhere in all of that, the trailer, the excavator, the harvester, and the fleet of vehicles just sit there. Perfectly good assets. Quietly ignored. Like that treadmill in the spare room — technically useful, currently a coat rack.

Of course, it cannot be denied that interest rates against the use of equity in real estate are lower, and equity from real estate can be used to provide finance for everything in this chapter. A tip when using equity in real estate is to allocate extra money to ensure the debt acquired to purchase a non-real estate asset is paid off over the same time as obtaining non-real estate asset finance against the asset.

A bank will happily take your money over 30 years and will happily earn more from you for the non-real estate asset than what you would pay on a 5-year loan term against the asset itself. Private lenders can sometimes provide an alternative. Given that many private lending facilities are designed as shorter-term loans, often ranging from 1 to 3 years, this can encourage borrowers to repay the debt more quickly rather than carrying it for decades. Although the interest rate on a private loan may be higher than that of a standard home loan, the shorter loan term can reduce the time the debt remains outstanding. This will likely be way cheaper than a bank when comparing the loan terms.

However, real estate may not hold enough equity to purchase a non-real-estate asset. Likewise, the advice for purchasing something for a business may be to compartmentalise it (ring-fence it) from all real estate that is not part of the business, so understanding this chapter could be quite beneficial.

This chapter is about changing that conversation. Not just for business owners. For anyone who has built something of value and does not yet realise they can use it.

Asset finance can solve problems faster than property finance — sometimes dramatically faster. It can preserve equity that took years to build. It can fund growth without putting the family home into the equation. And it has been the engine behind Australian agriculture, construction, transport, and healthcare for decades. Most people just never noticed, because no one framed it as a strategy.

They are about to.

The Psychology of Asset Lending

Before we get into structures, asset classes, and LVR ratios, it is worth spending a moment on something nobody puts in the brochure: the way people feel about borrowing against the things they own.

We are taught, from a fairly young age, that debt is something to be cautious about. That borrowing is a last resort. That a sensible person pays things off and does not go back for more. These are not unreasonable values. In the right context, they are genuinely sensible. But applied without nuance to a business or investment decision, they become a quiet tax on growth — a mental ceiling that keeps capable people from using the tools available to them.

The result is a particular kind of paralysis that shows up constantly in lending conversations. A business owner has assets. They have equity. They have a clear purpose for the capital. And yet they hesitate — not because the numbers do not work, but because borrowing feels like an admission of something. Like things are not going as well as they should be. Like someone will find out and think less of them.

Borrowing strategically against an asset you have already built is not a sign of struggle. It is a sign that you understand how capital works.

The most financially sophisticated operators in any industry — construction, agriculture, transport, manufacturing, healthcare — use asset finance as a deliberate, ongoing strategy. Not because they cannot afford to pay cash. Sometimes precisely because they can and choose not to. Tying up capital in a depreciating asset when that same capital could be working elsewhere is not prudence. It is inefficiency wearing the costume of responsibility.

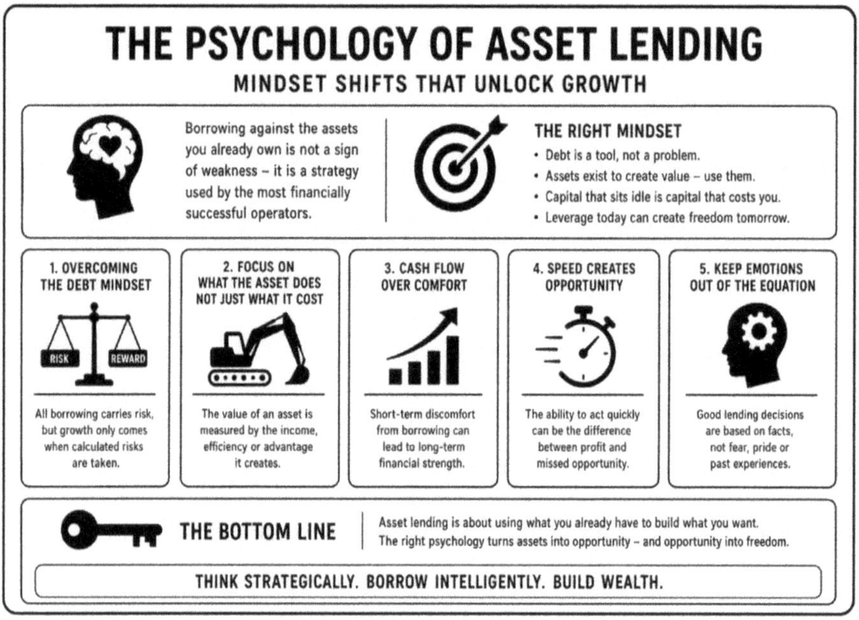

Why Banks Dislike Urgency

Banks do not hate people generally, well, at least not all the time. They just hate uncertainty — and urgency looks a lot like uncertainty from behind a compliance framework. A large institution processes thousands of loans every month. To do that at scale, it needs rules written by committees, reviewed by legal teams, and administered by people assessed on how closely they follow the process — not how creatively they solve an individual's problem on a Thursday afternoon.

Urgency, in this system, is suspicious. A borrower who needs something done quickly is asking the machine to skip steps. Banks initially use machines, not people, unlike private lenders. And skipping steps is precisely what large lenders have spent decades training their staff not to do. This is not a character flaw. It is architecture. Think of a mainstream bank like a freeway: excellent for moving large numbers of vehicles from A to B efficiently, provided everyone follows the same route. The moment your destination is slightly off the main road, the freeway cannot help you — not because the people in it are unhelpful, but because the road only goes one way.

Why Asset Finance Companies Charge for Certainty

Non-bank and private asset lenders were built for people who needed to go somewhere the freeway does not reach. They move faster. They use discretion. They can look at a situation as a whole rather than filtering it through a checklist. That flexibility has a price — and that price can often be a higher rate.

This is not gouging. It is honest pricing of a genuinely different service. Certainty of outcome, speed of decision, and the ability to consider context rather than just criteria — these are real things with real value. The borrower paying a higher rate for settlement in 48 hours is not being taken advantage of. They are buying something the bank simply does not sell.

Time Versus Interest Rate

Here is a scenario worth considering. A business needs equipment to fulfil a contract starting in three weeks. A mainstream bank offers a competitive rate — but approval takes at least six to eight weeks. A non-bank lender offers the same amount at a higher rate and settles in 48 hours.

Most people fixate on the rates. The lower number looks better. This is a very human response. But the rate comparison entirely misses the fact that the cheaper loan arrives five weeks after the contract has been awarded to someone else.

The real cost of finance is not the interest rate. It is the interest rate multiplied by the outcome it makes possible. Miss the window and the effective cost is infinity — because it funded nothing.

Why Borrowers Overvalue Headline Rates

Rate comparison tools are everywhere. Advertisements compete on decimal points. Aggregator websites rank products by rate as though rate were the only variable that matters. Borrowers, trained by years of this, arrive at lending conversations with a single number in their head and judge everything against it. It is the financial equivalent of choosing a restaurant purely on the price of the house wine.

Rate is one factor. Others include whether the loan will be approved, how long approval takes, whether the terms allow flexibility as circumstances change, whether the lender behaves reasonably when something goes wrong, and whether the structure fits its purpose. A lower rate inside the wrong structure — or secured against the family home when an asset would do — can be considerably more expensive than a higher rate that solves the problem cleanly.

Why Speed Changes Risk Pricing

Speed is not a luxury feature. For a business operating in the real world, timing is often the entire point. A lender who can make a decision in 24 hours is taking on a fundamentally different risk profile than one who takes six weeks — not because the borrower is riskier, but because less time means less information. That gap in information is priced into the rate. Understand this and the rate stops feeling like a penalty. It starts feeling like what it is: a fair exchange for a faster, more certain outcome.

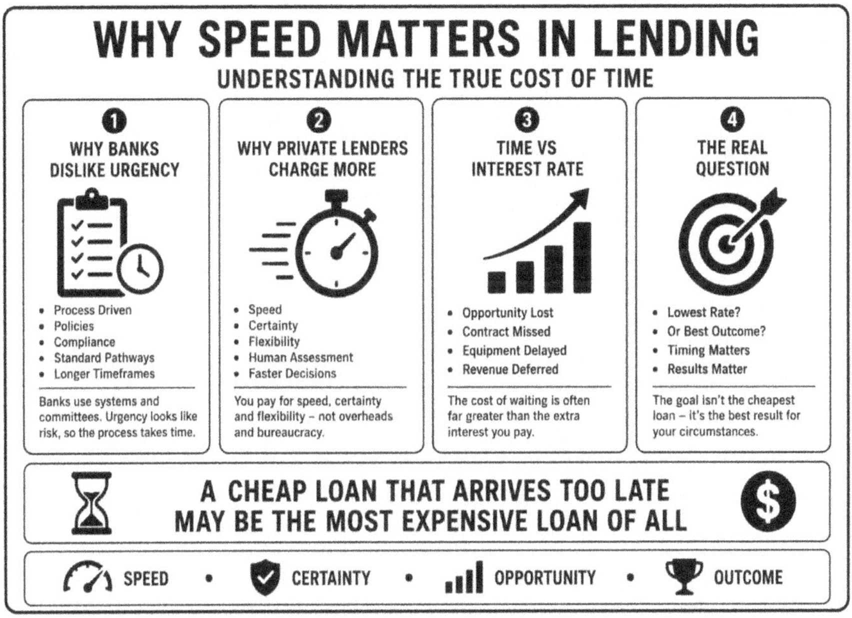

What Is Non-Real-Estate Asset Finance?

Asset finance is, at its core, a beautifully simple idea: if you own something valuable, or want to buy one, that thing itself can serve as collateral for a loan. Not your house. 'The thing', the asset.

The truck, the crane, the car, the piece of equipment, the commercial vehicle fleet, the harvester in the paddock, the caravan paid off three years ago and driven exactly twice — all of these can potentially serve as security for a loan. The asset does the same job as a property title does in a mortgage: it gives the lender something concrete to control or secure the finance against, something they can value and, if absolutely necessary, recover. Without involving your kitchen, bathroom, or your whole house.

Secured Versus Unsecured Lending

Secured lending means the lender has a registered interest in a specific asset. If the loan goes wrong, they have something to recover. The asset is the safety net — which is why rates on secured lending are generally lower than on unsecured. The lender is not just taking your word for it.

Unsecured lending means there is no specific asset behind the loan. The lender is assessing the borrower's cash flow, revenue, and business performance — lending against the business itself rather than against a physical asset. Higher risk for the lender means a higher rate for the borrower. Again, this is not punitive. It is just honest pricing.

Why Assets Behave Differently to Property as Security

Property, in Australia's lending landscape, has a near-mystical status. Values tend to go up over time. The secondary (resale) market is deep and active. Every lender in the country understands how to value a house. Assets behave differently. They depreciate. They have finite useful lives. Their secondary markets vary enormously — some assets can be sold at auction nationally within days; others are so specialised they have a buyer pool of maybe only three people.

This is why lenders assess assets differently. Not harder or worse, just differently. The questions they ask, the loan terms they offer, and the conditions they attach all reflect the specific characteristics of the asset in question.

How Lenders View Depreciation Versus Capital Growth

A property lender is generally comfortable with the value of their security increasing over time. An asset lender is managing the opposite: a security that, in most cases, loses value every month. This changes everything about how the loan is structured — the term, the repayment schedule, the LVR, the balloon payment provisions. The loan needs to stay ahead of the depreciation curve. The day the loan balance exceeds the asset's recoverable value is one no lender wants to reach.

Understanding this is the key to understanding why asset loans work the way they do. It is not arbitrary. It is the lender staying solvent.

Understanding Asset Classes — Not All Assets Are Equal

Walk into any asset finance conversation without understanding this, and you will be confused by the outcomes. Two borrowers with identical credit histories applying for the same loan amount can receive very different responses — simply because the assets they are financing fall into different lending categories.

Lenders assess every asset through roughly the same lens: how long it lasts, what the resale market is like, how liquid it is, and how quickly it loses value. The answers to those questions determine appetite, LVR, term, and rate. Knowing where your asset sits on that spectrum before you apply is not just useful — it is the difference between walking in prepared and walking in confused.

Passenger Vehicles and Motor Vehicle Finance

This is where most Australians first encounter asset finance without knowing it — the loan arranged in an afternoon at a dealership while someone in a shiny shirt offers coffee and suddenly it is your problem. Motor vehicle finance is the most mature, most competitive, and most accessible segment of the asset-lending market.

Cars and SUVs

Standard passenger vehicles and SUVs sit at the most straightforward end of the asset finance spectrum. Deep secondary markets, transparent pricing guides, national buyer demand, and well-understood depreciation curves mean lenders are comfortable and competitive. Terms of two to seven years are typical. LVRs of up to 100% are common on new vehicles and newer used stock.

Prestige Vehicles

Prestige vehicles — European marques, performance cars, high-end SUVs — attract a slightly different lending conversation. Not because lenders dislike them, but because the secondary market is narrower and the depreciation profile can be steeper. Some lenders specialise in this area and understand the market; others apply a standard used-vehicle discount that undervalues the asset. Knowing which lender, you are talking to matters more in this category than in most.

Electric Vehicles and Hybrids

Electric vehicle (EV) finance is evolving rapidly, and lender policies continue to adjust as the market matures. Unlike traditional petrol and diesel vehicles, EVs present additional considerations for lenders, including battery life, replacement costs, technological change, charging infrastructure, and uncertainty surrounding future resale values. While the long-term direction of the market appears clear, lenders are still determining how EVs will perform in the secondary market five to ten years from now.

One of the key concerns for lenders is residual value risk. Traditional motor vehicles have decades of historical data supporting valuations and depreciation trends. EVs do not yet have the same level of long-term data as other vehicles. Battery technology continues to improve rapidly, which can create uncertainty about how older models will be valued relative to newer vehicles with longer driving ranges and faster charging capabilities.

Hybrid vehicles often sit in a more comfortable position from a finance perspective. They provide some of the fuel-saving benefits associated with EVs while retaining the familiarity and flexibility of a petrol engine. Many borrowers view hybrids as a middle ground between traditional vehicles and full electric vehicles. As a result, lenders may sometimes view certain hybrid vehicles more favourably due to broader market acceptance and a larger potential resale market.

Government incentives have also played a role in supporting EV demand. In some cases, fringe benefits tax (FBT) concessions and other incentives have improved affordability for business owners and employees. These incentives can significantly influence borrowing decisions, particularly where the vehicle is being acquired for business purposes.

Recent geopolitical events have also demonstrated how quickly consumer demand can change. During the conflict involving Iran and the resulting concerns surrounding global oil supply, fuel prices increased sharply and many Australians began reassessing the long-term running costs of petrol and diesel vehicles. Industry reports showed a substantial increase in EV enquiries, vehicle searches, finance applications, and sales activity as consumers sought alternatives to rising fuel costs. EV sales in Australia nearly doubled year-on-year during parts of 2026, while searches for electric vehicles surged as motorists reacted to fuel price volatility.

This shift highlights an important aspect of asset finance: timing. Many borrowers who decided to purchase an EV or hybrid vehicle during periods of fuel uncertainty did not necessarily have months to wait for a traditional lending assessment. In many cases, buyers wanted to secure a vehicle immediately before stock became unavailable, prices increased, or delivery times lengthened. Fast asset finance solutions allowed borrowers to act quickly and secure the vehicle when they needed it rather than waiting for a slower approval process.

The Iran conflict also highlighted another reality often overlooked by borrowers. The cost of finance is only one part of the equation. A borrower who secures a vehicle quickly and reduces ongoing fuel expenses may be financially better off than someone who spends weeks chasing a marginally lower interest rate while continuing to absorb significantly higher fuel costs. The cheapest loan on paper is not always the cheapest outcome in practice.

From a lender's perspective, EVs, hybrids, and traditional vehicles are all assessed according to risk, resale value, and market demand. As EV adoption continues to increase across Australia, lenders' appetite is likely to continue to strengthen. However, hybrid vehicles may remain particularly attractive for some time due to their combination of fuel efficiency, established resale markets, and reduced dependence on charging infrastructure.

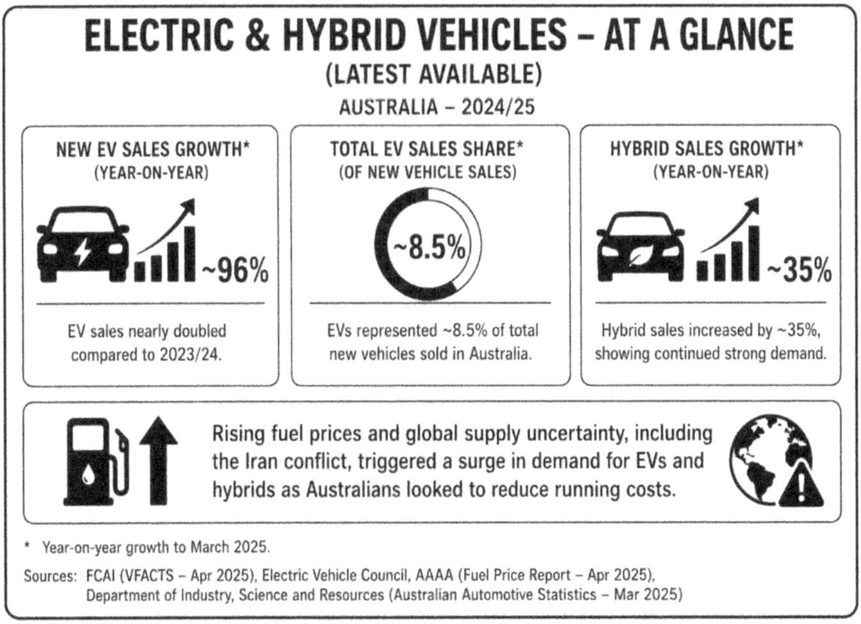

Perhaps the biggest lesson from recent events is that asset finance provides flexibility. Whether purchasing an EV, hybrid, or traditional vehicle, the ability to access funding quickly enables borrowers to respond to changing market conditions, fuel costs, and consumer demand without delaying important financial decisions. In many cases, speed and certainty of outcome can be just as valuable as the interest rate itself.

Demonstrator Vehicles

Demo vehicles sit in an interesting gap: they are technically used, but often with very low kilometres, full warranty, and a price discount of ten to twenty per cent versus new. For private buyers this is frequently the sweet spot — the first-year depreciation has already occurred, the warranty is largely intact, and manufacturer finance deals sometimes still apply. Worth asking about specifically rather than assuming they fall into the standard used-vehicle bucket.

New Versus Used — The Case Study

A buyer is looking at two options. A brand-new vehicle — full warranty, every modern feature, and that particular smell that makes otherwise sensible adults make financial decisions they will reconsider at a slightly lower speed than usual. Or a two-to-three-year-old version of the same vehicle with low kilometres, full-service history, and a meaningfully lower price.

The new car buyer reaches for reliable justifications. It has a warranty. Its history is known. The finance rate is better on new. And the classic: I deserve it, I've worked hard. None of these is unreasonable. But the maths tells a specific story.

A new vehicle loses a significant portion of its value the moment it leaves the dealership. The steepest depreciation occurs in the first 12 to 24 months. By the time a two-year-old version appears on the used market, that brutal early loss has already occurred — and the person buying it does not pay for it. The original owner did.

Think of it as a gift from a stranger who really needed a new car smell.

From a pure numbers perspective, the used vehicle is almost always the better financial decision for a private buyer. The gap between new and used is not just a savings on the purchase price — it is a savings on the depreciation the previous owner has already absorbed on your behalf.

But here is the flip side, and it matters enormously for business owners. That brutal first-year depreciation that private buyers want to avoid is, for a business, potentially the entire point. The drop in value is a tax-deductible expense. Under certain conditions — particularly with instant asset write-off provisions — a business may be able to claim a significant portion of a new vehicle's cost against taxable income in the year of purchase. The depreciation that hurts the private buyer works for the business owner, because the government is effectively subsidising part of the cost through reduced tax.

Same maths. There may be an entirely different outcome depending on who is buying and why. Private buyer paying out of pocket? A used vehicle is almost always wiser. Business owner with the right structure and advice? New might stack up better than it first appears — not in spite of the depreciation, but because of it. Talk to your accountant before assuming either way.

> The lesson: The most expensive time to own a vehicle is the first two years. If you buy used, someone else pays for that privilege. If you are a business, that same depreciation might be your best friend at tax time. Know which one you are before you decide.

Personal Versus Business Use

The distinction between personal and business use matters significantly in vehicle finance — for tax treatment, for the applicable finance structure, and for what the lender will offer. A vehicle used exclusively for business purposes has different options available than one used personally or for a mix of both. Novated leases, for example, are a salary packaging arrangement available through employers that can deliver genuine tax savings for employees — but they come with conditions, and understanding those conditions before signing is not optional.

Commercial Vehicle and Transport Finance

Commercial transport is one of the most active and lender-friendly areas of asset finance in Australia. Trucks, prime movers, trailers, vans, buses — these assets have strong secondary markets, national demand, and well-understood depreciation profiles. Lenders who specialise here understand the industry and can structure finance that reflects how transport businesses operate.

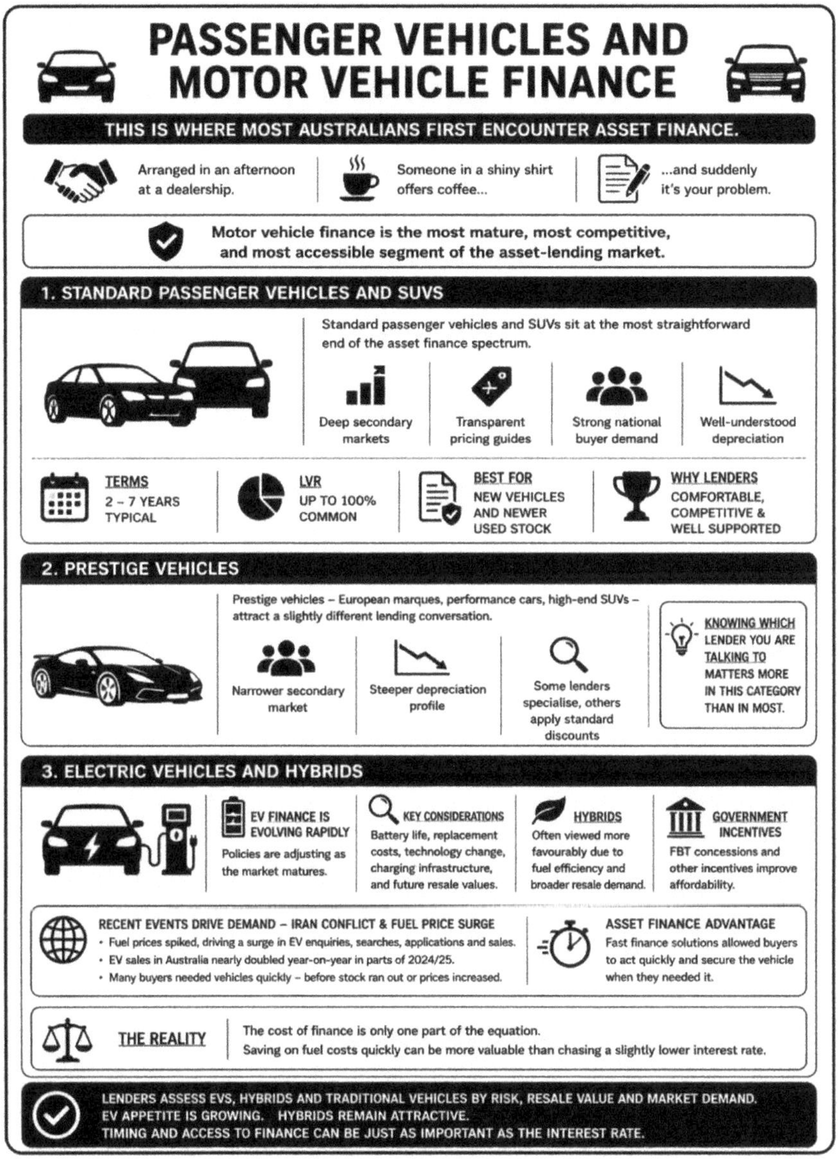

Trucks, Prime Movers and Trailers

Heavy vehicle finance is a specialised market. Loan amounts are larger, useful lives are longer, and the secondary market for well-maintained equipment from established manufacturers is genuinely strong. Lenders assess make, model, age, kilometres, and service history carefully. A prime mover with a full-service history and verifiable work contracts behind it is a very different proposition to one with gaps in the paperwork.

Vans, Buses and Coaches

Light commercial vehicles — vans and utes used for trade — sit at the more accessible end of commercial vehicle finance, with competitive terms and broad lender appetite. Buses and coaches occupy more specialised territory, with a narrower secondary market and more specific lending policies. Taxi and rideshare fleets have their own considerations, including platform income verification and the specific depreciation profiles of high-kilometre urban vehicles.

The Case Study — The Truckie Who Did Not Own His Home

A sole trader in transport had been running the same route for three years. Good operator. Clean history. Paid his bills on time, which in some circles is practically a personality trait. When his prime mover gave up the ghost in a manner that was both spectacular and expensive, he needed a replacement fast — he had a contract to fulfil and was roughly ten days away from someone else getting the call to complete the work.

He went to his bank. His bank explained that without property security and given the timeline, they were not in a position to assist. They suggested he come back when things were less urgent. He resisted the urge to explain how urgency works.

A non-bank transport lender approved the deal in 48 hours. Chattel mortgage, secured against the new vehicle. He was back on the road inside a week. The loan cost more than the bank would have charged. He did not care even slightly, because the bank's cheaper loan did not exist in any practical sense. The contract ran for fourteen months. He paid the loan out early. When he needed finance for a second unit two years later, he did not call the bank.

The lesson: A cheap loan that arrives too late is not cheap. It is a missed opportunity wearing a competitive rate.

Additionally, the other point mentioned sums up the entire book. "A bank's cheaper loan did not exist in any practical sense." So, a wise person will not live in denial; they will act by accepting a solution when a viable, affordable, and non-detrimental one is available.

Some borrowers become so focused on obtaining the perfect solution that they overlook a practical solution that is available today, when a solution is affordable, non-detrimental, and achieves the outcome, they sit on their hands in denial, complain about the cost of the solution, and not take up the offer, thereby missing out on what they wanted. Or what often happens (even when the solution is affordable, non-detrimental, and achieves the outcome) is they hold out their hands for money, putting the burden on friends and family to help them, dragging someone into their problem.

Many people involve family for help, which I accept only when the solution is unaffordable, detrimental, and fails to achieve the desired outcome. An exception is perhaps to approach parents without burdening anyone else, and only those who can easily afford it. Anecdotally, I have seen far too many grandparents and other family members and friends have been exploited, misled, unfairly burdened, unjustly treated and materially prejudiced by their grandchild

A lesson I learned early in life is that if you can't afford to buy something yourself, don't. Or, if a solution is available, albeit imperfect, don't be so selfish as to beg family for money rather than accept it. The biggest lesson in life, and often the worst mistake you can make, is to lend money to friends or family. It is very uncomfortable to ask for it back and can sour or end relationships if the money is not repaid when promised. At a minimum, if you are asked for money, let's say for a property investment, non-real estate asset investment or development opportunity aimed at making a profit, and you are not the parents (as parents have the strongest reason to help a child out of love and affection), draw up a joint venture agreement and demand a benefit. If you lend someone money, you may not earn interest. It is a huge risk for you to be dudded, stitched up, ripped off, or betrayed, and you may not get it back. Not only should it be in writing, but you must require a financial return and profit from it; otherwise, you are just being exploited, unfairly and selfishly burdened, or used.

Yellow Goods and Construction Equipment Finance

Excavators, loaders, dozers, cranes, graders, rollers, access equipment — the machinery that builds the physical world and makes a truly satisfying noise doing it. Yellow goods are among the most lender-friendly asset categories. The secondary market is strong, values are transparent through established industry guides, and there is consistent national demand for well-maintained equipment from recognised manufacturers.

A well-serviced Caterpillar or Komatsu machine is about as clean a security as asset finance offers. Lenders who specialise in this space understand the equipment, the industry, and the operators. They know what a machine is worth new, what it is worth at five years and ten thousand hours, and what it would fetch at auction on a Tuesday in regional Queensland. This depth of market knowledge produces confident lending — which generally means better terms for the borrower.

Specialised or unusual construction equipment — older machines, obscure manufacturers, highly modified assets — attracts more conservative lending. The principle is the same: the thinner the secondary market, the more cautious the lender.

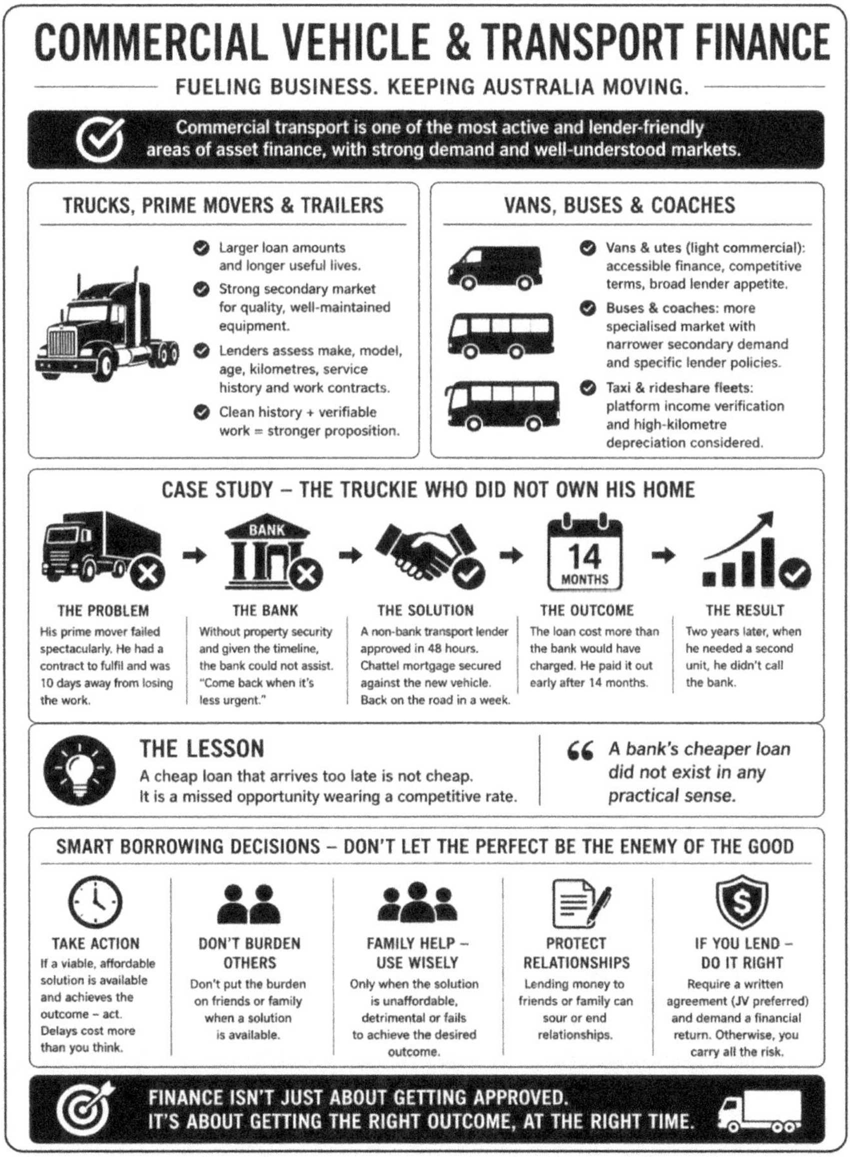

Plant and Equipment Finance

Manufacturing machinery, warehousing systems, printing equipment, medical equipment, commercial kitchen equipment — the category is broad, and lending appetite varies considerably within it.

Manufacturing and warehousing equipment from established suppliers with active secondary markets attracts reasonable lending terms. Medical equipment — particularly from major manufacturers with strong resale demand — can be financed competitively, and healthcare businesses have specific lending options worth exploring. Commercial kitchen equipment sits at the more conservative end; lenders know that restaurant-specific fit-outs have limited resale value, so finance tends to be structured accordingly.

Printing and production equipment follows the technology's useful life. A press that will be commercially viable for fifteen years is a different security to one that may be obsolete in three. Lenders in this space assess technology risk as carefully as they assess physical condition.

Case Study — The Manufacturer Who Kept the House Out of It

A small manufacturing business had an opportunity to add a capability that would let them take on work they were currently sending to a competitor. The equipment cost more than they had in cash and considerably less than they would need to justify touching the mortgage. Their accountant — a good one, the kind worth keeping — suggested equipment finance before going anywhere near the house.

A finance lease was structured over four years. The payments were fully deductible. The GST was claimable. The equipment was running within three weeks. Within six months, the new work it generated covered the repayments and contributed to the bottom line. The home equity was untouched. The equipment paid for itself, which is what equipment finance is supposed to do when everyone does their job properly.

> The lesson: Not every need for finance should come out of the house. Sometimes the smarter move is to let the asset fund itself.

Agricultural and Rural Equipment Finance

Tractors, harvesters, irrigation systems, livestock equipment — the rural lending market has its own rhythm, and lenders who understand it can be genuinely useful partners for farming businesses.

The key difference in agricultural lending is timing. Farm income is seasonal, commodity-exposed, and weather-dependent. Demanding monthly repayments from a cropping operation during a drought is not a lending policy; it is a recipe for default. Lenders who specialise in rural finance structure their products to reflect how farming income actually arrives — with seasonal repayment options, interest-only periods during growing seasons, and realistic assessments of income variability.

Geographic remoteness is also a consideration. An asset in a major city has one secondary market. The same asset in a remote farming community has a much smaller one. Lenders account for this in their LVR assessments.

Case Study — The Farmer Who Did Not Know What He Had

A cropping operation in regional South Australia had been paying down equipment finance for seven years. Consistent payments. Strong service records. The quiet discipline that rarely gets celebrated but absolutely should. When a water infrastructure opportunity arose that would meaningfully improve yields, the operator assumed his only option was a property-secured loan — a process he dreaded, having done it before and found it roughly as enjoyable as a root canal performed by someone who had recently completed an online course in root canals.

His finance broker pointed out something he had not considered: seven years of repayments had built substantial equity in the equipment. A refinance and equity release against the machinery covered the infrastructure cost without touching the property. The process took ten days. The crops are doing well. The operator now has a standing arrangement to review his equipment position annually — which has proved considerably more useful than he expected.

> The lesson: Equity builds in equipment just like it builds in property. Most people spend years creating it without realising it is there.

Specialised and Difficult-to-Finance Assets

Not every asset sits in a clean lending category with transparent values and an active resale market. Some assets are inherently harder to finance — not because they lack value, but because that value is harder to verify, harder to realise, and harder to recover in a worst-case scenario.

Aircraft and Marine Assets

Aircraft and boats occupy specialised lending territory. Values vary enormously based on type, age, condition, and maintenance history. Secondary markets are both national and international but relatively thin compared to those for motor vehicles. Lenders who operate here tend to be specialists with deep market knowledge — finding them is part of the work.

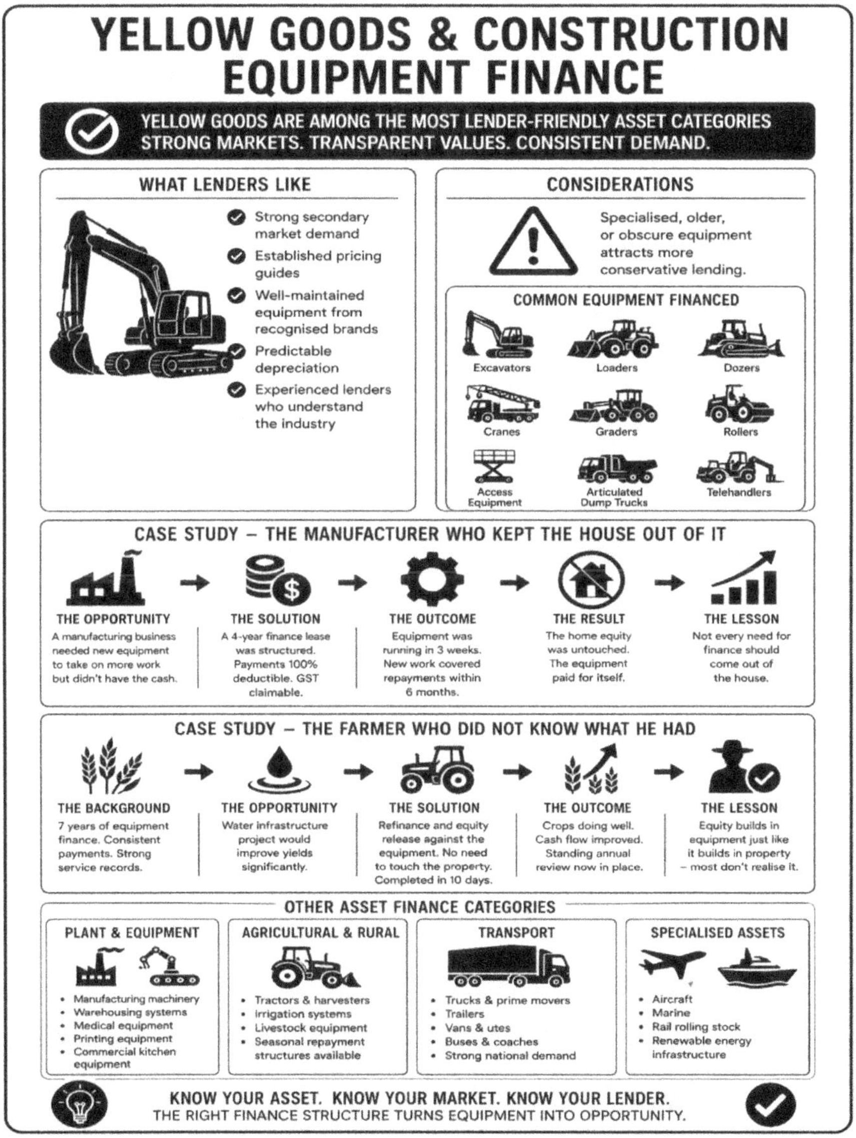

Caravans and Motorhomes

Caravans and motorhomes have become an increasingly popular asset class in Australia, supported by strong consumer demand, an active resale market, and a well-established dealer network. Unlike many consumer goods that depreciate rapidly, quality caravans and motorhomes from recognised manufacturers can often retain their value reasonably well, making them attractive security from a lender's perspective.

One of the key advantages of caravan and motorhome finance is that the asset itself can generally be used as security for the loan. Lenders assess factors such as the asset's age, manufacturer, condition, purchase price, and resale demand when determining how much they are prepared to lend. Well-known brands with strong resale histories are generally viewed more favourably than niche or imported models.

Australia has one of the largest caravan ownership markets in the world, creating a substantial secondary market for both new and used vehicles. This is important from a lending perspective because it provides confidence that the asset can be sold if necessary, thereby reducing the lender's risk.

Loan-to-value ratios (LVRs) vary between lenders and are influenced by the type and age of the asset. New caravans and motorhomes will generally qualify for higher LVRs, while older assets may attract lower lending limits or shorter loan terms. Many traditional lenders also impose maximum age restrictions, either when the loan is written or at the end of the loan term.

Retirees can sometimes encounter additional challenges when seeking finance. Traditional lenders often place significant emphasis on employment income and servicing calculations, which can disadvantage retirees despite them having substantial assets, strong net worth, significant superannuation balances, or being debt-free. As a result, some retirees may find it surprisingly difficult to obtain finance through mainstream channels, even when their overall financial position is strong.

Specialist and private lenders can often take a different approach. Rather than focusing solely on employment income, they may place greater emphasis on the value of the asset being financed, the borrower's overall financial position, available security, and the proposed repayment strategy. This can provide additional options for retirees who may not fit within standard bank policy but remain financially sound borrowers.

Private and specialist lenders may also offer solutions for older motorhomes, imported vehicles, custom-built conversions, and other assets that fall outside traditional lending guidelines. While each application is assessed on its own merits, this flexibility can be valuable where mainstream lenders have limited appetite for the transaction.

Another advantage of caravan and motorhome finance is the speed at which transactions can often be completed. Once the asset has been identified and the required documentation provided, approval and settlement can frequently occur within days. This can be particularly important when purchasing a sought-after vehicle and a prompt settlement is required.

Comprehensive insurance is generally a requirement for any caravan or motorhome finance facility. Given that many caravans and motorhomes can cost well in excess of $100,000, lenders will typically require their interest to be noted on the insurance policy to protect both parties against damage, theft, or loss.

From a finance perspective, caravans and motorhomes occupy a unique position within the asset finance market. Their identifiable value, active resale market, broad consumer demand, and ability to serve as standalone security help explain why they remain a popular lending category for banks, specialist financiers, and private lenders alike.

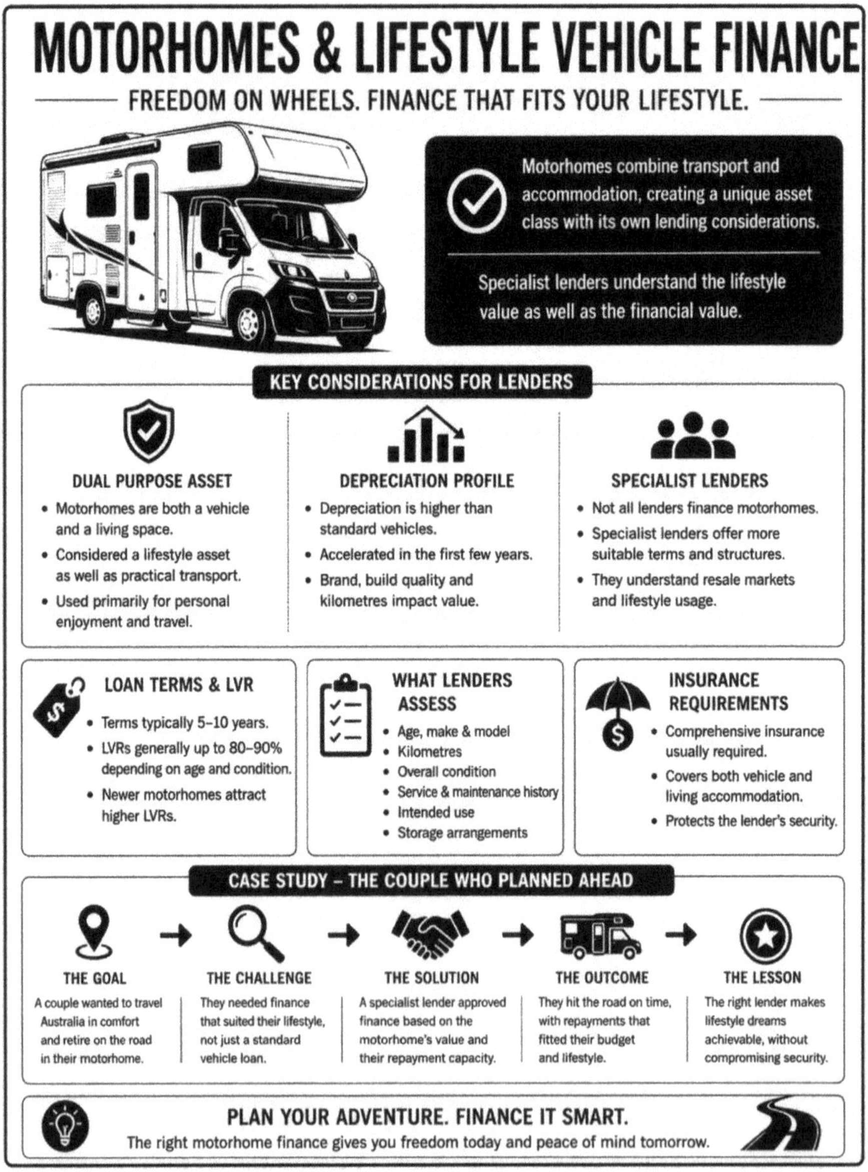

Mining Equipment

Mining equipment occupies an interesting middle ground. Large, well-known machinery from major manufacturers can attract strong lending given the deep secondary market — particularly for assets with low hours and documented service histories. Highly specialised or site-specific equipment is more difficult to value, as its value is largely tied to the operation it serves.

A side note: this is in stark contrast to the worthiness of investing in mining towns, especially in QLD or WA; I've seen sturdier investment strategies written on pub napkins. I'd rather buy a boat with a hole in it. Investing in a single-industry mining town can be like buying a parachute after you've jumped from the plane. Everything seems fine until you discover what was holding it up in the first place.

Aged, Imported and Difficult Assets

Assets banks simply do not like tend to share a few characteristics: age that places them outside standard lending parameters, obscure manufacturers with thin resale markets, significant modifications that affect value assessments, or provenance issues that complicate ownership verification. None of these is necessarily a deal-breaker. They are just conversations that need to happen with the right lender, not the most convenient one.

Asset Finance Structures Explained

Asset finance comes in several shapes. The differences matter, and getting the structure right is often worth more than getting the rate down by a fraction of a percentage point. A broker who understands both the structures and your specific situation is worth considerably more than one who just processes applications.

Chattel Mortgage

The most common business structure. You own the asset from day one, the lender registers a security interest over it, and the loan is repaid over an agreed term. The asset appears on your balance sheet. Interest and depreciation are generally tax-deductible for business use. GST on the purchase price can often be claimed upfront. Simple, well understood, and effective in most situations.

Finance Lease

Technically, the lender owns the asset during the loan period, and you use it. At the end of the term, you have options — purchase for a residual amount, extend the lease, or return the asset. Different balance sheet treatment than a chattel mortgage, which matters for some businesses. Lease payments are generally fully deductible as a business expense. Your accountant will have strong views on which structure suits your situation.

Operating Lease

Similar to a finance lease but structured so the asset does not appear on your balance sheet at all — it is treated as an operating expense. Useful for businesses that want to use an asset without the complexity of ownership. At the end of the term, the asset goes back. This structure suits businesses where the equipment will be upgraded regularly or where balance sheet presentation matters.

Hire Purchase and Commercial Hire Purchase

Hire purchase structures involve using the asset while making payments, with ownership transferring at the end of the term. The commercial variant has specific tax implications for GST and income tax that differ from a standard hire purchase. The distinction matters — again, accountant first.

Novated Lease

A salary packaging arrangement available through employers. The lease is between the employee, employer, and lender — with lease payments made from pre-tax salary, which can produce genuine tax savings. The employer assumes administrative responsibility during employment; if the employee leaves, the lease typically reverts to the employer. Not suitable for every situation, but genuinely useful for the right one.

Rent-to-Own

Structured as a rental with an option to purchase at the end. Payments are operating expenses. Useful for assets where the borrower is uncertain about long-term needs, or where cash flow is too variable for fixed repayments. Generally, a higher total cost than ownership structures, but the flexibility has genuine value in the right circumstances.

How Loan-to-Value Ratio Works in Asset Finance

LVR — loan-to-value ratio — once again, is the percentage of an asset's value that a lender will finance. In property lending, LVRs of 80% to 95% are standard. In asset finance, the picture is more varied — and understanding why helps explain a lot about how loan structures are built.

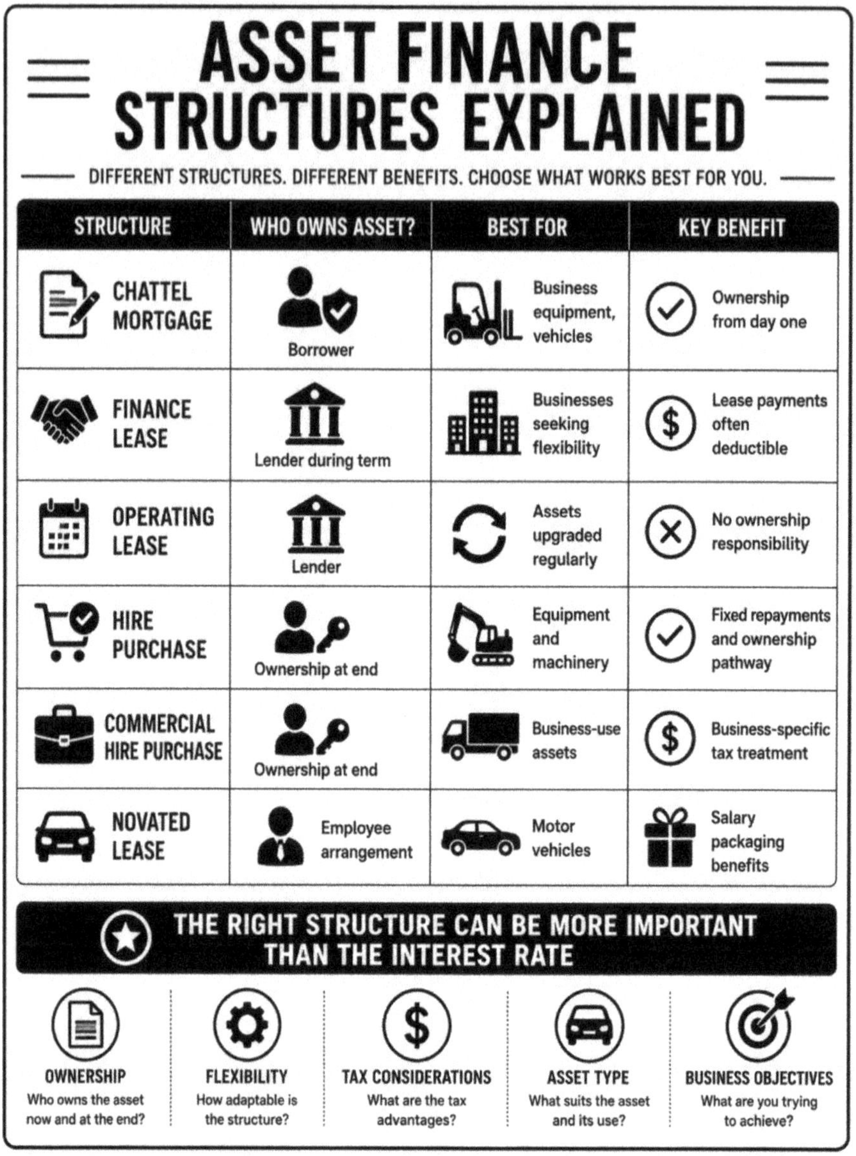

What LVR Means When the Security Depreciates

A property lender watches their security potentially grow in value over time. An asset lender watches it shrink. This means the loan needs to be structured so that repayments reduce the balance faster than the asset loses value — otherwise, the lender ends up in a position where the loan exceeds the asset's value. This is why asset loans are generally shorter than mortgages and why LVRs are more conservative on assets with steep depreciation curves.

Typical LVR Ranges by Asset Type

New passenger vehicles and popular commercial assets from major manufacturers can attract LVRs of up to 100% — meaning the lender will finance the full purchase price. This reflects the strength of the secondary market and the confidence in recovery values. Specialised, older, or less liquid assets attract more conservative LVRs — sometimes 60% to 70% of assessed value — because the recovery scenario is less predictable.

GST, Balloons and Residuals

GST inclusion in the financed amount matters because it affects the LVR calculation and the upfront cash required. For business buyers who can claim the GST back, financing the GST component means paying interest on money you will recover — worth considering when structuring the deal.

Balloon payments and residual values are agreed-upon amounts set aside for payment at the end of the loan term rather than through regular repayments. They reduce monthly payments by deferring a lump sum to the end. This can improve cash flow during the loan period, but the balloon needs to be planned for — either through refinancing, from cash, or from the sale or trade of the asset. Walking into a balloon payment with no plan is the kind of adventure nobody orders on purpose.

When 100% Finance Exists — and When It Does Not

100% finance — borrowing the full purchase price without a deposit — is available on certain assets, particularly new vehicles from established manufacturers with predictable

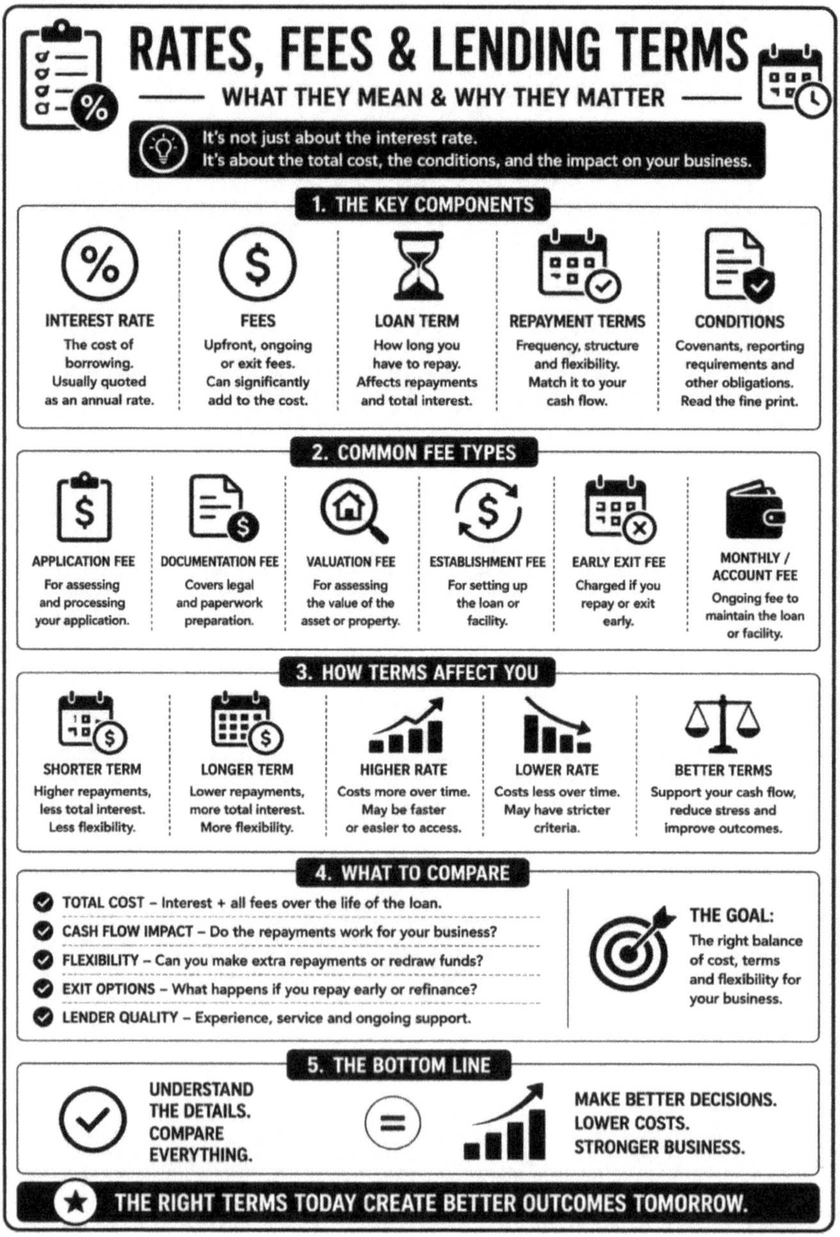

resale values. It does not apply to older assets, specialised equipment, or situations where the lender has no confidence in the recovery values. Expecting 100% finance on an asset the lender views as difficult is a conversation that will go poorly for everyone involved.

Residuals, Balloon Payments and End Debt

A balloon or residual payment is not a trap. It is a tool. Used correctly, it reduces repayments during the loan period and defers a lump sum until the borrower has more options — refinance the residual, pay it from cash, trade the asset, or sell it. Used without a plan, it becomes a problem that arrives with a bow on it and a due date.

Lower repayments during the term mean better cash flow now, at the cost of a larger obligation later. Whether that trade-off makes sense depends entirely on the borrower's circumstances, the expected value of the asset at the end of the term, and whether the exit strategy has been properly thought through. A broker who helps structure the balloon but does not discuss the exit plan is only doing half the job.

Refinancing residual debt is common and usually straightforward for assets that have held their value reasonably well. For assets that have depreciated more than expected, refinancing a balloon can result in a loan balance that exceeds the asset value — which is exactly the situation nobody wants and that proper planning at the outset largely prevents.

Unsecured Business Loans — Lending Without Security

Not every situation comes with a readily available asset to offer as collateral. Sometimes the need is for working capital, cash flow bridging, or a fast opportunity that does not have time to wait for an asset assessment. This is where unsecured business lending exists — and where the rate-versus-purpose trade-off becomes most acute.

What Unsecured Business Lending Actually Means

Unsecured lending means there is no specific asset registered as security. The lender is assessing the business's revenue, cash flow, and trading history — lending against the business itself. Higher risk for the lender means a higher rate for the borrower. This is not punitive. It is honest pricing of a genuinely different risk position. The lender has nothing to recover except hope, legal fees, and an increasingly awkward series of phone calls if things go sideways.

Revenue-Based Assessment and Working Capital Facilities

Many unsecured lenders assess borrowing capacity against monthly business turnover rather than against assets or property. This is the mechanism behind cash flow facilities and lines of credit — and it is one of the most underused tools in small-business finance.

A lender assesses your monthly turnover. Based on that, they offer access to a pool of funds — sometimes one month's turnover, sometimes two, in some cases up to three times monthly turnover depending on the lender and circumstances. That pool sits available. You pay nothing while it is unused. You draw on it when you need it, pay interest only on the amount drawn, and when cash comes in you put it back. Balance reduces. Interest stops. The facility is available again for the next time.

Some lenders charge a small monthly fee simply to keep the facility open and available — typically in the range of the price of a cup of coffee. A flat white, not a fancy double-shot oat milk situation with a name written on the side in text. For the peace of mind of knowing a financial buffer exists whenever you need it, most business owners who have one consider that an exceptionally good cup of coffee.

Case Study — The Facility Most Business Owners Do Not Know They Can Have

A small trades business. Three staff, consistent work, good reputation. The problem — the problem almost every small trades business has — is timing. Complete a job in week one. Invoice in week two. Client pays in week five, because clients have their own cash flow challenges and thirty-day payment terms that routinely become sixty days because someone in accounts is on an extended holiday in an undisclosed location.

In the meantime, wages are due in week two. Materials for the next job are needed in week three. The vehicle service that cannot be postponed happens in week four. The business has done the work, earned the money, and is completely unable to access it because it is sitting in someone else's accounts payable queue.

This is not a struggling business. This is a cash flow timing problem wearing the mask of a struggling business. And it is one of the most common reasons otherwise viable small businesses feel permanently stressed about money.

A cash flow facility fixes this. Draw on it to cover wages, materials, and the car service. The client pays in week five. Payment reduces the facility balance. Interest charged only on what was drawn, for three weeks. The cost is modest. The stress is gone. The business operates as though it always had a financial buffer — because now it does.

Extend that slightly. The same business, with a facility available, gets the opportunity to take on a larger project. Without the facility, the risk of a cash flow gap feels dangerous. With it, the gap is manageable. The project completes. Payment arrives. Facility reduces. The business has just grown in a way it would have avoided before.

> *This is not debt for debt's sake. This is working capital infrastructure — the difference between a business that can say yes to opportunities and one that has to let them pass because the timing does not work.*

Having access to a facility is not the same as needing to use it. The psychological value of knowing the buffer exists — even if it's never drawn on — is still significant. Businesses make better decisions when not operating from financial anxiety. The facility changes the quality of decisions across the business because those decisions stop being driven by what the account balance looks like on this particular Tuesday.

That is worth something. Probably more than the interest on the three weeks borrowed to cover payroll while waiting for a client who was definitely going to pay — honest, it is just that Brenda in accounts is very busy.

> The lesson: A cashflow facility is not a loan in the traditional sense. It is a financial safety net you pay for only when you actually need it. Most businesses that have one wonder how they operated without it. Most businesses that need one have never been told to ask.

Lease-Doc, Trail Book and Rent Roll Finance

Some unsecured or partially secured products are assessed against specific income streams rather than general business revenue. Lease-doc lending uses existing lease income as the primary basis for assessment — useful for property investors and some business operators whose income is documented through leases rather than standard financial statements. Trail book (mortgage broker: ongoing income while a loan remains where it was placed) and rent roll (rental managers' income from managing properties for investors): finance uses the recurring income streams from financial planning practices, mortgage broking businesses, or property management operations as security. The income stream itself becomes the asset. Niche products, but genuinely useful for the right businesses — and worth asking about if the income profile fits.

Merchant Cash Advances

A merchant cash advance is an advance against future card sales, repaid as a percentage of daily revenue. The repayment flexes with income — higher sales, faster repayment; slower periods, slower repayment. This can suit businesses with variable, card-heavy income streams such as retail or hospitality. The effective cost, when calculated as an annual percentage rate, is often higher than it initially appears. Not wrong for the right situation. Worth understanding fully before signing (this goes without saying for everything).

Why Unsecured Rates Are Higher — and When It Is Worth It

The rate is higher because the lender has less to recover if things go wrong. This is not gouging. It is math. The businesses that use unsecured lending well access it for a specific purpose with a clear repayment plan — either from the activity it funded or by refinancing into secured lending once circumstances allow. The businesses that use it as a chronic solution tend to compound their problems rather than solve them. Know the difference before you sign.

Why Non-Bank and Asset Lenders Work Differently — and Why It Matters

Borrower First Versus Asset First

Traditional lenders typically start with the asset or property — if the security does not fit the policy, the conversation ends quickly. Non-bank and private asset lenders are more likely to start with the borrower: who are they, what is the purpose, what does the exit look like, and can we structure something that works? This is a fundamentally different approach that produces different outcomes — particularly for borrowers whose situations are genuine but do not fit a standard checklist.

Policy Versus Discretion

Large lenders run on policy. The policy exists for good reasons — consistency, scalability, risk management. But policy cannot account for every situation, and the ones it cannot are often the most interesting. Non-bank lenders use more discretion. A file that would be declined by a policy system might be approved by a human who understands context. This is not a loophole. It is just a different way of doing business.

Automation Versus Common Sense

Increasingly, mainstream lending decisions are made by algorithms. The algorithm looks at inputs and produces an output. It does not understand that the borrower's income dipped two years ago because of a family medical situation and has since fully recovered. It does not understand that the business's most recent tax return does not reflect current trading because it was a transitional year. Common sense does not fit in a decision engine. Human lenders do — and they exist, predominantly in the non-bank space.

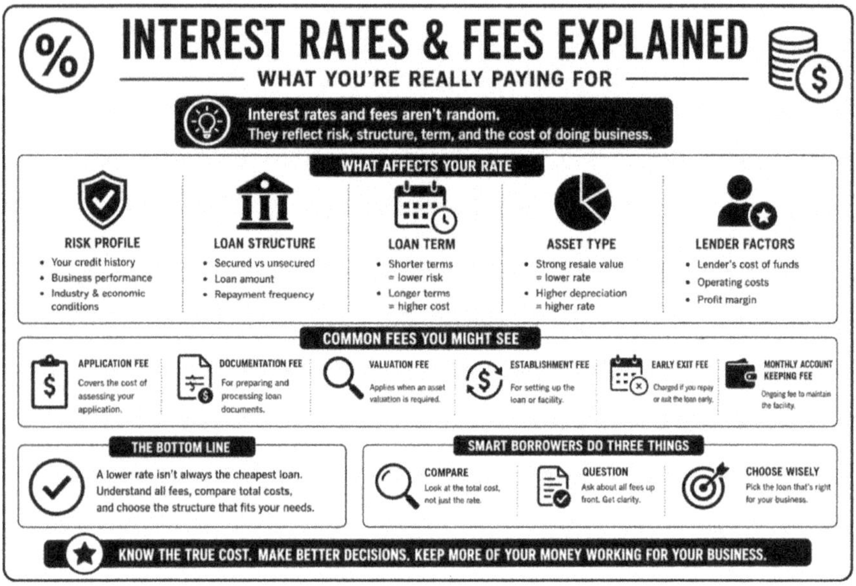

Settlement Timing — Why Speed Matters

Bank approval and settlement are not the same thing. Approval means the lender has agreed in principle. Settlement means the money has actually moved. The gap between those two events can be days or weeks, and for a business operating on a deadline, the difference matters enormously.

Same-day and sub-72-hour approval and settlement is genuinely available from specialist lenders for the right asset and borrower profile. This is not a marketing claim. It is a specific capability that some lenders have built to serve a need that banks structurally cannot meet. Knowing which lenders operate at that speed is part of what a good broker brings to the table.

Business interruption risk is real. Equipment downtime, missed contracts, and delayed operations — these costs are not always visible in a rate calculation, but they are very visible in a Profit and Loss (P&L) statement. The opportunity cost of waiting for a slow approval process needs to be part of the assessment. A loan that costs two per cent more per year but arrives in time to prevent a week of business interruption is almost certainly cheaper in total than the slower, cheaper alternative.

Asset Age, Condition and Marketability

Age matters in asset finance. Most lenders have hard cutoffs — assets beyond a certain age or with too many hours on the clock simply fall outside policy. These cutoffs exist because older assets have less predictable remaining life, thinner resale markets, and higher maintenance uncertainty. Knowing the age limits for the specific asset class you are financing avoids the frustration of getting deep into an application only to find the asset does not qualify.

Condition and service history affect not just whether an asset can be financed, but also at what LVR and rate. A well-maintained machine with complete service records from a recognised operator is a very different proposition to the same machine with gaps in its history. Documentation matters here in a way it does not always matter elsewhere.

Auction values versus retail values are a distinction worth understanding. What an asset sells for at retail — to a willing buyer with time to consider — is generally higher than what it fetches at a forced liquidation auction. Lenders are always considering a liquidation scenario, which is why their assessed values are sometimes more conservative than the borrower expects. The gap between what you think something is worth and what a lender can recover quickly is one of the more instructive conversations in finance.

Cash Out Against Existing Assets

One of the most underused strategies in asset finance is also the simplest: if you have been paying down an asset for years, you have probably built equity. That equity can often be accessed — without selling the asset, without refinancing the home, and without a full new loan application.

A business that has diligently paid down equipment finance for three years may have a meaningful cash position sitting quietly in the difference between the outstanding balance and the current market value. That position can be unlocked for working capital, a new acquisition, or to bridge a short-term gap. The equipment keeps working. The business keeps operating. The home equity stays untouched, minding its own business.

Equity release against vehicles and equipment is genuinely useful for debt consolidation, too — rolling several smaller, higher-rate obligations into a single facility secured by equipment can improve cash flow and reduce total interest costs. This requires careful structuring and an accountant's input, but the outcome is often significantly cleaner than the starting position.

This is not magic. It is just using what you have already built — which is the whole point.

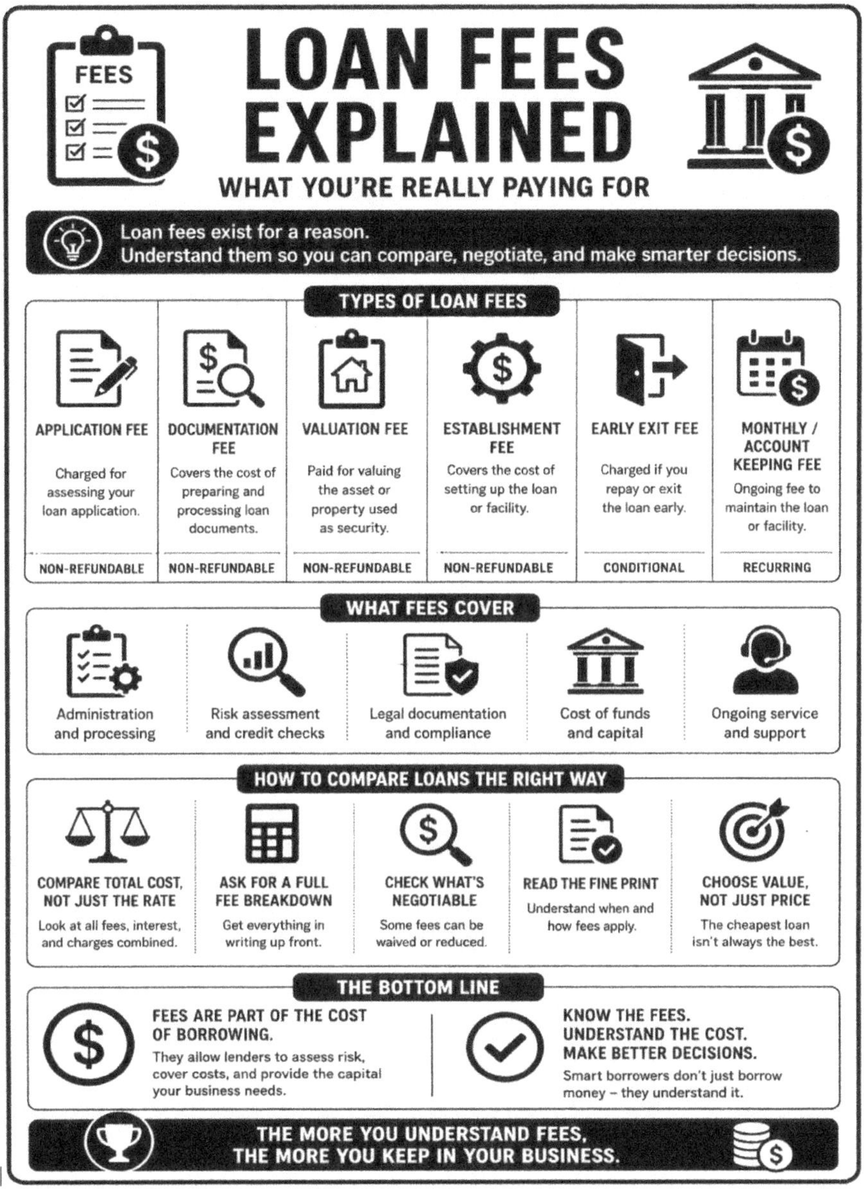

Using Asset Finance Instead of Property Finance

Preserving Property Equity

Property equity is finite. Once used, it is unavailable until circumstances slowly rebuild it. Businesses and individuals who reflexively draw on property equity for every capital need are consuming a resource that may be needed for something more important later — something where no asset alternative exists. Using asset finance for equipment, vehicles, and working capital keeps property equity intact and available for genuinely property-specific purposes.

Avoiding Cross-Collateralisation

Cross-collateralisation is the practice of using a single asset — usually the family home — as security across multiple lending facilities. It can also mean that several assets are collectively exposed to a loan. It sounds efficient. In practice, it gives one lender significant leverage over decisions that should belong to the borrower. Want to refinance one facility for a better rate? Want to sell one asset? Want to change lenders? If everything is tied together by the same security or several securities, none of those decisions is as free as it appears. You are not negotiating. You are asking permission.

Keeping lending clean and specific — each loan secured against the asset it funded — preserves flexibility. In finance, flexibility is almost always worth paying something to preserve.

When Asset Finance Can Make More Sense Than a Mortgage

Australia has a deep, committed, and somewhat irrational relationship with residential property. We treat homes like savings accounts, retirement plans, barbecue conversation topics, and the answer to every financial question ever asked. House, house, house, house.

This is not entirely without logic. Property in Australia has been a genuinely strong store of wealth over many decades. It is familiar. Lenders understand it deeply. It is the financial equivalent of a meat pie — everyone knows what it is and no one questions why it keeps showing up.

But treating your home as the answer to every financial question is a bit like using your emergency generator to power the kettle. It will work. But it is probably not the best use of that resource — especially when the actual emergency has not happened yet.

Buying income-producing equipment — machinery that will generate revenue to cover its own repayments and contribute to the business — is the clearest argument for asset finance over property finance. The asset funds itself. The home stays out of it. The equity that took years to build remains available for genuinely property-specific purposes. Maintaining liquidity and enabling faster growth strategies are logical extensions of the same argument: capital tied up in a paid-off vehicle or piece of equipment is capital that could be working elsewhere.

Case Studies — Real People, Real Situations

Case Study: Buying Something Without Property Security

A retail operator with three established locations found a fourth site with great lease terms and a motivated landlord. The problem: their existing lender needed four to six weeks to assess fit-out funding. The window was two weeks. Maybe less.

They went to an unsecured business lender. Approval in 24 hours. The rate was — let us be honest — genuinely confronting when expressed as an annual percentage. The operator accepted it with clear eyes and a specific plan: fund the fit-out, open the location, trade for six months, then refinance into conventional lending once trading history satisfied a mainstream lender. That is exactly what happened. The fourth location is now the second-best performer in the group.

The lesson: Expensive money used correctly is a tool. Expensive money used without a plan is a problem. Know the difference before you sign.

Case Study: Using Asset Finance to Grow Revenue

A manufacturing business had an opportunity to bring in-housework they were currently outsourcing to a competitor. The required equipment cost more than the available cash and less than the threshold for tapping into the mortgage. Equipment finance was structured over four years. Fully deductible payments. GST claimable. Equipment operational within three weeks of application. Within six months, the new capability was covering repayments and contributing to profit. Home equity untouched. Business stronger. Equipment paid for itself.

The lesson: Not every capital need should come out of the house. Sometimes the smarter move is to let the asset fund itself.

Case Study: Unsecured Business Finance

A trades business with three staff and consistent work had a persistent problem: cash flow timing. Work completed. Invoice sent. Payment arrived thirty to sixty days later. Wages, materials, and vehicle costs arrived in between. The business was viable — it just operated in a permanent state of financial anxiety because the timing never quite lined up.

A cash flow facility was established against monthly turnover. The business drew on it to cover the gaps, repaid it when client payments arrived, and paid interest only on what was drawn. The cost over a year was modest. The anxiety disappeared.

Within twelve months, the business had taken on two larger projects it would previously have declined — not because the work was risky, but because the cash flow gap would have been unmanageable without the facility.

> The lesson: The facility does not just solve cash flow problems. It changes the quality of decisions made across the business because those decisions stop being driven by the account balance on any particular day.

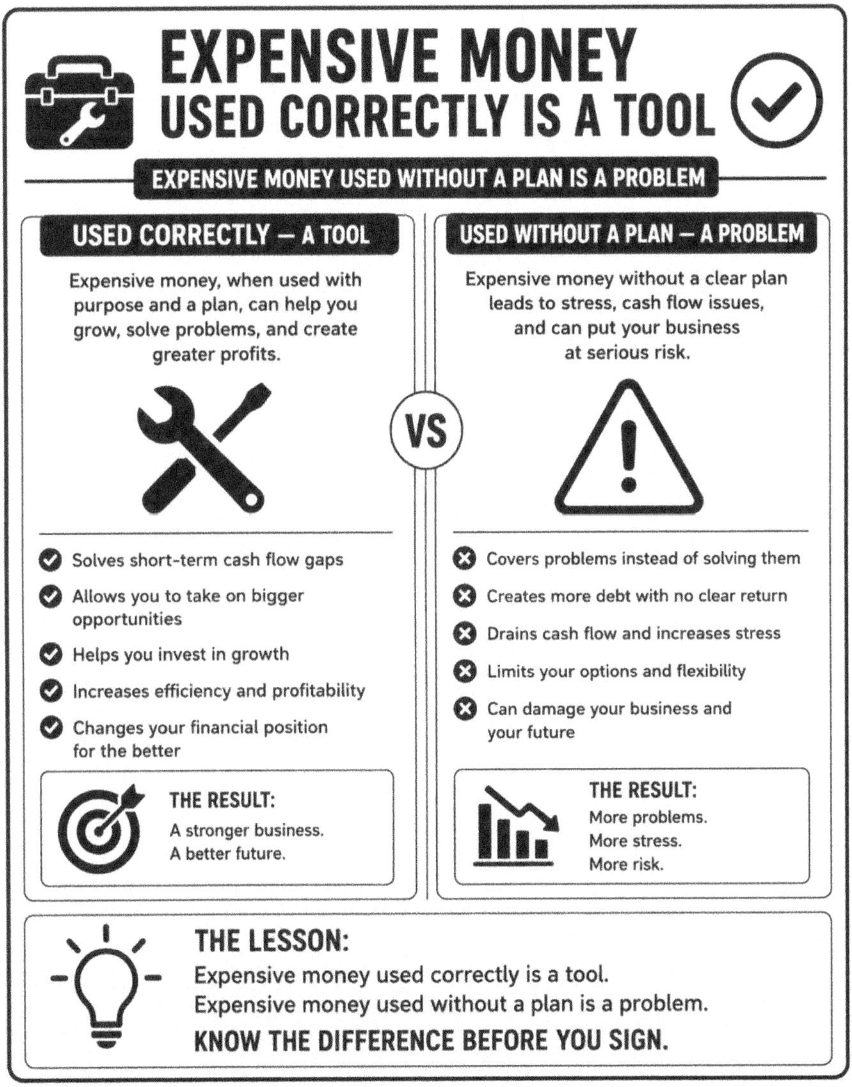

Private Lending Correlation — Same Principles, Different Security

Private lending and asset finance share more DNA than most people realise. The fundamentals of how a private lender assesses a non-bank lending proposition — asset quality, exit strategy, loan term, equity buffer, and borrower behaviour — apply directly to asset finance, just with different security types.

Asset quality is the starting point in both cases. A private lender considering a real estate deal asks what the property is worth and how certain the value is. An asset lender asks the same question about a truck or a piece of equipment. The methodology differs; the principle does not.

Exit strategy is equally central. How does the loan get repaid? What happens at the end of the term? In property-backed private lending, the exit might be a sale or refinance. In asset finance, it might be the completion of a contract, the sale of the asset, or a refinance into conventional lending. Both conversations require the answer to exist before the loan is advanced.

Borrower behaviour — track record, transparency, the quality of the information presented — matters in both contexts. Lenders in both markets are making judgments about people, not just assets. A well-presented case with clear purpose and honest disclosure of the challenges is consistently treated better than a polished application that falls apart under scrutiny.

Private lending extends beyond real estate, not because lenders got adventurous but because the same logic applies. Security, exit, equity, and borrower quality are the variables. The asset class is just the context.

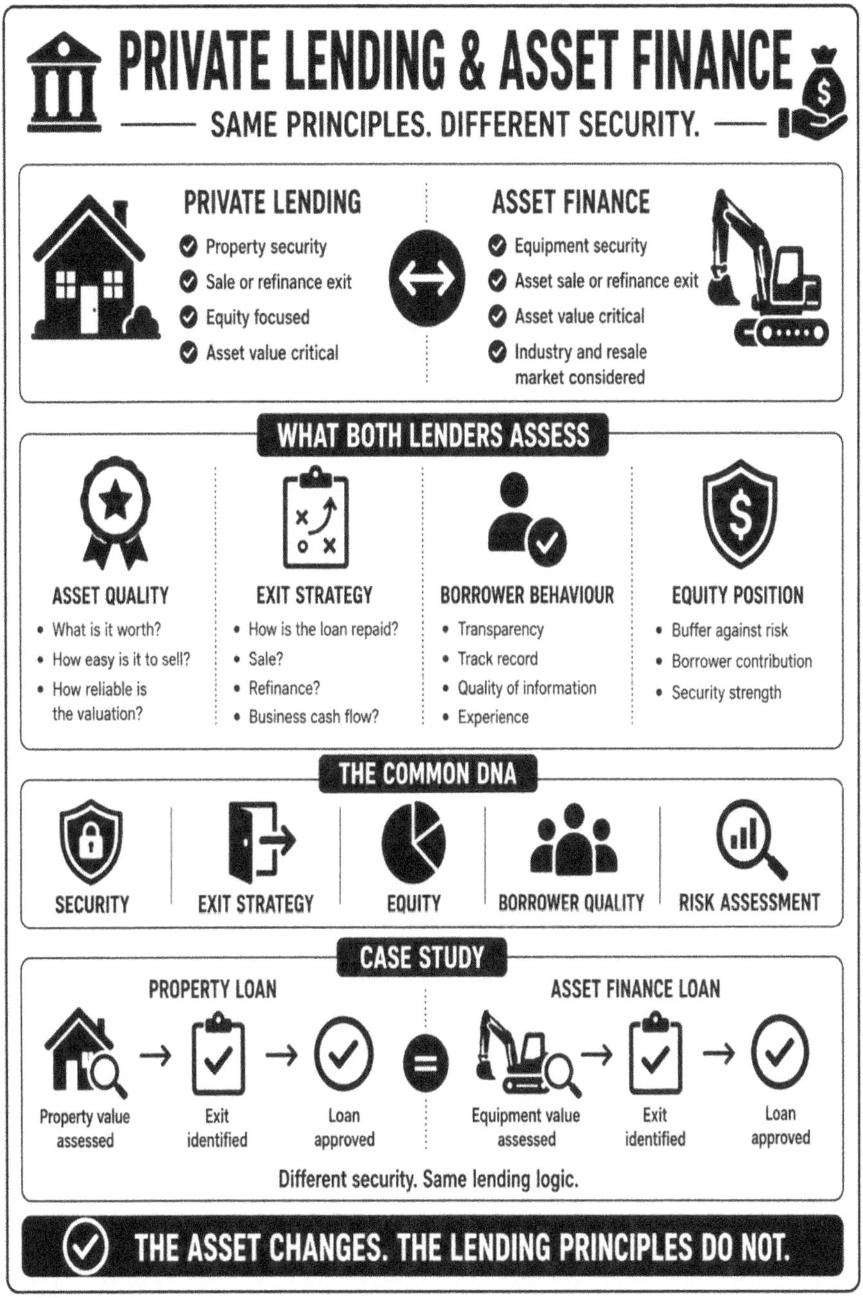
PRIVATE LENDING & ASSET FINANCE
SAME PRINCIPLES. DIFFERENT SECURITY.
PRIVATE LENDING
Property security
Sale or refinance exit
Equity focused
Asset value critical
ASSET FINANCE
Equipment security
Asset sale or refinance exit
Asset value critical
Industry and resale market considered
WHAT BOTH LENDERS ASSESS
ASSET QUALITY
What is it worth?
How easy is it to sell?
How reliable is the valuation?
EXIT STRATEGY
How is the loan repaid?
Sale?
Refinance?
Business cash flow?
BORROWER BEHAVIOUR
Transparency
Track record
Quality of information
Experience
EQUITY POSITION
Buffer against risk
Borrower contribution
Security strength
THE COMMON DNA
SECURITY
EXIT STRATEGY
EQUITY
BORROWER QUALITY
RISK ASSESSMENT
CASE STUDY
PROPERTY LOAN
Property value assessed
Exit identified
Loan approved
ASSET FINANCE LOAN
Equipment value assessed
Exit identified
Loan approved
Different security. Same lending logic.
THE ASSET CHANGES. THE LENDING PRINCIPLES DO NOT.

Checklist — Questions to Ask Before Applying for Asset Finance

Reading a chapter and nodding along is satisfying. This is the part where it becomes useful.

☐ What is the asset worth today — and how did you establish that value?

☐ Is there any existing finance registered against the asset? Check the Personal Property Security Register (PPSR) before proceeding.

☐ What is the asset's age, hours, and service history — and does it fall within standard lending parameters?

☐ What structure best fits your situation — chattel mortgage, finance lease, operating lease, or something else? Have you discussed this with your accountant?

☐ What is the after-tax cost of the finance, not just the headline rate?

☐ Does speed of settlement matter to this decision? If so, have you factored it into the lender selection?

☐ What is the balloon or residual at the end of the term, and what is the plan for it?

☐ Is property security required — and if so, is there an alternative that keeps the house out of it?

☐ Have you spoken to a broker who specialises in this asset class specifically?

☐ If you have existing equipment with equity, do you know how much that equity is and whether it can be accessed?

☐ Have you been told no by a mainstream lender? Have you then asked a non-bank lender the same question?

☐ Do you have a working capital facility in place, and if not, do you know what you could access based on your monthly turnover?

Summary — Stop Thinking Only in Real Estate

Australia's lending landscape is considerably bigger than most people realise. The house is one piece of it — an important piece, a familiar piece, one with a track record that deserves genuine respect. But it is not the only piece.

The assets people build through work — the equipment, the vehicles, the machinery, the professional tools of the trade — are legitimate, useful, and chronically underappreciated sources of borrowing power. Using them strategically does not mean taking on dangerous risk. It means using the resources available in the way that best serves the situation.

The shifts that matter are not complicated. Stop thinking the house is the only answer. Start asking what you actually own and whether it can do more work for you. Stop evaluating finance purely on rate. Start evaluating it on whether the structure, timing, and terms actually fit the purpose. Stop treating urgency as something to hide. Start to understand that speed has a legitimate price, and that price is often worth paying. Stop treating a bank decline as the end of the conversation — it is just the end of the conversation with that institution.

Banks do not lend against dreams. They lend against evidence. The job of a strategic borrower is to make the evidence as clear, compelling, and well-presented as possible — and to find the lender whose appetite matches the specific situation rather than just the most familiar one.

The house is not the only thing worth lending against.

It never was.

One final note, offered with genuine warmth: the people who get the best outcomes from lending are not the cleverest or the wealthiest. They are the ones who ask better questions, find better advisors, and refuse to accept that the first answer they receive is the only one available.

That is not finance. That is just stubbornness applied usefully.

> *Before entering any asset finance or lending arrangement, speak to a qualified finance broker and your accountant. Structure matters. Tax treatment matters. The right advice at the start is worth considerably more than the cheapest loan you can find without it.*

15.

Subdividing, Constructing, and Developing

Property development: scary, a piece of cake, or somewhere in between?

Your response will probably depend on whether you are a first-timer, a second-timer, or a veteran, and how much you know about the process. Of course, if you do have experience in property development, then your response will also be based on whether that experience was painless or painful.

Ultimately, in finance, the lender will require council-approved plans and specifications, along with the fixed-price building contract. It is reasonable to consider that you do not sign a building contract unless it is a fixed-price contract.

Having said that, most contracts will include a provisional sum to cover the builder for expenses that cannot reasonably be foreseen. An example of this could be discovering rock in the ground during excavation. Builders are then able to draw down on the provisional sum. Imagine $5000 is the provisional sum allowed. In the example just given, the removal of rock may cost $3000, and this would be invoiced to you. Unless another unforeseen scenario occurs, you would not need to pay the balance of $2000. It is important that you agree with the provisional sum included.

Subdividing and Strata

These are the two methods used to create new titles and more value in a property. Almost anyone can do this with the right sized block of land in the right area by applying to council to split the block. Subdividing one block may mean that you create two smaller land lots with individual titles, and you can then create smaller developments.

Bear in mind that a property does not necessarily have to be subdivided to build more than one dwelling on the land; you can strata the titles. Strata title refers to a situation where an individual or entity owns part of the property, such as the dwelling (e.g. townhouse, unit, or office), but they share ownership of the rest of the property, such as some or all of the land, driveways, gardens, foyers, or corridors in apartment buildings. Normally, more than two dwellings that share a driveway or common land require a body corporate/owner's corporation to be established to insure the land and manage the responsibility of the shared areas.

Caravan parks, resorts, and retirement villages are more obvious examples of this. Strata titles are great for generating immediate value, as you can then sell separate parts of the property off. You may have heard the saying, "the sum of the parts are worth more than the whole."

You do not have to develop or build to gain value from applying to strata a title. A good friend of mine purchased several blocks of three or four units on a single title and successfully applied to the council for a strata title, resulting in a 200K uplift in value.

Subdivision

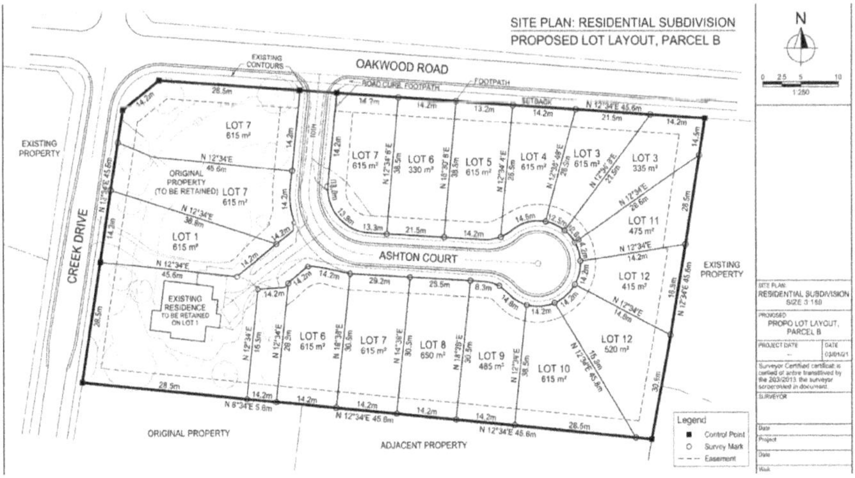

Strata

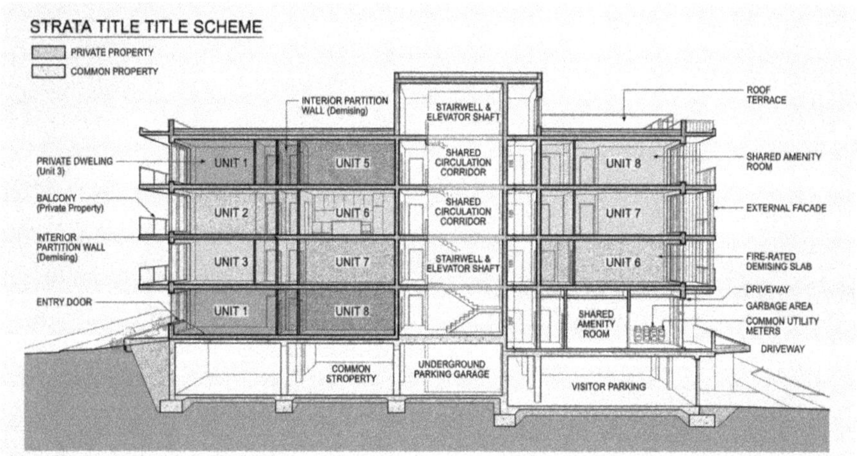

Process

Be patient reading this; there are a number of considerations and processes. Remember, councils are obliged to follow specific timelines prescribed in the planning scheme. The statutory requirement is sixty days; however, the clock starts and stops at various intervals, primarily because councils require and request additional information. This may not suit your timeline and could increase your costs (e.g. holding costs such as interest or rent if you have to live elsewhere). However, the end result can be very rewarding and profitable, especially if you have been able to get the house you want by extending, rather than buying again and moving. You can save a lot in sales costs and taxes.

When it comes to property development, there are many rules and regulations. As boring as they may seem, it is important to try to come to grips with them. You also need to understand some basic terms or definitions. Getting your head around these is critical to helping you along the way and with any future projects you may undertake.

Property development is not just about building a structure. It includes all activities that add value to a piece of land or property or change how the land may be used (which can also be considered to add value).

Examples of property development include:

- building a new home
- a renovation or extension, obtaining a planning permit, which is permission to use the land in a certain way (e.g. creating units or townhouses)
- obtaining a building permit (permission to construct a project)
- ‘change of use’ permits (e.g. turning a warehouse into a 24-hour gym or indoor trampoline centre)
- The actual construction of projects.

If you are a current or potential investor, let’s get one thing sorted straight up: any investment carries risk, and that includes property development. There are absolutely no guarantees.

But with research, planning, and experience, the level of risk can be minimised. So, let's get into the nitty-gritty!

Councils have a document called a planning scheme, which incorporates their long-term vision and specifies how land will be used in their area (in keeping with their vision). You can, if you wish, read these on your local council website. This document will clarify whether you need a planning permit for your project. Sometimes the planning scheme is not as clear as you might hope, and it may be worthwhile having someone qualified and familiar with these types of matters to help you with interpretation. It can be complex, with lots of 'if this, then that.'

A planning permit is permission from your council to use or develop land in a certain way. There are allowable uses with a planning permit, allowable uses without a planning permit, and prohibited uses. A simple example is that you cannot have an industrial building/use of land in a residential area, or an extreme example is that a brothel will not be permitted in a residential area (thank goodness). Generally, a planning permit is required for units or commercial projects, but it may also be needed for some residential developments.

If a planning permit is required for your project, you will need to apply to the council for this. The application requires preliminary (conceptual) designs to be prepared and submitted, along with various plans and reports, depending on the type of proposed development and the council involved (as they often differ in their requirements). The regulations are complex, and it is wise to check before buying land.

A planning permit does not belong to a person or persons; it is issued *to* an applicant *for a particular property*. Often, properties are sold with a planning permit in place, and therefore, a buyer can proceed with the development as specified by the permit and approved plans. They will then complete the next stage in applying for the building permit. It is very important to know that plans/permits for one property cannot be used on another property. You must obtain a separate permit for each one.

The process of applying for a planning permit is outlined in the next flowchart/diagram.

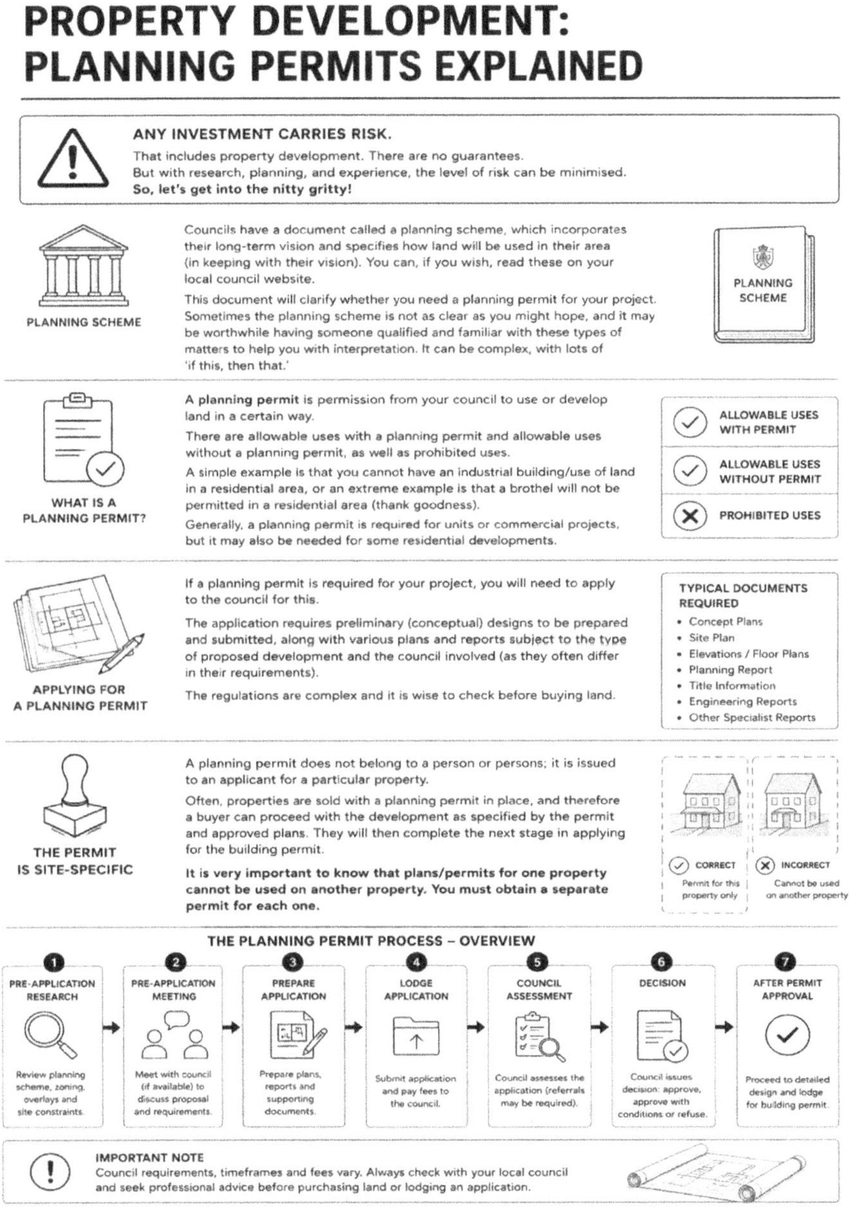

A building permit, now more commonly issued by a private building surveyor (though some councils still issue them), is permission to build the proposed development.

The application requires the preparation of construction plans (or working drawings) and the relevant design documentation. These are the plans a builder will work from during the construction of your project.

If a planning permit is required for the project, the building permit application plans must match the concept designs/drawings approved for the planning permit.

A registered building practitioner is required to complete the plans and documentation for both planning and building permit applications.

The Land

If you already have your land, the first item to check off is your Certificate of Title. This will not only give you the site's dimensions but also detail any restrictions imposed on the site. Some of the restrictions include:

Easements

An easement is a section of land registered on your property title where you cannot build, such as where there may be drains. It gives someone the right to use the land for a specific purpose, even if they are not the landowners. Permission may be granted to build eaves over the easement, but this should not be taken for granted.

Covenants

Covenants were placed on titles many years ago, usually at the time of the original subdivision, to create some certainty about the type(s) of development that would occur on the land within the original subdivision.

Many residential lots have titles that contain restrictive covenants. Covenants can limit the use and development of land in various ways and *may therefore* cause difficulties if the landowner wishes to develop their land.

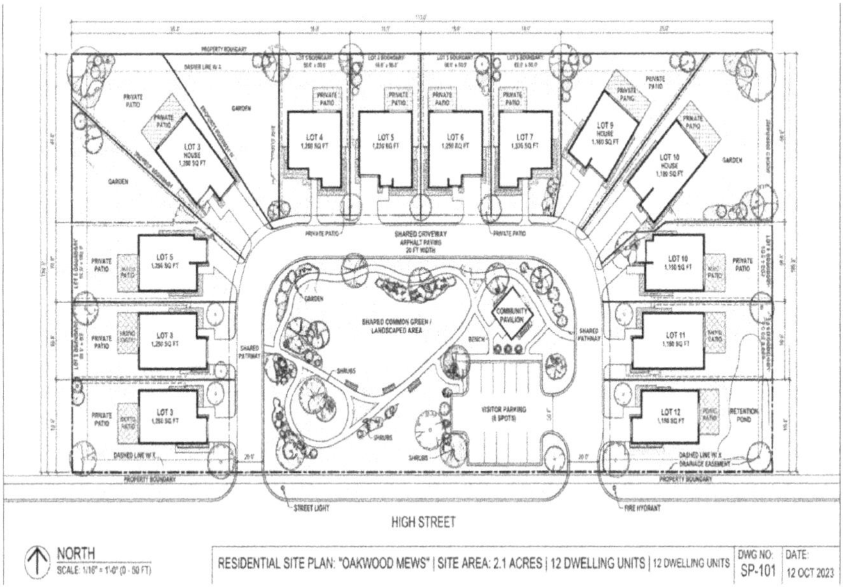

The most common restrictions of covenants are as follows:

- No more than one dwelling house and associated outbuilding may be erected.
- Only single-storey dwellings may be erected.
- Construction of a dwelling must be done with brick or any other approved (specified) material.
- The roof of any building must be slate or tiles (as opposed to metal deck).

- The value of the dwelling must not be less than a specified amount.
- No sand or earth may be removed from the land, nor may any quarrying be done on the land.

Covenants can, in some cases, be removed when applying for a planning permit. As part of this process, or with the assistance of a solicitor, covenants may be removed by making an application through the courts.

Section 173 Agreements

This is an agreement reached under the named section of the Planning and Environment Act 1987 and is usually made with the council (the responsible authority) and the owner or potential purchaser of the land. The agreement will detail various conditions and/or restrictions on how the land can be developed or used, which can also be registered on the title.

If you are on the hunt for just the right block, then request the sale documents, specifically the Section 32 Statement or equivalent in the relevant state. This is a statement by the owner/seller to potential purchasers, detailing certain information about the property title that should be known before signing a contract to buy the land.

The information noted above (re: easements, covenants, and Section 173 agreements) can form part of your research so that you do not end up purchasing property that you cannot use as you would like.

You may like to consider employing the services of a buyer's agent, who can source land specific to your project, or approach someone or a business with specific knowledge and experience in planning and design prior to purchase/signing contracts.

The next step is to check the zoning for your land. This is part of the planning scheme mentioned earlier. Land is earmarked or zoned by councils for use in a specific way, such as housing (residential), business, or industrial use. For example, there are currently forty-eight zones in Victoria. Each one will have its own set of requirements and – dare I say it – restrictions. It will also specify whether a planning permit is required and the information that must be provided and submitted to the council with an application for a planning permit.

Overlays should also be considered. Overlays are a special feature of the land; examples include significant vegetation, heritage, or flood risks. As another example, there are 26 types of overlays in Victoria. You can find out how your land is zoned and if any overlays apply in a number of ways, including:

- contacting your local council
- checking the Section 32 Statement/equivalent
- contacting a consultant.

Designing Your 'For Now' Home, Your Dream Home, or Maximising the Return on Your Investment?

This can be nerve-wracking because there is, without a doubt, a lot of money involved. So, it is important to be realistic. With *careful* planning, you can keep expenses to a minimum. There are a lot of things to consider, and I will try to cover them all here.

Decisions, decisions! You could choose a spec home builder, a design-and-construct company, or a company that prepares custom designs. There are advantages and disadvantages to each option.

Spec Home Builder

Traditionally, this term means a new house is designed and constructed (display home), with the expectation that sales of that design will result from an inspection. That is, you can purchase this house design for the company's fixed price on your land (but remember, conditions apply). Because of the volume build, the builder may receive bulk buying discounts and could pass some of those discounts on to the purchaser.

Disadvantages include that the design may not suit your site, or take into account orientation to the sun, views, or neighbours. It is less likely to be in keeping with the character of the neighbourhood, and most likely unsuitable for land with fall (slope). As the term 'volume build' implies, there may be a number of similar dwellings in an area, thereby reducing resale value.

Design and Construct Company

This is where a building company quotes to build, renovate, or extend your home and includes the design process as part of the package. It is a good way to know the final costs from the beginning, and some companies use in-house building designers to complete the design work.

Advantages include that these projects are designed specifically for your site and needs. The total cost includes the design process, and saves you the time and trouble of finding a builder and going to tender.

Disadvantages include that the projects are designed for profitability rather than for inspirational, functional design. You cannot have this type of company design your project and then choose another builder. Furthermore, not every home style is suitable for this kind of service. For example, some companies will only complete second-storey additions to certain types of homes.

A Custom-Designed Home or Renovation

This is where you engage a company that specialises in creating personalised custom designs, such as a building designer. They will consult you regarding the land (pre-purchase, if required), your wish list for your home or renovation, and the regulations. They will create a design to marry your goals, the site's potential, and council regulations.

Advantages often include obtaining a better result, such as a custom-designed home or renovation tailored to your individual needs. Your design choices are only limited by site or council restrictions. The property will be designed to take advantage of the sun, any views, and to enhance the privacy and enjoyment of your home. Further, resale value is generally higher for custom-designed homes.

The biggest disadvantage is that this option is more expensive than the other two. Most will say this downside is outweighed by the advantage of a personalised, custom design that suits your lifestyle or investment goals.

The custom design process will consider:

- your budget
- your family (existing/planned)
- lifestyle
- the land, including all the items noted earlier, such as the easements and other restrictions

- trees; there may be trees on the site that can be retained, or some may need to be removed. In some areas, permits are required for tree removal, and this should be thoroughly investigated before work begins
- there may be a building envelope, which means you can only build within that area on the site
- the type of property you're looking for (e.g. modern, period style, or open-plan living).

So, What's The Important Stuff to Think About When Designing a New Dwelling?

Whilst there is no crystal ball, there are quite a few things that warrant attention and can produce better results:

- think about how long you may live in the property, or what your goal is with it (e.g., buy-and-hold, flip, or rent it out and live in it later).
- It should have an owner-occupier appeal.
- Corridors take up lots of space, so it could be worth keeping them to a minimum.
- think ahead - children become teenagers, and then adults, quickly. They need and want their own space(s), such as study areas. If you can afford it, there are many advantages to adding en-suites (albeit smaller ones) off their rooms; this would appeal to a wider demographic and perhaps have better resale value.
- if the home you are planning is two-storey, think about cavity and storage spaces under the stairs, as well as sitting/storage areas at the landings.
- if the budget is tight, you may also like to consider designing a bigger home, completing the 'shell' (exterior walls), and fitting out some of it later (rather than doing

an extension, which can be even more costly). Again, it depends on the purpose.

- consider the home's orientation on the land (e.g., outdoor living areas facing north to capture passive solar energy and warmth).
- the connection between your indoor and outdoor living areas should flow.
- street appeal; I hear of so many people who love living in their property, whether it is their own or a rental, but dislike the house's first impression.
- given the location of the windows and the furniture you may already have, the design will need to account for any slope on the land and other natural features.

This list can seem quite extensive, but a great designer should challenge you to think of all the above, and then some!

Once you have finalised your design and sketch plans have been completed to a sufficient level of detail, a preliminary costing can be prepared by either a quantity surveyor (QS), building cost estimator, or a builder. This will give you a gauge of how much it will cost to build. This could be an important step before proceeding with the construction (working drawings), because it is easier to change the design at this point if the indicative build cost comes in too high. If you wait until the construction drawings are complete or the building permit has been issued, changes after this point will incur additional design/documentation fees (most likely for the building surveyor to amend the permit).

It is well worth discussing your overall budget with the designer, as this can significantly impact the designer's approach and the suggestions they make to you. For example:

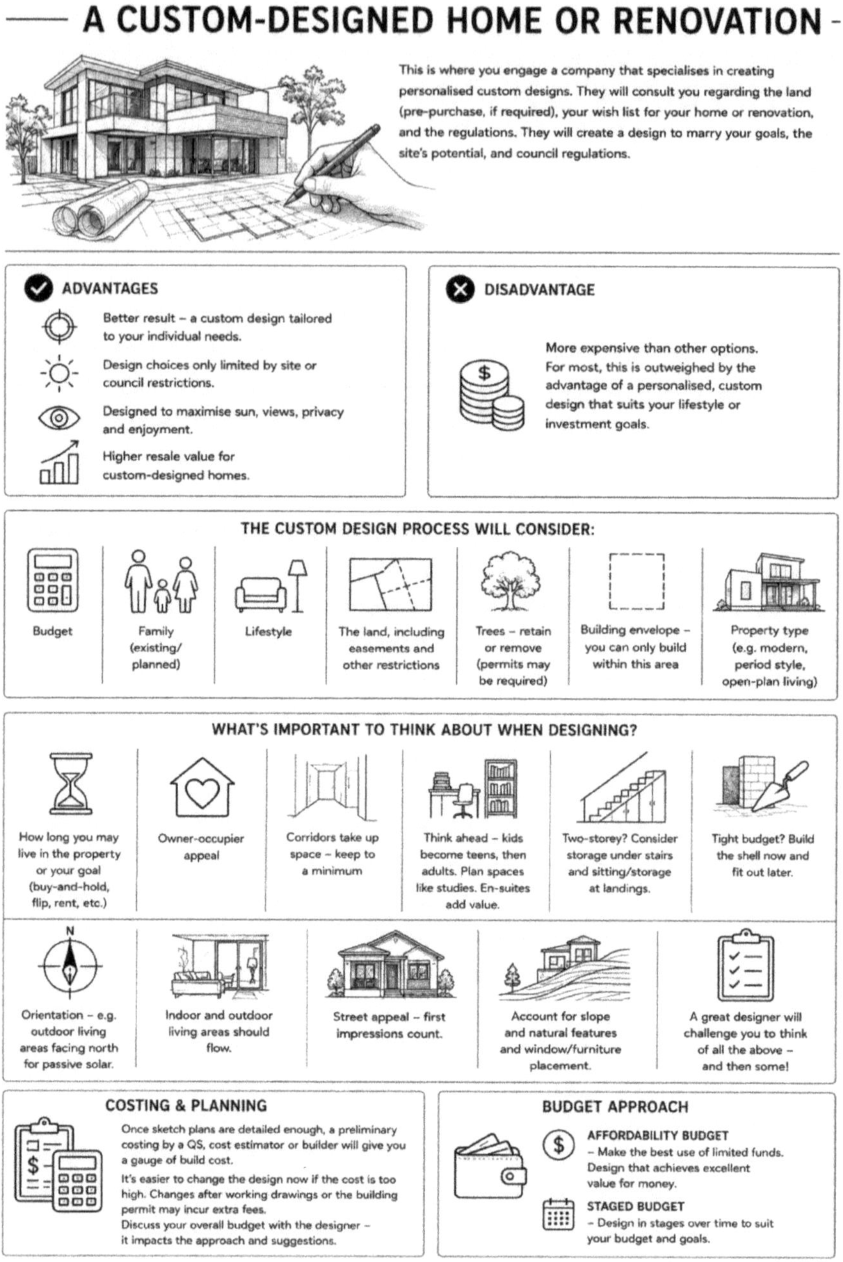

Affordability Budget

– making the best use of the limited funds available. This requires a design that achieves excellent value for money.

Staged Budget

– The entire budget is not available in one lump sum but may be available over time in a couple of or multiple instalments. The designer would create the overall design of the build that could be completed in stages. Generally, planning permits and building permits are valid for two years (you can also apply for extensions, although this should not be relied upon).

Development Budget

– The primary goal is to obtain a profit on the sale of the property within a couple of years.

Capitalisation Conscious Budget

– The owner and designer are trying to reduce the risk of overcapitalisation on the property. Overcapitalisation may occur if the money spent on the home exceeds its potential resale value. Several factors come into play when assessing the risk of overcapitalisation, including location, the quality of the work, the size of the home (or renovation), and the state of the market at the time.

On another note, some believe that the quality of life and lifestyle is more important in the family home than the risk of overcapitalising. If this is an investment property, you should not have your owner-occupier hat on, but you should have your commercial hat on. Yes, the property should have appeal, but many things can be appealing with less expensive inclusions.

Investment Budget

– The aim is to achieve long-term rents from the investment property (and, quite likely, capital growth and low maintenance costs).

The cost of building your home (or renovation/extension) can vary considerably based upon:

- whether you are renovating or building new (the former is often more expensive per square metre)
- the size of the project
- the type of construction (e.g. the type of roof or exterior cladding)
- the number of areas requiring fittings and fixtures, such as bathrooms, en-suites, kitchens, and laundries, as well as the quality of the fittings and fixtures, and the slope of the site – the steeper the site, the more it usually costs to build on. Because foundations and supporting structures differ, additional excavation may be needed, along with retaining walls, for example.
- access to the site for the delivery and handling of materials
- the type of soil conditions on the site, which may impact upon the foundations needed
- whether rock is present on the site, potentially requiring additional excavation
- availability of services, such as water supply, storm water, sewer lines, electricity, gas, and phone
- a contingency sum: an amount usually allowed by most builders to cover unforeseen costs. For example, undertaking a renovation/extension has been known to lead to the discovery of termites in the frame, which then requires replacement and treatment for further protection. A contingency sum could usually be around 5–10% of the budget.
- accurate and complete documents, which will minimise delays in the planning and building process.

Developing your Backyard (more traditionally known as 'Dual-Occupancy')

If two or more dwellings are proposed for a block of land, a planning permit is required.

It is essential that you have a designer who can determine if your project is feasible. Feasibility means that, based upon the designer's knowledge of the council planning scheme, the zone for the land, their understanding of any restrictions, and the council's preferred developments for the area, you are more likely to achieve a permit than not. And if it *is* feasible, what exactly does that mean? There is no 100% guarantee that your project will receive a planning permit (or permission from council).

When a planning permit is required, the following information needs to be gathered and prepared:

Planning Permit Application Form

Complete the application form for a planning permit and pay the relevant application fee.

Copy of Title

A clear, legible copy of the certificate of title, showing current ownership of the land, needs to be provided and submitted with the application when it is lodged with council. The copy of title must be current and could range from one month to three months old (depending on the relevant council). Details of any registered covenants/restrictions on the land must also be provided.

Reports

These reports detail the proposal's consistency with the objectives of the State Planning Framework, Local Planning Policy Framework, and the Municipal Strategic Statement.

Site Re-Establishment and Feature Surveys

These surveys are prepared by a licensed land surveyor and provide information about the site, including elevations, contours, and the positions of fences and trees. You may contact a surveyor of your choice, or your designer may be able to arrange an external consultant on your behalf.

Neighbourhood and Site Description Plan and the Design Response Plan

These plans detail all properties within a fifty-metre radius (at a minimum) of the subject site and address all the requirements of the relevant clauses of the local council's planning scheme, as well as how the proposed development responds to the neighbourhood.

Photographs

Detailed photographs of the subject site and surrounding properties (including those opposite the site) must be submitted with the application.

Site/Floor Plan

The site/floor plan is required to include the following:

- the dimensions of the land as detailed on the certificate of title
- a floor plan, with a description indicating the use of all rooms

- the location and internal dimensions of any garages, car spaces, and/or carport structures
- setbacks from all boundaries
- adjoining building envelopes/windows facing the subject site within nine metres of the property boundaries
- location and width of existing and/or proposed vehicle crossovers (driveways)
- location, height, and the construction materials of existing and/or proposed fencing
- site levels and finished floor levels to the Australian Height Datum (AHD)
- any existing vegetation proposed to be retained – with details including height and full botanical name
- location and size of any easements on/or adjacent to the site.

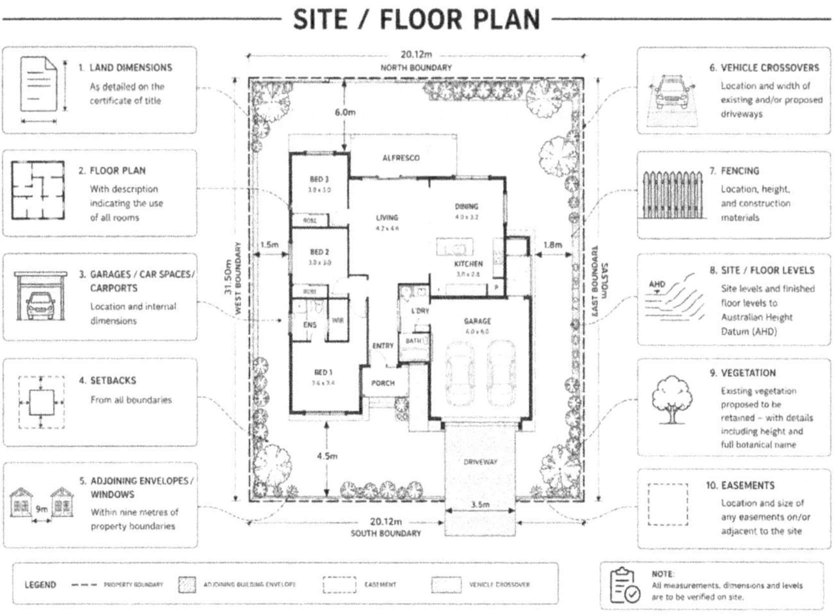

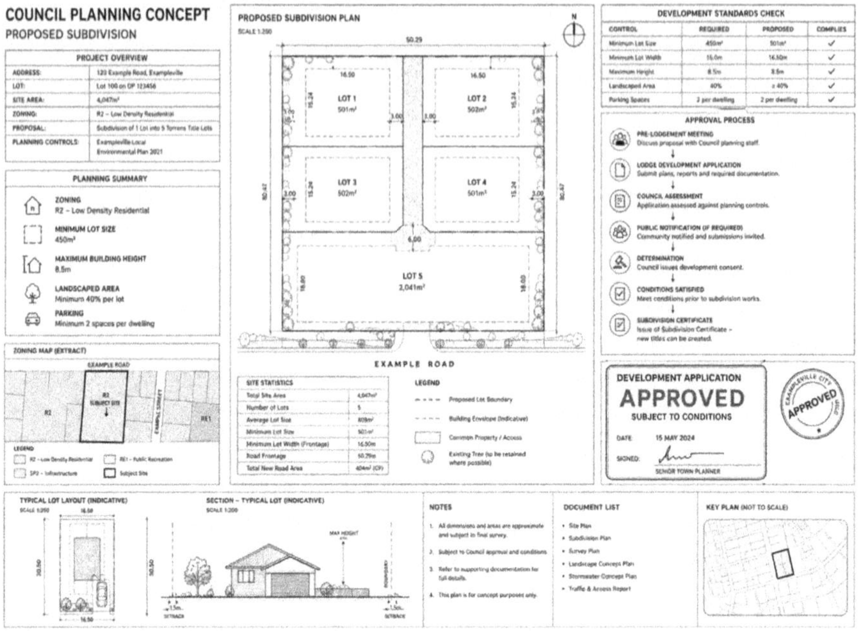

Elevations

Dwelling

The elevations must be provided for all sides (of all dwellings) and detail the following:

- the natural ground level, and the height of the finished floor levels above the natural ground level
- external wall heights and overall building heights, measured from natural ground level
- the position of all windows, along with the sill height of the windows, measured from the finished floor level
- the location and extent of any proposed cut and fill.

Front Fence

The elevations of the front fence are required to detail:

- construction materials and finishes
- dimensions of all components of the fence, as measured above natural ground level.

Shadow Diagrams

On separate plans, shadow diagrams must be supplied at 9.00 am, 12.00 noon, and 3.00 pm on the 22nd of September (this date is midway between the shortest and longest days of the year).

Schedule of External Finishes, Materials, and Colours, including:

- All external walls
- Roof
- Fascia
- Window frames
- External doors
- Paving, including car park surfacing.

Arborist Report

The Arborist Report should detail all established, significant trees on-site, or on adjoining land within five metres of the property boundary. The condition of the trees will be assessed, including:

- accurate location
- full botanical name

- DBH (diameter of trunk at breast height) – i.e. trunk calliper at approximately 1.4 metres above ground
- critical root zone
- health, structure, and form of the trees
- the tolerance of each tree to the proposed development works
- suitability for retention
- tree protection measures, if retained.

Development Summary

The development summary will provide information for both existing and proposed conditions, including:

- site area
- number of dwellings
- floor areas
- number of car spaces
- area of private/total open space
- building site coverage
- percentage of impervious surfaces.

Plans and Elevations

Copies of all plans and elevations will be required in either A3 or A4 size, in addition to A1 plans submitted with the application.

Additional Information

Additional information may be required if the land is subject to a Heritage Overlay, a Special Building Overlay, or any other overlay. An overlay, as I have previously touched on, is a council control. It could relate to, for example, tree/vegetation protection, siting, or the specified size of subdivisions. Note: There may be more than one overlay that applies to an area.

Development Contributions

Some councils impose a development contribution fee, which is used to establish and/or maintain parks and council infrastructure.

Landscape Plan

These details address the areas of the site to be landscaped, as well as specify the materials and plants to be used for both the common and private areas of the proposed development.

Councils may differ slightly in their requirements for planning applications because they have their own Housing Strategy or municipal planning scheme. Examples of this include coastal, rural, and metropolitan. As these areas can differ greatly, it makes sense that their planning schemes would too.

It is difficult to determine how long a typical town planning application will take. This depends upon the size of the project and the council involved. Generally, four to six months would be needed. A quick turnaround can be completed in as little as 45 days, while the longer side of things could stretch to 2 years, or, if you are unlucky, even more.

Once a planning permit has been received, the next step is to obtain a building permit. Refer to the "project flowchart" for an outline of the process. The building permit process is usually quite straightforward and does not take as long as a planning permit. Approximately four to six weeks should be allowed.

If a planning application is refused a permit, you could have the option to appeal at VCAT (Victorian Civil Administrative Tribunal) or your state equivalent. This is also detailed on the "Planning Permit Process" flowchart.

Renovations and Extensions

Hereafter, these projects will be affectionately called 'renos.' Let's be honest – they are not for the fainthearted!

They can be challenging at worst, and frustrating at best, but they can also be extremely rewarding if one thinks laterally, begins with the end in mind, has a bucketload of patience, and is willing to be flexible. And you might need to get used to a bit – ok, a lot – of dust as well. For some people, and depending on the size of the renovation, you might want to factor in accommodation in the budget!

Renos can be more expensive per square metre, so a realistic budget and a bit of cash (or a loan) will not go astray. Bear in mind that if you were to sell your home and buy elsewhere, the buying and selling costs alone can equate to $100,000. So, redirecting this money to your current place of residence or the house you have just purchased can be very worthwhile.

The first message is to dig deep. Get real about your goals. Ask yourself what you are trying to achieve in doing the reno in the first instance?

Some might argue that you can never overcapitalise on your own home/lifestyle, but this does not mean that making your house a mansion in the worst street or the worst suburb is the wisest choice. Having said that, if you are planning to stay for the long term, at least seven to ten years post-reno (which is the next property cycle), you will most likely see a return on your financial investment.

Unless you were the original designer of the home and know exactly what happened on-site during the construction process, you will not know what is behind the walls or under the roof until the various materials are removed in the demolition part of your renovation. This means your reno will be designed based on the current floorplan, and what is reasonable to assume is behind the walls and under the roof. This is true regardless of whether you have the original plans. If you do not have an original/current copy of the plans, a full measure-up and redraw of the existing house will be required.

It is important to know that sometimes builders and/or carpenters will make changes along the way during the construction process, as do homeowners. These changes may be to get a better result on-site. Once the plaster has been removed and what is behind is revealed, the construction may need to be done differently from what was planned (e.g., as drawn on the plans).

The advantage of being on-site throughout the renovation process is that decisions can be made on the spot if need be. In some instances, these changes may need to and/or should go back to the council and/or a building surveyor for approval, but often they do not.

So, the plans are prepared, based on what can be seen at the time and what the homeowner wants. All structural work will require a building permit, and most renovations will be in this category. Some will require a planning permit too. For example, if your property has a foothill overlay or a bushfire management overlay, these will trigger the need for a planning permit.

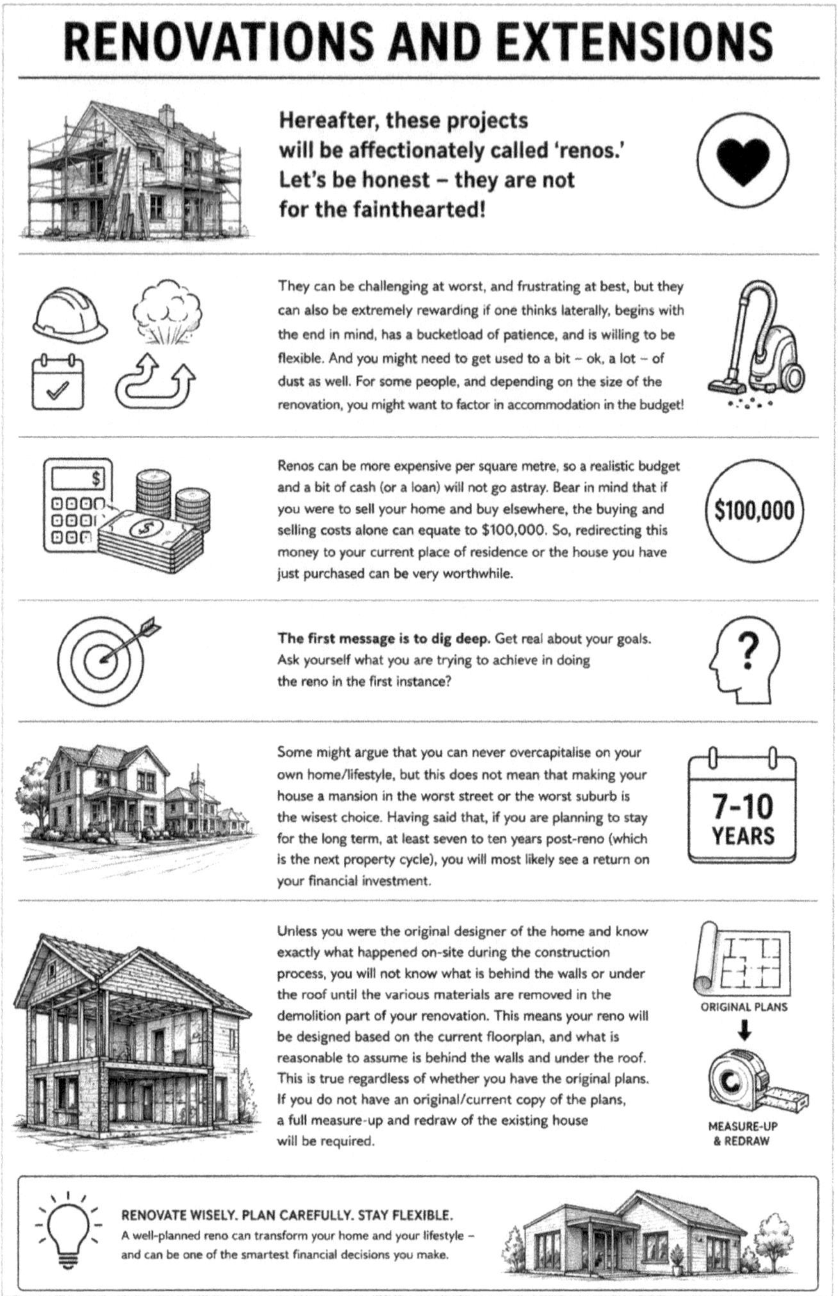

The next section will feature a case study about a significant renovation (and, yes, extension).

Scenario

Client:

Mum, Dad, and three children (6, 9, and 12 years old respectively).

Project:

Second-storey addition to the house, and renovation/upgrade of other areas.

Specifics:

New master bedroom, ensuite, study, and retreat area.

Combine kitchen, existing study, family room, and part of existing deck into one, open plan area.

Design/fit out new kitchen.

Construct new deck.

Required removal of load bearing walls, and engineering computations for beams (to replace the load bearing walls). Additional footings were also required underneath the existing house.

Goal:

No one in the family wanted to move. The house was aging, and the parents had a desire for better living spaces for their growing family in the longer term (ten years or longer).

Constraints:

Slope of the land.

An overlay on the site meant that the overall size of the house (and deck) could not exceed 40% site cover.

Permits:

The renovation required a planning permit and building permit.

This type of project is significant and involved quite a few thousand dollars. A builder was engaged, rather than the clients managing the project and all the tradespeople required themselves. This is completely recommended when you are not in the building industry or do not have experience in renovating a property.

The project commenced in February and took approximately six months to complete. The family only moved out for one week whilst the new flooring was laid/sealed.

Challenges:

Dust, dust, and more dust. This meant nightly vacuuming sessions to reduce dust and make living in the space as easy as possible.

At one point, a tradesperson's foot went through the ceiling (in an area not even being renovated)! One of the carpenters working on the new upper-storey frame accidentally stepped onto and through the ceiling below. The builder was required to patch and repair this (at his expense).

Managing the renovation and everyday life through winter, particularly with a makeshift kitchen and huge tarpaulins on the roof for an extended period. To begin with, the tradies were able to complete a fair proportion of the renovation without entering the house. However, an upper-storey renovation requires removing a portion of the existing roof at some point. A tarpaulin was then placed over the makeshift roof, which is often not watertight nor wind resistant.

Some of the local wildlife invited themselves inside – thanks to the tarpaulin roof, there were many nooks that made this possible. The family would hear the rustling of said wildlife in the night and have to evict them.

Another challenge was looking after the family pets and making sure they did not escape with so many people coming and going was also a challenge at times.

The "TARDIS" (a.k.a. the builders loo) at the front of the property was a bit of an eyesore.

Their front lawn was, essentially, murdered, and some of their plants suffered the same fate.

A final challenge was cleaning up after tradespeople, as each person's definition of clean can be completely different! As mentioned earlier, the vacuum cleaner worked overtime and ultimately had to be replaced!

Outcome:

The final product was an updated and much more modern, appealing home. It contained fabulous new living spaces, with separate areas for study and quiet times. As a result, family members no longer had the feeling that they were 'on top of one another.'

There were no budget blowouts as considerable thought had gone into the design (which is always a good thing).

Would They Have Done Anything Differently?

The family only wished that they had done the renovation/extension years earlier so that they could have had more time to enjoy the new areas. It was the best thing they ever did.

Renos can be a daunting, confronting, and messy exercise, but with appropriate planning and guidance, a fabulous result can be achieved. Try not to be swayed by horror stories; often, these are the result of trying to cut corners and/or doing the project on the smell of an oily rag. Be guided by the experts, and what you really want and need for you and your family!

In Summary

Extending, subdividing, constructing, and developing are not projects to be undertaken by those who are time poor! They are projects better suited to those who wish to buy and hold or buy and flip.

Mistakes often made by owner-builders include using credit cards to pay for work, letting emotion into the decision-making process (regarding upgrades and inclusions), not allowing a buffer, and/or not fully assessing feasibility.

With many, if not all, of these projects, they can carry slightly higher risk (which is variable, based upon who undertakes them) in that more time and expertise are usually needed. However, the results can be positive, with higher yields, greater growth, and profit potential, thereby increasing wealth.

It is important to understand all the financial aspects involved, including costs, risks, time, effort versus reward, sell versus hold, and allowances for profit (around 20%). Tax and time can dilute the return on investment, plus one should consider opportunity costs.

Private Lending in Construction and Development: Where It Truly Comes Into Its Own

There is a point in every property journey where planning ends and reality begins. On paper, construction appears controlled. Numbers align, timelines are mapped, and the outcome looks predictable. In practice, construction is fluid. It shifts, adapts, and often challenges the very assumptions it began with. This is the point where traditional lending begins to struggle, and where private lending not only assists but leads.

This chapter is not about theory. It is about what happens on site, in real projects, with real borrowers. Builders, developers, and everyday investors all eventually reach a stage where they need a lender that understands movement rather than resisting it. That is where private lending comes into its own.

Construction Is Not Linear — And Lending Should Not Be Either

The starting point is simple. Construction does not follow a straight line.

A borrower might begin with a clear plan. They acquire land, obtain permits, engage a builder, and set a budget. At that moment, the project fits perfectly within a traditional lending framework. But construction rarely stays within that initial boundary.

Costs rise. Materials become scarce. Labour availability tightens. Weather intervenes. Variations are introduced, sometimes by necessity, sometimes by ambition. A project that began modestly becomes something more substantial.

At the same time, external pressures may arise. Interest rates shift. Market sentiment changes. Builders encounter financial difficulty. In recent years, builder collapses have become more common, leaving partially completed projects across the country.

Traditional lenders are not designed for this environment. They require the certainty that exists at the beginning of the project to remain intact throughout. Once that certainty breaks, the structure no longer fits.

Private lending is built around the understanding that certainty will not hold.

Entering a Project Mid-Stream — The Defining Advantage

One of the most powerful aspects of private lending is its ability to step into a project after it has already begun. This is not a minor feature that sits quietly in the background. It is the defining advantage that separates private lending from traditional finance in the construction space.

In reality, very few projects go exactly to plan from day one through to completion. Borrowers rarely run out of ambition, but they often run out of capital. A project might begin with strong intent and sufficient funds, but as construction progresses, the financial demands evolve. Costs increase, variations are introduced, and what once seemed comfortably funded begins to tighten.

At this point, borrowers start looking for additional funding, and the timing of that need is rarely convenient. They do not seek funding at the beginning, when everything is neat and policy-compliant. They seek funding when the project is already underway.

This commonly occurs when:

- The slab has been poured, but the original funding has been exhausted
- The frame is complete, yet the builder cannot continue without further payment
- The property has reached the lock-up stage, but finishing costs have increased significantly
- The project is more than halfway complete, but there is no remaining capital to finish

Each of these scenarios represents a project in motion, not a project at the starting line. For a traditional lender, this is precisely the problem. Their preference is to assess the entire transaction at the outset, with all variables defined. When a project is already in progress, it no longer fits that model.

Private lending takes the opposite view. It does not attempt to rewind the project back to day one. Instead, it accepts the project as it exists today and asks a different set of questions. What matters is not how the project started, but where it stands now and how it can be completed.

The lender looks at the land, the improvements already made, the remaining cost to complete, and the value once the work is finished. From this position, a funding structure is built.

This approach changes the outcome entirely. Instead of a project being declined because it no longer fits policy, it is assessed based on its current reality. This is how incomplete projects move forward rather than remain stalled indefinitely.

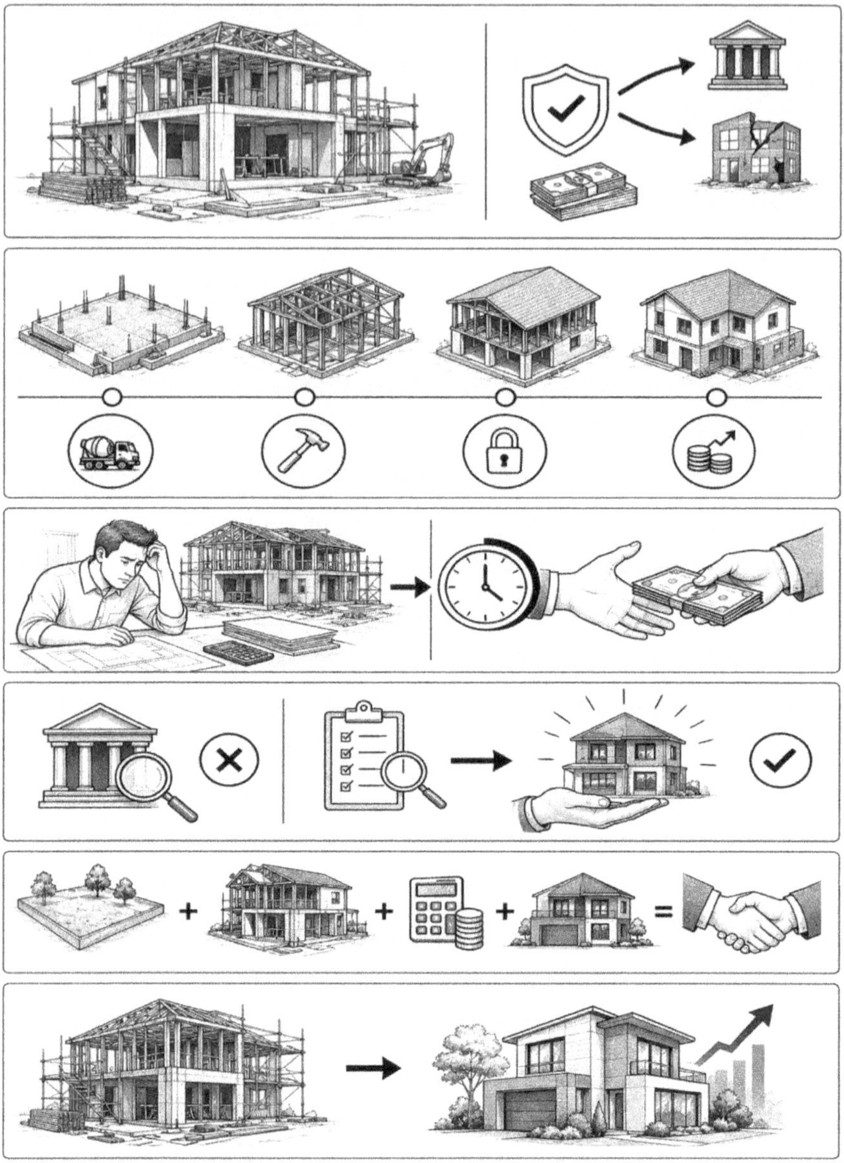

A Real Scenario: The Half-Built Dream

To understand this in practical terms, consider a borrower who sets out to build a duplex. They begin with equity in their land and enough capital to commence construction. The early stages progress well. The slab is poured, the frame goes up, and the property reaches lock-up.

At this point, the project looks successful from the outside. Structure is in place, and the end product is within sight. However, beneath the surface, the financial position has changed.

During construction, the borrower has made a series of decisions. They upgrade finishes, improve design elements, and add features that enhance the final product. Each decision appears reasonable on its own. Collectively, they increase the total cost beyond the original budget.

By the time the project reaches lock-up, the borrower has exhausted their funds.

They approach a bank for additional finance. The response is structured and predictable. The bank requests updated financials, a fixed-price contract for completion, confirmation of remaining funds, and evidence of serviceability at current interest rates.

The borrower cannot satisfy these requirements. The project does not meet policy. The application is declined.

At this point, the borrower is left with a partially completed asset. It cannot be sold at full value because it is not finished. It cannot be refinanced because it does not meet lending criteria. It exists in a financial gap.

Private lending steps into that gap.

The lender assesses the land, the completed works, the remaining cost, and the end value of the finished duplex. Based on this, funding is provided to complete the build.

Once completed, the borrower regains control. They can sell at full market value or refinance into a traditional loan.

The difference between these two outcomes is not the project itself. It is the lending structure applied to it.

Understanding GRV — The Forward View That Changes Everything

At the centre of private construction lending is a concept that shifts the entire assessment: Gross Realisable Value, or GRV.

GRV represents the value of the project once it is completed. It is not speculative in the casual sense. It is based on comparable sales, market demand, and the characteristics of the finished product. It is a grounded estimate of the asset's value when it is no longer a work in progress.

Private lenders use this forward view to structure their loans. Instead of relying solely on the current value, they consider the project's trajectory.

This allows lending to be based on:

- The value of the land
- The value of completed works
- The projected end value

In many cases, lending reaches approximately 65-70% of GRV, depending on the nature of the project and whether it is an investment or owner-occupied.

This is a fundamental shift. It recognises that value is not static. It is created through completion.

Traditional lenders remain anchored to the present. Their assessment is heavily weighted toward current valuation and strict cost certainty. This limits their ability to support projects that are not fully formed.

Private lending recognises that a project in motion carries future value, and that value can be responsibly used to structure funding.

No Pre-Sales — Retaining Control of the Project

In traditional development finance, pre-sales are often a requirement. Developers must secure buyers before construction begins, locking in contracts to demonstrate demand and reduce lender risk.

While this provides comfort to the lender, it creates constraints for the developer. Pre-sales often require discounted pricing, extended marketing periods, and a level of commitment from buyers who have not yet seen the finished product.

Private lending removes this requirement in many cases. Developments can proceed based on value and structure, rather than pre-commitment.

This allows developers to build first and sell later. It allows them to present a completed product to the market and achieve pricing that reflects actual demand rather than early-stage assumptions.

Control remains with the developer. They are not forced to shape their project around lender requirements. Instead, the lending structure adapts to the project.

Borrowing Capacity — When It Stops Being the Centrepiece

Traditional lending begins with income. It is the foundation of every assessment. The borrower must demonstrate the ability to service the loan over time.

Private lending shifts the focus entirely. The central question is no longer whether the borrower can service the loan indefinitely, but how the loan will be repaid within a defined timeframe.

Where the exit is clear—through sale or refinance—ongoing income becomes less critical.

This allows borrowers to proceed with projects even where traditional serviceability models would prevent them. It recognises that not all loans are designed to be held long-term.

Owner-Builders — The Reality That Cannot Be Ignored

Owner-builders represent a practical reality that sits outside traditional policy. Many borrowers have the skill and experience to manage their own construction projects. They engage trades directly, control costs, and shape the build according to their vision.

Banks, however, generally avoid these scenarios. The absence of a licensed builder and fixed-price contract introduces uncertainty that does not align with standard lending frameworks.

Private lending addresses this gap. It does not assume failure simply because the structure is different. Instead, it assesses the project on its merits.

The key questions remain consistent:

- What has been built
- What remains
- What will the final outcome be

This allows owner-builder projects to move forward when they would otherwise stall.

Builder Collapse — When the System Needs a Second Chance

Builder insolvency has left many projects incomplete. Borrowers are often left in a position where they have invested significant funds but cannot proceed.

Traditional lenders rarely step into these situations. The uncertainty is too great.

Private lenders treat incomplete construction as a scenario to be assessed, not avoided. Funding is structured to complete the project, restore value, and enable an exit.

This provides a second chance for projects that would otherwise remain unfinished.

Cost-Plus Contracts — Flexibility That Requires Discipline

Not all construction can be fixed at the outset. Cost-plus contracts allow projects to evolve, providing flexibility in materials and design.

Private lending accepts this reality. However, flexibility introduces risk.

Without careful management, costs can expand beyond expectations. This can reduce equity and place pressure on the project.

To manage this, lenders rely on structured oversight, including detailed cost analysis and independent verification.

Flexibility is allowed, but it must be supported by discipline.

Quantity Surveyors — Bringing Structure to a Moving Process

In a dynamic construction environment, independent verification becomes essential. Quantity surveyors provide this structure.

They assess what has been completed, what remains, and whether the project is financially viable.

Their role ensures that funding decisions are based on measurable reality rather than assumptions.

Without this layer of verification, lending would rely too heavily on projections. With it, the process becomes controlled and accountable.

Closing Thought

Each of these points is not isolated. They work together.

Private lending does not succeed just because of one feature; it succeeds because it aligns with how construction actually works.

Projects do not need to be perfect. They need to be understood.

And that is the difference.

Construction is not static. It moves, evolves, and adapts.

Lending that supports construction must do the same.

Private lending does not attempt to impose a rigid structure on a dynamic process. It works within that process, providing funding where and when it is needed, based on what the project is today and what it will become.

For builders, developers, and investors, this is not just another lending option.

It is the mechanism that turns incomplete projects into completed ones.

And that is where its value is most clearly seen.

16.

Commercial Finance and Property

In Australia, more than half of the workforce is employed by over two million small to medium enterprises:

Industrial, office space, and retail properties make up the commercial landscape. Demographic patterns will influence some commercial sectors. Infrastructure for healthcare and aged care is becoming the norm in holiday destinations, with baby boomers seeking out a sea change. The growing demand for childcare services has created a need for this type of commercial property, while the rise of online shopping has increased demand for warehouses.

Our growing population has put pressure on parking availability and costs in capital cities; investing in a single or commercial car park is becoming increasingly popular.

The biggest difference between this market and the residential market is that it is more macro, and Government policy conditions affect the commercial space. Economics, as distinct from market conditions, can vary across commercial property grades and regions, driven by consumer spending and interest rates. This, in turn, influences the success of the tenant occupying your property and their ability to stay in business, which will all impact your property. Commercial property is riskier when it comes to vacancy. More macro-level classifications apply to commercial property; entire sectors can be affected at any one time within a region, rather than being more specific to a particular suburb. Tourist accommodation, retail property, offices, and industrial spaces can all suffer across an entire region.

On the whole, it is investors seeking yield who support the demand for commercial property. The problem with commercial property is its inherent lack of long-term, stable growth – just like the stock market, which is directly linked to the corporate world.

Many experts say that there is a high percentage of business failure in the first two years. 60% of small businesses fail in the first three years, according to *Inside Small Business*. Vacancy rates can be high, which soon offset the higher yields of around 8%.

Commercial property may include businesses, shops, retail, resort-style offices, factories, farms, multi-unit developments, warehouses, industrial units, mixed residential and commercial use, and income-producing properties. The list goes on. The value of the properties in question is based on their rental returns. Often, the tenant pays all the outgoings (e.g., insurance, rates, and fit-out). This is a separate market from residential, which requires different knowledge and due diligence. This type of property can possibly be good for diversifying your portfolio, given that it can typically have higher yields.

Strata offices are becoming popular because tenants can rent them near where they live, allowing them to escape distractions and interruptions at home while expanding their business. Remember, strata title refers to a situation where an individual/entity owns part of the property, such as the dwelling (e.g., townhouse, unit, or office), but shares ownership of the rest of the property.

Standard residential and commercial lenders will generally lend up to 75% and can lend over $2.5 million for a commercial investment property. Whilst fifteen-year terms are more common, thirty-year terms are also possible. Lenders have dedicated lending teams for commercial property due to the industry's bespoke nature and the diversity of economic conditions that may bear on a credit decision. The biggest difference with commercial finance is that it does not fit neatly into predefined boxes as easily as residential lending, because it is less predictable. The required documentation is similar to that for a residential loan, whether low- or full-documentation. However, in commercial lending, future cash flow forecasts can be considered, rather than the black-and-white approach used in residential lending. Commercial lending is normally a non-coded loan.

Repayment frequency can be the same as residential lending (weekly, fortnightly, or monthly) with additional repayments allowed on fixed rates, though monthly repayments are normally used. There are sometimes early termination fees attached to the loan. Some lenders do provide unlimited cash out to 75% LVR (Loan-to-Value Ratio), which can also be used for working capital and the purchase of business equipment.

Trading businesses are more popular with lenders, providing a product or service as distinct from property sales activities, as these are less impacted (generally speaking) by the property industry as an economy. Non-developer businesses are nimbler, whereas a developer would find it problematic to reduce a thirty-unit development to fifteen.

Brokers are even more important in commercial finance; they can add significant value in packaging a deal and selling its strengths to the funder. Policy is less straightforward with commercial finance. Factors such as inventory finance, asset finance, unsecured finance, cash flow, and equipment and car finance must all be factored in (these financial details are beyond the scope of this book).

Commercial finance is the offering of loans for business purposes. The lender will need to be satisfied as to the business purpose, and any such lending is not covered under the *National Consumer Credit Protection Act 2009*.

A few examples of commercial finance include the purchase of a motor vehicle that is used predominantly for business use, commercial property (by nature and/or use), and business overdrafts and trade facilities (such as letters of credit, cash flow funding, or simply a loan to set up or purchase a business). However, for the purpose of this chapter, we will focus primarily on finance for commercial property.

The Upside of Commercial Property

Purchasing a commercial property for investment purposes is a genuine alternative to investing in residential property. One of the main benefits of owning commercial property over residential property is that the tenant generally covers all outgoings (property ownership costs), which are paid in addition to the rent. This means that the tenant pays for the rates, insurance, body corporate, and any other property ownership costs (other than land tax) that apply to the commercial property. Furthermore, the cost of preparing a commercial lease may be the tenant's responsibility. This generally results in a much higher yield to the owner.

Another benefit of commercial property is that the tenant may update and improve the property to better suit their business needs (e.g., fitting out the property for use is generally at the tenant's cost). Any modifications to the property may also require the tenant to 'make good' the property at the end of the lease. Tenants will generally maintain the property in top condition, as it is important to their business image, staff, and customers. Compare this to a residential investment; the landlord of a residential property has to ensure the property is presented at its best in order to attract a tenant, and the costs of any improvements are generally at the hand of the landlord.

Commercial properties also tend to have longer lease terms, which offer the landlord greater comfort and the ability to forecast cash flow. Leases normally have annual reviews, often last more than three years, and may also include options for further terms.

The Downside of Commercial Property

On the downside, commercial property may be more sensitive to the state of the economy, and values can be greatly affected at times of economic downturns. A commercial property may remain unoccupied for longer periods as businesses seek to reduce costs or downsize when the economy slows. Furthermore, commercial properties tend to lag behind residential properties in capital growth during economic upturns. Values are closely aligned with economic performance and business sentiment. As for residential property, we all need a roof over our heads, whether we rent or own an owner-occupied property. Therefore, residential property is less aligned with the performance of the economy and more aligned with supply-and-demand factors, which are directly affected by population growth and the number of new dwellings constructed.

Commercial property supply and demand can be influenced by a range of factors, including changes in infrastructure, local supply levels, specific requirements of potential business tenants, and business sentiment. Importantly, the value of a commercial property is largely influenced by the quality of the tenant and the lease term, so a higher level of expertise is required when considering the investment value equation.

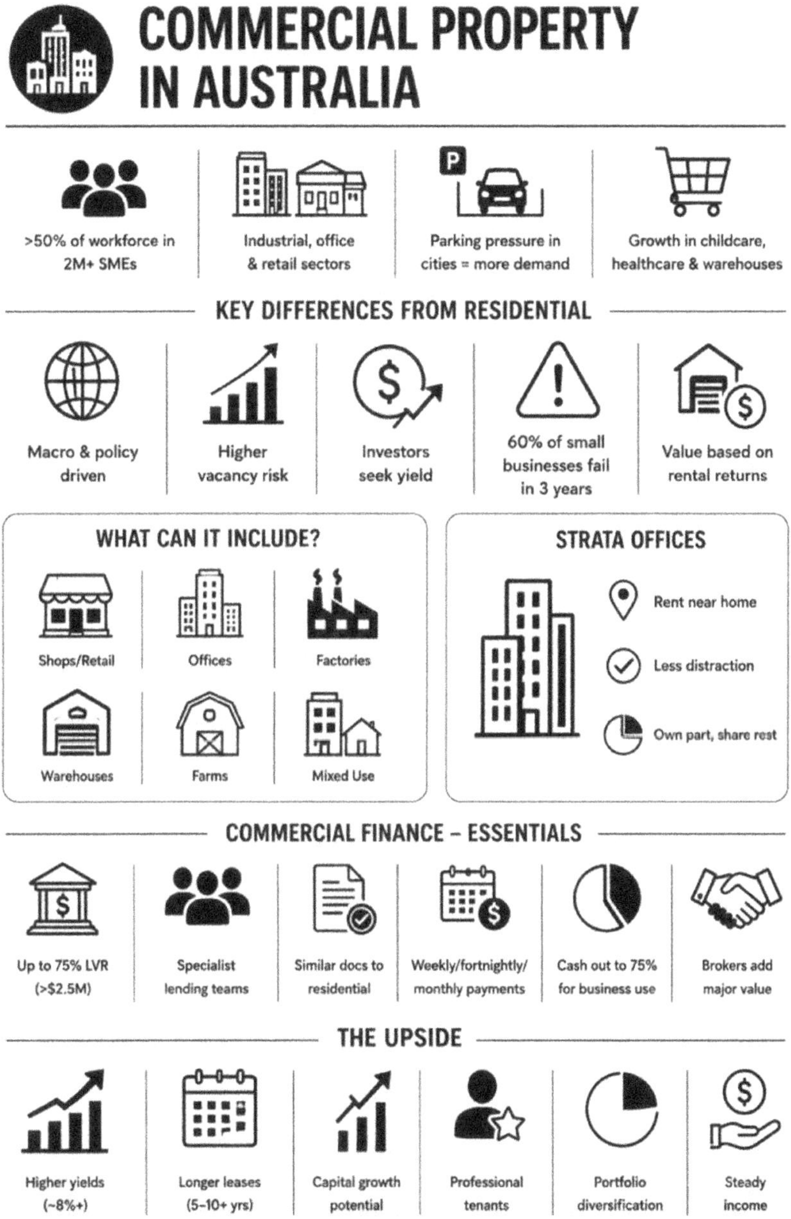

Financing Commercial Property

Commercial properties can take many forms. A lender will assess the property to establish its business purpose and will also consider a number of other variables, including the property's zoning, any existing permits, current and future use, and the property's income-generating nature. Examples of commercial properties include offices, car parks, warehouses, retail shops, farmland, hotels and pubs, petrol stations, and properties with specialised uses (e.g., aged care and hospitals). Residential property development (as a general rule, greater than four dwellings on one title) can also qualify under commercial lending, as such development demonstrates an intention to generate profit. Because of its wide range of uses, commercial property finance is more complex than residential property lending. Each application is often reviewed on a case-by-case basis, allowing the lender to take a more flexible approach to lending criteria. Lending criteria can vary significantly from one lender to another.

Before you seek commercial finance from a lender, you should prepare a business plan and cash flow forecast. These two reports will assist the lender in its credit assessment of your application. The quality of your submission could potentially impact the final interest rate the lender attributes to your loan. It would be a good idea to involve your lawyer to review potentially complex commercial lease agreements, and your accountant for financial advice and preparation of cash flow forecasts. Also seek the services of a finance broker with strong commercial lending experience.

Unlike residential property loans, which can have a term of up to 30 years, commercial property loans generally have a maximum term of 15 years. Lenders will sometimes consider providing you with an interest-only period (although you will generally be asked to justify this request), and you will have to take into consideration the cash flow impact of paying principal and interest repayments over a shorter loan term.

As a rule, you will need to have a larger upfront deposit contribution when purchasing commercial property. This requirement varies by lender, and most lenders will only lend between 65–80% of the commercial property valuation (this percentage is the LVR). The overall LVR can be influenced by a number of factors, including bank policy, the applicant's strength, security risk as outlined in the valuation report, the quality of the tenant and lease, and the term of the loan sought.

There is no mortgage insurance available for commercial property finance; lender fees and charges are generally higher than in residential property finance. You should expect to pay a higher interest rate compared to a residential home loan. You will often have to cover upfront costs, including a lender establishment fee, a risk fee, a bank valuation fee, and a legal documentation fee.

Most loan accounts also come with monthly or quarterly account maintenance fees. Most lenders will negotiate pricing; however, the stronger the application and risk mitigants, the better the chances of achieving a lower overall pricing outcome. The interest rate offered by a lender will be influenced by an assessed risk margin, which the lender calculates after considering the credit strengths and weaknesses specific to your application. You should also factor in any monthly, quarterly, or annual bank fees when calculating the effective interest rate.

Some lenders primarily focus on residential loans but want exposure to the commercial property market. These lenders often offer more simplified commercial loan products (which are highly competitive) and more straightforward criteria, and they offer what is referred to as a 'pure asset lend' against established commercial properties. These types of loans are very similar to your standard home loan in that they are 'set and forget'. The lender does not implement any financial covenants on your loan that sometimes require the borrower to provide annual financial statements for review and/or maintain the LVR at a minimum level (therefore avoiding any potential future lender's request for revaluation of your property in the future).

When considering commercial property for rental purposes, some lenders may offer a 'lease doc' product. This type of loan criterion relies on the rental income from a commercial lease to service the loan. These commercial loan products are niche. Gross rental income of 1.5 multiplied by interest cover (150% of the interest repayment amount) is a good guide when seeking a lease doc commercial product. Furthermore, the tenant's quality may also influence credit decision-making. For example, a large corporation as a tenant would be looked on more favourably than a start-up business.

When considering a commercial loan agreement, you should pay particular attention to any financial covenants outlined in the loan contract. A financial covenant is a requirement on the borrower to ensure that, during the term of the loan, you are able to demonstrate compliance with the requirement(s) stated in your loan contract. As mentioned above, financial covenants may include minimum net profit (EBITDA – Earnings before interest, tax, depreciation and amortisation), minimum LVR, and reference to annual turnover.

If you fail to meet the financial covenants outlined in your loan contract, you may be required to pay down your loan or even repay the whole debt, which could put you under significant financial stress. Making the loan repayments on time and in full does not mean you can abandon your financial covenants. Sometimes you may be better off securing a loan with a higher annual interest cost and no financial covenants than a lower annual interest cost loan with strict financial covenants.

When seeking a commercial loan for property, you should engage the services of a finance broker, as the range of products and lender credit criteria, as well as the subjective assessment nature of commercial lending, may be overwhelming.

Deposit Requirements

The LVR is more conservative under commercial property lending, as the financial risk factors are generally exposed to a greater number of variables. There is no 'one size fits all' solution when it comes to commercial finance. Each application is assessed on a case-by-case basis.

The four major Australian banks have traditionally had a stronghold on commercial finance; however, private lenders give the banks a run for their money, often providing a simpler approach to financing. An example of a simplified approach is a lease doc loan product. The lender is generally looking at the tenant's creditworthiness and the strength of the lease. Often, a lender will require that an existing lease be in effect for a minimum of 12 months. Lease doc products are generally short-term (one to five years) and align with the remaining term of the lease in place. Private lenders don't actually require a lease; if the borrower were to say they will sell the property, even if they refinance it later, borrowing capacity is not required.

Should you Lease or Buy a Premises?

This is an ongoing dilemma for many businesses. When a business commences operation, it is important to concentrate on cash flow and establishing the business. It is probably wise to not outlay unnecessary capital until the business is established. Over time, the choice may be out of the owner's hands as growth and the need for more size, among many other factors, may lead to the decision being made for the owner.

There are a number of considerations, drawbacks, and benefits when deciding whether to lease or buy a business premises. The starting point (besides the considerations detailed below) could be to seek advice from an accountant to model the costs of purchasing a premises and compare this to leasing costs.

The business's fundamental needs must be assessed first.

Considerations

Floor space: the cost per square metre can impact the affordability of purchasing the premises; it may be more cost-effective to lease the space. Licenses, permits, and allowable use need to be factored in.

Visibility: Better-placed premises in a suburb can cost more to purchase than to lease, in which case leasing may be better.

Signage: This is important for many service and product businesses alike.

Parking: It is very important to have parking available for clients. Clients are required to come to the business, rather than the business coming to them. Restaurants, cafés, and hotels (to name a few) list access (parking and wheelchair/disabled access) near the top of their priority list. Access, with a consideration of anti-discrimination laws, is important.

Location: With the internet, location is becoming less important. The suitability of the environment and the demographics of the business's clients can inform the decision for the owner, depending on affordability, so that they can be situated in an appropriate location. Proximity of suppliers, distributors, and clients, as well as complementary services offered by other businesses, all play their roles

Budget: The bottom line, having the borrowing capacity, the deposit, and the ability to borrow based on tax returns or income, will ultimately determine the choices that a business has.

Purchasing a separate commercial property is a matter of comparing the cost to rent your own premises versus the cost of having a mortgage against an owned property. Consider the location, the opportunity cost with respect to whether there is a better location you could purchase a commercial property in for investment, and whether rental income from another premises could earn you or save you more money than purchasing your own premises (and the growth of the property in its location).

Joint Ventures

Joint ventures are commonly used in property developments and various other commercial enterprises, including mining syndicates and research and development ventures. They are usually set up for specific purposes (rather than a long-term commercial arrangement, such as a partnership), and they can be highly profitable when you choose the right business(es) to enter into the arrangement with you. This section will not discuss partnerships, specifically, but may refer to them for comparative purposes.

There are many traps for the unwary, and it is important that a joint venture is structured appropriately to achieve the desired commercial outcomes.

What is a Joint Venture?

The High Court has defined a joint venture as "an association of persons for the purposes of a particular trading, commercial, mining or other financial undertaking or endeavour with a view to mutual profit, with each participant usually (but not necessarily) contributing money, property or skill"

Joint ventures are often confused with partnerships, but there are some important differences, namely:

- Joint ventures are set up for a specific purpose and generally cease to exist once that purpose is achieved, whereas partnerships are ongoing.
- In joint ventures, the parties maintain their status as separate entities, whereas a partnership is not a separate legal entity and every partner has unlimited liability. This is an important distinction, as in a partnership, each partner is "jointly and severally" liable for the actions of the others in all legal situations, including being criminally liable. Joint venturers are only liable to the extent stipulated in their joint venture agreement (for example, each entity is only liable for a fixed percentage of the debts of the joint venture). Getting this distinction right is also important for tax purposes.
- As the High Court definition implies, joint venturers can contribute "money, property or skill." In property developments, it is not uncommon for one party to provide the property or the finance, and the other to either provide the labour and skills to build the development or to do the research to locate a suitable development site and undertake the feasibility assessment of its profitability.
- With joint ventures, the parties are not necessarily in a fiduciary relationship (e.g. one involving trust), whereas this is an important aspect of a partnership.

Types of Joint Ventures

Joint ventures are generally either:

- An 'unincorporated joint venture,' where the parties use their existing corporate structures without setting up a new business entity.
- An 'incorporated joint venture,' where a new entity, such as a company or a unit trust, is set up to manage the joint venture. In this case, the joint venture partners are the shareholders of the new company (or unit holders of the unit trust), and the joint venturers appoint the directors of the joint venture entity. There are variations on this structure, but this is often how it works. This type of joint venture also has better asset protection for the parties, because the liabilities of the venture can be limited to the joint venture company, rather than being passed on to the joint venturers themselves.

The type of joint venture used often depends on the scale of the operation.

Tips for the Uninitiated

In planning a joint venture, there are a number of issues that should be considered:

Do proper due diligence on your proposed joint venture partner. Have they done this before? Were they successful? Do they have a positive existing profile in the marketplace? Are they prepared to let you speak with previous clients or joint-venture partners, and if not, why not? These are just a few of the things you should consider.

Get proper legal, accounting, and tax advice. A lot can go wrong if you do not structure the venture correctly.

Clearly define the objectives and roles of the respective parties. This can be done in conjunction with your professional advisors.

Draw up a formal agreement. This should cover the following issues, at least (this list is not exhaustive):

- the structure and objectives of the venture
- the management structure of the venture and its powers
- rights and obligations of the respective parties
- financial contributions, and how profits and losses will be allocated to the parties
- other financial issues, such as financial reporting and accounting
- ownership of intellectual property developed for the venture (this issue is often overlooked)
- marketing, and appointment of estate agents and other professionals
- a suitable dispute resolution provision
- exit strategies and dissolution of the venture.

Maintain Proper Financial Records

Plan regular meetings to monitor objectives and assess key performance indicators.

Proper planning will never guarantee success, but it will go a long way to mitigating the risks involved in a business venture with another party.

Leases

Commercial Leases

The law in relation to commercial and, in particular, retail leases vary from state to state. The law referred to in this section is applicable in the state of Victoria, Australia.

What are Commercial Leases?

The term 'commercial leases' is used rather loosely to refer to genuine commercial and retail leases. Retail leases are really just another type of commercial lease, which (in Victoria) relates specifically to premises used for the retailing of goods or services. Both the Law Institute of Victoria (LIV) and the Real Estate Institute of Victoria (REIV) publish commercial leases, which can be used in both retail and non-retail situations, but landlords are not required to use the standard form contracts. They may use contracts tailored to their specific needs, provided they comply with any relevant legislation.

In Victoria, general commercial leases are not governed by any specific legislation, other than the *Property Law Act 1958* (generally), while the *Retail Leases Act 2003* governs retail leases. All states have retail tenancy legislation.

Retail Leases

Retail leasing legislation was introduced in Victoria in the mid-1980s to curb the domination of the marketplace by a small group of landlords and to even the playing field for landlords and tenants alike. The current legislation relates to premises which are used "wholly or predominantly" for the retailing of goods or services, but does not include leases:

- for less than a year;
- where one party is a listed corporation, or a subsidiary of the listed corporation;
- where the cost of occupancy is more than $1 million a year;
- relating to premises above the third floor of a multi-storey building, or;
- relating to wholesaling, manufacturing, or storage businesses.

The Retail Leases Act includes a number of important protections for tenants, including:

- a requirement that the landlord provide a disclosure statement, outlining key provisions of the lease and the Victorian Small Business Commissioner information sheet, together with the lease agreement itself. The disclosure statement must set out the annual estimate of outgoings under the lease.
- the tenant is entitled to a minimum five-year lease term, including renewal periods, although the tenant can waive this right.
- landlords cannot recover legal expenses relating to the costs of drafting the lease, land tax, capital costs for the premises, or key money (a demand by the landlord for money to grant or transfer a lease).

These are only some of the protections afforded by the legislation.

Not surprisingly, some landlords try to argue that the retail tenancy legislation does not apply to their premises, but the law is clear that if the premises are used for retail purposes, the relevant legislation does and will apply. This is because Australian courts and tribunals generally consider the real substance, rather than the form of a contract. The old analogy of "if it looks like a duck and quacks like a duck, then it is probably a duck" comes to mind.

Although the definition of retail premises may seem fairly clear, there can be some grey areas (for example, whether premises that are used for supplying commercial services to other businesses are covered by the legislation). The short answer (in Victoria) is that where premises are used for supplying services to other businesses, who are the "ultimate consumers" of those services, then the legislation still applies. This may come as a surprise to some landlords and tenants, who may have thought that they were parties merely to a general commercial lease.

Examples of this would be the sale of shelves by a business to a retail outlet which uses them to display their goods, or the sale of ingredients to another business which makes biscuits and cakes. These would be retail sales of the shelves and ingredients, respectively.

This is just a broad overview of commercial/retail leases, as it is quite a complex area of law and is beyond the scope of this book. However, here are some guidelines for both landlords and tenants about entering into commercial leases.

17.

Summary; Private Lending Compared to Other Lenders

Private Lenders Versus Standard Banks

Understanding the Real Differences in Modern Lending

One of the biggest misconceptions in the lending industry is that private lending exists outside responsible lending obligations or operates without structure, assessment, or regulation. That is not necessarily correct. While private lending is far more flexible than traditional bank lending, some private lenders still operate within regulated lending environments and still undertake significant due diligence and assessment. The difference is not that private lenders ignore risk or compliance. The difference is that they assess transactions differently and structure loans around solutions rather than rigid policy.

Traditional banks and private lenders serve different purposes within the lending market. Banks are designed around long-term standard lending, predictable borrowers, and policy consistency. Private lenders are designed around flexibility, asset strength, and solving situations that banks either cannot or will not accommodate.

Understanding these differences is essential because many borrowers assume that if a bank declines them, then no finance options remain. In reality, the lending market is significantly broader than the major banks, and private lenders often provide pathways that mainstream institutions simply do not offer.

The Traditional Bank Model

Banks are highly structured institutions. They operate under extensive regulation, internal governance frameworks, responsible lending obligations, APRA oversight, shareholder expectations, and risk management systems. Often it's the shareholders that take precedent over borrowers, in my opinion.

As a result, banks generally prefer borrowers who fit neatly within policy.

A traditional bank wants to see:

- stable income;
- strong borrowing capacity;
- low living expenses;
- clean credit history;
- long-term employment;
- standard residential property;
- predictable repayment history; and
- long-term servicing ability.

Banks are fundamentally designed to assess whether the borrower can comfortably meet repayments over an extended period, often across a 25- or 30-year loan term.

This is why banks rely heavily on:

- servicing calculators;
- debt-to-income ratios;
- credit scoring;

- repayment buffers;
- sensitised interest rates; and detailed income verification.

For straightforward borrowers, this system works well. However, many borrowers do not fit perfectly within these frameworks.

The Private Lending Model

Private lending approaches lending from an entirely different perspective.

Rather than focusing primarily on long-term servicing calculators, private lenders commonly focus on:

- the security property;
- available equity;
- the loan-to-value ratio;
- the exit strategy; and
- the overall commercial strength of the transaction.

Banks generally assess the borrower first and the asset second.

Private lenders often assess the asset and exit strategy first, then the borrower.

This distinction changes everything.

A private lender may still approve a transaction where:

- income evidence is weak;
- the borrower is self-employed;
- tax returns are unavailable;
- the property type is unusual;
- credit impairment exists;

- the borrower is on a temporary visa;
- tax debt is present; or
- the borrower lacks traditional borrowing capacity.

The reason is simple. Private lenders are often more concerned with how the debt will ultimately be repaid than whether the borrower fits a standard servicing calculator today.

Regulated Versus Non-Regulated Private Lending

A major misunderstanding within the market is that all private lending operates outside regulation. That is incorrect.

Private lenders can operate in both:

- regulated environments; and
- non-regulated environments;

whether a loan is regulated often depends on:

- the borrower structure;
- whether the borrower is a natural person;
- the purpose of the loan; and
- whether the debt is wholly or predominantly for business purposes.

If the loan falls within consumer lending legislation, responsible lending obligations may still apply.

This means the lender may still need to:

- assess suitability;
- undertake enquiries into the borrower's position;
- review objectives and requirements; and
- ensure the loan is not unsuitable.

Many high-quality private lenders take these obligations seriously and still undertake substantial due diligence even where flexibility exists.

The idea that private lending is simply "easy money" is inaccurate.

When Servicing May Not Be Required

One of the key advantages of private lending is that traditional borrowing capacity may not always be required.

This usually occurs where:

- the loan term is short;
- interest is capitalised;
- no ongoing repayments are required; and
- there is a strong and credible exit strategy.

Examples of acceptable exit strategies may include:

- sale of property;
- refinance after construction completion;
- refinance to a bank later;
- receipt of inheritance;
- business sale;
- maturing investment;
- settlement of litigation; or
- sale of another asset.

In these scenarios, the private lender may place greater emphasis on the certainty of the exit rather than ongoing income.

This is one of the reasons private lending has become so important in:

- bridging finance;
- development lending;
- construction lending;
- renovation finance;
- tax debt lending; and
- short-term commercial transactions.

When Servicing Still Matters

However, private lending does not mean servicing is always irrelevant.

There are many situations where servicing absolutely does matter, even with private lenders.

For example, if:

- the proposed exit strategy is refinance;
- the borrower intends to retain the property long-term;
- the property is owner-occupied, and the loan purpose is not predominately for business or commercial purposes;
- the property is the borrower's only property and is not unconditionally sold; or
- the loan is in the borrower's personal name, and the loan purpose is not predominately for business or commercial purposes;

then servicing may still need to be clearly evident.

This is particularly important from both:

- a responsible lending perspective; and
- a practical repayment perspective.

A lender cannot simply ignore the reality that if a borrower intends to refinance later, another lender will eventually need to assess servicing capacity. If there is no realistic prospect of refinancing, then the proposed exit strategy may not be credible.

Similarly, where a borrower's only property is involved, lenders must exercise significant caution.

If the borrower's sole property is being used as security and there is no clear ability to refinance or repay the debt, then the lender risks placing the borrower into a position where they could lose the only property they own.

This becomes particularly sensitive where:

- the borrower is older;
- retirement income is limited;
- servicing is weak; or
- the borrower would effectively move from ownership to renting if enforcement occurred.

Good private lenders recognise these concerns and assess them carefully.

The Importance of Exit Strategy;

The exit strategy is perhaps the single most important aspect of private lending.

A private lender is rarely focused solely on the beginning of the transaction. The lender is equally focused on how the debt will end.

An exit strategy must generally be:

- identifiable;
- realistic;
- measurable; and
- plausible within the loan term.

For example:

"I hope property prices rise" is not an exit strategy.

"The property is already listed for sale with significant equity" maybe.

"The borrower will refinance after construction completion" may be acceptable if servicing is likely at that future point.

"An inheritance is expected" may require strong evidence.

Private lending is therefore highly strategic lending.

Interest Capitalisation and Cash Flow Relief

Banks usually require monthly repayments from day one.

Private lenders commonly allow interest capitalisation.

This means:

the interest is added to the loan balance; and

no repayments are required during the loan term.

This can significantly reduce financial pressure during:

- renovations;
- construction;
- bridging periods;
- business transitions; or
- temporary financial stress.

However, even where repayments are not required, the lender still needs confidence that the debt can ultimately be repaid.

Again, the focus returns to:

- equity;
- security; and
- exit strategy.

Speed and Flexibility

Another major advantage of private lending is speed.

Traditional banks may take:

weeks;

months; or

multiple assessment stages

to approve a transaction.

Private lenders are generally structured to move much faster.

In many cases they can:

assess transactions quickly;

review valuations rapidly;

make commercial decisions directly; and

settle within days.

This becomes critical where:

auction deadlines exist;

settlement is urgent;

tax debt enforcement is occurring;

caveats are registered;

bridging is required; or

an opportunity would otherwise be lost.

Speed itself becomes part of the value proposition.

Property Types Banks Often Avoid

Traditional banks prefer simple residential property because it is easier to:

value;

insure;

understand; and

sell in recovery situations.

Private lenders are generally more flexible regarding property types.

Examples include:

- owner-builder projects;
- incomplete construction;
- acreage;
- rural property;
- hobby farms;
- rooming houses;
- residual stock;

- multiple dwellings on one title;
- NDIS property;
- specialised commercial property;
- display homes;
- serviced apartments; and
- unusual zoning.

Banks may:

- reduce LVRs;
- impose excessive conditions; or
- decline outright.

Private lenders commonly focus instead on:

- equity;
- marketability;
- location; and
- exit strength.

Construction and Development Finance

Private lending becomes particularly powerful in construction and development lending.

Banks often require:

- fixed-price contracts;
- extensive pre-sales;
- strong servicing;
- detailed QS reports; and
- lengthy approval processes.

Private lenders may:

- enter projects mid-construction;
- fund incomplete builds;
- lend against GRV;
- fund owner-builders;
- accept staged completion; and
- structure funding around the end value of the project.

This flexibility can allow developers to:

- finish projects;
- unlock equity;
- refinance later; or
- sell completed stock;
- credit Impairment.

Traditional banks rely heavily on:

- credit scoring;
- repayment history; and
- automated risk systems.

Private lenders generally assess credit impairment differently.

Rather than focusing solely on:

- defaults;
- enquiries;
- arrears; or
- judgments;

Private lenders commonly assess:

- why the issue occurred;
- whether it is ongoing;
- whether equity exists; and
- whether the transaction resolves the problem.

This means borrowers with:

- defaults;
- discharged bankruptcy;
- tax debt;
- missed repayments; or
- impaired credit history

May still access funding through private lending.

The higher interest rate reflects the increased risk and flexibility.

Non-Residents and Visa Holders

Banks can be extremely restrictive regarding:

- visa subclasses;
- foreign income;
- country restrictions; and
- residency status.

Private lenders are often far more flexible.

They commonly assess:

- the asset;
- the equity;
- FIRB compliance; and
- the proposed exit rather than rigid residency policy alone.

This flexibility can assist:

- temporary residents;
- foreign income earners;
- newly arrived migrants; and
- international business owners.

The Cost of Flexibility

Private lending is more expensive than standard bank lending.

That reality must be acknowledged.

The higher rates and fees reflect:

- increased risk;
- reduced documentation;
- flexibility;
- speed;
- specialised property types; and
- short-term loan structures.

However, borrowers often misunderstand how these loans should be evaluated.

The question should not simply be:
"What is the rate?"

The better question is:
"What problem does the loan solve?"

A private loan may:

- save a development;
- preserve a deposit;

- stop enforcement action;
- complete construction;
- clear tax debt;
- unlock equity; or
- create future profit.

In many situations, obtaining the solution matters more than obtaining the cheapest possible interest rate.

Final Thoughts

Private lending and standard bank lending are fundamentally different lending models designed for different purposes.

Banks prioritise:

- consistency;
- long-term servicing;
- low-risk borrowers; and
- policy compliance.

Private lenders prioritise:

- flexibility;
- asset strength;
- equity;
- timing; and
- exit strategy.

Importantly, private lending does not mean the absence of assessment or regulation. Many private lenders operate within regulated environments and still undertake careful due diligence, particularly where:

the borrower is an individual;

the loan is consumer-related;

the property is owner-occupied; or

refinance forms part of the proposed exit strategy.

Where the borrower's only property is involved, or where the proposed exit relies on refinance, servicing often still needs to be evident. A credible exit strategy cannot exist without realistic future repayment capacity.

The best private lenders understand this balance. They provide flexibility without ignoring responsibility.

***

Ultimately, private lending exists because real life does not always fit neatly within bank policy. It provides borrowers with opportunities, solutions, and flexibility where traditional lenders often cannot assist.

For many borrowers, private lending is not merely an alternative to a bank. It is the pathway that allows the transaction, project, or opportunity to proceed.

www.ingramcontent.com/pod-product-compliance
Lightning Source LLC
LaVergne TN
LVHW051920051126
851857LV00021B/2087
* 9 7 8 1 9 2 3 5 0 1 9 0 4 *